A

WOMEN OF
THE WORD

WOMEN OF THE WORD

JEWISH WOMEN

AND

JEWISH WRITING

EDITED BY

JUDITH R. BASKIN

Wayne State University Press   Detroit

Library of Congress Cataloging-in-Publication Data

Women of the word : Jewish women and Jewish writing / edited by
Judith R. Baskin.
    p. cm.
    Includes bibliographical references and index.
    ISBN 0-8143-2422-3. — ISBN 0-8143-2423-1 (pbk. : alk. paper)
    1. Jewish literature—Women authors—History and criticism.
2. Women in Judaism. 3. Women in literature. I. Baskin, Judith
Reesa, 1950– .
PN842.W66   1994
809′.89287—dc20   94-12697

Designer: *S.R. Tenenbaum*

Frontispiece: A page from the Darmstadt Haggadah,
fol. 48v, ca. 1430 Upper Rhine Valley, Germany.
(Courtesy of Hessische Landes- und
Hochschulbibliothek, Darmstadt, Germany.)

Grateful acknowledgment is made to the
Lucius N. Littauer Foundation for
financial assistance in the
publication of this volume.

◆

For my brother DAVID BASKIN and my sister SUSAN BASKIN,

and their families, JOAN GARSON, JACOB and REBECCA,

and JACK MICAY, NATHAN and RACHEL

CONTENTS

ACKNOWLEDGMENTS

I acknowledge with gratitude the enthusiastic participation of the fine scholars who have contributed to this volume. I have learned a great deal from them and from their essays.

A one-semester sabbatical leave during the spring semester, 1992, allowed me precious time in which to undertake many of the tasks connected with editing this volume. I am indebted to the University at Albany, State University of New York, for that valuable respite from teaching and administration. My participation in the Jewish Studies Women's Caucus has been an important influence in my professional life and in the direction of my scholarship. I am thankful for the support and guidance my colleagues in the Caucus have consistently offered as together we find our way into the new territory of Jewish Women's Studies. I am very grateful for the ongoing interest of Arthur Evans, Director of Wayne State University Press, in the projects I have proposed, and for the enthusiasm and care the editors with whom I have worked, Kathy Wildfong and Lynn H. Trease, have shown in bringing these undertakings to completion. I would also like to thank the Lucius N. Littauer Foundation for its generous subvention of this volume, and for the Foundation's continuing support of my efforts to further the study of Jewish women's lives and cultural achievements.

9

Once again, my husband Warren Ginsberg, and our children Sam and Shira, have patiently endured my preoccupation with a demanding project. I thank them for their forebearance and for their love. My brother David and my sister Susan, and their families, have been constant sources of warmth and encouragement over the years. I am pleased to dedicate this book to them.

CONTRIBUTORS

HOWARD ADELMAN is director of the Program in Jewish Studies at Smith College, where his courses include the study of Jewish women. In addition to his work on women in Italian Jewish life, he has published on Italian Jewish history, especially the life and thought of Leon Modena, a seventeenth-century Venetian rabbi.

RUTH ADLER teaches Jewish studies and comparative literature at Baruch College of the City University of New York. She is the author of *Women of the Shtetl—Through the Eyes of Y. L. Peretz: A Socio-psychological Study* and numerous articles on female characters in Hebrew, Yiddish, and American Jewish literature.

JUDITH R. BASKIN, chair of the Department of Judaic Studies at the State University of New York at Albany, is the author of *Pharaoh's Counsellors: Job, Jethro and Balaam in Rabbinic and Patristic Tradition,* the editor of *Jewish Women in Historical Perspective,* and coeditor, with Shelly Tenenbaum, of *Gender and Jewish Studies: A Curriculum Guide.* She writes about Jewish women in late antiquity and the Middle Ages.

JANET BURSTEIN, associate professor of English at Drew University, teaches courses in Victorian literature and Jewish American literature at the undergraduate and graduate levels. She is the author of *Charting the Minefields: A Critical Analysis of Israelis and Americans in Dialogue* and numerous articles on Jewish American and British literature.

SARAH BLACHER COHEN, professor of English at the State University of New York at Albany, is the author of *Saul Bellow's Enigmatic Laughter* and the editor of *From Hester Street to Hollywood, Jewish Wry,* and *Comic Relief: Humor in Contemporary American Literature.* The general editor of the SUNY Press series *Modern Jewish Literature,* her most recent book is *Cynthia Ozick's Comic Art: From Levity to Liturgy.*

JUDITH DISHON is the head of the medieval section in the Department of Literature of the Jewish People at Bar Ilan University. She received bachelor's and master of arts degrees from Hebrew University in Jerusalem and a Ph.D. from Columbia University. Her publications include articles and books on medieval Hebrew literature.

YAEL FELDMAN, an associate professor in the Skirball Department of Hebrew and Judaica at New York University, is the author of *Modernism and Cultural Transfer: Gabriel Preil and the Tradition of Jewish Literary Bilingualism* and the coeditor of *Teaching the Hebrew Bible as Literature.* She has published widely on topics connected with Hebrew literature.

NORA GLICKMAN is an associate professor of Spanish and Latin American literature at Queens College. She is the author of two books of short stories, *Uno de sus juanes* and *Mujeres, memories, malagros*; a study of the white slave trade, *La Trata de blancas*; and many articles on Jewish themes and authors in Latin American literature.

KATHRYN HELLERSTEIN has taught literature and writing at Wellesley, Haverford, and Gratz colleges and the University of Pennsylvania. She translated and edited Moyshe-Leyb Halpern's early poems, *In New York: A Selection,* and is now completing *The Selected Poems of Kadya Molodowsky,* as well as an anthology of women Yiddish poets and a critical book on these poets.

SARA R. HOROWITZ, director of the Jewish Studies Program at the University of Delaware, received her doctorate from the Joint Program of Literary Studies/ Comparative Literature at Brandeis University. Her research centers on representations of the Holocaust in fiction, film, and autobiography.

CAROLE S. KESSNER is a member of the Department of Comparative Literature at the State University of New York at Stony Brook. She is the author of *The Other New York Jewish Intellectuals* and articles exploring the Jewish impact on English and American literature.

MIRI KUBOVY is professor of Near Eastern Languages and Civilizations at Harvard University and has served as a visiting professor at Wesleyan and Tel Aviv Universities. She has published numerous papers on modern Hebrew literature, especially the narratives of S. Y. Agnon, and has translated three books, short stories, and poetry from Hebrew to English.

ANNE LAPIDUS LERNER is the dean of Albert List College of Jewish Studies and an assistant professor of Jewish Literature at the Jewish Theological Seminary of America. She wrote *Passing the Love of Women: Gide's Saul and its Biblical Roots,* coedited *Gender and Text in Modern Hebrew and Yiddish Literature,* and has written many articles in the fields of Jewish literature and Jewish women's studies.

SHMUEL NIGER, pseudonym of Shmuel Charney, is widely considered the foremost Yiddish literary critic of the twentieth century. He was born in 1883 in the Minsk region, White Russia. In Vilna in 1908 he was one of the founders of *Literarishe monatshriften,* and in 1912 he edited the new monthly, *Di yidishe velt.* Together with philologist and Zionist leader Ber Borokhov he edited *Der pinkes* (1913), a volume devoted to the history of Yiddish literature, folklore, criticism, and bibliography. In 1914 he edited Zalmen Rejzen's first *Leksikon fun der yidisher literatur un prese,* and much later, in the fifties in America, he became the editor of a similar, expanded literary encyclopedia, *Leksikon fun der nayer yidisher literatur.* For the thirty-five years from his arrival in the United States in 1920 until his death in 1955, Niger worked as literary critic for the Yiddish daily *Der tog.* From 1941–1947 he coedited the prestigious literary monthly *Di zukunft.* The many books he wrote include *Shmuesn vegn bikher* (1922) and the posthumous *Yidishe shrayber in Sovet-Rusland* (1958), *Bleter geshikhte fun der yidisher literatur* (1959), *Kritik un kritiker* (1959), and *Sholem Asch* (1960).

NORMA FAIN PRATT, who teaches women's history at Mt. San Antonio College, has published widely in the field of American Jewish history. Her work includes *Morris Hillquit: A Political Biography of an American Jewish Socialist, The History of Jewish Women in Southern California,* and articles dealing with the history of Jewish women.

NAOMI B. SOKOLOFF teaches Hebrew and modern Jewish literature at the University of Washington in Seattle. She has published articles on Israeli authors and other Jewish writers and a book, *The Imagination of the Child in Modern Jewish Fiction.* She is a coeditor of *Gender and Text in Modern Hebrew and Yiddish Literature.*

LAURA WEXLER teaches American studies and women's studies at Yale University. She is co-author of the forthcoming *Pregnant Pictures: Women in the Age of Mechanical Reproduction*, and has written extensively on American history and culture.

SHEVA ZUCKER teaches Yiddish and Jewish literature at Duke University. She has written articles on women writers and the image of women in modern Yiddish literature and is editing an anthology of Yiddish women prose writers in translation. She recently published a textbook, *Yiddish: An Introduction to the Language, Literature, and Culture*.

EDITOR'S NOTE

Transliteration of Hebrew and Yiddish varies from chapter to chapter according to the author's preference. Some words and names which appear frequently have been transliterated consistently throughout the volume, occasionally leading to inconsistencies within individual chapters.

1 ♦ JUDITH R. BASKIN

Women of the Word: An Introduction

"I am a Russian Jewess, a flame—a longing," declares the protagonist of Anzia Yezierska's 1923 novel, *Salome of the Tenements*: "A soul consumed with hunger for heights beyond reach. I am the ache of unvoiced dreams, the clamor of suppressed desires. . . . I am the urge of ages for the free, the beautiful that never was yet on land or sea."[1] In her novels and short stories, Yezierska wrote about Jewish women expressing previously "unvoiced dreams." Her passionate *cri de coeur* is one of many that were heard as Jewish women in Europe, the land of Israel, and the Americas began to explore the greatly enlarged opportunities for self-expression offered by modern secular culture. In both poetry and prose, in Hebrew, Yiddish, and many other languages, an unprecedented number of Jewish women, at the end of the nineteenth and in the early decades of the twentieth century, began to write creatively from the raw material of their own experiences and feelings. The essays in this volume

17

present the ways these writers reclaimed their Jewish heritage as "women of the word," even as they also record the painful choices and sacrifices demanded by lives devoted to literary expression.

For with the opportunity for self-realization came estrangement from a traditional Jewish culture that had strictly limited women's access to learning and literary accomplishment. To become a Jewish woman writer was to become a cultural anomaly; often the price of such an achievement was equivocal exile from a male society profoundly uncomfortable with female intellectual assertiveness. Yezierka's heroine Sara Smolinsky in *Bread Givers* acknowledges at the novel's end that despite her astounding success in achieving an education, gaining employment as a public school teacher in New York City, and turning herself into a "person," she still feels the overwhelming and inescapable burden of a less accepting past: "It wasn't just my father, but the generations who made my father whose weight was still upon me."[2] And, as the Yiddish poet Kadya Molodowsky (1894–1975) laments to the "kosher grandmothers" who hound her flight from the restrictions of traditional Jewish life, what has driven her away is what will forever haunt her and render her incomplete:

> Your sighs were the whips that lashed me
> and drove my young life to the threshold
> to escape from your kosher beds.
> But wherever the street grows dark you pursue me—
> wherever a shadow falls.
>
> Your whimperings race like the autumn wind past me,
> and your words are the silken cord
> still binding my thoughts.
> My life is a page ripped out of a holy book
> and part of the first line is missing. [3]

Jewish women writers of the early twentieth century, like Molodowsky and Yezierska, lived with a sense of painful connection to a culture that rejected their aspirations. They knew they would always feel loss and cultural dislocation in their fight to establish their own voices and identities as literary women in a wider world that was only marginally more sympathetic to their ambitions.

Responding to a variety of Jewish women's voices in Hebrew, Yiddish, English, and Spanish, from the Middle Ages to the present, these essays chronicle the Jewish encounter with modernity and document female strategies for constructing intellectual and emotional identities amidst the competing demands of traditional norms, familial obligations, and economic survival. The themes of repression and equivocal liberation resonate throughout this compilation, as the authors reflect on the silencing of the female voice in a traditional Jewish culture that most often denied women the education and the empowerment requisite for recording their thoughts and feelings. And while the individual essays reveal literary discoveries of self and forgings of identity by women rising to the opportunities and challenges of drastically altered Jewish social realities, a significant number also show the sad declines of women writers upon whom silence was reimposed.

While *Women of the Word: Jewish Women and Jewish Writing* stands alone as a collection of insightful literary essays on this little-explored topic, it was conceived, in part, as a companion study and complement to *Jewish Women in Historical Perspective*[4] a similar anthology that explores the lives and activities of Jewish women in various times and places. The present essays fill certain significant gaps in the earlier volume, which lacked historical studies of Jewish women's lives in Eastern Europe, the land of Israel, and Latin America. Thus, while the focus of these essays is overwhelmingly secular Jewish literature,[5] whether prose, poetry, or fiction, studied as literature, an underlying intent of the collection is to demonstrate the ways in which literature tells us about women's lives in particular circumstances. This perspective, which privileges "voice" over "writing," does not deny the validity of text as text, but does reveal my

own historian's concern to recover the realia of Jewish women's experiences from written texts of all kinds.[6]

Still, these are literary essays. Although each author approaches her or his topic differently, in general the essays
divide into two unequal categories. Four essays deal with
the ways women are depicted in particular literary works or
bodies of Jewish literature written by a man or men, while
twelve essays explore the literary productions of Jewish
women. In fact, with this division, the chapters in this volume epitomize the two predominant theoretical approaches
of recent feminist criticism.

As feminist critic Elaine Showalter has noted, the first of
these theoretical modes of feminist literary criticism is ideological, "concerned with the feminist as reader."[7] Such readings consider the ways certain texts or literatures portray
women, and examine what female characters have symbolized and what the larger cultural meanings implicit in female
representation are. Feminist readers also seek to revise the
literary criticism of the past, which has generally been im-
pervious to the difference and the distinctiveness of female
experience. Such feminist criticism, as Sandra Gilbert has
declared, "wants to decode and demystify all the disguised
questions and answers that have always shadowed the connections between textuality and sexuality, genre and gender, psychosexual identity and cultural authority,"[8] and
these concerns underlie those fours essays here that analyze how women are imagined in works by male authors.

A second mode of feminist criticism, represented in the
remaining twelve essays, is the study of women as writers,
and an exploration of the qualities that make women's writing different from men's, an approach that Showalter has
dubbed "gynocritics."[9] In her discussion of a cultural theory
of women's writing, Showalter suggests that while differences in class, race, nationality, and history are literary de-
terminants as significant as gender, "nonetheless, women's
culture forms a collective experience within the cultural
whole, an experience that binds women writers to each

other over time and space."[10] Yet, as Showalter recognizes, women's cultures are rarely autonomous. Few women live their lives apart from men. As Gerda Lerner has noted,

> Women live their social existence within the general culture and, whenever they are confined by patriarchal restraint or segregation into separateness (which always has subordination as its purpose), they transform this restraint into complementarity (asserting the importance of woman's function, even its "superiority") and redefine it. Thus, women live a duality—as members of the general culture and as partakers of women's culture.[11]

These insights are particularly significant in a discussion of what writer Norma Rosen has called the "accidents of influence"[12] that situate Jewish women writers within more than one world at the same time. Thus, Jewish women not only experience the duality of living as women in a male-dominated culture, but also keenly feel the equally significant duality of being part of a Jewish minority in often uncongenial cultural environments. Women in general, who are simultaneously "inside and outside of the male tradition," are most often reduced to "undercurrents of the mainstream."[13] So Jewish women, as other minority women, participate as "others" in several traditions at once. The intensified estrangement this kind of experience engenders is a recurring subtext in the studies of Jewish women authors collected here.

This volume is ordered roughly chronologically; this arrangement juxtaposes analyses of contemporaneous literature by and about women written in Hebrew, Yiddish, English, and Spanish, indicative, though hardly inclusive, of a Jewish female struggle across geographical and linguistic boundaries to find a voice with which to express that imaginative transmutation of experience and aspiration we call literature. Yet the chapters fall into natural categories by language groups as well, and it is in this configuration, generally speaking, that each chapter is discussed here. *Women of the Word* was not intended to record or analyze every Jewish female writer, past or present. Instead, this volume attempts to provide a representative survey of literary genres and individual writers in several significant Jewish languages of the modern period. That so much remains to be said, and so many writers to be discussed, suggests the wealth of ways in which Jewish women in the modern era are claiming their own access to the word.

Women of the Word begins with Judith Dishon's study of portrayals of women in secular Hebrew literature of the Middle Ages.[14] Dishon finds that, as in earlier Jewish literatures, two contradictory attitudes toward women prevail. Some medieval texts depict women positively, praising the wife who brings warmth and comfort to her husband's life and enables him to fulfill his religious obligations in security. Occasionally, as in other medieval literatures, such exemplary wives undergo great suffering or even sacrifice their lives in order to help their husbands. But such texts, designed to teach a man what to look for in a spouse, are in the minority; the large majority of secular Hebrew texts, most of which were intended as popular entertainment, portray women harshly, as seductive, perfidious, and selfish. While the male authors of these works borrowed liberally from literary traditions with frequent negative stereotypes of women, it is also true that they were able to build on ambiguous images of women already present in biblical and rabbinic literature. As Dishon notes, whatever the intent of these stories may have been, they succeeded in sustaining an overwhelmingly unfavorable view of women that endured in subsequent Jewish writing.

Howard Adelman's essay, which analyzes portrayals of women in Italian Jewish authors from the late Middle Ages to the nineteenth century, finds a similarly ambivalent attitude in the tracts, poetry, and sermons he examines. He is particularly struck by the hostility expressed toward women for studying traditional texts, speaking in public, or writing, indications that in parts of early modern Italy, Jewish women were beginning to expand the range of their activities, despite strong disapproval from some men. Adelman also describes the career of Rachel Luzzatto Morpurgo (1790–1871). Deeply learned in traditional Jewish sources and the first female modern Hebrew poet, she lived and wrote in a time and place where the possibilities for a woman were tightly circumscribed, particularly for a wife and mother.

Dishon and Adelman provide the historical and literary backdrop for the creative concerns and original voices of more recent Jewish women writers. At the same time, Adelman's essay chronicles the emergence of a Jewish female literary voice of unusual learning and great potential who was trapped and limited by the prejudices and conventions of her times.

The literary critic Shmuel Niger's 1919 essay, "Yiddish Literature and the Female Reader," translated and abridged by Sheva Zucker, with Zucker's additional annotations, relates the simultaneous development of female literacy and Yiddish literature. While the modern reader may not always be comfortable with some of Niger's views as to "feminine" qualities and tendencies, his generally sympathetic essay is, as his translator says, the starting point for anyone wanting to learn about women and Yiddish literature.[15] Niger describes the development of a spiritual literature for women and "plain folk who could not study the Torah," thus revealing how Yiddish became a permitted literary language in the service of female piety at the same time as it tacitly met the needs of the masses of uneducated Jewish men. Niger discusses the development of ethical *musar* writings and of the *tkhines,* supplicatory prayers for women, and he enumerates the women who wrote such Yiddish literature. Not surprisingly, they were generally elite and privileged individuals who were often closely connected with the world of rabbinic learning, usually as both daughters and wives. He concludes his article with a brief discussion of Glückel of Hameln (1645–1724), a preeminent example of the exceptional woman whose excellent education, immersion in Yiddish pietistic writings, including the tradition of the ethical will, and relative prosperity gave her the prerequisites for literary creation once widowhood and the marriages of her children allowed her the silence and space necessary to record her memoirs. The source of Glückel's conviction that her own life and experiences mattered and resonated beyond herself, however, and the origins of the reservoirs of energy upon which she drew to record them are harder to fathom, and for the modern reader remain among the most striking aspects of this wonderful writer's singularity.[16]

Norma Fain Pratt carries the story of women and Yiddish literature further in her study of fifty women writers of Yiddish whose literary works were published mainly in the United States between 1890 and 1940. These self-made women from the poorer classes of East European Jewry were typical of first-generation immigrants to America who, as Pratt writes, "interpreted their own lives in their own language," even as they spoke for the ideals of the politically radical secular Jewish subculture to which they belonged. Yet as Pratt points out in her conclusion, most of these women were undercut by gender-based discrimination, including from within their own political circles, and they painfully experienced the bitter contradiction of seeming acceptance and implicit exclusion.

Kathryn Hellerstein describes this exclusion further in her study of the gender politics inherent in the formation of the literary canon of Yiddish poetry. Examining which poems by which female poets were included in two early twentieth-century anthologies of Yiddish poetry published in the United States, Hellerstein demonstrates how male expectations of poetry by women, together with a conviction of women's secondary place within Yiddish literature, determined which poets and which of their poems would be most widely read and remembered. This cautionary essay reminds us that the absence of female Yiddish poets and certain of their poems from anthologies, both past and present, should not be taken as a final statement of their value.

Hebrew, the language of Jewish prayer and study, was at once the central language of Jewish religious and spiritual life and the language from which Jewish women were furthest removed. Traditional Jewish culture enforced this separation, advising that women pray in the vernacular and lending its approval to the production of spiritual works for women in Yiddish. Ironically, it was historical imperatives that broke down this invisible barrier as Hebrew reemerged in the early modern era as the privileged language of a new, "enlightened" Jewish literature, and ultimately became the symbolic vehicle of Jewish national aspirations. From such endeavors women could not be excluded, although their relationship to Hebrew literature long remained ambiguous.[17]

A prime example of this ambiguity is Dvora Baron, the subject of Ruth Adler's chapter. Baron, the daughter of a rabbi from a small Lithuanian shtetl, was the sole female among her enlightened East European literary peers. Educated by her father in traditional rabbinic sources generally taught only to boys, and identifying deeply with her loving and gentle male parent, Baron stands apart from other writers of her milieu in her positive representations of East European Jewish religious tradition, and in her attention to the details of women's lives. Anomalous not only on account of her gender, Baron insisted on using Hebrew rather than Yiddish to describe the homely details of shtetl life and refused to abandon her subject matter even after immigrating to the land of Israel. There, perhaps disappointed and worn down by the demands of family life and discouraged by the criticisms of other writers, she eventually withdrew into silence and seclusion.

The expression and repression of female voice that are exemplified in Baron's writings and her life are a major concern, too, in Naomi B. Sokoloff's analysis of *In the Prime of Her Life,* by Israel's preeminent novelist of the first half of this century, Nobel laureate S. Y. Agnon. Here Sokoloff explores Agnon's legitimation of gender concerns as an appropriate topic for literary art, also demonstrating how Agnon

aligns the past, present, and future of the Hebrew language
with the tentative and ultimately blighted yearnings of a
female protagonist unable to actuate her personality or potential in any concrete way. It is clear that this juxtaposition
of Hebrew with an unfulfilled female is no accident; Agnon's
deep pessimism as to the possibilities of female enlightenment and self-realization appears to mirror his apprehen-
sions for the rebirth and future of a vibrant vernacular Hebrew in the protean crucible of a Jewish state.

Women like Dvora Baron who wrote imaginative Hebrew
prose remained anomalies in Israeli culture until quite recently, when a few women writers have begun to attempt
the short story and novel forms. Yael Feldman's essay discusses the strategies such contemporary novelists as Shulamit Hareven and Shulamit Lapid employ to avoid autobiographical representation of themselves or reflections on the
condition of contemporary Israeli woman in their work. Yet,
she argues, they do reveal themselves and their concerns
with questions of female subjectivity and gender boundaries
in the characters and situations they depict in their historical novels, apparently set in periods long past. She suggests
that it is in these quasi-historical settings that Israeli woman
writers are able to register vicariously their social critique
of a contemporary Israel in which feminist concerns continue to be seen as peripheral and inimical to the larger
issues of collective identity and national survival, and in
whose literary culture the voices of women continue to be
muted.

Female writers of Hebrew in this century, as women writing in Yiddish, have most frequently been poets. As Anita
Norich has pointed out, the issues raised by this "gender
and genre discussion" are complicated and must be viewed
in a critical context that addresses "questions about tradition, canon, genre, gender, and culture" simultaneously.[18]
She suggests that the Jewish literary world has rarely been
open to women in the ways it has to men, resulting in "a
kind of rootedness in culture which, for Jews in general and

still more recently for Israelis, has been remarkably different for men and women."[19] In the dislocations occasioned by the cultural transformations, historic horrors, and physical uprootedness that have characterized the Jewish encounter with modernity, it may be that poetry rather than prose offered aspiring literary women the most accessible entry into the worlds of Yiddish and Hebrew letters.

Anne Lapidus Lerner and Miri Kubovy provide close readings of the works of two very different Hebrew poets, one tied to the natural history and physical landmarks of the land of Israel, the other fascinated by the technology of modernity that attempts to transcend the boundaries of the natural world itself.

Lerner explores the poetry of Esther Raab (1894–1981), known as the poet who first and perhaps best incorporated the Israeli landscape into modern Hebrew poetry. Born in the land of Israel to early pioneers from Eastern Europe, Raab was enamored from childhood of the Near Eastern landscape, and her deep knowledge of the natural world profoundly informs her poetry. In her writing, uniquely indigenous to the biblical landscape, she merges eroticism and images of the land, both fecund and sun bleached, into a new distillation of Hebrew in the female voice, a transformation as self-made and unexpected as the new Jewish experience of which she was a part.

In her study of the very contemporary Hebrew poetry of Maya Bejerano, Miri Kubovy examines Bejerano's use of scientific innovation and high technology in her journey from the physical truth of the external world to the truth within, a voyage to the self that transcends the particularity of national boundaries. Whether "riding an invisible optical fiber" to the unreachable star of the soul, a destination as distant as the remotest realms of space and as intimately present as a human touch, or whether celebrating sexual passion even as she is saddened by the transitory nature of physical love, Bejerano's wonder at the infinite variety of the natural world is expressed in combination with her fas-

cination with the speed of cars and and the flickering images
of film. All of existence enriches her realm of poetic experience, in which no natural phenomenon or startling new
technology, no matter how wondrous, can fully minister to
the cravings and yearnings of the human heart. Bejerano is
a product of sophisticated Israel, a cosmopolitan poet
whose use of Hebrew transforms traditional nuances while
resonating in universal cadences.

The United States, to which over two million Jews immigrated in the nineteenth and twentieth centuries, has offered Jews unimagined liberty as well as the concomitant
predicaments of conflicted identity, societal accommoda-
tion, and the ever-present option of disappearance into the
mainstream culture. Out of such pressures literature is
born, and just as American shores offered a haven for the
Yiddish poets discussed by Pratt and Hellerstein, so too
America's pluralistic cultural marketplace has supported a
vibrant American Jewish literary outpouring in English to
which women have made significant contributions.[20] Laura
Wexler discusses one of the first female immigrant writers
who chose to write English prose rather than Yiddish poetry. For Wexler, Anzia Yezierska's story is that of every
immigrant to America who must accept a state of historical amnesia in return for admission to a new cultural consciousness and world of social values. In discussing what
Yezierska was willing to negotiate for American cultural
acceptance and what she was not, Wexler highlights not
only Yezierska's estrangement from Old World Jewish patriarchs like her father, but also her disillusionment with
his American equivalent, the "Anglo-Saxon" male authority
figure like her mentor and erstwhile lover John Dewey,
whom she perceived as equally rejecting because he viewed
her as an exotic "other." While the Old World patriarch
denounces his daughter's attempts at secular education and
Americanization with scorn, the "Anglo-Saxon" authority
figure demands a self-transformation that requires the
obliteration of historical memory. What Yezierska perceives
and rebels against is America's demand that the immigrant

erase her own experience and replace it with the values of another, and she argues instead for the possibility of reconciliation of the present and past. Yet for Yezierska, gender constitutes the obstacle that cannot be overcome in either realm, whether in the lives of her fictional characters or in her own. As Wexler remarks, Yezierska's abandonment of her marriage and her painful relinquishment of her small daughter to her former husband's care in order to write her novels of immigrant life is an indication to us of how little we know about the choices demanded of immigrant Jewish women at the turn of the century, or what those choices cost.

Janet Burstein explores some of these painful choices in her discussion of Jewish women's writing of the 1920s whose themes focus upon the sacrifices exacted of women by the achievement of American middle-class success. By placing mothers at the centers of their stories, the writers she examines find a way of representing the tension they felt between fulfilling their own aspirations and honoring the cultural dictates that directed them toward service and duty to others. Coming from a European milieu in which women's activities, however essential to their families' survival, were secondary to male endeavors, Jewish mothers in America responded to middle-class imperatives by withdrawing from the marketplace to the home, where their care of their families was seen as subordinate to male wage earning activities. Self-sacrificing Jewish mothers in the autobiographical writings of Rebekah Kohut (1864–1951), the semiautobiographical work of "Leah Morton" (Elizabeth Stern 1890–1954), and the 1920s fiction of Emanie Sachs remain faithful to congruent bourgeois American and traditional Jewish values that women must "look outward to the needs of others, rather than inward, to the demands of their own soul," even as their experience reveals the ways those imperatives constrain and devalue them. In the cultural moment Burstein describes, when the conflict between competing needs is visible but cannot be resolved, the conventional middle-class, married protagonists of the works she studies must

stop short of self-realization, and instead accept their con-
stricting social roles as nurturers and consumers.

Carole S. Kessner's essay continues this theme of matri-
archal service and self-denial as she considers the idealism
and social activism that links nineteenth-century American
Jewish women writers and their twentieth-century spiritual
descendants. Kessner studies "the rhetoric of zeal" in the
lives and oeuvres of two American Jewish writers, Emma
Lazarus (1849–89) and Marie Syrkin (1899–1989), and extends this ongoing tradition to the contemporary writer
Cynthia Ozick. Kessner's subjects are analogous to Yezierska in their determination to pursue their own literary goals
despite the costs, yet their circumstances are very different.
Lazarus, Syrkin, and Ozick received excellent secular educations in the United States; all had read broadly in English
literature; and all came to their Jewish concerns only in
early adulthood, when they began to combine their literary
art with influential essays on topics of Jewish concern. Supporters of Zionism, all remained firmly anchored in the
American Diaspora, aware of its dangers but refusing to re-
pudiate its claims as a Jewish haven. For none of these pro-
digiously talented women was feminism a predominant concern. Rather, each found her true literary self through
Jewish self-identification and passionate involvement in en-
hancing and improving the lives of other Jews.

Sarah Blacher Cohen carries Kessner's topic further in
her discussion of Cynthia Ozick as a "prophet for parochialism," one of several American Jewish writers who feels
free to express her artistic vision in Jewish terms and is
committed to the creation of an authentic and sustainable
American Judaism for the future. Ozick speaks in her public
rhetoric of the formation of a new Jewish language for the
American Diaspora, "Judeo-English" or "New Yiddish,"
through which Jews may inject a Jewish sensibility into a
distinctively Jewish English, and as Cohen demonstrates,
these themes have long been part of Ozick's fiction as well.
Offering no easy answers, her writings call American Jewry
to judgment, warning of the dangers of assimilation into the

American intellectual mainstream, and reminding them in prophetic language of their historic connection to Jewish sources of creativity and sustenance.

Nora Glickman's essay on Jewish women writers in Latin America delves into a large body of literature little known to the English-speaking reader. She finds that the novels, poetry, plays, and screenplays written by Jewish women in countries from Mexico to Argentina are remarkable in the similarity of their authors' concerns with issues of assimilation and integration, generational differences, and the contrasts between their own East European Jewish heritage and Latin American society. As nonpracticing Jews in overwhelmingly Catholic countries, and as professionals and intellectuals, often of deep political commitment, who are strongly identified with Latin American culture, Jewish women writers are ambivalent about the meaning of their Jewish identities but convinced of the centrality of their Jewishness to their lives and writing. Living within two groups simultaneously, as women in a male Jewish literary tradition and as Jews in a Latin American Catholic culture, they try to transmit this duality in their writing, which retains an obsessive emphasis on the complexities of the Jewish past, particularly as reflected in family relationships, even as their works direct themselves to the human situation in general.

Sara R. Horowitz's chapter looks at the transmutations of memory, testimony, and survival in the words of women who have survived the Holocaust. Drawing on diverse genres, including oral history, memoirs, interviews, and Holocaust-based fiction, Horowitz argues that there is something characteristically "female" about women's responses to their experiences of the unthinkable, and concludes that survivors' reflections are inevitably gendered. Yet she demonstrates the ways women's experiences have been marginalized in much of the writing about the Nazi genocide: in many frequently read narratives, women figure peripherally; their memoirs and testimony are not considered central; the conditions that pertained to women particularly are rarely considered. Horowitz believes that women's experiences, and their mediation through memory and literature, reveal different patterns of experience and reflection, intrinsic both in women's physical differences from men and in their particular orientation toward family relationships. Women's experiences, she argues, do matter, in and of themselves, and as they focus our attention on the particularities of a horror beyond understanding.

The essays in this collection are part of a nascent but dynamic effort to listen to the voices of Jewish women past and present. Neither inclusive nor exclusive, *Women of the Word: Jewish Women and Jewish Writing* attempts to illuminate moments, both painful and exhilarating, from the struggle of Jewish women to find literary legitimacy, often in Jewish cultures wary of female aspirations and feminist concerns. Written in a present when Jewish women writers internationally are creating a wealth of diverse literary works, these studies remind us of the short span of time in which Jewish women's writing has flourished and inspire us with the richness of the literature that Jewish women writers have already produced, often through great pain and struggle.

NOTES

1. Anzia Yezierska, *Salome of the Tenements* (New York, 1923), 65.

2. Anzia Yezierska, *Bread Givers* (New York, 1925; repr. 1975), 297.

3. Kadya Molodowsky, from *"Froyen lider* I" ("Women Songs"), transl. Adrienne Rich, in *A Treasury of Yiddish Poetry,* ed. Irving Howe and Eliezer Greenberg (New York, 1969), 284.

4. *Jewish Women in Historical Perspective,* ed. Judith R. Baskin (Detroit, 1991).

5. For Jewish women's religious writing see *Four Centuries of Jewish Women's Spirituality: A Sourcebook,* ed. Ellen M. Umansky and Dianne Ashton (Boston, 1992).

6. Anita Norich discusses this distinction in "Jewish Literatures and Feminist Criticism: An Introduction to Gender and Text," in *Gender and*

Text in Modern Hebrew and Yiddish Literature, ed. Naomi B. Sokoloff, Anne Lapidus Lerner, and Anita Norich (New York and Jerusalem, 1992), 5.

7. Elaine Showalter, "Feminist Criticism in the Wilderness," in her edited collection, *The New Feminist Criticism: Essays on Women, Literature, and Theory* (New York, 1985), 245.

8. Sandra M. Gilbert, "What Do Feminist Critics Want? A Postcard from the Volcano," in Showalter, ed., *New Feminist Criticism,* 36.

9. Showalter, "Criticism in the Wilderness," 249.

10. *Ibid.,* 260.

11. Gerda Lerner, "The Challenge of Women's History," in her *The Majority Finds Its Past: Placing Women in History* (New York, 1979), 52; quoted in Showalter, "Criticism in the Wilderness," 261.

12. Norma Rosen, *Accidents of Influence: Writing as a Woman and Jew in America* (Albany, N.Y., 1992), xiii, and throughout, discusses being a woman and a Jew "who writes in an America . . . stunningly indifferent to both."

13. Showalter, "Criticism in the Wilderness," 264. She notes that the metaphor of "undercurrents" derives from Ellen Moers, *Literary Women: The Great Writers* (New York, 1976).

14. For images of women in biblical, Greco-Roman Diaspora, and rabbinic literatures, see Susan Niditch, "Portrayals of Women in the Hebrew Bible"; Ross S. Kraemer, "Jewish Women in the Diaspora World of Late Antiquity"; and Judith Romney Wegner, "The Image and Status of Women in Classical Rabbinic Judaism," in Baskin, *Historical Perspective.* For a study of portrayals of women in the Jewish pietistic religious literature of twelfth- and thirteenth-century Germany, see Judith R. Baskin, "From Separation to Displacement: The Problem of Women in *Sefer Hasidim,*" *Association for Jewish Studies Review* 19:1 (1994), 1–10.

15. For an annotated bibliography of recent works on women and Yiddish literature, see Kathryn Hellerstein, "Gender Studies and Yiddish Literature," in Sokoloff et al., *Gender and Text,* 249–55.

16. For a recent study of Glückel's memoirs, see Dorothy Bilik, "The Memoirs of Glikl of Hameln: The Archeology of the Text," *Yiddish* 8:2 (1992), 1–18.

17. For an annotated bibliography of feminist criticism of modern Hebrew writing, see Naomi Sokoloff, "Gender Studies and Modern Hebrew Literature," in Sokoloff et al., *Gender and Text,* 257–63. In the same book, see Anita Norich, "Jewish Literatures" 3–8, for a discussion of the cultural implications of Jewish women's writing in both Yiddish and Hebrew.

18. Norich, "Jewish Literatures," 11, 13. On women's contributions to modern Hebrew poetry, see Dan Miron, "Why Was There No Women's Poetry in Hebrew Before 1920?" in Sokoloff et al., *Gender and Text,* 65–92.

19. Norich, "Jewish Literatures," 11.

20. There is a large body of literature by American Jewish women writers, and much critical writing about their works. For some comprehensive overviews with extensive bibliographical references, see Joyce Antler's introduction to her edited collection *America and I: Short Stories by American Jewish Women Writers* (Boston, 1990), 1–24, and Sylvia Barack Fishman, "The Faces of Women: An Introductory Essay," in her

anthology of readings *Follow My Footprints: Changing Images of Women in American Jewish Fiction* (Hanover, N.H., 1992), 1–60. Two recent critical studies of American Jewish women writers are Diane Lichtenstein, *Writing Their Names: The Tradition of Nineteenth-Century American Jewish Women Writers* (Bloomington, Ind., 1992), and Ellen Uffen, *Strands in the Cable: The Place of the Past in American Jewish Women's Writing* (New York, 1992).

2 ◆ JUDITH DISHON

Images of Women in Medieval Hebrew Literature

Two contradictory attitudes toward women prevail in ancient and medieval literatures of both East and West. According to the first, women are virtuous and good, and without them life would not be worth living. But according to the second, women are evil creatures who cause men much suffering, and woe to the unfortunate who fall into their trap. In Hebrew literature this ambivalence is already evident in the Bible, where Proverbs 8:22, for example, advises that "He who finds a wife has found happiness," while Ecclesiastes 7:26 states, "And I find woman more bitter than death; she is all traps, her hands are fetters, her heart is snares. He who is pleasing to God escapes from her, and he who is displeasing is caught by her."[1]

This equivocal approach to women continues in rabbinic writings. Some sages cited in the Babylonian Talmud hold that women love and care for their husbands, give charity, act hospitably to guests (B. Berakhot 10b), and are compassionate (B. Megilla 14b). Such sources state that an extra measure of wisdom was given to women (B. Nidda 45b), and that "there is no blessing in a man's house except for the sake of his wife" (B. Baba Metzia 59a). But there are also negative talmudic statements characterizing women as chatterers (B. Kiddushin 49b) and as light-headed (B. Kiddushin 80b). Stories and anecdotes are related about bad women, such as the wives of Rav and his son, R. Hiyya (B. Yevamot 63a-b) who were consistently contrary and unresponsive to their husbands' wishes.[2]

This duality appears prominently in Jewish secular literature of the Middle Ages, as well, where the topic of women occupies an important place.[3] In the twelfth and thirteenth centuries, in particular, a sudden abundance of Hebrew prose dealing with women appears in Spain, Italy, Provence, and Ashkenaz (Germany/northern France).[4] In some cases entire volumes are devoted to women, while other books assign one or more chapters to the topic. The sophisticated composition of some of these works indicates how important the subject was to their authors; indeed, an entirely new literary genre, the debate about female virtues and vices, emerges at this time and continues well into the seventeenth century.

Some medieval Hebrew writers regard women as a blessing to mankind and an essential element of life. Husbands find repose with their wives, because "man cannot rest without a helpmate."[5] Such wives are attentive to their husbands' needs and well-being, and they merit the biblical designation of "women of valor" (Proverbs 31). Good women are neither gluttonous nor quarrelsome; their voices are soft and pleasant. They are wise, modest, and loyal, and withstand all temptation even if this causes them great suffering. They are God fearing and righteous, and may even sacrifice their own lives to save their husbands from death. These authors do not amuse themselves at the expense of good women, nor do they write words of mockery and satire; such women are treated with respect and seriousness, and nothing ironic or amusing is written about them. Rather, anecdotes and stories about good wives are intended to teach men what kind of wife to look for.

Wise women appear in both medieval Hebrew prose stories and rhymed humorous narratives, or *maqamat*. For example, Rachel, wife of Hovav, in the *maqama Ezrat Nashim* saves her husband by her wits from all his troubles.[6] Other wise women are the wives of the king in the framework story of the extremely popular *Tales of Sendebar,* and in the story told by the first sage.[7] The origins of this beloved collection of tales, some of which also portray women quite negatively, are unclear. Some researchers believe that the original book was written in India at the end of the eighth century and was translated into Arabic by the ninth century. During the Middle Ages the book was translated in different versions into Syriac, Greek, and Hebrew, and into many other European languages where it was called *The Seven Sages of Rome.*

Two stories in the *Book of Comfort (Hibbur Yafeh me-ha-Yeshu'ah)*, written by Rabbenu Nissim in the eleventh century in Qairwan (North Africa), describe female self-sacrifice. "The Shining Gown" tells about a woman who persuades her husband to sell her as a servant and give the money he gets to charity, so that his gown in the world to come will be complete. She promises to withstand all temptations and does so, suffering greatly until she is freed. Similarly, the story "Nathan de Susita" tells of a poor man's wife who desperately needs money to free her husband from jail. Nathan, a rich man, is willing to give her the money only if she sleeps with him, but she chastises him about committing such a sin. He listens to her and suppresses his desires, meriting a great reward.[8] Similar are the stories about the bride who saves her groom from death on their wedding day, when the Angel of Death comes to take his soul.[9]

But far more frequent than these positive images are the negative representations of women in medieval Hebrew literature. These women are not modest but seductive, not loyal but perfidious, and not devoted to their husbands but uncaring and selfish. Such monstrous and one-sided portrayals represent women as the enemy of men, and the cause of all their troubles in life since the beginning of human history. As the fourteenth-century Italian Hebrew writer Immanuel of Rome laments, "How many were burned because of her, / Stoned with rocks / How many were hung, how many / Were tortured, because of her. / Eve, she was the first and she / Will testify to those who understand."[10]

Popular sayings predict that disgrace and shame will befall a man because of women: "A woman is a month's joy and a lifetime of agony."[11] When wives are still young they may delight their husbands, but soon enough they will turn into old bags,[12] and even when young and beautiful, they are able to make the lives of their husbands unbearable by their constant nagging. In the story "The Wood Worker" in his *Book of Delight*, the twelfth-century Spanish Hebrew writer Joseph Ibn Zabara describes the ultimately fatal catastrophes that befall a couple when the wife nags.[13] Women are criticized, too, for their endless chattering and their insatiable desire for clothing and luxuries; it is said that a wife may easily impoverish her husband by her greed and gluttony. Thus, Immanuel of Rome recounts: "As soon as she marries / She will want clothes / Even ornaments / Head-dresses, veils / Nose-rings and pearls / Turbans and scarves . . . / Therefore the early books / Of proverbs say / That woman is the reason for / The lack of property."[14] Especially objectionable is the voice of a woman that disturbs her husband's rest. That voice is described as thunder; together with the meal, such a wife serves her husband a mouthful of curses and abuse.[15]

It is, therefore, not astounding to find stories and sayings in which women are likened to the devil himself, sometimes even surpassing him in wickedness.[16] This negative attitude, which finds in women the essence of all evil, is also expressed in the similes used in these compositions. Often women are compared to beasts, wolves, snakes, and cattle; in short, to cunning and mischievous animals or to stupid and stubborn creatures that can be handled only with a stick. Thus, Moshe Ibn Haviv, who was born in Lisbon in the mid-fifteenth century and later lived in Italy, writes in his

Darkhei No'am, "If your wife is evil and will not listen to your voice to serve you and plots against you, know that with a strong stick a rebellious cow will straighten her furrows and plough."[17]

Sometimes women are compared to a terrible storm because of the damage they cause.[18] A very insulting simile likens women to leprosy, the most horrible disease of the Middle Ages, a comparison that is already found in the Talmud.[19] The Arabian king in *The Book of Delight* neatly sums up such negative thinking: "Never has there been seen or heard of a woman who was good and virtuous, endowed with understanding and knowledge. Their love is only for their own pleasure and their own benefit. They have no control over their desires and they sin against themselves" (26).

The Hebrew authors who depicted women in such a hateful manner were strongly influenced by misogynistic traditions in the Muslim and Christian cultures in which they lived. Thus, the feminine stereotypes in their writing were often based on the descriptions of women in other literatures of medieval Europe. Building, for example, on an existing story in Eastern literature, the Hebrew author would first provide a Jewish background and give the heroes Hebrew names. Often the story started and ended with a verse from the Bible, adding authenticity to its contents. Interspersed into the story were more verses and citations from biblical and rabbinic sources, while the language of the story itself was biblical Hebrew. The reader of a story that had been changed in these ways would be easily convinced that it was rooted in centuries-old Jewish tradition.

The most common shortcomings of women to appear in medieval Hebrew prose works can be grouped into three somewhat contradictory sets of qualities: fearfulness and cruelty; laziness and greed or gluttony; and light-headedness and shrewdness or unending deceitfulness. The inherent fearfulness of women is depicted so vividly that it becomes a symbol for all forms of cowardice and weakness. Thus, in *The Book of Delight*, a male character is admonished, "Do not see my face again for you are not a man; your

heart is as soft as a woman's" (29), and in the fourteenth-
century Spanish Hebrew text, *Even Bohan*, the author laments, "I have almost grown old and have lost my strength,
like a woman."[20] But, despite their weakness, women do not
hesitate to employ cruelty to better their lot. They are even
ready to commit murder for material gain, as in the story in
The Book of Delight (and earlier in *The Book of Comfort*)
about a rich merchant's wife who is willing to kill her husband in order to become queen.[21]

Women can be immensely lazy. Although their task is to
take care of their homes and raise their children, they often
prefer to be idle, and demand pampering, slaves, maids, and
all kinds of delicacies. Wives plot to obtain whatever they
desire, without caring how much the husbands have to toil
for it. The wife in Judah Ibn Shabbetai's *Minhat Yehudah*
even threatens to deny her husband entry to his own house
if he does not fulfill her demands.[22] Fourteenth-century Immanuel of Rome depicts the combined laziness and greed of
women as follows: "They dress in finery, eat delicacies,
drink nectar. They repose on their side on coaches, eat nuts
and call for the singer to sing them songs."[23] In short,
women love to dress in expensive clothes, show off their
jewelry, and will always demand more; as Immanuel puts it:
"She made a covenant with the mirror / And I will always
find it in her hands / As if she cannot live without it."[24] Such
a wife even gives her husband advice on how to get richer,
but only a fool would listen to her and he finds out soon
enough that a woman's advice leads to calamity, as in the
story about the jeweler's wife who promises to make him
rich if he creates a golden idol. It is her idea to sell the idol
to the princess, who, she thinks, will reward them both with
a large sum of money. The foolish husband listens to his
wife and makes the idol, forgetting that he lives in a country
where idols are forbidden. Instead of getting a big reward,
his hand is cut off when the king finds out that he sold an
idol.[25]

Light-headedness and stupidity are two vices that are attributed to women in many medieval Hebrew works, based

on the talmudic saying that women are light-headed. "To seek cleverness in a woman is as hard as to seek modesty in a whore," says Immanuel of Rome,[26] and "as beautiful as they are," complains Jedaiah Ha-Penini in fourteenth-century Provence, "so are they stupid."[27] Yet, while women are depicted as light-headed and obtuse, they are also portrayed as shrewd, deceitful, and fickle. Seductiveness and allure were believed to be inborn qualities of women, stemming from the ceaseless lust that dominates most of their activities. Thus, Judah Alharizi, who lived in Spain at the turn of the twelfth century, wrote in *The Book of Tahkemoni,* "Three things will not be satiated by three things, an ear by words, land by rain, and women by men."[28]

Many medieval Hebrew proverbs and short stories center around the supposed female traits of deceit and infidelity. The pronounced emphasis on this theme in medieval Hebrew writing may have its origins in the sources from which this literature is drawn, since frequently Hebrew stories are in fact translations and adaptations of works originating in the East, mainly in Persian and Indian literatures. The themes of female infidelity and deceit are central in Arabic and medieval European literatures, too, and may also have derived to some extent from similar sources.[29] Such works in Hebrew include *Tales of Sendebar, The Prince and the Hermit,* and *Kalila ve-Dimna. The Prince and the Hermit* is apparently based on an Indian source that describes Buddha's life. It was translated into Arabic and European languages and became one of the most popular books in European literature during the Middle Ages under the title *Barlaam and Josaphat.* In the thirteenth century it was translated into Hebrew from an Arabic source no longer extant, by Abraham Ibn Hasdai, who put it into the style of a *maqama.* The very popular *Kalila ve-Dimna (Kalila and Dimna)* is an eighth-century Arabic adaptation of an ancient Indian book of animal tales, *The Panchatantra,* and is named after two of its central animal characters who are jackals.[30]

In these and similar books, women's wiles are expressed through the three interrelated characteristics of hypocrisy,

deceit, and betrayal, qualities said to be deeply imbedded in
the female soul, which are used to betray husbands or to
acquire a lover. The authors warn males repeatedly about
this phenomenon: "Who can understand women's deceit
and wiles? How many great men have they brought low and
how much agony have they bequeathed, how many brave
men have fallen because of them and could not be raised?"
(*Minhat Yehudah*, 4). Men are especially warned against women's treachery, as the hermit tells the prince in *The Prince
and the Hermit*: "My son, be aware of the wiles of women and
their betrayal and their machinations, because their
thoughts are many" (108). The wiles and deceptions of
women are also at the heart of *Tales of Sendebar,* where the
sages warn the king not to listen to his wife's advice to kill
his son, because all women are treacherous and liars. To
elucidate further, the seven sages tell stories about women's
deceit and machinations.[31]

Among the many images of female treachery in medieval
Hebrew literature is "the treacherous woman and her paramour."[32] This theme is found in anthologies of stories from
non-Jewish sources, such as *Kalila and Dimna*, *Tales of
Sendebar*, and *The Prince and the Hermit,* but it is also found
in other Hebrew medieval works, such as the pre-eleventh-
century *Midrash Aseret ha-Dibberot,*[33] in *Meshal Ha-Kadmoni,*
composed by Yitzhak Ibn Sahula in thirteenth-century
Spain,[34] and in the somewhat later *Proverbs of King Solomon.*[35] All these stories tell about a wife who betrays her
husband with a lover, often employing considerable cunning
to deceive her husband upon his unexpected return while
her lover is still with her. In these tales, the wife always
succeeds in "proving" that her husband is mistaken and
that his suspicions are unfounded. She generally manages to
escape punishment, and sometimes even extracts an apol-
ogy from her husband, either in words or in gifts.[36] These
stories, like the contemporaneous French *fabliaux,* are generally written so that the sympathy of the reader is with the
shrewd duper, the wife, and not with the dupe, her husband.

Stories built around the theme of "the deceitful wife" or

"the wife who did not withstand the test of trust" also deal extensively with the treachery of women. Mostly, this theme concerns a test that a king gives to a couple to prove his conjecture that women are worse than death, treacherous, and untrustworthy. The king first tries to persuade the husband to kill his wife, promising his daughter in marriage as a reward. The husband withstands the temptation and does not harm his wife. Then the king tries to entice the wife to kill her husband, promising he will marry her if she does. But knowing the folly of women, the king gives her a tin sword, which crumples harmlessly when she immediately attempts to despatch her spouse. This is how the king proves his claim that all women are treacherous. Stories with this theme appear in many Hebrew medieval works.[37]

A third paradigm of female treachery is known in world literature as "the matron of Ephesus." A widow cries over the grave of her husband and refuses to be comforted. But soon enough, she falls in love with a watchman who comes to discover who is crying in the middle of the night. Because the watchman neglects his post in the cemetery to dally with the widow, the body of a hung man is stolen, and he is now afraid that he will be hung in its place. To save the watchman, the widow unearths the body of her deceased husband. She desecrates the body to make it look similar to the one that was stolen, and hangs the mutilated body of her husband in place of the stolen one.[38]

Another popular theme deals with female vengeance. When a male refuses to be seduced by a treacherous woman, she can become cruel and make false accusations against him. This is the way the young wife of the king behaves in the framework story of *Tales of Sendebar*. She tries to seduce the king's son with her charms and have him join her machinations against his father. When the son refuses her, she accuses him of trying to sleep with her, and as a result he is almost executed. In some of the stories, the false accusations of a woman may actually bring about the death of an innocent man, as in the story about a scholar who, according to custom, leaves his phylacteries outside a lav-

atory. A woman who passes by takes them and claims that
the scholar gave them to her as harlot's pay. Unable to
refute the false accusation, the scholar throws himself off
the roof. Similar is the story "R. Meir and the Unfaithful
Woman." R. Meir's custom is to lodge in Tiberias with someone named Judah. Once, when R. Meir is intoxicated, Judah's second wife nestles against him during the night, and
in the morning she tells him that relations have occurred,
giving him a sign that she has seen his body. R. Meir runs
away from the house and decrees a fast upon himself, convinced that he is an adulterer. Then a voice calls out from
Heaven that he is slated for the world to come, and he understands that the woman had lied.[39]

In Hebrew medieval tales the deceitfulness of a woman
may be so fierce that no man can withstand her. Such a
woman knows her great powers and will seduce a man with
all the means at her disposal. *Tales of Sendebar* relates the
story of a simple woman (the wife of an innkeeper) who
proves to a wise man, who claims to be an expert on the
subject of female arts and cunning, that a man can never
really understand all of women's wiles and deceptions, nor
be alert to all of them. After this wise man falls into the trap
she sets for him, he agrees: no man can escape a woman's
stratagems. He then burns his treatise on women's deceptions, over which he has labored for years.[40]

In the book *Mishlei Arav,* by Yitzhak, a writer of the late
twelfth or early thirteenth century, chapter 46, an old man
summarizes his experiences in a similar fashion:

> And I have had experience for years with men and
> women. I have found out that if a man will sit together
> for a day or two with another man whom he has not
> known before, or if he will go with him for a few days'
> journey, he will be able to know his ideas and under-
> stand his customs, and will be able to recognize his
> inner thoughts on his face. But a man may be together
> with a woman for many years and he will discover that
> every day she will display a new manner and will act

differently, as is said, "One man out of a thousand I found, but a woman out of all these I did not find."

Men are warned against women's seductiveness, treachery, and cunning in many medieval Hebrew texts. *Minhat Yehudah* 3, for example, offers the following proverbs, "It is better to be among thorns than to be among women"; "It is better to cook on a stove than to be between two breasts"; and "Meet an enraged bear, meet a pack of wolves in the forest, but do not meet privately with a woman." In other sayings women are described as repugnant and loathsome.[41] Yet almost all these warnings are in vain; in many works the woman succeeds in seducing the male simply because he cannot resist her.[42]

All medieval Hebrew writers whose works survive were men. They built on the ambiguous images of women present in biblical and rabbinic literature and borrowed liberally from other literary traditions where negative stereotypes of women were a standard convention. Some writers may have genuinely dreaded women and resented their fearsome powers,[43] while others were simply content to play on popular stereotypes in order to entertain their readers. Often, authorial use of humor, irony, parody, and satire in portraying women leaves the intended message unclear. Thus, evil protagonists (male or female) may say positive things about women, and vice versa,[44] while some authors use a framework story whose tone is positive toward women, while the stories within the framework are extremely negative.[45] Another device found in many works is the double entendre, where the literal level of a story may depict women as evil, while the second, hidden level reveals her male counterpart as equally despicable.[46]

Nevertheless, whether one interprets these works as unabashedly misogynistic, as satire and parody criticizing popular opinion, or as observations on the failings of human nature among both men and women, one cannot escape the unpleasant portrayals of women. The bitter taste of these antifemale stories persists even in works that ultimately make clear that a villain has used misogynistic tales only for the sake of harming one of the heroes. It is the regrettable fact that whatever the intended aim of these stories and sayings may have been, they succeeded in creating an overwhelmingly negative stereotype of women in medieval Hebrew writing that reinforced earlier, similar traditions, and remained as an enduring feature of subsequent Jewish literature.

NOTES

1. Recent scholarship on women in biblical literature includes Tikva Frymer-Kensky, *In the Wake of the Goddesses: Women, Culture and the Biblical Transformation of Pagan Myth* (New York, 1992); Susan Niditch, "Portrayals of Women in the Hebrew Bible," in *Jewish Women in Historical Perspective,* ed. Judith R. Baskin (Detroit, 1991), 25–42; *The Women's Bible Commentary,* ed. Carol A. Newsom and Sharon H. Ringe (Louisville, Ky., 1992); Ilana Pardes, *Countertraditions in the Bible: A Feminist Approach* (Cambridge, Mass., 1992).

2. For more details on attitudes expressed toward women in such rabbinic texts as the Mishnah and Talmud, see Judith Hauptman, "Images of Women in the Talmud," in *Religion and Sexism,* ed. R. R. Ruether (New York, 1974), 184–212; Rachel Biale, *Women and Jewish Law: An Exploration of Women's Issues in Halakhic Sources* (New York, 1984); Judith R. Baskin, "The Separation of Women in Rabbinic Judaism," in *Women, Religion, and Social Change,* ed. Y. Y. Haddad and E. B. Findly (Albany, N.Y., 1985), 3–18; Judith Romney Wegner, *Chattel or Person: The Status of Women in the Mishnah* (New York and Oxford, 1988), and "The Image and Status of Women in Classical Rabbinic Judaism," in Baskin, *Historical Perspective,* 68–93.

3. Not much research has been done on women in Hebrew and Muslim literatures of the Middle Ages, in contrast with the abundance of research on women in other medieval European literatures. Works of this latter type include J. M. Ferrante, *Woman as Image in Medieval Literature from the Twelfth Century to Dante* (New York, 1975); E. Power, *Medieval Women* (Cambridge, Mass., 1975); *The Roles and Images of Women in the Middle Ages and Renaissance,* ed. D. Radcliff Umstead, *University of Pittsburgh Publications on the Middle Ages and Renaissance* 3 (1975); K. M. Wilson and E. M. Makowski, *Wykked Wyves and the Woes of Marriage* (Albany, N.Y., 1990); and R. Howard Bloch, *Medieval Misogyny and the Invention of Western Romantic Love* (Chicago, 1991).

4. For the image of women in Hebrew poetry of the Middle Ages in Spain, see Raymond P. Scheindlin, *Wine, Women, and Death: Medieval Hebrew Poems on the Good Life* (Philadelphia, 1986), 77–138.

5. Shmuel Ha-Nagid, *The Collected Poetry of Shmuel Ha-Nagid* [Hebrew], 2 vols., ed. Dov Jarden (Jerusalem, 1982), 2: *Ben Mishle* no. 722.

6. This *maqama* was published by A. M. Habermann in *Three Maqamat on Women* [Hebrew] (Jerusalem, 1971), 32–44.

7. Morris Epstein, *Tales of Sendebar: An Edition and Translation of the Hebrew Version of the Seven Sages. Based on Unpublished Manuscripts* (Philadelphia, 1967).

8. For a Hebrew translation of this work, which was composed in Arabic, see H. Z. Hirschberg, *Book of Comfort (Hibbur Yafeh me-ha-Yeshu'ah)* [Hebrew], (Jerusalem, 1970); these stories are found on 26–28, 73–76. The story of Nathan de Susita appears in other versions, for example as story 13 in *Sefer Ma'asim*, an unpublished story collection compiled by an unknown author in twelfth-century northern France or Germany, now in the Bodleian Library, ms. Or 135. See Eli Yassif, *"Sefer Ma'asim,"* [Hebrew] *Tarbiz* 53 (1984), 409–29.

9. See story 139 in M. Gaster, *The Exempla of the Rabbis,* rev. ed. (New York, 1968); "The Hero Predestined to Die on His Wedding Day," in H. Schwarzbaum, *Jewish Folklore Between East and West,* ed. Eli Yassif (Beer Sheva, Israel, 1989), 143–72.

10. *The Cantos of Immanuel of Rome* [Hebrew], ed. Dov Jarden (Jerusalem, 1957), 1:32. Similar negative attitudes are expressed by the thirteenth-century Spanish writer Judah Ibn Shabbetai, in such satiric writings as his 1208 *Minhat Yehudah Sonei Hanashim (Hater of Women)*, which is in *Ta'am Zeqenim,* ed. A. Ashkenazi (Frankfurt am Main, 1854); the Provençal writer Jedaiah Ha-Penini, (c. 1270–1340), whose rejoinder, "In Defense of Women," is collected in Habermann, *Three Maqamat on Women.*

11. Abraham Ibn Hasdai, *The Prince and the Hermit (Ben Ha-Melekh ve-ha-Nazir)* [Hebrew], ed. S. Levin (Warsaw, 1922).

12. Ha-Penini, "Defense of Women," 66.

13. Joseph Ibn Zabara, *The Book of Delight (Sefer ha-Sha'shu'im)* [Hebrew], ed. I. Davidson (Berlin, 1925), 26. Similar in theme is *Ma'amar Midyenei Isha (A Short Book on the Wickedness of Women)*, written in Spain in the fourteenth century by Maimon Galipapa, ed. I. Davidson in *Shalosh Halatzot* (New York, 1904).

14. Jarden, *Cantos of Immanuel,* 31.

15. Ibn Zabara, *Book of Delight,* 141; Judah Al-Harizi, *The Book of Tahkemoni* [Hebrew], ed. A. Kaminka (Warsaw, 1899), 71; Hirschberg, *Book of Comfort,* 44. See also T. Rosen, "On Tongues Being Bound and Let Loose: Women in Medieval Hebrew Literature," *Prooftexts* 8 (1988), 67–87.

16. In the story "The Washerwoman and the Devil," in Ibn Zabara's *Book of Delight,* 138–40, a woman is described as worse than the devil.

17. Moshe Ibn Habib, *Ways of Pleasantness (Darkkei No'am)*, ed. H. Schirmann, in *Ha-Shira ha-Ivrit bi-Sefarad uvi-Provence* 2 (1956), 664.

18. Judah Ibn Shabbetai, *Minhat Yehudah,* 3.

19. Ibn Zabara, *Book of Delight,* 22; Galipapa, *Ma'amar Midyenei Isha,* 28; based on B. Yevamot 63a–b.

20. Kalonimus ben Kalonimus, *Even Bohan*, ed. A. M. Habermann (Tel Aviv, 1956), 11.

21. Ibn Zabara, *Book of Delight*, 26–30, and also 32–33, the story of the widow weeping on her husband's grave; see also J. Dishon, *"The Book of Delight," Composed by Joseph ben Meir Zabara* [Hebrew] (Jerusalem, 1985), 61–77.

22. Ibn Shabbetai, *Minhat Yehudah*, 9.

23. Jarden, *Cantos of Immanuel*, 33.

24. *Ibid.*, 365.

25. Ibn Zabara, *Book of Delight*, 26.

26. Jarden, *Cantos of Immanuel*, 338.

27. Ha-Penini, "Defense of Women," 18.

28. Alharizi, *Book of Tahkemoni*, 337–38.

29. There is, for example, a comprehensive chapter on women and their negative traits in the literary thesaurus *Uyun al-akhbar* (*The Fountains of Story*) by the ninth-century Arab philologist Ibn Qutaiba. Christian European literature of the Middle Ages often preached against women and their perfidiousness. The subject of the deception and treachery of women is dealt with in sermons, in the didactic literature, and in belles lettres, such as the monumental French thirteenth-century poem *The Romance of the Rose* by Guillaume de Lorris and Jean de Meun, and in the French *fabliaux*. For more on this literature, see Bloch, *Medieval Misogyny*.

30. See Joseph Derenbourg, *Deux versions hébraïques du livre de Kalila et Dimnah* (Paris, 1881).

31. For more on the subject of women's deceit and wiles, see, for example, ch. 45 and 46 of *Mishlei Arav*, by Yitzhak, published in *Ha-Levanon* (1868); Jarden, *Cantos of Immanuel*, 30: "Listen, O Prince, to my knowledge of women's deceit. They hunt the souls of men and they ensnare them. A person cannot fathom the multitude of their deceit and evil."

32. See Judith Dishon, "The Deceitful Woman and Her Paramour" [Hebrew], *Criticism and Interpretation* 30.

33. This early collection of stories was republished by A. Jellinek in *Beit ha-Midrash*, part I, 3d ed. (Jerusalem, 1967), 86–87.

34. Yitzhak ben Shlomo Ibn Sahula, *Meshal ha-Kadmoni*, ed. Yisrael Zmora (Tel Aviv, 1952).

35. *Proverbs of King Solomon* (*Meshalim shel Shlomo ha-Melekh*) first appeared in print in 1516 in Constantinople. Originally, the book consisted of five short stories that take place in the time of King Solomon (or of his father, King David), but the number of stories varies in later versions. The book was republished by A. Jellinek, *Beit ha-Midrash*, part IV, 3d ed. (Jerusalem, 1967), 145–52. A condensed English translation appears under the title "Parables of Solomon" in Moses Gaster, *The Exempla of the Rabbis*.

36. Dishon, "Deceitful Woman."

37. See, for example, Hirschberg, *Book of Comfort* 30–33; Ibn Zabara, *Book of Delight*, 26–30; *Sefer Ma'asim*, story 49; in the *Proverbs of King Solomon*, 146–48; and in a slightly different form in *Kalila and Dimna*, "The Deceitful Dove," 282–305.

38. Ibn Zabara, *Book of Delight,* 32–33.
39. Hirshberg, *Book of Comfort,* 68–70. A slightly different version of this story appears in *Midrash Aseret ha-Dibberot* (A. Jellinek, *Beit ha-Midrash,* part I), 81–83.
40. *Tales of Sendebar,* lines 1042–76.
41. In an argument between a man and a woman as to who is more important in the forty-first *maqama* in *The Book of Tahkemoni,* 322, the man says to the woman: "If the woman is the foundation of man, then it is a bad and evil-smelling foundation."
42. There are a number of stories where the male is almost seduced but is saved at the last moment, as, for example, in the story "Matya ben Harash" in *Midrash Aseret ha-Dibberot,* 79–80, and in Gaster, *The Exempla of the Rabbis,* story 136 (see the bibliography there), where Satan disguises himself as a beautiful woman who attempts to seduce R. Matya ben Harash to test him. When R. Matya cannot withstand the temptation anymore, he takes out his own eyes and refuses to let the angel Rafael heal him so he won't fall prey to temptation again.
43. For analyses of medieval fears of women, see, for example W. Lederer, *The Fear of Women* (New York, 1960); H. Goldberg, "Sexual Humor in Misogynist Medieval Exempla" in *Women in Hispanic Literature,* ed. B. Miller (Berkeley, Calif., 1983), 67–83; M. Hallissy, *Venomous Woman: Fear of the Female in Literature,* (New York, 1987); R. Howard Bloch, "Medieval Misogyny," *Representations* 20 (1987), 1–24; and *Misogyny, Misandry and Misanthropy,* ed. R. Howard Bloch and F. Ferguson (Berkeley, Calif., 1989).
44. In *Minhat Yehudah,* for example, the villains, Sheker and Kozbi, say positive things about women, while in *The Book of Delight* the sly fox tells antifemale stories to make the tiger disbelieve his wife and ignore her good advice. In the end it turns out that the fox has lied and the tiger's wife has tried in vain to rescue her husband from his evil grasp. A similar theme is developed in Ibn Sahula, *Meshal ha-Kadmoni,* 71–90.
45. The outer framework of *The Book of Delight* presents a positive attitude toward women, while the inner stories, such as those of the tiger and the fox, are negative.
46. This is a common device in medieval Hebrew prose; see Dishon, *"The Book of Delight,"* 58–61; 75–77.

3 ◆ HOWARD ADELMAN

Finding Women's Voices in Italian Jewish Literature

AMON: **Many tell me that the counsel of a child or a woman, who speaks impulsively and without due consideration, is words of prophecy.**

RAV HEMDAN: **Thus the spirit in a woman, a fool, or a minor is prophecy, but they do not know it.**

—Judah Sommo (1527–92)
***A Comedy of Betrothal* II:7[1]**

To learn what Italian Jewish women thought, said, and did before the modern period, one must study the writings of male authors. The literary texts of Italian Jewry, such as biblical commentaries, sermons, philosophical writing, ethical tracts, and poetry, often reflect hostility toward women's attempts to assume power and to pursue activities that many men deemed inappropriate for them. That male writers inveighed against women who studied traditional texts, spoke in public, and wrote implies that there were women who did these things. Moreover, that such strong cases for female subjugation had to be made may also indicate that efforts to limit women's endeavors and their spheres of action were not accepted as a matter of course by either sex.[2]

One of the most striking features of Italian Hebrew poems about women from the period of the Renaissance is their specific references to Jewish women with political and economic power. For example, *Magen nashim* (*Protector of Women*) by Judah Sommo (1527–92) begins with a dedication to Hannah Rieti, a prominent woman related to a family of well-educated women. In the course of the poem he makes many references to other leading Jewish women of Italy, including Benvenida, "the Princess" Abravanel, and her daugher, Dona Gioia, "who has a name among the mighty."[3] Sommo, and other Italian Jewish writers who refer to powerful Jewish women, are following conventions established by such Italian Renaissance writers as Ariosto, Gogio, and Castiglione, whose works about women not only are dedicated to women, but are inspired by the contradiction their authors saw between traditional negative attitudes toward females, and the actual political power held by Lucrezia Borgia, Elizabeth Gonzaga, Isabella and Beatrice d'Este, and others.[4] The Jewish writers, following this model, attempted to place "great" Jewish women of their own era into the tradition of great Jewish women of the Bible, and included the great women of pagan antiquity and the Christian patronesses of the Renaissance. Yet, as with Christian writing, hostility also accompanied praise, perhaps indicating male resentment of the authority a few elite women had acquired. The fifteenth-century Hebrew poet Jacob Fano, for instance, attacks Sommo for having tried to ingratiate himself with powerful women in his poem, writing sarcastically and referring to the blessing thanking God on the occasion of significant events: "Say the *sheheheyanu* for our time, to see women who possess Torah and greatness together."[5]

This ambivalence is also evident in *Eshet hayyil*, (*A Woman of Valor*), by Abraham Yagel (1553–c. 1623), a rabbi, teacher, and scholar from the Reggio area of northern Italy, which typifies many Jewish writings about women from early modern Italy. This extended commentary on Proverbs

31:10–31, a biblical hymn of praise to the good wife, described by the author as a "small sermon," was finished in
late 1605, published during the next year, and never republished.[6] The content of this text written for men, which is
primarily based in rabbinic exegesis, provides insights into
contemporary discourse about the roles of men and women.
The central theme of the book is the comparison of the
woman of valor, the dutiful wife, with her opposite, the *ishah
zarah,* or "other woman," of Proverbs 6–7.

The woman of valor serves her husband and does everything that is necessary to make him happy and to preserve
his honor. She is gentle, kind, and calm, and views her husband as the master and lord appointed over her by God as
a lord rules over a state (6b). If she does not please him she
will suffer great pain (6b). This remark is the closest Yagel
comes to suggesting that a wife may merit physical abuse,
although he mentions elsewhere that part of her work includes administering corporal punishment to the young
women under her supervision as well as to her own children
(12b).

The husband trusts his wife, places his house and possessions in her charge, and she takes care of them and
raises the children. The woman of valor takes the initiative
in meeting her husband's needs and requires no prompting
from him. All her thoughts are directed toward his needs
(10a, 18b), motivated by a mixture of fear, love, and duty
(17b). For the purpose of further serving her husband, she is
involved in business, which includes meeting many merchants from abroad; she is careful not to leave her house,
where she carries out most of her transactions (11a, 14a–b).
She even tries to put aside a third of her income to invest in
land (12a) and to give as charity (12b); these efforts may not
always be appreciated by her husband (12a). One of the
most important aspects of her work, as for most women,
historically, is her spinning. The text mentions that the spindle and distaff are the principal outlets for women's creativity and intellect, expressive of the concern that a woman's
idleness may lead to lewdness (12b, 17b).[7]

Commenting on Proverbs 31:22, "Fine linen and purple are her clothing," Yagel finds biblical justification for women adorning themselves with expensive finery as a sign of their honor, yet he is also concerned for vanity and needless expenses and suggests a balanced middle way where the things that are necessary for the man's honor and reputation are acquired without funds being expended on fleeting frivolities (13b–14a). He reinforces this point by connecting it with the next verse from Proverbs (31:23), "Her husband is known at the gates," suggesting that the man's honor is dependent upon his wife's behavior and appearance (14a). Yagel's remarks reflect the thinking behind the Italian Jewish community's sumptuary laws that tried to limit conspicuous consumption, especially for women.[8]

According to Yagel, a woman's nature is satisfied in caring for her home and raising children (14a). He warns (15a):

> her voice must never be heard in public like a screaming virago [*kolanit*]; all the women who want to be like men raise their voices to speak assertively [*ledaber gevohah*] like cocks croak, raising their voice so their tongue becomes a sharp sword. But [the woman of valor] does not dare to open her mouth except with wisdom "as words of the sages are heard quietly" (Ecclesiastes 9:17). In addition she will not give in to much speech or the idle chatter of women. Rather, all her speech will be leveled with proper correction, and her words will be in suitable conformity to the rest of her ways.

For a fleeting moment he appears to sanction the acquisition, if not the expression, of wisdom by women. However, the next sentence, accompanied by all of the prejudices of the period, makes clear that this is a concession for ornamental and aesthetic purposes only: "In order that we do not think that she is like one of the blacks who do not have the mind or heart to speak because of the weakness of their intellect and the grief of their heart and their natural fear that the little that they speak, their words will be rebuke and absurd thoughts." Rather, basing himself on Proverbs 31:26, "She opens with wisdom and the teaching (*torat*) of kindness is on her tongue," Yagel explains that the woman is encouraged to arrange her words in a splendid way and with great kindness so that she will find favor with all who see her and so that her words will be acceptable to all who hear her. In describing her words not only as pearls and precious objects, but as words of Torah more precious than fine gold, he presents the woman's words as an ornament and concedes that she must have access to the study of some Torah, at least, to be successful in her decorative role (15a).

The second half of Yagel's sermon/commentary is devoted to describing the opposite of a woman of valor, "the other woman," who represents the majority of her sex (16a). Such a woman, bound by neither fear nor love, abandons not only her husband but God. The first sign of her recklessness is that she is noisy, rebellious in the house, she ventures outside, and stops doing her work. Soon, owing to idleness, she is committing adultery and causing shame to her cuckold husband (17b–18a). So great is Yagel's concern for the consequences of a woman's neglecting any of her duties to her husband, home, and family that, in a fascinating reference to early modern Jewish women's spirituality, he explicitly singles out for rebuke women who adopt ascetic practices such as daily fasting, prayer, placing ashes on their heads, wearing sackcloth, denying themselves enjoyment of even the smallest earthly matters, or vowing to abstain from all pleasure. Even though Yagel admits that the intentions of these women are good and holy, he declares their single-minded devotion to God as a dereliction of their other duties. By pursuing this course, a woman has not fulfilled her obligations to God, because she has abandoned her husband and her home. A man will turn against his wife and hate her for taking such a course (18b–19a).

From Yagel's rhetoric, it seems likely that women did not always serve their husbands, preserve their honor, act gently, kindly, and calmly toward them, and accept their authority. It was sometimes necessary for men to threaten their wives with suffering and great pain to ensure their attentive service. Yagel's writing seems to indicate that some women did not adequately manage their homes, raise their children, and pursue businesses. Others may have pursued their business, as indicated in contemporary Jewish literature, at the expense of their household duties, perhaps not only outside the house but in loud, public altercations.[9] This may be the reason why their activities were not always appreciated by their husbands. In an apparent contradiction of some of his earlier pronouncements, Yagel later cautions the husband not to consider saying that God has made him lord and master (*patron*) over his wife as a master over a slave, a king over servants, or a shepherd over a flock (23a). A final admonition is that it is also a disgrace for him to raise his voice to his wife before others or to engage in sexual frolic with her in public (23b). These prohibitions show that Yagel was more interested in protesting the behavior of independent women than in sanctioning oppressive treatment of women by men.

The key to understanding Yagel's nuanced description of the marital relationship is that the education, wealth, and refinement attained by a woman must accrue to the honor, prestige, and position of her husband. Similar views, also rooted in scripture, tradition, law, and custom, were expressed throughout Europe at this time.[10] Thus, many of the aspects of economic and intellectual life that were possible areas of empowerment for women, such as fiscal independence, educational attainment, rich dress, and even family relations,[11] were areas of domestic life in which Yagel tried to present women as functioning for the benefit of their husbands and families.[12]

Another example of an early modern Hebrew commentary on Proverbs 31 is found in a manuscript called *Shevah hanashim* (*In Praise of Women*) by David ben Judah Messer Leon (c. 1465–c. 1536), an Italian rabbi and intellectual who later settled in Constantinople.[13] Many aspects of his discourse about women resemble Yagel's.[14] David ben Judah

praises good women (*shevah hanashim hatovot*, 109b) effu-
sively because they are so hard to find (110b). While he is
away, her husband can depend upon such a wife to super-
vise the house and his funds, which she will not waste on
pleasures or clothing. She makes his desires her own, and
can earn income through her industry so that he can be idle
(115b). In his absence he trusts her not to commit adultery
as "evil women" do (see Proverbs 6–7). Because of his trust
in his good, modest, and loving wife, he can travel on business and better support his family. Men who distrust their
wives are not as free to travel and to prosper. They become
angry and beat their wives cruelly.[15] David ben Judah notes
that wives who have been beaten might be expected to take
vengeance against their husbands; however, these women
avoid doing so even when the opportunity arises. Instead,
they respond with kindness to their abusive husbands. This
is further to their credit. David ben Judah comments on
Proverbs, stating that women should always be happy with
their husbands' lot, be occupied with projects, and not take
part in idle conversations. Even if wealthy, a wife must work
so that she does not become bored or promiscuous. Following Proverbs closely, he praises the good wife for her good
sense in business and her diligence in housework, particularly her willingness to rise early to care for her family. She
also buys land, spins voluntarily, gives charity, and shows
herself to be enlightened (116b–118a). Although her ability
to speak intelligently is considered secondary to her moral
qualities and her domestic diligence, nevertheless, when
she engages in intellectual matters her words should be
informed by Torah (118a). His prescription of these qualities seems to undermine his acceptance of the notion that
"women are simple minded" (B. Kiddushin 80b–81a). Thus,
David ben Judah's emphasis on the qualities that make a
woman trustworthy also reveals an awareness of the traits
of untrustworthy women who express discontent with their
husbands and an unwillingness to accept emotional or physical abuse.

The delineation of the ideal woman based on a combination of textual exegesis, philosophical terminology, contemporary social norms, and personal fears is also found in Italian Jewish sermons. These were probably delivered in Italian, but they were recorded in Hebrew.[16] One of the earliest extant Jewish sermons from Italy was preached by Moses ben Joab of Florence in about 1456 at the betrothal of Abraham Montalcino to an unnamed woman.[17] Moses ben Joab begins by citing Proverbs 18:22: "He who finds a wife finds good and obtains the favor of the Lord." He explains, using terminology from philosophy, that by her nature the woman is a deficient and incomplete creation by herself in both substance and form, better suited for passivity and affect (*hipa'alut*) than for taking an active role.[18] Mixing Renaissance notions of physiology with biblical and talmudic references, he argues that a wife should, therefore, serve her husband and help him in his activities (1 Kings 1:2,4). This is the best way for the woman to engage in activity without disrupting the passivity that is her nature. Her honor is to stay at home without being involved in his activities, because the nature of the man is the opposite of the woman. Because of her nature the woman suffers from a serious lack of imagination, the faculty which frees the intellect to bind concrete impressions and words "wherein there is no light" (Isaiah 8:20). She also is constitutionally incapable of imagining material things or understanding the spiritual because she cannot rise above her lowly position. Thus, when a man finds a suitable woman he has found something good.

Moses ben Joab then turns to Genesis 2:23, "because from man woman was taken," and seems for a moment almost to contradict his argument by stating that the good wife, provided by divine providence, is similar to her husband in her activities and compatible with him in substance and form. Nevertheless, even this woman, whom God formed for her husband and who is bone of his bones and flesh of his flesh (Genesis 2:23), brought death to his window (Jeremiah 9:20) because she was seduced by the advice of the serpent. The sermon thus moves from men and women in general to the original biblical couple. Then it shifts from Adam and Eve to the difficulties of finding a good wife in the fifteenth century as Moses ben Joab asks how, if God could not provide Adam with an adequate mate, can a man living in a generation of sin surrounded by purveyors of evil do any better? After lamenting the small amounts that the parents of the bride now receive from the groom compared to what once was, he complains further about the behavior of married women, invoking tradition to accuse men who take unworthy wives of destroying the race (*posel zaro*) and to warn women who rebel that they will produce deficient children.

Through this description of the unworthy wife, Moses ben Joab offers further confirmation of the ways in which women during this period attained power and independence. They pursued many activities, possibly including creative endeavors in religion, literature, or art, which threatened their husbands' authority and honor.

Another sermon showing the limits that men attempted to place on women was preached by Samuel Judah Katzenellenbogen (1521–97), a leading rabbi in Padua and Venice.[19] He constructed his sermon around the biblical verse, "Assemble the nation, the men, the women, and the children. . . . in order that they may obey and in order that they may learn and fear the Lord their God and observe to do all the words of this Torah" (Deuteronomy 31:12), together with the comment of Rabbi Eleazar ben Azariah in the Talmud, "If the men come to study and the women come to obey, why do the children come? To give reward to those who bring them" (B. Hagigah 3a). Katzenellenbogen raises the possibility that this interpretation is in error because it connects the men, who are listed first, with learning, which is listed second, and the women, who are listed second, with obeying, which is listed first. The biblical verse appears to imply that "they may obey" refers to the men and "they may learn" refers to the women, because women may need to learn more so that they can conduct themselves properly in the fulfillment of commandments. He then rules out this possibility by arguing that Rabbi Eleazar ben Azariah had correctly assigned the men and women their duties according to what was suitable and necessary for each. The men should study Torah, but not the women; it is not their way. As proof he refers to the Mishnah: "R. Eliezer says: Everyone who teaches his daughter Torah, it is as if he taught her lechery" (M. Sota 3:4). He argues that Eleazar ben Azariah had warned the women to be obedient because, according to the Talmud, "they are simple minded" (B. Kiddushin 80b–81a) and tend to trivialize many things. Women must obey the teachers even if they do not approve of what they are told to do.

Katzenellenbogen then launches into his specific concern: Jewish women should cover their hair and not wear hairpieces. To justify this position he cites first the Talmud, "women's hair is sexually provocative" (B. Berakot 24a), and then tradition: generations of Ashkenazic rabbis have even forbidden silk ties (*binde*) that match the natural hair color. His own view is that most hairpieces look too much like a woman's natural hair; he appeals, as well, to comparative practices: even non-Jewish women, including nuns, cover their hair.

Another of the sermon's topics is the many different intentions that a man can have when he marries a women. These may include the desire for a helper in the management of his house and in watching his possessions, the enjoyment of sexual intercourse, or the generation of sons (*banim*; perhaps "children") who will inherit his property. Indeed, fulfilling the commandment to be fruitful and multiply by fathering a son (*ben*) who will serve the Lord is the ultimate purpose of life. Katzenellenbogen's text makes it clear that men had to be urged to study, and women, who flaunted their femininity, physical presence, and economic resources in public, to be obedient.

Each of these two preachers roots his views about women in a range of materials, including the Bible, rabbinic literature, what he calls the laws of nature, and secular sources. Ultimately, the preacher's concern, however, is the independent behavior of Jewish women in his day. None of these writers tried in any way to empower women, yet each, through his protestations, serves as witness to activities in which Jewish women participated.

One example of Jews absorbing attitudes about women from non-Jewish sources is apparent in a manuscript by Leone Romano (Judah ben Moses ben Daniel ben Jekutiel, Rabbi Yehudah Haphilosoph, or Leone de Sere Daniel, 1292–1350). He selected and translated into Hebrew selected passages of Egidius or Aegidius Colonna, also known as Romanus, or Giles of Rome (1247–1316). This famous student of Thomas Aquinas taught at the University of Paris and was the tutor to the young Philip IV of France for whom he wrote *De regimine principum*. One of the passages translated discusses the inability of women to keep secrets (II, I, 21).[20] This specific trait of women is attributed to three weaknesses: their lack of intellect, their soft-heartedness (cowardice), and their craving for luxury. In the discussion that follows, further deficiencies of women are described. They do not have the strength to control their desires. Prevention and warnings only stimulate their desires. They are easily seduced and believe that every flatterer loves them dearly. These traits lead them to reveal their husbands' secrets to other women with whom they feel a sense of solidarity. Lurking behind this discussion and its subsequent Hebrew translation is the realization on the part of men that the woman's tongue is a source of power, and the fear that by creating alliances with each other and by revealing their husbands' secrets to other women, women may be able to hold power over their husbands.[21]

Immanuel Frances (1618–1710), one of the leading Hebrew poets of early modern Italy, expresses a hostility against women of learning in his poem "Against Women Who Pursue Religious Studies":[22]

> To teach the religion of God to the female
> Is like putting a treasure in the furnace, . . .
> And pairing thoughts of a woman with the secret of
> God,

Is like putting a black woman in the bosom of a
    distinguished man.
When she wears the garment of Torah and its mystery,
For an adulterous man she will be naked.
She plans her evil designs for lechery
And her study in the law of being fruitful and
    multiplying.
Thus the Torah whines in the mouth of a woman. . . .
There is no wealth like a foolish woman who is
Impoverished in the Torah of God and from all
    understanding,
Who only teaches her son the Shema. . . .
With a pure heart she makes her prayers,
In every language without deceit,
Thus she obtains from God her requests
And her supplications will always be desirable.
So we have investigated and found it undoubtably true,
And the proof is Beruriah.

This poem continues the theme of the good woman and the bad woman. According to Frances, the evil woman's debauchery is inspired by her religious study. The good woman's primary concern is fostering the piety of her sons. For this she is rewarded by God, and presumably by her husband. Frances's poem reflects fear of women's studying and anxiety over the possible opportunities it could bring them, in both the domestic and public spheres. Central to the ambivalence expressed toward women is his ambiguous characterization of the rabbinic figure Beruriah. In medieval Jewish tradition, as witnessed by the eleventh-century French commentator Rashi's remarks on B. Avodah Zara 18b, Beruriah exemplified an educated woman who became sexually promiscuous. In the present instance it is not clear if she represents a woman who prays with a pure heart or an example of one who does not. For other Italian Jews, such as Gedaliah ibn Yahya, Beruriah personifies the virtue of quality of character (*tekhunah* or *qualità*).[23]

Given the predominantly negative attitudes toward educated women that the leaders of the Jewish community held in early modern Italy, it is not surprising that there are very few Jewish women whose accomplishments in learning and literature are widely known. Among those women who did attain high levels of learning in Torah, Mishnah, Talmud, Midrash, and Zohar, mainly from wealthy and powerful families, were Fioretta Modena, Diena Rieti, and Benvenida Abravanel. Many others, including female teachers and women with advanced abilities in Hebrew, left a mark without leaving a record of their names.[24]

One of the frequently cited examples of a Jewish woman writer from Italy may never have actually existed. Giustina Levi-Perotti of Sassoferrato was long thought to have sent a poem to the Italian writer Francesco Petrarca (1304–14), to which he replied with one of his own, preserved in his published works. Levi-Perotti's poem, however, is now widely considered a sixteenth-century forgery. Nevertheless, even if Levi-Perotti did not actually write the poem, such an attribution is still indicative of significant literary activities by Jewish women in the sixteenth century. Clearly, enough women were involved in similar endeavors for the forgery to have been believable at that time.[25] Such Jewish women writers included Debora Ascarelli, whose Italian poetry may be the first work by a Jewish woman ever published; Rosa Levi, who sent an Italian sonnet to the Venetian poet Luigi Grotto; and Sarra Copia Sullam, a well-educated woman who conducted a major salon for Jewish and Christian intellectuals in Venice in the early seventeenth century and whose prose and poetry were published during her lifetime.[26] Another source that preserves an Italian Jewish woman's voice is the account by Anna del Monte of her thirteen days in a house for new converts to the Catholic Church in 1749.[27]

Symbolic of the transition into the modern world for Italian Jewish women writers is the Hebrew poet Rachel Luzzatto Morpurgo (1790–1871) of Trieste.[28] Her younger cousin Samuel David Luzzatto, known as Shadal (1800–65), was born ten years later in the same house. They studied Hebrew and discussed philosophical and religious topics together for many years. He would become a prominent figure in modern Jewish thought and Hebrew literature as well as her confidant and patron in Hebrew letters. He attributes to her a major role in influencing his love for Jewish learning in general and Hebrew poetry in particular.[29]

Morpurgo's youth was occupied with the study of the Hebrew classics, first Bible with commentaries, then Talmud under the tutelage of a rabbi and her uncle, and finally, the mystical classic, the Zohar, which Shadal purchased for her in 1817. Rachel Luzzatto, like most Jewish women with any education, acquired all her learning at home, alongside her brother and cousin, from private tutors and family members. Her home had a excellent Hebrew library. Like Italian Jewish women of previous generations she worked in the family business, in this case as a turner on a lathe (*haratut* or *drechsler*), a skill she learned from her uncle and father. She also sewed, making most of her own clothes. Morpurgo polished her Hebrew skills in correspondence and conversations with Shadal. In 1816 he wrote a Hebrew poem chiding her for disliking every young man ("Every good young man and doer of valor is contemptible?"). She responded in Hebrew, mimicking his meter, form, content, and even vocabulary, describing how she had found a young man but her parents did not approve of him. Finally her parents relented and allowed her to marry Jacob Morpurgo in 1819, when she was twenty-nine years old. After her marriage she was no longer able to devote much time or energy to study and writing. Her husband disapproved of these activities, and as mandated by centuries of Jewish tradition, she devoted herself to serving him, doing housework, and rearing children. The only time she found for writing was late at night and on Rosh Hodesh, the first day of each month, when Jewish women traditionally did no work. In 1847, Shadal had their poetic correspondence published in *Kokhavei yitzhak*, a journal devoted to modern Hebrew literature and enlightenment, thirty years after it had been written. Even her husband was proud of the recognition she received for her talent.[30] Some of the enlightened readers of the journal, a few of whom wrote Hebrew poems in her honor, called her

"Queen of the Hebrew Versifiers." Several observed that she had left the way of women, whom they characterized as without understanding and with wisdom only in making veils and scarfs, but they praised her for rising above them by pursuing her studies and acquiring wisdom. Others lamented the long silence of the woman's voice and the silence of female music. One compared her to the contemporary French Jewish actress also of the name Rachel (Eliza Rachel Felix, 1821–58). However, others had difficulty accepting that her Hebrew poems were actually written by a woman, claiming that they were really by a man using a female pseudonym.[31]

Rachel Morpurgo refers to gender and its consequences in her writing. On the one hand, in a letter to Shadal, she pridefully invokes not only the traditional patriarchs but the matriarchs as well: "may he who blessed our ancestors (*avotenu*) Abraham, Isaac, and Jacob, Sarah, Rebecca, and Leah, bless the entire community of the congregation of Israel and may we merit and live and go up to offer paschal sacrifices upon the altar."[32] Her writings also include a rare Hebrew description of a relationship between women in her farewell poem to Rachel Luzzatto on her marriage to Solomon Sulam:

> Rachel with Rachel is bonded
> Like a necklace on the neck
> Your love for me is an ornament
> On my head you are a crown. (15)

Her poems in Hebrew and Aramaic regularly refer to the poetry of others in Hebrew periodical literature, and comment on the accomplishments of other literary Jewish women, such as the "Rabbanit" Tamar Luzzatto, wife of Mordecai Samuel Ghirondi (22). She also refers to a commentary on the Passover Haggadah that was published by the unnamed daughter of Meyer Randegger (23) and mentions the visit that the English philanthropist Moses Montefiore and his (unnamed) wife Judith paid to Trieste in 1855 on their way to Palestine, and Rachel's desire at the age of sixty-five to accompany them as a servant (29). She refers, as well, to the burdens of raising her children (25). On the other hand, in a letter to Mendel Stern, editor of *Kokhavei yitzhak*, she writes, "The truth is that it is not for a woman to come forward (*lekadem*) . . . but I feared that you would cast me into the depths of the sea when you saw that there was nothing substantial in my words but the way of women."[33] Similarly, in 1847, on learning about the praise that her work was receiving in the Hebrew periodical literature, Rachel wrote a poem that included references to her fears of humiliation, and to the traditional citations against women, such as that "women are simple minded" and "there is no wisdom for woman except the spindle."[34] Rachel Morpurgo regularly signed herself as the "Worm," or *Rimah*, the initials of Rachel Morpugo *Haketanah*, which in Hebrew means, "Little Rachel Morpurgo." Such expressions of modesty were often employed by prominent rabbis. Rachel Morpurgo's poetry was translated into several European languages, was included in a few anthologies of modern Hebrew poetry, and is remembered in some of the histories of modern Hebrew literature. Scholars emphasize her novelty as the first female modern Hebrew poet, calling her an "*Unicum*."[35]

Italian Hebrew literature about women contains nothing that approximates what would now be characterized as feminism. There are no entreaties by men or women for any sort of gender equity or equality. There are no pleas, such as those found among some Christian writers, for greater involvement of women in society.[36] Even in the attempts to praise women, outright hostility is often expressed, and the conviction that a wife should be subordinate to her husband is always there. Such views are often justified as an intrinsic consequence of biological destiny, not as the results of the needs of men. The writers never seem to doubt that these attitudes are in perfect harmony with Jewish tradition, natural law, and non-Jewish practice. They insist that woman's arena is the home and family, where she must be secondary to her husband, and they cast aspersions on any person who might act or consider acting against this order.[37] Perhaps the male authors try so hard to state the inferiority of women in order to counter a quite different social reality, in which some women were asserting themselves in many ways, including expressing themselves in public, in matters of religion, and in literature. Apparently male protestations were efficacious, for these nascent feminist activities did not culminate in a movement or in major changes in Italian Jewish life for many years, and even then the results were not widespread—but that is another story.[38]

NOTES

1. I would like to thank Arnold Adelman, Judith R. Baskin, Marc Gopin, Benjamin C. I. Ravid, Binyamin Richler, David B. Ruderman, Cheryl Tallan, and the Smith College Committee on Faculty Compensation and Development for their help. This chapter supplements my earlier "Images of Women in Italian Jewish Literature in the Late Middle Ages," *Proceedings of the Tenth World Congress of Jewish Studies* (Jerusalem, 1990), division B, vol.II, 99–106.

1. Judah Sommo, *Hamahazeh ha'ivri harishon: tzahut bedihuta dekiddushin*, ed. Hayyim Schirmann (Jerusalem, 1965), 50; translated as *A Comedy of Betrothal* by Albert S. Golding (Ottawa, 1988), 90.

2. For the opportunities of and limitations on Italian Jewish women, see my "Italian Jewish Women," in *Jewish Women in Historical Perspective*, ed. Judith R. Baskin (Detroit, 1991), 135–58.

3. On Sommo and his poem, see *Tzahut bedihuta dekiddushin*, 121–45. Benvenida Abravanel was praised by David Reuveni, a contemporary messianic pretender, for sending him gifts and money, ransoming captives, giving charity, and fasting every day. She also served as a teacher for a duchess. See A. Z. Eshkoly, *Sippur david hareuveni* (Jerusalem, 1940), introduction 115–19, 151, 193–94, 223; text 57, 82.

4. See, for example, Maryanne Cline Horowitz, "The Woman Question in Renaissance Texts," *History of European Ideas* 8 (1987), 581–95.

5. On Fano, see my "Images of Jewish Women," 100.

6. Abraham Yagel, *Eshet hayyil* (Venice, 1605–06), 24 fols. For discussion of Yagel, see David Ruderman, *Kabbalah, Magic, and Science* (Cambridge, Mass., 1988), especially 16, and his edition *A Valley of Vision: The Heavenly Journey of Abraham ben Hananiah Yagel* (Philadelphia, 1990), especially 64, 197; cf. 33, 185–89, 193–99.

7. For a discussion of the domestic education of Jewish women, see my paper "Servants and Sexuality: Seduction, Surrogacy, and Rape: Some Observations concerning Class, Gender, and Race in Early Modern Italian Jewish Families," in *Gender and Judaism*, ed. Tamar Rudavsky (New York, 1994), based in part upon Jerusalem ms. Benayahu 9-vav, fols. 8a–9b.

8. On sumptuary laws, see my "Rabbis and Reality: The Public Roles of Jewish Women in the Renaissance and Catholic Restoration," *Jewish History* 5:1 (1991), 27–40.

9. See my "Rabbis and Reality," and the discussion of the career of Madame Rina in Yagel's *Valley of Vision*, ed. Ruderman, 87, 98–100, 129–35, 156–61, 175–83, 202–13.

10. See, for example, Bonnie S. Anderson and Judith P. Zinsser, *A History of Their Own*, 2 vols. (New York, 1989), 1:256–59, 290, 440–43; 2: 27–29; and Judith R. Baskin, "Some Parallels in the Education of Medieval Jewish and Christian Women," *Jewish History* 5:1 (1991), 41–51.

11. See my "Custom, Law, and Gender: Levirate Union among Ashkenazim and Sephardim after the Expulsion from Spain," in *Expulsion of the Jews: 1492 and After. Garland Studies in the Renaissance,* ed. R. Waddington (New York, 1994).

12. Yagel's typology of good and bad women is also presented in great detail in his *Valley of Vision*, 183–99, and is discussed in Ruderman's introduction, 32–33.

13. Biblioteca palatina, Parma, Codice de Rossi, no. 2651 (1395), fols. 89a–121b; Jewish National and University Library, Institute for Microfilmed Hebrew Manuscripts, no. 13566.

14. On David ben Judah, see Hava Tirosh-Rothschild, *Between Worlds: The Life and Thought of Rabbi David ben Judah Messer Leon* (Albany, N.Y., 1991), 62–77.

15. See my "Wife-Beating among Early Modern Italian Jews," *Proceedings of the Eleventh World Congress of Jewish Studies* (Jerusalem, 1994).

16. On Jewish preaching in Italy, see *Preachers of the Italian Ghetto,* ed. David B. Ruderman (Los Angeles, 1992).

17. Umberto Cassuto, *Un Rabbino Fiorentino del Secolo XV* (Florence, 1908), 29–33; *Revista israelitica* 4 (1907), 225–29; this sermon is discussed by Marc Saperstein, "Italian Jewish Preaching: An Overview," in Ruderman, *Preachers of the Ghetto,* 24, 32.

18. The comment in my "Images of Women," 102, that there are no references to female passivity, should be modified. See Constance Jordan, *Renaissance Feminism: Literary Texts and Political Models* (Ithaca, N.Y., 1990), 30–34.

19. Samuel Judah Katzenellenbogen, *Shnem asar derashot* (Venice, 1594; Lemberg [Lvov], 1811), no. 1, fols. 2a–5a; see Gedaliah Nigal, "The Sermons of Samuel Judah Katzenellenbogen," [Hebrew], *Sinai* 36 (1972), 79–85; Saperstein, "Italian Jewish Preaching," 30–31.

20. Biblioteca medicea laurenziana, Plut. 1.22, fols. 8a–7b; Institute for Microfilmed Hebrew Manuscripts, no. 17643. See Umberto Cassuto, "Manoscritti ebraici della R. Biblioteca Laurenziana in Firenze," *Festschrift für Aron Freimann zum 60. Geburtstage* (Berlin, 1935), 17–21; *Del Reggimento de' Principi di Egidio Romano* (Florence, 1858), 157–58.

21. See Jordan, *Renaissance Feminism,* 4; Lisa Jardine, *Still Harping on Daughters: Women and Drama in the Age of Shakespeare* (New York, 1989), 107.

22. Jacob Frances, "Neged nashim ha'oskot belimmudei kodesh," in *Kol shirei yaakov frances,* ed. Peninah Naveh (Jerusalem, 1969), 347–49.

23. Gedaliah ibn Yahya, "Shevah hanashim," cited in A. Neubauer and M. Steinschneider, "Zür Frauenliteratur," *Israelitische Letterbode* 10 (1884), 142. See also my "Images of Women." On Beruriah see David Goodblatt, "The Beruriah Traditions," *Journal of Jewish Studies* 26 (1975), 68–85; Rachel Adler, "The Virgin in the Brothel and Other Anomalies: Character and Context in the Legend of Beruriah," *Tikkun* (November/December 1988), 28–32, 102–05.

24. For the names and accomplishments of other women see Eshkoly, *Sippur david hareuveni.*

25. Medardo Morici, "Giustina Levi-Perotti e le petrarchiste marchigiane: contributo alla storia delle falsificazioni letterarie nei sec. XVI e XVII," *Rassegna nazionale* 21 (August 16, 1899): 662–95; see also Mario Emilio Cosenza, *Biographical and Bibliographical Dictionary of the Italian Humanists and of the World of Classical Scholarship in Italy, 1300–1800,* vol.3 (Boston, 1962), 2668–69. On other apocryphal learned Jewish women, see Baskin, "Some Parallels," 46.

26. See my "Educational and Literary Activities of Jewish Women in Italy during the Renaissance and the Counter Reformation," *Sefer hayovel leprofessor shlomo simonsohn* (Tel Aviv, 1993), 9–23.

27. See Joseph B. Sermonetta, "Tredici giorni nella casa dei conversi: dal diario di una giovane ebrea del 18° secolo," *Michael* 1 (1972), 261–315.

28. On Rachel Morpurgo see *Ugav rahel: shirim ve'iggrot,* ed. Isaac Hayyim Castiglione (Cracow, 1891; repr. Tel Aviv, 1943); Nina Salaman, *Rahel Morpurgo and the Contemporary Hebrew Poets in Italy* (London, 1924); Joseph Klausner, *Historiah shel hasifrut ha'ivrit hehadashah* 4:1 (Jerusalem, 1941), 44–56; and Sondra Henry and Emily Taitz, *Written Out of History* (New York, 1978), 199–206 and 279–80. For another assessment, see Dan Miron, "Why Was There No Women's Poetry in Hebrew Before 1920?," in *Gender and Text in Modern Hebrew and Yiddish Literature,* ed. Naomi B. Sokoloff et al. (New York and Jerusalem, 1992), 65. Page references here are to the 1943 edition of *Ugav Rahel.*

29. Marc Gopin, in his recent Brandeis dissertation on Samuel David Luzzatto, confirms that Rachel Luzzatto Morpurgo played a major role in Shadal's development; see S. D. Luzzatto, *Autobiografia di S. D. Luzzatto* (Padua, 1882), 59–60, and his "Toledot shmuel david luzzatto," *Hamagid* 2 (1858), 74.

30. Much of what is known about Rachel Morpurgo's life comes from Shadal himself. S. D. Luzzatto, "Mikhtav," *Kokhavei yitzhak* 35 (1868), 15–19.

31. These views were published primarily in *Kokhavei yitzhak.* A complete list of citations is found in Bernhard Wachstein, *Die Hebräische Publizistik in Wien,* vol. 1 (Vienna, 1930), 151–53; see also xcvii–xcviii. Many are cited by Klausner, *Historiah,* 52–55.

32. Morpurgo, *Ugav rahel,* letter no. I, 2, p. 74.

33. Morpurgo, *Ugav rahel,* letter no. II, 1, p. 76.
34. Morpurgo, *Ugav rahel,* 12.
35. Klausner, *Historiah,* 52. For information about a contemporary Jewish woman writer in Lemberg, Jetty Wohllerner (c. 1810–91), see Wachstein, *Hebräische Publizistik,* 245–46, 92, and XCVIII.
36. See, for example, Jardine, *Still Harping on Daughters,* 42–67, and my "Rabbis and Reality."
37. For similar conclusions, see Jordan, *Renaissance Feminism,* 18–19.
38. In the Italian Jewish periodical literature of the late nineteenth century, there is much material on the impact of the first wave of feminism on Italian Jewish women. See *Vessillo israelitico* beginning in the mid-1850s and continuing through at least the 1920s.

4 ♦ SHMUEL NIGER

Yiddish Literature and the Female Reader

Translated and abridged by Sheva Zucker

---

*This article by the Yiddish literary critic Shmuel Niger
(1883–1955) first appeared in 1919, just before the period of real blossoming of female creativity on the Yiddish literary scene that we have come to associate with
figures such as Kadya Molodowsky, Anna Margolin,
and Rokhl Korn, to name but a few. Even at the height
of this period, critics and fellow writers referred to
women writers always as "female writers" rather than
"writers," and judged their artistic virtues and shortcomings to be those supposedly characteristic of their
sex. Niger's use of phrases and unexamined generalizations (only some of which appear in this translation)
such as "purely feminine topics and concerns" (as opposed not to "masculine" but to "universal concerns"),
"feminine loquaciousness," "the lyrical disposition of
the woman," or "the female tendency to concreteness"
may annoy but should certainly not surprise the contemporary reader.*

*Even so, "Yiddish Literature and the Female
Reader" represents an invaluable contribution to Yid-*

dish literary history, and remains the starting point for anyone wanting to learn about that subject. Niger's study is comprehensive and largely original. At the same time that he underlines the more universal appeal of modern Yiddish writing, he writes with a keen sense of historic truth. Rather than trying to reject the literary past, he appreciates it for the piety, simplicity, intimacy, lyricism, folksiness, and, indeed, femininity that he saw as its hallmarks. Perhaps in arguing for this literature he is arguing for a greater acceptance of the "female voice" that could no longer be ignored in the literature of his own day.

OLD YIDDISH LITERATURE AND ITS AUDIENCE

The generally accepted opinion that Old Yiddish literature[1] was intended only for women and unlearned men is something of an exaggeration. Folklore, an important component of Yiddish folk literature, was, at least in part, the creation of scholars and educated people. Folksongs were sung not only by servant girls and artisans but also by students and scholars at their celebrations. Yeshiva students often performed Yiddish plays based on biblical stories on festivals and joyous occasions, while preachers and Hasidic rabbis liked to hear and tell stories about saintly men.

Yiddish writers and translators also wrote for a broader audience. Avrom ben Moyshe, the author of a rhymed translation of the biblical book of Ezekiel (Cracow, 1586), prefaced his work with the couplet, "In modest Yiddish, for women and girls to read with delight, / Young men and householders we also invite."[2] The preface to the 1753 Redlheim edition of the famous *Mayse-bukh*[3] explicitly states that "No scholar need be ashamed to read this storybook."

The Kabbalists (Jewish mystics) and the Hasidim did not generally distinguish between a scholar and an ordinary Jew, or between their languages. Because the Hasidim valued the heart above all, they respected Yiddish, for in it they could express themselves most freely. Thus, Rabbi Nahman of Bratslav[4] wrote his celebrated stories (*Sipurey mayses,* 1815) in Yiddish, and exhorted everyone, learned and ignorant alike, to pray privately to God in the mother tongue. He and his disciples also composed prayers in Yiddish.

Later, in the nineteenth century, learned Jews read secular Yiddish books, although they still considered it beneath their dignity to read religious books in Yiddish. Even people who scorned women's books read the stories of the nineteenth-century *maskil*[5] Isaac Meyer Dik.[6] In his autobiography, Abraham Cahan, the first editor of the New York newspaper the *Forverts* (*Jewish Daily Forward*) writes: "A boy who studied *gemore* was not supposed to read stories in *zhargon* [jargon, or Yiddish] and yet yeshiva boys devoured them."[7] Indeed, *maskilim* in the first half of the nineteenth century often acquired their "heretical" ideas from Yiddish secular books, which proliferated in both printed and manuscript form.

Still, while the opinion that only women and simple men read Old Yiddish literature may be somewhat overstated, it is nevertheless basically correct. Even writers who intended their works to be read by scholars were still primarily concerned with "those women and the plain folk who could not study the Torah." Although the preface to Eliyohu Bokher's translation of Psalms mentions teachers, it begins with the words, "You pious and devoted women."[8] Publishers would address their appeals primarily to female customers. The title page and preface to most Old Yiddish publications bore the rhyme "*Basheydlekh, far vayber un meydlekh*" ("Modestly, for women and girls"). The word "men" in the phrase "For men and women" generally referred to simple men— those who were on the same level as women in terms of learning. Such men always existed, as did both religious and secular authors who wrote for them. The author of the *musar* (morality) book *Brantshpigl* writes: "This book is made in Yiddish for women and for men who are like women and cannot learn much."[9] Even in wills, the part pertaining to the daughters or to other women was in Yiddish while the rest was in Hebrew.[10]

Not all women were illiterate in Hebrew.[11] The more prominent families sometimes sent their daughters to school with their sons. Glückel of Hameln and Pauline Wengeroff,[12] who grew up in seventeenth-century Germany and nineteenth-century Russia, respectively, both received extensive educations that included instruction in Hebrew. But they, like the other women writers mentioned below, were exceptions; generally, Jewish girls were taught to pray and to read only in Yiddish. The differing attitudes toward the education of boys and girls among European Jews are expressed in this typical lullaby, in which a little boy is rocked to sleep with the words "What is the best of wares? The child will study the Torah, the Torah will he study, he will write learned volumes, and he will always be a good Jew," and a girl with the words, "What is the best of wares? Sorele's groom will study the Torah, Torah will he study, learned volumes will he write; Sorele will remain good and pious."[13] Girls, in fact, had no time to study: they had to help their mothers at home and in the store, and when they were a little older, they were married off. When a girl got married, she had to run the household and shoulder the responsibility of earning a living. Whether by choice or by force of circumstance, she became an *eyshes khayil* ("woman of valor"),[14] minding the store and often traveling to villages and fairs with her wares. Both the store and her husband might bear her name. Literary examples of this are Y. L. Peretz's Mendl Brayne's, in the story by the same name, and S. Y. Abramovich's Khayim-Khone Khaye-Trayne's in the novel *Fishke der krumer*. In real life, some of the earlier maskilic writers, like Mendl Lefin and Shloyme Ettinger, were largely supported by their wives.

Indeed, the *eyshes khayil* type, beginning with Ettinger's Serkele,[15] left a deep imprint on Yiddish literature. In one of his novels, Sholem Aleichem delivers an interesting discourse on this authentically Jewish type:

While other nations are still considering the question of whether or not the woman is a human being, . . . the

Jews of Mazepevke stand at a distance and laugh at all their ideas and so-called achievements, because in Mazepevke the woman has since time immemorial played as important a role as the man. In fact, one could say that almost all the business in Mazepevke is in the hands of the women. Often the wife's reputation completely overshadows the husband's.

Despite or perhaps because of the Jewish woman's important economic role, she was not easily allowed into the man's spiritual world. Today, economic power leads to a certain level of spiritual emancipation, but in those days the woman's economic importance led to her economic exploitation. Her male counterpart saw himself as belonging to a higher race chosen by God to study and observe the laws of the holy Torah. The silly, sinful female, who lived only by the merits of her husband, was to consider herself fortunate to be his provider in this world and his footstool in the next.

The women's section of the synagogue was a sort of spiritual ghetto in which females were confined from childhood. Seldom were they sent to school. While even the most ignorant man could read some Hebrew, many women could not. On the Sabbath and holidays, a learned woman, called a *zogerke* (sayer), would chant from the *sidur* (prayer book), or read *tkhines* (supplicatory prayers) in the synagogue, and everyone would repeat after her. She might also read the Yiddish Bible to her friends at her home.

Because women were on the whole uneducated, they needed a literature in the language that they spoke, a literature that would mediate between them and the holy texts. They needed a literature that would be a *zogerke*. Yiddish literature and women were so closely associated that for a time women's books were even printed in a special typeface called *vayber taytch* (women's German). Many books had female-oriented titles, such as *One Lovely Book for Women,* and *A God-Fearing Song in Honor of Women and Girls.* Even as late as the nineteenth century, the *maskil* Isaac Meyer Dik was addressing the "dear female reader."

Yiddish literature is perhaps the only literature in the world that until recently was sustained by the female and not the male reader. Until the birth of modern Yiddish literature, and for a short time thereafter, even an uneducated male would have been embarrassed to read "women's books," and he read them only in secret, if at all, so as not to be taken for a "woman."[16] Women not only bought and read Yiddish books, they also encouraged writers to write in Yiddish—and to write in their honor. For example, a handwritten translation of Psalms (c. 1532) by Reb Eliezer ben Yisroyel carries this dedication: "This book of Psalms was written with diligence for my patroness Pesl bas Reb Yisroyel. I hope that she will read it."

THE CONTENTS OF OLD YIDDISH LITERATURE

Until the start of the Haskala movement, which began to erode traditional Jewish life, Yiddish literature was mainly nurtured by Hebrew literature. The most important works in Yiddish were translations and adaptations of the Hebrew Bible, together with excerpts from rabbinic writings considered suitable for a female audience. Rabbinic literature consists of *halakha* (legal writings) and *agada* (legends and other nonlegal materials). While Jewish men devoted their entire lives to the study of the *halakhic* aspects of the Talmud and its commentaries, they considered *agada* much less important. In Yiddish literature, however, the emphasis was on biblical, *agadic*, and *musar* books; very little *halakha* was translated into Yiddish. Even had translations of the major *halakhic* rabbinic texts made these works more linguistically accessible, women and ignorant men would still not have shown great interest in them, because the difficulty lay in the subject matter itself and not in the language. Rather, the laws essential for women and unlearned men were published in Yiddish in separate little booklets.[17] *Halakha* for its own sake, with no practical purpose, so important in the "masculine" literature, is completely nonexistent in Yiddish.

The most common texts for women were translations of the Bible. Those from the fifteenth century were the first books to be written and printed in Yiddish. The rabbinic sages' injunction against women's learning was believed to apply to Talmud study but not to the Bible and practical *halakha*. On Saturday afternoons, when men studied the Talmud, their wives read the weekly Torah portion in Yiddish. Although literal translations abounded of the *khumash* (the Torah, or five books of Moses), none was ever as popular as the *Taytsh-khumesh*,[18] first published by Sheftl Hurwitz in Prague in 1608 or 1610, or the *Tsenerene*, by Yankev ben Itzkhok Ashkenazy (c.1590–1618). Not simply translations, these and other such books included homilies on the weekly biblical readings from the Torah and Prophets, as well as stories, legends, parables, and words of chastisement and comfort, drawn from rabbinic literature, the Zohar and other mystical texts, and histories and travel accounts.[19]

Both the biblical-*agadic* content and the topics of specific works reflect the "feminine" character of the Yiddish books. Books were often published with parallel Hebrew and Yiddish texts so that husband and wife would not have to buy two separate volumes. The contents, however, frequently differed. In Reb Shloyme London's *Koheles Shloyme* (3d ed., Amsterdam, 1772), an anthology and a veritable treasure of Old Yiddish literature, a mystical quotation from Kabbala precedes the laws of the blessings over food on the Hebrew side. The Yiddish on the left offers simply: "A pretty prayer that we should say after the meal." Many Yiddish *musar* books have sections devoted to women's topics. *Sheyvet Musar* (*Staff of Morality*, Warsaw, 1889) devotes chapter 24 to the qualities "that a pious woman must have so that her husband will love her and not, God forbid, have thoughts about other women, which will make his children not good." The *Brantshpigl* and *Sheyn froyen-bikhl* ("Pretty Book for Women" [Cracow, 1577]) discuss proper female conduct, the woman's religious obligations, and her relations with her husband.

Although all Hebrew and Aramaic prayers—including the

High Holiday prayer book and the penitential prayers, as well as lamentations, Sabbath songs, liturgical poems, and the daily portions from biblical and rabbinic literature to be read after morning prayers—were translated into Yiddish, these "masculine" prayers were never as important as *tkhines,*[20] the prayers that were originally intended for, and often written by, women. Intimate and warm, they concentrate more on the individual than the collective. One prays that God forgive one's sins and grant sustenance and long life. The patriarchs and matriarchs and other saintly men and women are often invoked, and one prays that their merits may come to our aid. The *tkhines* are full of scenes and characters that stir the imagination, as well as words that touch the heart and cause tears to flow.

The first original *tkhine* appears to have been composed by Avrom Apoteker at the end of the sixteenth century. Unfortunately, no extant copy is known. However, an early collection of *tkhines* by Aron ben Shmuel (Fürth, 1709) called *Liblekhe tfile (Lovely prayer)*, or *Greftike arznay fur guf un neshome (Powerful Medicines for Body and Soul)*, is a valuable source of information on early *tkhines*. Although Ben Shmuel's intended audience consisted primarily of women, his collection also includes prayers for men.

These *tkhines,* like *tkhines* in general, are for the most part intimate, personal, and even private. There is a *tkhine* for every sort of person and occasion; indeed, many were created originally for purely female occasions. The collection *Tkhines uvakoshes (Supplications and Petitions),*[21] for example, includes the following: "*tkhine* for oneself and for one's husband and children," several *tkhines* "for good children," "a *tkhine* before one takes *challah*," "a *tkhine* before kindling the Sabbath and holiday candles," "a prayer for a widow," and "a *tkhine* to say for a husband on a journey." The *Seyder tkhines (Order of tkhines)* published in Frankfurt am Main in 1732, contains *tkhines* to be said before and after the woman immerses herself in the *mikva* (ritual bath); when she is in her seventh month of pregnancy; when she is going to give birth; and when she has relations with her husband. Even *tkhines* that do not deal specifically with women's matters often mention women. Authors and supplicants alike take pride in famous women, referring wherever appropriate to the matriarchs and other righteous women such as Obadiah's wife, Batya the daughter of Pharaoh, and Serakh the daughter of Asher.[22]

It is harder to identify the specifically feminine in the secular literature, because men often read chronicles, travel accounts, grammars, and popular science and medical books. Some Yiddish medical books were devoted entirely to "women's" topics; these include *Derekh noshim veyoldos* (*The Way of Women and Childbearing*), and *Matsil nefoshes* (*Saving Human Beings*), about children's hygiene. Adaptations of German entertainment literature such as chivalric and folk books were read mainly by women. *Artish hauf* (*King Arthur's Court*) begins with the verse: "When you read what I write, your heart will delight."[23] Pious writers waged war against this literature for "idlers." Like the author of the *Mayse-bukh,* they tried to divert the Jewish readership away from it by adapting interesting tales from the *agada,* the Zohar and other sacred sources.

Paradoxically, while sixteenth-century authors tried to draw women away from secular literature in Yiddish, the later Haskala writers tried to draw them to it. They concentrated on women because they, in contrast to men, were not immersed in religious books. In one of his booklets, Isaac Meyer Dik writes:

> Your heart, my dear female reader, is still quite free of all other distorted ideas. You are not conceited about your learning nor about your holy role. You are not fanatic and you will therefore be an impartial (truthful and honest) judge of my booklets; they will make a good impression on your gentle nature and you will share them with your husband, your bridegroom, and you will influence him if he himself hasn't read them. That influence that one clever woman can have on her husband's heart, no holy text or book can have. As our

sages say, "Everything is from the wife." You will understand me and my booklets much better than your husband, were he to read them himself, because you are at home much more and the burdens of life weigh on you more than they do on him who drowns all his worries in the house of study.

While Dik did not write only for women, and hoped that the "dear reader" would convey his ideas to her husband, some of his stories explore purely feminine concerns. Although these stories were written by an "enlightened" author, they have the flavor of old *musar* books for women.

THE FEMININE STYLE OF OLD YIDDISH LITERATURE

The style of Old Yiddish literature was also distinctively feminine. For the woman the *agada* became the intermediary between the ancient and the medieval imagination, bringing the Bible closer to her own times. And so, the *Khumash* became the *Taytsh-khumesh,* a synthesis of the Bible and *agada*, and not merely a literal translation into Yiddish. Nowhere did the Bible and the *agada* grow together so naturally as in the *Tsenerene*; here the last boundaries between commentary and text, interpretation and literal meaning were erased and united in a new spiritual oneness.

The essential femininity of the Yiddish style is perhaps most apparent in *musar* books and *tkhines*. Morality literature achieves its true style and charm when translated into and revised in Yiddish, or when it is actually first written in Yiddish, a language that has within it the necessary softness and sweetness for this genre. *Musar* books not only took the place of legal codes, educational institutions, and the agadic texts that men studied in synagogue every day after prayers, they also took the place of preachers. Many parables and translations of sacred passages from Hebrew *musar* books have the quality of sermons spoken from the pulpit rather than of written language. The preachers, in turn, were living, speaking *musar* books. It is no coincidence that many such books were published in Yiddish in the seventeenth century, at the same time that preaching was becoming popular. Like preachers, *musar* books told marvelous tales and instructive parables. Both appealed to the spirit and imagination of the woman and the common man, and not to the intellect.[24] Both were soft and lyrical, intimate, folksy, and feminine.

The *tkhines* were even more so. Passages were not simply translated literally from Hebrew. For example, in Hebrew, this prayer published in *Brokhes hakoydesh* (*Blessings of Holiness,* 1879), a bilingual collection of *tkhines*, reads: "May my prayer come before you and may you turn your ear to my outcry." The Yiddish says: "I pray to you, God, dear God, the God of my ancestors Abraham, Isaac, and Jacob, and Sarah, Rebecca, Rachel, and Leah that my prayer may come before you and that you may turn your ears to my outcry."[25] The greater length of the Yiddish is a function not only of the wonderful succinctness of Hebrew but of the female tendency towards concreteness. This tendency, as well as a concern with people and historical figures rather than abstract concepts, manifests itself not only in the fact that *tkhines* are less universal than men's prayers, but also in their personal, private quality: in almost every *tkhine* the supplicant mentions her name, "I, so-and-so, daughter of so-and-so." She may also add her own words. The *tkhine* is more lyrical than the prayer, as the very name *tkhine* (supplication) suggests. The word *tfile* (prayer) means "to ask" or "to pray." *Tkhine* means "to implore" or "to entreat," and it was created expressly for the intimate outpouring of the heart. The woman does not pray to God, rather she spends time with Him, arguing with Him and complaining as if He were a close friend. She even addresses him with *du,* the familiar form in Yiddish of "you." The *tkhine* is not only lyrical, it is elegiac:

> Almighty God, here come I, sad widow, to pray to you with a broken heart. . . . My God, my Lord, what can be

worse in this world than being a widow? Almighty God, how can my heart be free when I can only think of how I have become a widow? You, dear God, you do every-thing right, I accept it with love, so I say, were I not sinful, you would not have brought this upon me. . . . But I beg that you take these tears which I have shed since I became a widow and since this trouble befell me. . . . O, dear God, when I think that my children are saying, "We have become orphans . . ."[26]

This tearful tone pervades almost all the *tkhines*. For the Jewish woman, God is not a God of vengeance, but a com-passionate, kind, and gracious God, a merciful father in heaven who becomes part of the family. The God of the *tkhines* has a soft heart, and cannot stand tears; He has become, as it were, feminized.

Not only were *tkhines* recited by women, many were also written by women. While most *tkhines* are anonymous, many are signed by a person who calls herself Soreh bas Toyvim.[27] Later authors imitated and published *tkhines* un-der this pseudonym, raising significant doubts as to the ac-tual existence of a Soreh bas Toyvim, but there definitely was such a person.[28] In the preface to her *tkhine* "*Shloyshe she'orim*" ("Three gates") she writes:

I (Soreh bas Toyvim) do this for the sake of the dear God, blessed be He and blessed be His name, and ar-range another beautiful new *tkhine* (concerning the three gates). . . . I take for my help the living God, blessed be He, who lives forever and eternally, and ren-der this *tkhine* in Yiddish with great love and with awe and trembling with fear and broken limbs and with much prayer because of the merits of our matriarchs (Sarah, Rebecca, Rachel, and Leah). May my dear moth-ers intercede for me to God (blessed be He) and may my wandering be an (atonement) for my (sins) and may God, blessed be He, forgive me for talking in synagogue when the beloved Torah was being read.

The Yiddish text is preceded by the Hebrew sentence: "This gate is based on the three commandments that are given to women and my name Soreh is at the beginning of the verses." Concluding with a bit of autobiography, she says: "I (Soreh) offer this prayer to God that He may care for me in my old age so that our children will not be driven away from us and I composed the other new *tkhine* for you that we may be restored from our sins and from the Angel of Death and that because of its merit may God, blessed be He, spare our lives." These bits of personal information are not only biographically interesting, they also suggest that she is actually writing of her own experiences and trials.

Ironically, Isaac Meyer Dik, who, more than anyone else, was heir to the feminine Yiddish style, was highly critical of the *tkhines*: "They are completely senseless, worthless," he writes, "and offer no thoughts to warm the heart or elevate the spirit."[29] Perhaps Dik's Haskalah outlook biased him against them, or perhaps he was not familiar with the authentic *tkhines* and was directing his condemnation at the lame, error-ridden literal translations of Hebrew prayers. Even so, his attitude seems particularly puzzling given that his writing is so close in spirit to the works that he scorns. Lines from his work could be interpolated into the early women's *musar* books and pass for the actual writing of that period. Dik and then later his pupil Yaakov Dinezon provide the natural, gradual, careful transition from the early feminine folk literature to that part of later Yiddish literature that is only psychologically feminine. Shomer,[30] the notorious writer of *shund* (trashy) novels, like Dik wrote for the "dear female reader" and tried to satisfy her needs by writing in her spirit and style. The only difference was that Dik wrote for an earlier generation of readers and Shomer for a later one. The Yiddish writer Y. L. Peretz describes this older reader in his sketch *A farshterter Shabes* (*A Ruined Sabbath*): "Serl is a woman of many accomplishments, she reads Yiddish fluently; she knows the Yiddish Bible and the *Kav hayosher* and the *Reyshis khokhme* and several more *musar* books, almost by heart; she is well versed in Hell;

she's at home in every corner, she knows where the boiling hot tar is." In *Di Lezerin* (*The Female Reader*) he delineates the new reader as follows:

> One of the Sabbath candles is still flickering, and one of the members of the household is still up—the oldest daughter. Her flowing hair is red; her face—yellow, nourished by too few potatoes. Her eyes burn; her sagging breast rises and falls, her thin hands quiver. . . . By the flickering candle she reads one of Shomer's novels. Her lips quiver with impatience. She is agitated. She is afraid: what if her candle goes out and she doesn't find out what happened to the dragon?[31]

The mother reads the Yiddish Bible; the daughter reads Shomer's novels. Reading the Yiddish Bible and *musar* books was both a religious obligation and a need, enjoyed as one enjoys doing a good deed. Shomer awakened the Jewish woman's imagination for this world rather than the next. He stirred in her a longing for life and love, teaching her to read for pleasure and curiosity.

With the change in the content and style of Yiddish literature came a change in the female reader. But only in the last several decades of the nineteenth century, when a folk intelligentsia arose and when the masses began to articulate secular, spiritual needs, did Yiddish literature cease being for women readers only.

WOMEN WRITERS

Perhaps the first woman who wrote in Yiddish in the early modern period was Rebecca (Rifka) Tiktiner, the daughter of Reb Meyer Tiktiner, who lived in Poland in the early years of the sixteenth century. Known as a preacher, she translated the well-known medieval *musar* book *Khoyves halevoves* (*Duties of the Heart*, 1609), and wrote, among other things, a *musar* book, *Minekes Rifka* (*Rifka the Wet Nurse*, Cracow, 1618), both of which were published posthumously in 1550.[32]

Other female writers include Khane bas Reb Yehuda Leyb Katz, the wife of Reb Yitskhok Ashkenazi, who wrote *tkhines* and also a rhymed Yiddish "sermon" that was published in Amsterdam around 1700. Serl bas Reb Yankev Segal of Dubno composed the very popular *Tkhine imohes* (*Supplication for the Matriarchs*) for the beginning of the month of Elul. This *tkhine* has prayers to each of the matriarchs, Sarah, Rebecca, Rachel, and Leah, and is infused with a gentle, warm, motherly feeling. Henna bas Reb Yehuda, the wife of Rabbi Arye Leyb Safra of Brod, translated Hebrew works into Yiddish. The title page of the *tkhine* she translated explains that this "*tkhine* in a weeping voice was brought from the land of Israel. It was written in the Sacred Tongue and was copied into Yiddish by the chaste, God-fearing woman, Mistress Henna." At the end there is "a prayer to God, blessed be He, for the woman who has no children." Eydl bas Reb Moyshe Mendls published a shortened version of the histories of Josephus in Yiddish (Cracow, 1670).[33]

The best and best-known female Yiddish author is Glückel of Hameln. In the seven books of her *Memoirs,* she describes her life from her birth in 1645 until 1719, five years before her death at the age of seventy-nine. The *Memoirs,* which were preserved by Glückel's descendants until their publication in 1896, remain the most culturally and historically valuable work in Yiddish literature.[34]

Glückel's father, Reb Leyb Pinkerle, was one of the most important figures in the Jewish community of Hamburg. His house was the center of all communal affairs. When the Jews were to be expelled from Hamburg, it was he who managed to get the decree revoked. Thus, since her childhood, Glückel lived in an atmosphere of community service and communal life. While still a child, she married Reb Khayim Hamel and settled in Hameln. Thanks to the matches she later arranged for her twelve children, she came to know and be connected with the Jewish elite of various cities and countries across Europe. Her *Memoirs* describe these people, as well as the turmoil, upheavals, and movements of her time, providing a wonderful historical source on Jewish life at the end of the seventeenth and beginning of the eighteenth century in Germany, France, Denmark, Holland, Austria, and Poland.

From a purely literary standpoint, the *Memoirs* are a first-rate work of Yiddish women's literature. Only the better *tkhines* and the authentically feminine *musar* books share their touching lyricism and bare but chaste intimacy. Their publisher was right in saying: "When one opens this book, one does not open a grave but rather a human heart." Glückel's motives for writing her memoirs were purely personal and subjective. By writing she wanted to drive away her melancholy and restore her shattered spirit after her husband's death in 1691. "In the year 5451, in my great grief and heartache, I shall begin to write," she starts in Hebrew and then continues in Yiddish: "My dear children, I began to write this, with God's help, after the death of your pious father, to relieve my soul of the melancholy thoughts that came over me." And so she wrote, little by little, until she married the banker Cerf Levy of Metz in 1700, and only in 1712 after his death, when melancholy thoughts came to her once more, did she again take to writing her *Memoirs*. She completed them in 1719.

With her *Memoirs,* Glückel intended not only to acquaint her children with the important events that happened to their large, rich, and distinguished family scattered the world over, but also to leave them a sort of ethical will. She wanted to teach them how to live in this world. Her *Memoirs* begin, like the *musar* books in which she was so well versed, with praise for God, blessed be He, who "created everything with mercy and compassion, so that everything is of use to us sinners." It may very well be that she had meant to write a *musar* book, but she found that the *musar* and the praise and plea to God inevitably came together, just as personal memories, joys, and sorrows had earlier merged in the work of Soreh bas Toyvim. In this way, *musar* was transformed into autobiography, while maintaining the function and ul-

timately the style of a morality text: "For example, a ship full
of people was traveling at sea and somebody was walking on
the ship's deck and he bent over and fell into the sea and
seemed to have drowned. The captain saw this and threw
out some rope and warned him to hold on tightly so that he
would not fall as we, sinning mortals, fall."[35]

There are many such parables and stories written in the
style of an authentic preacher, a style which Glückel, clever,
experienced, and well-read woman that she was, had heard
and read in Yiddish books. Had Glückel's *Memoirs* been published not by an academic at the end of the nineteenth century in Germany, but rather by an ordinary Jewish printer
and bookseller at the time when such books were a requirement, a delight, and a jewel in the home of every educated
Jewish woman, then they would certainly have been among
the most popular and beloved of Yiddish *musar* books. They
represent the best example of the feminine voice, that is to
say, the tender-spirited, intimate-lyrical quality that is so
deeply characteristic of Old Yiddish literature.

NOTES

Translator's note: This is a translation and abridgment of Shmuel Niger's
essay "*Di Yidishe literatur un di lezerin*" ("Yiddish Literature and the
Female Reader") first published as a separate volume of *Der pinkes*, 1913;
repr. Vilna, 1919. The Yiddish reader will probably find it easier to locate
the later reprint in Niger, *Bleter geshikhte fun der Yidisher literatur (Pages
from the history of Yiddish literature)* (New York: Congress for Jewish Culture, 1959). The essay has been reduced to about a third of its original
length. While this translation incorporates almost all of Niger's main
points (except his discussion of masculine and feminine letter writing
styles), Yiddish readers are strongly urged to read the original for the
wonderful quotations and examples, which limited space, unfortunately,
prevented us from including here.

The notes which follow are a compilation of Niger's and my own. Most
bibliographic references predating Niger's essay are from the original.
However, I felt it necessary to explain certain terms and characters that
would have needed no elaboration for Niger's Yiddish-speaking audience.

Thus, notes on such terms as "Old Yiddish literature," "*Mayse-bukh,*" and "*eyshes-khayil,*" or people such as Isaac Meyer Dik and Shomer are generally additions to the Niger text.

I would like to express my gratitude to Richard Fein of Cambridge, Mass. and Judith Ruderman of Durham, N.C., for reading the English manuscript, and to Ernst Manasse of Durham for his help with German words and phrases. The transliteration of Yiddish and Hebrew words follows the standard system devised by the YIVO Institute for Jewish Research. Hebrew words, and Hebrew words that have also come into Yiddish but are generally known to the English reader from the Hebrew, such as *halakha, musar,* etc., are transliterated according to the modern Sephardic pronunciation. Titles of books, names of people, and other Yiddish terms deriving from Hebrew or Hebrew-Aramaic relating to Old Yiddish literature are transcribed according to their Yiddish pronunciation. I have translated titles of works where I felt it would enhance the reader's understanding of the subject.

This translation is published with the permission of the Congress for Jewish Culture.

1. Early or Old Yiddish literature, the period on which Niger concentrates in this article, developed during the Middle Yiddish period (1500–1700) and thereafter. A useful source for the history of Old Yiddish literature is Israel Zinberg, *A History of Jewish Literature,* vol. 7, transl. Bernard Martin (New York and Cincinnati, 1975). See also Max Weinreich, *History of the Yiddish Language,* transl. Sh. Noble (Chicago, 1980), 270–77; and *Encyclopedia Judaica,* "Yiddish literature."

2. Eliezer Shulman, "*Sfat yehudit ashkenazit vesifruteha,*" in *Hazman: me'asef lesifrut ulemada* (St. Petersburg, 1903), vol.1:20.

3. The *Mayse-bukh (Story Book)* was one of the most popular works of Old Yiddish literature. The oldest printed edition extant was published in 1602 in Basel by Jacob ben Abraham of Mezhirech. Scholars date the first edition thirty to fifty years earlier than this. The *Mayse-bukh* consists of over three hundred stories taken from rabbinic and medieval Hebrew literature. Because all the tales are placed within the framework of moral lessons, the rabbis saw this work as an antidote to pure entertainment literature.

4. On Rabbi Nahman see Sh. A. Horodetsky, *Lekorot hahasidut* (Berditchev, 1906), 39, 58; *Shivhei Haran* (Lemberg [Lvov], 1911); Arthur Green, *Tormented Master: A Life of Rabbi Nahman of Bratslav* (University, Ala., 1979).

5. A *maskil* (enlightener) is a proponent of the Haskala (Jewish Enlightenment), which was introduced into Germany by Moses Mendelssohn in the 1770s, and then spread into Eastern Europe, where it lasted until the 1880s. Although most of the East European *maskilim* viewed Yiddish as an inferior jargon they could not totally renounce the language, for it was much too deeply entrenched among the Jewish masses whom they sought to enlighten. In the hands of the *maskilim,* the Yiddish vernacular became the vehicle for the development of a modern secular literature through which they sought to lead Jews away from the ills of traditional life and into the modern world.

6. Isaac Meyer Dik (1814–93) was the first popular writer of Yiddish fiction. A *maskil* who used literature to popularize the ideas of the Haskala, he wrote over three hundred stories and short novels in Yiddish and Hebrew. Dik was the natural transition between Old and Modern Yiddish literature, serving as the link between the traditional didactic and ethical tales of the older literature and the modernistic trends of the Haskala.

7. Abraham Cahan, *Bleter fun mayn lebn* (New York, 1926–28), 1:89. The term *zhargon* for Yiddish will doubtless strike the reader as pejorative. While the reasons behind the name may in fact be negative, many Yiddish speakers used the term in a neutral fashion until the beginning of the twentieth century; see Weinreich, *History*, 320–33.

8. Eliohu Bokher, *Tilim iberzetsung* (Venice, 1545), quoted in Shulman, "Sfat yehudit ashkenazit," 1:20.

9. M. Grünbaum, *Jüdisch-Deutsche Chrestomatie* (Leipzig, 1882), 231. There exists in Yiddish a large *musar* (morality) ethical literature, often translated from Hebrew ethical literature, which teaches ideal religious and social behavior for both the individual and society. Directed mostly toward women, such works are also dedicated to them. Even when only a translation, the style of the Yiddish *musar* books—clear, simple, popular, and rich in stories and parables—is distinct from its Hebrew prototype. The first musar book is *Sefer middot* (*Book of Good Qualities*, 1542). Other well-known examples include *Orhot tsadikim* (*The Ways of the Righteous*, 1542) and *Lev tov* (*Good Heart*, Prague, 1620). The *Brantshpigl* (*The Mirror*, 1602) by Moses Hanoch of Prague is the first original *musar* work in Yiddish. The author purports to hold a mirror up to the life around him. He prescribes good behavior in practical terms, addressing such topics as how to raise children and train servants.

10. Ezriel Nosn Frank and Yisroeyel Khaim Zagorodsky, *Di familie Davidzon* (Warsaw, 1924), 18.

11. For lists of women who were learned enough to study the Talmud and its commentaries, see M. Kayserling, *Die Jüdischen Frauen in der Geschichte, Literatur und Kunst* (Leipzig, 1879); A. Berliner, *Hayey hayehudim be'ashkenaz biyemey habeynayim* (n.p.: Akhiasef, 1900), 8–9; M. Güdemann, *Hatorah vehahayim be'artsot hama'arav biyemey habeynayim* (Warsaw, 1897), 190–98.

12. For Glückel of Hameln, see below. Pauline Wengeroff (1833–1916) also wrote memoirs in which she portrays her life as a member of a wealthy Jewish family in Russia before the Haskala, *Memoiren einer Grossmutter: Bilder aus der Kulturgeschichte der Juden Russlands im 19 Jahrhundert* (Berlin, 1910, 1913). Niger implies that Glückel went to school with her brothers. Glückel simply writes that she went to heder (traditional Jewish school for young children, usually boys) and that her father gave his children, girls and boys, a secular as well as religious education, leaving the matter somewhat ambiguous. According to Sondra Henry and Emily Taitz, *Written Out of History: Our Jewish Foremothers* (Fresh Meadows, New York, 1983), 169, girls in Germany sometimes did go to schools especially for girls.

13. Shoyel Ginsberg and Peysakh Marek, *Yevreyskie narodniye piesni v'rosii* (St. Petersburg, 1901), nos. 60 and 67.

14. The term *eyshes khayil* (literally "woman of valor") derives from Proverbs 31:10–31. For a scholarly analysis of this phenomenon, see Immanuel Etkes, "Marriage and Torah Study among the Lomdim in Lithuania in the Nineteenth Century," in *The Jewish Family: Metaphor and Memory*, ed. David Kraemer (New York, 1989).

15. Shloyme Ettinger's *eyshes khayil,* Serkele, in the 1825–30 drama by the same name, is among the best-known female figures in Yiddish literature of the Haskala. Although the *eyshes khayil* is usually a positive type, Serkele is an antiheroine; the author sees her control of the family and the family pursestrings as the mark not of positive power or liberation, but rather of a backward society where women's assumption of power is a sign of the weakness and impotence of the men.

16. See S. Y. Abramovich's autobiography in *Seyfer hazikaron* (Warsaw, 1888), 123; and Sholem Aleichem, *Funem yarid* (Kiev: Yidishe folksbibliotek), 2:66.

17. Such books of laws especially for women and unlearned men include *Tares Arn* (1728), *Bris melakh* by Reb Yomtov Lipman Heller, *Seyder melikhe* (Venice, n.d.), *Seyder hanikor* (Cracow, 1644), and various editions of *Shkhites uvedikes*. These deal with laws of purity, salting and porging meat, and slaughtering and inspecting meat.

18. The *Taytsh-khumesh,* published by Reb Sheftl Hurwitz in 1608 or 1610 in Prague, includes literal and homiletical interpretations of the Pentateuch and Rashi's commentary in Yiddish.

19. Histories included Josephus, *Tsemakh Dovid* and *Sheyvet Yehuda. Masoyes Reb Binyomin* was a popular travel account.

20. On *tkhines* see Israel Zinberg, *History* 7:249–59; Chava Weissler, "The Traditional Piety of Ashkenazic Women," in *Jewish Spirituality,* ed. Arthur Green (New York, 1987) 2:245–75; *idem,* "Prayers in Yiddish and the Religious World of Ashkenazic Women," in *Jewish Women in Historical Perspective,* ed. Judith R. Baskin (Detroit, 1991), 159–81.

21. *Tkhines uvakoshes* (Vilna, 1864). There are many editions of this work; the word *seyder* is often included at the beginning of the title. See Weissler, "Traditional Piety," 247–52, and "Prayers in Yiddish," 162–68.

22. Also frequently mentioned is Hannah, the mother of the prophet Samuel, who is invoked particularly in *tkhines* for barren women.

23. Johann Christof Wagenseil, *Belehrung der Jüdisch-Teutschen Red- und Schreibart* (Königsberg, 1699), 157.

24. For more on the similarity between *musar* literature and preaching, see Grünbaum, *Chrestomatie,* 196.

25. *Brokhes hakoydesh* (Vilna, 1879, 1883).

26. *Tkhines uvakoshes* (Vilna, 1861), 40.

27. For more information on Soreh bas Toyvim, see Zinberg, *History,* 253–56; Weissler, "Prayers in Yiddish," 172–76.

28. On the controversy over the historicity of Soreh bas Toyvim, see Weissler, "Prayers in Yiddish," 174, and Zinberg, *History,* 7:252–54. Weissler believes that much of *Shloyshe she'orim* was written by a woman who, for convenience, may be referred to as Soreh bas Toyvim and whose text "contains a distinctive and powerful literary voice."

29. Isaac Meyer Dik, Preface to *Shivim moltsayt* (Vilna, 1877).

30. Shomer was the pseudonym of the Yiddish novelist and dramatist Nahum Meyer Shaikevich (1849–1905) whose name became synonymous with the *shundroman,* the trashy novel.

31. Y. L. Peretz, *Ale verk fun Y. L. Peretz* (Warsaw, 1911), 2:28, 24.

32. On Rebecca Tiktiner, see Henry and Taitz, *Written Out of History,* 92–100.

33. Other female writers of Old Yiddish literature mentioned by Niger in the Yiddish original include the *tkhine* writers Rokhl bas Reb Mordkhe, Dvoyre the wife of Rabbi Naftoli, Mamael Matl, Rokhl Hinde, Beyle bas Reb Ber son of Reb Khezkio Hurvitz (perhaps only a publisher), and of course Soreh bas Toyvim; the translators of prayers or *tkhines* include Laza wife of Yankev ben Mordkhe Shverin, Elis bas Reb Mordkhe Mikhals of Slutzk, Shifre bas Reb Yehuda Leyb of Lublin, Rozl Fishels (also a publisher), and the poet Toybe Pan.

34. Yiddish readers may read a modern Yiddish "translation," *Glikl Hamil—zikhroynes, Musterverk fun der yidisher literatur* 26 (Buenos Aires, 1967). For an English version see *The Memoirs of Glückel of Hameln,* transl. Marvin Lowenthal (New York, 1977).

35. Glückel of Hameln, *Zikhroynes,* 22. Niger himself does not quote the end of the parable, *Zikhroynes,* 22, which is translated by Lowenthal, *Memoirs,* 1, as follows: "Just so, our Torah is like a rope which the great and gracious God has thrown to us as we drown in the stormy sea of life, that we may seize hold of it and be saved."

5 ♦ RUTH ADLER

Dvora Baron: Daughter of the Shtetl

Photographs of Hebrew and Yiddish writers in Vilna, taken in 1909, include twenty men and one woman—Dvora Baron. These pictures make a statement about the literati of the period. They also explain why most of what we know about the small town Jewish life of Eastern Europe in the nineteenth and early twentieth centuries stems from the works of male authors, such as Mendele Mocher Sforim (Shalom Jacob Abramowitz), Sholem Aleichem (Shalom Rabinowitz), Y. L. Peretz, Y. H. Brenner, and Y. D. Berkowitz. Yet, these portrayals of the shtetl are, at best, partial representations and, at worst, flawed, for they are often ideologically tainted by writers who had left the physical confines of the shtetl but were still seeking to separate themselves from its emotional grip. They paint a grim picture, emphasizing the shtetl's defects and filling it with shadowy figures like those who inhabit Peretz's "Dead Town," people staggering under the load of eking out a meager existence, neither engaging in daily activities, loving or caring for one another, nor striving for ideals.

Many of these male writers were sensitive to woman's plight. Mendele and Peretz decried arranged marriages, bemoaned women's excessive economic burdens, and even noted their lack of equal educational opportunities. Berkowitz saw how harassed and overburdened women were with child rearing and housework. Influenced by the Haskalah and socialism, these writers buttressed their ideological rejection of the shtetl by describing women as pathetic victims of an antiquated social and economic system.[1] Other authors, such as Sholem Aleichem, sometimes depicted women as stereotypical shrews and nags. Daughters, interestingly, tended to be romanticized by all.

Dvora Baron (1887–1957) is the only female Hebrew prose writer known to have emerged from the shtetl milieu in the last century. Like many of her contemporaries, she also wrote in Yiddish at the beginning of her career, but she soon turned to Hebrew as her primary literary language. Her works, which are an important and neglected source of information about shtetl life in general and the lives of women in particular, reflect her own unique experiences and perceptions, often quite different from those presented by men. There are similarities, to be sure, since Baron also focuses on the alienated and depicts social injustice, but her perspective on the shtetl differs from her male contemporaries', and she colors her stories with other hues.

In her collected works, Baron does not write as a critic wishing to condemn or reform an outdated system. Baron sought to capture the spirit of the people who inhabited Uzda, the small Lithuanian town she knew so well, and she depicts the beauty as well as the ugliness that lay beneath the shtetl's bleak surface. Baron's shtetl has a flowing quality; it is a place where people live, give birth, and die; they celebrate holidays as seasons come and go. Generations also come and go; people leave the shtetl and emigrate to America while relatives stay behind in loneliness. True, Baron was annoyed by some of the shtetl's mores, particularly as they applied to women. But her overall approach is humanistic, and her works are pathos-filled and lyrical, composed by one who was in tune with the tempo of the shtetl, acquainted with its values, and able to empathize with its struggles. She can well be compared to the photographer son of Mousha in her story "The Thorny Path," who captures the inner essence of his subjects and brings out the best in everyone, noting even barely discernible aspects of their personalities.

Most of the works discussed here are from *Parshiyot*,[2] a one-volume compilation of Baron's short story collections. However, Baron began to write and publish at fifteen, and there are quite a number of writings in Hebrew and Yiddish that she chose to leave out of her collected works. These early efforts were recently collected and published, together with commentary about Baron's early life, by Nurit Govrin.[3] The tone of many of these writings is far starker than the subtle style Baron adopted later on; it may be that she was intent on imitating the cynical stance of the male writers. She may also have been trying to establish herself as a respected female writer in a man's world by flaunting her ability to utilize talmudic idiom. (Her readers, in fact, asked her to write more simply.)[4] Still, while most of these early works lack the lyricism, compassion, and polish of Baron's later writing, they are instructive in revealing her recurring themes and style, and they will be referred to here for that purpose.[5]

In her collected works, Baron introduces the reader to both men and women of the shtetl, but the women and their point of view predominate. Baron's shtetl is primarily a woman's world, even if it does revolve around men. Women appear in almost every shtetl story. Sometimes, like the widow who lives next door to Fradel, they are mentioned briefly. In other instances, they occupy center stage, as Fradel, who, after suffering incessant emotional abuse from a uncaring husband, decides to leave a loveless marriage, or Mina, whose ugliness vanishes when she is no longer subjected to her city mother's loathing and finds friendship and respect in the shtetl. We become acquainted even with tangential characters, through simple and vivid details of their lives which Baron weaves into her tales. Like a Greek chorus, Baron's women constantly comment on and react to events going on around them.

Most of all we get to know the author herself. Baron is at the same time a teller of others' tales and a narrator of her own. She is a participant-observer: when she writes about other women, she is writing about herself; when she writes about herself, she is writing about other shtetl women as well. Present in almost every shtetl story is Chana, Baron's narrative persona, named after her deceased sister and fashioned after Dvora Baron herself. Chana is either an observer—the events take place "in Chana's town"—or one of the characters in her stories.[6] Baron was an extremely private person; many details about her life have come to light only after her death. It was not known until recently, for instance, that before immigrating to the land of Israel she had been engaged to a fellow writer, Moshe Ben-Eliezer (Moshe Glembotski) (1880–1944), for ten years.[7] It is therefore paradoxical that Baron's stories tend to be quasi-autobiographical and appear to reveal so much about her own early life.

Although Baron left the shtetl for the city at the age of fifteen, and lived in the land of Israel from twenty-three on, the shtetl locale and its culture continued to frame her stories. Whereas some stories take place in the land of Israel, some in Egypt, where she lived with her family during the First World War, and a few in East European urban settings, the bulk are set in the small Lithuanian shtetl in which she was reared. But she was aware that the Uzda she depicted was a microcosm of the world at large, and comments that the vignettes of life she portrays are but a mirror of universal life. Thus, she writes at the end of "The Bricklayer" that the lot of that unfortunate man "is the lot of most people on earth. They work and they toil and they die in the mud" (220).

Dvora Baron was considered something of a phenomenon

among the writers of her generation. Some women in Eastern Europe were able to read Hebrew from the *siddur*, but
they generally could not speak or understand the language,
or even write Hebrew letters. Baron demonstrated mastery
of the traditional sources that boys learned in the heder or
the yeshiva, which was generally inaccessible to girls. This
is even more surprising since she grew up in a shtetl where
opportunities for girls to study were especially rare. Her
colleagues referred to her as "the rabbi's daughter" and
spoke of her with wonderment. They went out of their way
to seek her out.[8] One writer even came to Uzda to meet "the
woman writer, the rabbi's daughter." Dvora was at the well
washing dishes at the time and came running barefoot when
her brother informed her of a visitor.[9] It was unusual for a
woman to be knowledgeable in rabbinic sources, and the
readers of her early stories were astonished by her familiarity with the Talmud.[10] The fact that women were generally not able to gain such knowledge in the shtetl grieved
Baron greatly, and she deals with the theme in her earliest
writings.

Being a rabbi's daughter had a profound impact on Baron's work. It enabled her to learn first hand about aspects of
shtetl life she otherwise might not have known. People came
to the rabbi for rulings on religious matters and resolution
of disputes. But they also came to discuss personal problems, confer about delicate family matters, receive blessings
before leaving the country, have nightmares reinterpreted,
or to pour out the anguish of their hearts to a learned and
sympathetic ear. Almost everyone in Uzda needed to consult with the rabbi at some time, and so Baron was able to
perceive the shtetl in its totality while noting its diversity as
well. The community room where people came to consult
with the rabbi was actually part of the rabbi's living quar-
ters, separated from the rest of the living space by a curtain.
From her perch in the room, or seated behind the curtain,
little Dvora saw and heard all. Small wonder that many of
her stories are written as reminiscences or that the narrative voice is that of Chana, the rabbi's daughter. Baron was

able to bring to her stories descriptions of relatively unknown rituals and intimate family situations. She learned
about good and evil, about human tears and striving. She
came to understand what troubled people and how they
related to each other. And from her father, she learned to
care about the unfortunates of the world.

Her father was the most important influence in her life.
She describes him as a loving, wise, and compassionate being. It was he who gave her entry into the male intellectual
world of rabbinic literature, providing the tools she would
need to become a Hebrew writer. He taught her to read
Rashi script, and we know from the recollections of a friend
that Dvora would sit in the women's gallery and listen to her
father teaching Talmud to the boys. She would occasionally
call out some question about the *mishnayot* or *Ain Ya'akov*
she was studying.[11] Baron describes how Chana would hear
her father preparing his sermons. He would frequently share
his ideas with her, or she would tag along while he discussed his thoughts with a fellow talmudic scholar (230–31).

One of the unusual aspects of Baron's works is that they
provide the reader with details about the life of a shtetl
rabbi. She depicts his relationships with his family and his
interactions with shtetl folk. Her father was, apparently, an
inspiring speaker. Baron describes the effect of his sermons
(243): How excited people became about participating in the
geniza ceremony![12] He inspired even his impoverished con-
gregants to provide "eating days" for yeshiva students.
Through her depiction of Chana's father, Baron remembers
a father who was kind and sensitive to everyone. He is the
only one who speaks respectfully to an idiot lad who delivers the milk. When some rude boys shove an old woman
aside at the *geniza* ceremony, it is Chana's father who notices the unfortunate woman, calls her over, and graciously
accepts the frayed pages from her hand (244). Baron even
records the rabbi's relationship to gentiles. He is on most
friendly terms with the priest. And he is always depicted
with a smile on his face, even when ill and in pain (208).

Baron's positive descriptions of a rabbi father diverge

from her contemporaries' depictions of rabbis as fanatical reactionary forces, intolerant of enlightenment. Both rabbis and fathers are generally portrayed in modern Hebrew literature as destructive elements. Where a more positive approach is employed, as in the works of Peretz or Agnon, a layer of irony or satire usually accompanies it. But Baron's view is different and reflects her reality: her father was, in fact, a warm and tolerant person, who is said to have read modern Hebrew prose. Baron's nephew concurs, and describes his grandfather as brilliant, filled with humility, loving, and ready to help the unfortunate.[13] The rabbi's love for his children is apparent in the letters he wrote to Dvora and her brother after they left the shtetl. Baron's depiction also contradicts the *luftmentsh* image usually associated with the talmudic scholar in modern Hebrew literature: this rabbi appears to have been a practical person who could chat with a priest or put up shelves in their summer dwelling (210). Baron's picture then, counterbalances the generally negative picture of the shtetl rabbi in the works of her contemporaries. There is no doubt that it also reflects the Jewish-Lithuanian milieu, which was generally more enlightened and tolerant than other parts of Eastern Europe.

Baron's father apparently served as a role model for her. Friends and relatives report that she was quite similar to him.[14] As one of Baron's writer friends noted, "there was not another writer who showed as much sympathy for the oppressed."[15] It is probably because of her close relationship with her father that no generation gaps are portrayed in her works. She didn't sever her ties with the shtetl she left at fifteen, and in her stories, too, young people who move on retain loving relationships with parents and come back to visit or even to marry childhood sweethearts ("Fradel," "The Thorny Path").

Dvora Baron's father provided her with the skills to develop as a writer and may well have affected her style of writing, which has a homiletic quality, much like his sermons. He was wont to begin a sermon with a biblical passage on which he would then expound. Baron similarly starts each shtetl story with a biblical verse; she comments on it and then elaborates it through the characters and events of her narrative. The very first story in her collected works, "Family," illustrates this style. Before she begins to tell about a specific family in the shtetl, she relates the genealogy of Genesis. With this narrative mode, Baron also adopted the shtetl inhabitant's manner of speaking and viewing the world in the context of traditional sources, where everything was colored by the Bible, Midrash, and Talmud. In Baron's Lithuanian milieu, even the women quoted religious sources constantly. A grandmother, for instance, cites talmudic passages about the advantage of a son over a daughter in the apparently autobiographical story "The First Day."

It is not surprising that many of Baron's stories center about a nurturing father. In "The First Day," it is the father who comes to his daughter's rescue after her grandmother rejects her because of her gender, and her bedridden mother is too ill to care for the newborn. Baron's narrator Chana states that it was his smile that "she would come to know and love as a comfort throughout her life." Everything in the room is altered when her father, "the person who would be dearer to her than anything," enters. The lights go on and her mother and grandmother both cheer up. She describes her father as always knowing "the exact word of comfort" to offer her mother and others. When Chana awakened from a bad dream, her father would be there, bending over her, "the sickly father, in rabbinic garb, with immense love in his gaze" (283). When she arrives home after he has died, she writes, "Daddy, Daddy, my heart cried within me, when I suddenly grasped the sharpness of my being orphaned and knowing that there was no one who would find the right word . . . to say to comfort me in the long night" (298).

In general, Baron portrays fathers in nurturing roles. She writes that her father comforted and rocked her, "as all fathers do." One of her most touching tales describes a poor man who takes on the most demeaning tasks, and endures ridicule and hardship, in order to support his family and, particularly, to attain the means to buy cocoa for an ailing son. When the man returns home from work, he is greeted warmly by his children, who climb on his back and clamor for his attention. One of the most touching scenes describes how the man carefully raises the cup to his ill child's mouth so as not to lose a drop of the precious liquid and then, mindful of the other children, gives each one a lick of the cocoa dregs remaining in the cup (197). Portrayals of loving fathers transcend class structure. "Gilgulim" describes a hard-headed businessman who becomes loving and tender in the presence of his daughter. Fathers consistently show affection to their children, especially to their daughters. In "The Thorny Path" the father caresses his daughter's hair lovingly; the ailing father of "What Has Been" comforts the crying daughter and shares with her his most prized possession, an orange. It has been noted that a warm relationship existed between fathers and daughters in the shtetl and Baron's stories bear this out.[16]

However, Baron's descriptions of mothers are more ambivalent. On the one hand, she seems to idealize her mother. Quasi-autobiographical accounts reveal a beautiful, aristocratic, and loving woman, a blend of tradition and modernity, somber and modest with a blond wig, urbane, blue-eyed, well mannered, and educated. A photograph of Baron's mother bears out this description. Her story "In the Beginning" vividly portrays Chana's chic city-bred mother's first encounter with the shtetl. The newly wed rebbetzin (rabbi's wife) is shocked by the poverty, filth, and grayness she sees around her and is horrified by the sense of sameness everywhere. When the elegantly dressed woman is about to enter her new dwelling, she comes upon a goat ambling about outside and breaks down and weeps. By providing this view of the shtetl through her mother's eyes, Baron is giving the reader an outsider's view, an objective rendering, of the environment in which she was reared. To some extent Baron must be describing her own feelings about the shtetl that in the end led her to leave it. The

sophisticated newcomer, however, soon adjusted and before long was emulating her neighbors and baking the identical cheesecakes she so despised at first. She even began to
sell yeast, a shtetl prerogative of the rabbi's wife, to help out
financially.

Much as fathers, mothers too are compassionate. Baron
has Chana's mother comment frequently on shtetl occur-
rences she considers unjust. The mother is especially em-
pathetic to unfortunate women. At a divorce proceeding she
adamantly refuses to give a divorced man's relatives goblets
for the wine they brought to celebrate the occasion. She
tries instead to comfort the ex-wife. Baron does not deny the
mother the nurturing role. When little Chana is born, her
mother rejoices and bends over her daughter's crib with a
radiant smile. Later, her mother insists on obtaining a goose
to make goose-fat for her daughter to take with her when
she departs for the city "so that Chana will have *shmaltz* to
put on her bread while studying late into the night" (293). As
she leaves, her mother kisses her and says, "Don't forget to
take good care of the jar of jam." Thus, in Baron's shtetl, the
fathers provided words of comfort, while the mothers supplied the comfort of warmth and food.

But other sketches depict betrayal, negligence, and a
yearning for a mother's love that is prevalent in much of
shtetl literature.[17] Baron describes in amazement an infant's
cries in the crib going unheeded. The mother, she says,
should have comforted and loved her daughter, thereby en-
abling her to sustain pain in later life. Another story, "Deception," indicts the mother even more strongly, recounting
a traumatic incident which metamorphoses into a symbol of
maternal treachery. Chana is assured by her mother that the
barber will not cut her hair short, only to discover that her
mother had actually instructed him to have her pretty
tresses snipped while distracting her with a cookie. Chana
learns what has happened when her friends ridicule her for
her "boy's haircut." She is astounded at her mother's betrayal. "This was my mother whom I trusted!" she declares,
and says that this incident became a symbol for all other

acts of deception she was to experience in life. A storm that hits the shtetl right after this event appears to be a projection of the anger she felt but could not express. The story is also interesting from a psychological perspective. Baron retained her long, braided hair all her life and was obviously proud of it. Since it is the mother who wanted her daughter to look like a boy, we must also ask if Baron thought that her mother would actually have preferred a son.

There are even malevolent mothers in Baron's stories. The mother in "What Has Been" could have stepped out of Grimms' fairy tales, so unbelievably hateful is she to her daughter, Mina. Once, when her daughter was being fitted for a dress, the mother angrily pounced on her, tore the lovely dress around the neckline, and snipped one of the girl's braids. Mina ran into the cellar, wanting to harm herself, plagued by her feeling of being despised. "The Thorny Path" describes a stepmother who makes her stepdaughter, Mousha, do all the work. When Mousha herself gives birth to a son, she cannot care for him and has to give him away to be raised by others. A strongly socialistic tale, "Shifra," describes an impoverished mother who sends her widowed daughter to become a wet nurse in the city, forcing her to abandon her own two-month-old infant. Poor Shifra cries constantly, is sent back to the shtetl, and dies en route. Although the mother brings about her daughter's death, it is her desire to seek sustenance for the daughter that led her to send the girl away. Indeed, in most instances, Baron's descriptions of maternal cruelty are offset by extenuating circumstances or mitigated by the appearance of surrogate mothers, such as aunts or family friends who provide nurturance ("What Has Been," "The Thorny Path"). In Baron's stories, mothers curse or slap children only when exasperated and in great pain, as in an early story, "Pain," where the mother is critically ill and dying of a tumor.

Baron captures the subtle nuances of marital relationships within the shtetl. Her narrator, Chana, frequently reflects on the marriage of her parents. It was a loving one. Her mother would look up to her father admiringly, radiant when walking with him. At one point, she is so taken with the sound of her husband's Torah study that she runs into the room with outstretched hands, as if to embrace him. "There is no need," Baron writes, "to describe the words of comfort that were exchanged between the two in the middle of the night." It is obvious that her parents did not display affection to each other publicly. Chana sees her parents walking together for the first time in a summer resort.

Indeed, Baron describes a well-known aspect of shtetl marriage rarely touched upon by others. Laws of ritual purity were an integral part of married life in the shtetl. They involved the woman's immersion in a *mikvah*, a ritual bath, about a week after the completion of a menstrual cycle, and the avoidance of sexual contact from the onset of the menses until then. In "Fradel" Baron lauds Jewish women for their diligence and self-sacrifice in adhering to this tradition in the face of considerable hardship. The law requires that the bathing be done at night. Baron describes women making their way to the *mikvah* along icy ground on wintry nights, faces flushed with embarrassment as they try to avoid the inquisitive gazes of their neighbors "in order to preserve a holy tradition passed down from mother to daughter" (110). These words sound as if they could have been delivered by a rabbi from the pulpit in praise of observance of the laws of purity. However, an awareness of women's embarrassment could only have been conveyed by a sensitive female writer attuned to women's feelings.

The laws of ritual purity appear in her earliest stories. But there she describes the practice in uncomplimentary contexts. In one of her earliest works, "A Couple Quarrels," composed in 1905 while she still lived in the shtetl, a husband mistreats his wife, who says to him, "You lustful person! For two weeks I am 'Darling' and 'Dear' and then for two weeks you cannot stand me." In another early work, "In the Darkness," a husband insists that his wife go to the *mikvah* so that he can have relations with her. She does not want to go, because she needs to feed the hungry children. But, she consents, goes unwillingly, and then reluctantly accedes to his desire to have sex. Govrin claims that this story reveals Baron's true feelings about the laws of ritual purity.[18] It is possible, however, that it is more indicative of her ambivalence to sexuality, framed within the traditional Jewish context as she knew it.

Other marital relationships are also not described idyllically. Husbands either ignore or neglect their wives, want them only for childbearing, and even beat them. The story "Agunah" describes a husband who distances himself emotionally from his wife: an old woman attempts to share her excitement about an itinerant preacher's speech with her husband, but he pretends to be asleep and ignores her pleas to wake up and listen to her. The woman knows he is really awake and ruminates "that is the way men have always been" (306). Baron is probably one of the few authors of this time and place who describes battered wives, a theme in one of her earliest works, "A Couple Quarrels," written in 1905. In "Trifles," the shoemaker's wife pathetically seeks refuge in the rabbi's house for fear that her husband will beat her because she has again given birth to a girl. One cannot help comparing this glimpse of a real, though rare, social evil of the shtetl with some of Mendele's and Peretz's works, where it is the woman who runs after the man with a rolling pin!

Some of Baron's most pathos-filled tales are about divorce.[19] She writes: "Of all those who came in years past for judgment to my father's rabbinic court, those who seemed most unfortunate were the women about to be divorced by their husbands" (185). Divorce was rare in the shtetl and women endured much, even lovelessness, to avoid it at all cost. Baron describes the sequence of events that led up to the dissolution of a marriage. First, the husband found fault with his wife, either because his family had turned him against her or because he was enamored with another. From the moment that divorce appeared imminent, the wife's status in the town deteriorated—storekeepers refused to extend credit, acquaintances stared at her and pretended they did not know her. A particularly sad circumstance that led to divorce was the wife's presumed barrenness. According to Jewish law, a primary function of wedlock is procreation. In the event that a woman has not borne children within ten years of marriage, the husband is entitled to divorce her and marry another. Baron describes a man's arrival at the rabbi's house in preparation for the divorce in such a situation. He is surrounded by his relatives, who form a fortress around him and are even prepared to celebrate the divorce. The woman, however, is ignored and left to sit forlornly with only the rabbi's wife to offer support. Baron describes how these unfortunate women would walk unsteadily away into the darkness of loneliness and shattered dreams to confront the reality of struggling to subsist without a husband. Subsequently they had to see their seat in the synagogue occupied by the new wife, as they disappeared into a corner. There were writers, such as Mendele and Peretz, who themselves experienced divorce, but they did not write about it. Others, such as Y. L. Gordon, used it to mock the rabbinic system. Despite her deep sympathy for these tragic divorcées, Baron, unlike her peers who used these events to thunder against rabbinic authority, accepted misfortune as part of life's existential mystery, perhaps because of the respect for tradition instilled in her by her father.

One of the most unusual aspects of Baron's works is the friendship she depicts among women. Her shtetl is truly a community of women, with women caring for one another, commenting on one another's sorrows, and helping one another survive courageously. Her women characters never seem to be lonely or overworked, though they are always busy. They are constantly interacting with other women, as they go about their housework and engage in handiwork. Nor does Baron describe housework as drudgery; rather she views handiwork as healing. In "What Has Been," Mina's nervous, abusive mother is calmed by learning to do handiwork. Friends reported that in her own life Baron occupied herself with handiwork when living in Israel, and that she was a meticulous and efficient housewife.[20] One of the most heartwarming illustrations of bonding and courage is Baron's description of Chaya-Chava and Reizel. After Chaya-Chava's husband is murdered in a pogrom, she comes to the shtetl with her six children and learns to bake cookies to sell in the marketplace. When Reizel loses her husband in similar fashion, Chaya-Chava reaches out to her, gives her part of her dwelling, teaches her how to bake, and together they go to the marketplace to sell their wares, while other women in the shtetl care for their children and help however they can. Baron marvels at the courage of these women (426). Baron also describes loving relationships between her aunt and the shoemaker's wife, the friendship between Chana and Mina, through which Mina gains self-respect, and Chana's friendship with Gitel in "Gilgulim".

Baron saw friendship everywhere in the shtetl. There are many loving women in her stories and also good male friends who are ready to offer support whenever possible. Among the loving figures who reappear are the cook and the aunt. Baron herself seems to have been sociable. She was close to her students when she taught in the cities of Europe and her room was a center for friends to gather.[21] One marvels at the illness, and other factors perhaps, that combined to turn such a sociable woman into a recluse in later life. In contrast with her emphasis on friendship, Baron also describes the sinister power of gossip in many of her tales. It is not as strong a motif as friendship, but is obviously condemned in "The Thorny Path." Baron apparently experienced its ill effects personally and instructed her daughter to destroy any revealing letters after her death.[22]

Despite her positive portrayals of certain aspects of female lives and her acceptance of tradition, Baron is aware of the complexity and dark side of being a woman in the shtetl. Although she herself was able to transcend many of the obstacles of gender, she was still well informed about the disadvantages for women intrinsic to the shtetl milieu. Thus, Baron dwells upon an acknowledged aspect of shtetl life not commented upon by male authors—the preference for the male child.[23] One of the harshest depictions of this occurs in her work "Trifles," in which a shoemaker's wife has given birth to a succession of daughters. Following each birth, the woman was beaten by her husband and forcibly led to the rabbi with threat of divorce. One of the most heartrending scenes is of the poor woman, weak from childbirth, following an enraged husband to the rabbi's house with little girls clutching fearfully at her skirt. In her seemingly autobiographical story "The First Day," Baron describes her own experience of this oppression. Since the birth of a daughter was not hailed as an occasion of great rejoicing, her father was called away from his newborn daughter to officiate at a circumcision ceremony of a distant relative's child. The two births provide a study in contrasts. The circumcision was heralded with rejoicing and festive fare; the home of the newborn girl is filled with gloom. In the darkened house, the grandmother piously recites passages from the Talmud extolling male virtue and returns the sumptuous food ordered in anticipation of the birth of a male child. The infant girl remains in her crib, unfed and unattended, crying incessantly. While lying in her crib, she perceives a single screw oddly protruding from the ceiling, and sees herself as that screw, a "symbol of every unfortunate superfluous being in life."

The superiority of the male in the traditional setting of the shtetl preoccupied Baron from early on. Many of her early works address the topic centrally or tangentially. As early as 1904 she wrote "A Superfluous One," about a girl who felt she was extraneous. She continued to decry women's exclusion from the intellectual and religious sphere of Jewish tradition. In *"Kadisha"* (a feminine version of Kaddish [the Jewish mourner's prayer] that does not exist in Hebrew), a grandfather says to his granddaughter, "If only you were a boy," suggesting that she would then be able to recite the Kaddish for him after his death. In one story a mother rejoices when her son studies the Talmud, but insists that her daughter cannot do the same and must learn housework instead. In another, a woman seeks to find a man to make the kiddush (sanctification of the wine) for her on the Sabbath, assuming that she cannot do it for herself, and in a third, the narrator is disturbed that as a girl she cannot make Havdalah, the service that ends the Sabbath. Baron's tone of resentment, strident in her early works, became more subtle, but remains a powerful theme in her collected works. In *"Geniza,"* for instance, the men want to reject a book of *tkhines* (prayers for women in Yiddish) that a woman brings because they don't deem her prayer book legitimately holy. The woman mumbles to herself about how difficult woman's lot is. This issue was obviously close to Baron's heart as a daughter of the shtetl and concerned her even after she entered the larger world of Hebrew letters, where she continued to feel the effects of these traditional attitudes.[24]

Baron's obvious ambivalence over her gender are echoed in her depictions of sexuality. In contrast to her collected stories, her earlier writings are blatantly erotic. Her peers were, in fact, surprised by the degree of eroticism and spoke about her "strange themes,"[25] which were foreign to Hebrew letters of that time. After reading her works, writers were surprised to meet a demure, modestly attired Baron.[26] Her works seemed so brazen that they expected to find a "loose" woman who believed in free love. Her early tale "In the Darkness" comes as close to describing sex as was possible at that time. She depicts a husband demanding to have relations with his wife, displacing a toddler from his usual sleeping area so that he could share the woman's bed. In the darkness, the child cries out that he sees a big red tongue coming at him and a bitch entering the room.

Many of Baron's descriptions in her collected works, however, carry only the subtlest hint of eroticism, as when she describes Dina, freshly bathed and shampooed, eagerly awaiting her husband's arrival for the Sabbath. It may be that Baron inserted eroticism into her early works in order to dispel any doubts about her ability and readiness to deal with naturalistic themes despite being a rabbi's daughter. Yet her collected works emphasize instead an idealized picture of platonic relationships between husband and wife. In "Gilgulim," for example, Gitel and Reuven get married en route to Israel. The innkeeper provides them with private accomodations to consummate the marriage and is surprised to find them shortly after sitting on opposite sides of the room, engrossed in packing their things, "like a brother and a sister." What is noteworthy about these words is that Baron's description of "brother and sister" is similar to her view of a perfect relationship between the sexes expressed in a conversation with her fiancé, Ben Eliezer.[27] Much has been made of this apparent avoidance of eroticism in Baron's collected works, as well as her reclusiveness in the last decades of her life. Her seclusion was due, at least in part, to illness, for she had been frail much of her life. But Baron is also known to have held some negative views about marriage, allegedly remarking that marriage is akin to death for a woman.[28] If these words sound harsh, they can perhaps best be understood as alluding to her artistic self. Baron found that the myriad tasks of managing a household efficiently on a meager income required all her daytime hours, and she was forced to appropriate the wee hours of the night for her writing.[29] Considering her weak physical state, this must have been quite a strain on her health. In "What Has Been," Baron faults the environment for not knowing how to nurture the poetic Ephraim, who died prematurely. Baron may have felt that her own surroundings after marriage hindered her development as a creative artist. Baron's marriage to Yosef Aharonson has been much analyzed. Her husband was noted for his uprightness and was similar to her father in character, a likely source of his attraction for her.[30] It is known that when Yosef Aharonson resigned from the editorship of *Hapo'el Hatsa'ir*, Baron resigned with him, apparently as a sign of solidarity. Aharonson went on to another career. But Baron's life took an odd turn. Shortly thereafter she became a recluse and isolated herself in her room. These factors would indicate that Baron's marriage did engender a kind of death of her creative muse. Baron spent many years translating *Madame Bovary* into Hebrew because she admired Flaubert's succinct and precise prose. It may well be, however, that like Madame Bovary, she found herself stifled in her marriage.

Like the bird in her story, "Goose," Baron flew away from the shtetl. But, like Chana in the story, she took with her some of the *shmaltz* from her parents' home. Although her fellow writers in the land of Israel enjoined her to write only about her new milieu and denigrated her for not doing so, she endured their mockery.[31] Unlike her peers, she courageously continued to write about the shtetl and viewed Zionism as an extension of the shtetl and not as its antithesis. In Baron's story "Gilgulim," Chana's childhood friend Gitel, who has settled in Israel, is overjoyed when her shtetl father joins her there.[32] So, too, Baron carried the memory of her father and her father's home with her to the new homeland and kept them alive in her writing.

NOTES

1. See Ruth Adler, *Women of the Shtetl Through the Eyes of Y. L. Peretz* (Cranbury N.J., 1980) 21–25, for a fuller discussion.

2. Dvora Baron, *Parshiyot* (Jerusalem, 1968).

3. Nurit Govrin, *The First Half: Dvora Baron, Her Life and Work 1887– 1922* [Hebrew] (Jerusalem, 1988), and *Dvora Baron; Early Stories 1902– 1920* [Hebrew], ed. Avner Holtzman (Jerusalem, 1988).

4. Govrin, *First Half*, 106.

5. Page references are to *Parshiyot* (see n. 2); the early stories are all contained in Govrin's volume (see n. 3). The translations into English are my own. Some of Baron's stories have been translated into English in *The Thorny Path*, ed. I. Hanoch, transl. J. Schachter (Jerusalem, 1969).

6. Y. Fichman, *Contemporaries* [Hebrew] (Tel Aviv, 1954), 254–87, notes that despite the memoir-like quality of her work, Baron maintained an aesthetic distance between herself and her subject that allowed her to write with both compassion and objectivity.

7. Govrin, *First Half*, 43–69.

8. *Ibid.*, 32–35.

9. R. Alper, "About Dvora Baron" [Hebrew], *Agav urcha* (Tel Aviv, 1960), 242–48. *Agav urcha* is a collection of works from Baron's literary legacy, some of her correspondence, and reminiscences by various friends and relatives.

10. Govrin, *First Half*, 116.

11. M. Gitlin, "In Her Youth, The Recollections of a Neighbor" [He-

brew], *Agav urcha*, 208, 209. *Ain Yaakov* is a collection of allegorical and homiletical material from the Talmud.

12. According to Jewish tradition, holy books cannot be destroyed because they contain God's name. When they become frayed they are, therefore, buried in the ground. This burial ritual is known as *geniza*.

13. E. Pedarsky, "About Grandfather and His Home" [Hebrew], *Agav urcha,* 205–08.

14. Alper, "About Dvora Baron."

15. A. Kariv, *Chords and Arrangements* [Hebrew] (Jerusalem, 1972), 265.

16. M. Zborowski and E. Herzog, *Life Is with People* (New York, 1972), 332.

17. Ruth Adler, "The Real Jewish Mother," *Midstream* (Oct. 1977), 38–41.

18. Govrin, *First Half*, 152–154.

19. Some of the points made in this chapter were discussed briefly in my essay "Devorah Baron: Chronicler of East-European Jewish Women," *Midstream* (Aug.-Sept. 1988), 40–44.

20. D. Lachower, "In Her Memory" [Hebrew], *Agav urcha,* 229–230; and D. Zakai, "As I Saw Her" [Hebrew], *Agav urcha,* 225–229.

21. B. Ben-Yehuda, "Dvora: A Guide to the Young" [Hebrew], *Agav Urcha,* 209–22.

22. Govrin, *First Half*, 43, 50.

23. M. S. Zunser, *Yesterday,* (New York, 1978), 65, notes in her memoir of shtetl life that a popular shtetl maxim was "A daughter banishes laughter."

24. *Dvora Baron: A Selection of Critical Essays on Her Literary Prose* [Hebrew], ed. Ada Pagis (Tel Aviv, 1974). Pagis, 8–11, notes that critics focused on Baron's uniqueness as a woman writer from the shtetl, or on other aspects of her personal life, rather than discussing her literary pieces themselves.

25. Govrin, *First Half,* 76.

26. *Ibid.,* 114.

27. *Ibid.,* 54.

28. *Agav urcha,* 108.

29. Alper, "About Dvora Baron."

30. Y. Keshet, *Approximations: Essays in Literary Criticism* [Hebrew] (Jerusalem, 1969), 52–54.

31. Govrin, *First Half,* 204. Her colleagues also mocked her respect for tradition (211).

32. The Hebrew word *gilgulim* connotes both "wanderings" and "reincarnation." The story's title suggests that Baron believed that the shtetl could in some way be transplanted to Israel.

6 ✦ NORMA FAIN PRATT

Culture and Radical Politics: Yiddish Women Writers in America, 1890–1940

During the first two decades of the twentieth century, the cultural traditions East European Jewish immigrants brought with them to America were fundamentally recast, yet few cultural historians have considered the extent to which these transformations were an expression of class and gender. This study, based on the lives of some fifty Yiddish women writers whose extensive literary works appeared in the United States during the first half of the twentieth century, confronts diversity, class difference, and especially gender as sources of change in American Jewish life.[1]

All of the women under consideration came from the poorer classes of East European Jewry. A few were daughters of impoverished merchant families; others were raised in an artisan environment; but most came from the proletarianized Jewish classes of recently industrialized Russian Poland and the Austro-Hungarian Empire. Their parents, particularly their mothers, were barely literate. While few of

111

these women received advanced formal education either in
Eastern Europe or in America, in the New World they became journalists, poets, short story writers, and novelists,
representing a first generation of Jewish women, immigrant
and poor, who interpreted their own lives in their own language.

Emigrating mainly in the years between 1905 and 1920
and settling in large urban centers (New York, Chicago, and
Los Angeles), they wrote exclusively in Yiddish for audi-
ences who still communicated primarily in that language.
The Jewish anarchist, socialist, Yiddish avant-garde, and,
later in the 1920s and 1930s, the Jewish communist presses
regularly accepted the literary work of these women, whose
writing dealt primarily with female, Jewish, and working-
class immigrant issues rather than political concerns. Along
with their male counterparts, these writers were spokes-
women for a politically radical Jewish subculture that existed within the general American Jewish society but at the
same time possessed its own outlook and its own political,
social, and cultural institutions. This distinctive Jewish subculture, consisting mainly of needle trades workers, small
businesspeople, clerks, students, teachers, and artists, represented one form of secular Jewish existence in America.
These people were known as the *veltlikhe yidn* ("secular
Jews"): the *radikaln* of the Jewish Left. They rejected Orthodox Judaism with its rituals and rabbinical leadership and in
its place accepted a Jewish identity, *yiddishkeit*, that was
committed to the preservation of the Yiddish language, the
celebration of historic Jewish holidays, and the cultivation
of Jewish loyalties. Their *yiddishkeit* also included a special
devotion to the Jewish working class, the international
working class, and America, their adopted home. Committed to the creation of a distinct Jewish society as part of a
culturally pluralistic society in America, they wanted to be
American without assimilating; they wished to express politically radical ideals, especially in matters social and economic; and they hoped to remain Yiddish speakers and cultural Jews.

In the ideological paradigm of the secular radicals, these diverse goals and loyalties did not seem contradictory. Rather, with these purposes in mind, this Jewish subculture created Jewish radical political parties (the Anarchists, the socialist *Verband*, the Communist International Workers' Order, the Zionist-socialist *Po'ale Zion*) that in turn maintained Yiddish newspapers (*Tsukunft, Fraye arbeter shtime*), Yiddish literary journals (*Brikn, Signal, Hamer*), literary-political discussion groups, choruses, mutual insurance groups, drama clubs, recreational camps, children's Yiddish schools, and summer camps. It was an immigrants' society and an immigrants' dream that attracted thousands of people, at its center and at its margins, for several decades from the end of the nineteenth century until at least the fourth decade of the twentieth century. Women were an active force in creating and maintaining its institutions, and Yiddish women writers were the visible and vocal representatives of their gender.[2]

Yet those same women writers, although an important group, were also isolated from men and from each other. Their participation in the radical Yiddishist culture was not the same as male participation. Although members of the same anarchist, socialist, or communist parties and contributors to the same newspapers and journals, women writers functioned differently from men within the institutional structure of Jewish radical society. The hundreds of volumes of their fiction and nonfiction remain a distinct body of literature that documents, articulates, and serves as a guide for understanding the perceptions of an entire generation of immigrant women who came of age in the United States before the Second World War.

Had the fifty immigrant writers under discussion remained in Europe, they might have had some opportunity for educational and literary development, since East European Jewish society was becoming increasingly secularized at the turn of the century. Girls attended gymnasium; some even took higher degrees at the university level.[3] A vital Yiddish literature was also developing in twentieth-century

Europe, not only in America. Yet, as late as the 1930s only a few exceptional women, like Kadya Molodowsky in Warsaw and Devorah Fogel in Lemberg (Lvov), had attained any literary reputation of consequence.[4]

In America, on the other hand, a much larger number of Jewish women achieved an artistic and intellectual existence, albeit a circumscribed one. The emergence of women as writers was part of the blending of old and new social and intellectual forces at work in American Jewish life that provided a favorable climate for the acceptance of a female intelligentsia. Some of the Jewish women, especially socialist, Zionist-socialist, and anarchist immigrants, had already participated in cultural activities in Eastern Europe in the 1890s. In addition, immigrant society in America was in need of interpreters of its new experiences, and intellectuals and critics, with little formal education but with insight into the contemporary scene, were perceived as authentic spokesmen. There was an enormous growth of Yiddish publications, and talented and persevering women without academic credentials, like men in similar circumstances, were encouraged to express their views in print. Moreover, during the Progressive Era, American ideas of female emancipation reinforced favorable existing radical Jewish attitudes toward female intellectuality and competence. But most important of all, theoretical ideas of equality were concretized by the behavior of Jewish women, particularly working women, who belied all contemporary stereotypes of immigrant women as passive victims of industrial American society. In the period between 1909, the year of the famous shirtwaist makers' strike, and the 1920s, when Jewish women workers and trade unionists helped organize the garment industry unions, Jewish immigrant women were militant and tenacious. Therefore, those women who spoke on their behalf directly or indirectly received a hearing.

Under what circumstances did East European Jewish women become Yiddish writers? Scanty information exists in Yiddish biographical lexicons, rare autobiographies, and several oral history interviews.[5] From these sources, it appears that most of the Yiddish women writers, born into Orthodox Jewish households in small towns in Eastern Europe in the late 1800s, began to write before they left Europe for America. Their fathers often worked at a trade or were poor merchants and devoted part of their time to talmudic scholarship. Tending house, their barely literate mothers uttered prayers, the *tkhines,* written especially for women and used by women in the privacy of their homes to ask God for personal, family, and community happiness.[6] Orthodox Judaism as practiced in Eastern Europe severely circumscribed the role of women in public worship and in communal affairs, although women were permitted and even encouraged to practice a trade outside the home. Many women, in fact, supported the household while their husbands devoted their lives to religious study.[7]

The women born in the last decades of the nineteenth century were the first generation of East European Jewish women to receive a formal secular education.[8] Several of the writers began their literary careers as children, encouraged by teachers in the Yiddish *folkshules* or the state Russian schools of the Pale of Settlement, or by Hebrew tutors. For example, Zelda Knizshnik, one of the earliest Yiddish women poets, who was born in 1869 near Vilna, wrote her first poem in Hebrew at the age of nine. Her first Yiddish poem was published in 1900 in a Cracow literary journal, *Der yid.* Married at a young age, Knizshnik was unable to pursue a literary career because of poverty and domestic responsibilities, but she began to write again in her later years. Her poems were personal laments upon her sad and lonely fate:

> My husband is in America
> A son is in Baku;
> Another son is in Africa,
> A daughter—God, I wish I knew!
>
> Sent away, my little bird,
> Exiled from her tree,
> And I too wander, drift and dream
> Where, where is my home?

> A mother's heart is everywhere,
> The soul fragments and tears—
> I have, oh, so many homes
> But rest I do not have.[9]

Even though girls were sent to school, parents quite often disapproved if the young writers took their literary interests too seriously. At times parents regarded writing itself to be an irreligious act. For instance, Malke Lee, one of the few Yiddish poets to write an autobiography, recalled with intense bitterness that her father, a pious man, secretly burned her entire portfolio of poetry in the family oven because he believed it was against God's will for a girl to write.[10]

A considerable number of the women writers became radicals in Eastern Europe, and their writing was part of a more extensive political consciousness that often began with the rejection of traditional Orthodox Jewish values. Many of these writers, while still quite young, were repelled by standards set for female behavior. Lilly Bes recalled in an angry poem:

> Within me has burst my grandmother's sense of
>   modesty
> Revolt burns in me like effervescent wine.
> Let good folk curse and hate me,
> I can no longer be otherwise.[11]

In their adolescent years in Europe, several writers either joined illegal radical Jewish political organizations or had a relative who belonged. These political groups were particularly important for those young women, mainly manual workers, who did not receive a secondary education, the group providing the place of the school. Furthermore, at the turn of the century, European Jewish radicals lauded women as fellow workers and fellow intellectuals, in contrast to the manner in which they were regarded by the Orthodox male leadership. The hymn of the Bund, the socialist Jewish workers organization, the *Shvue* (Oath), which was intoned at every mass meeting and at strikes and demonstrations, called upon *"Brider un shvester fun arbet un noyt"* (Brothers and sisters, united in work and in need). Within the Bund, there were special worker education groups where women without much education were given positions of importance. Women were appointed to the Bund's executive committees; they acted as union organizers, prepared propaganda leaflets, and disseminated revolutionary literature.[12]

At the turn of the century, the women in the Bund did not attempt to organize separate socialist women's groups. Feminism, as an ideology, was considered to be bourgeois, serving the ambitions of middle-class women. As workers, these women identified primarily with the Jewish proletariat, although they were aware of the special problems of women workers, such as unequal pay, work-related health problems, and double work at home and in the factory. It was not until the 1920s, when the Bund became a legal party in Poland, that women's organizations were founded.[13]

Nevertheless, Jewish women in radical groups felt they had broken tradition and were acting outside the female roles assigned them in Jewish society. Their poems expressed these feelings. For instance, Kadya Molodowsky, poet, essayist, and editor of literary-political journals in the United States from the late 1930s until the early 1970s, described her estrangement from traditional Jewish life in her famous poem *"Froyen lider,"* written in Poland around 1919. Ambivalently, she expressed her sense of alienation, which combined with feelings of strong ties to the women in her family. Adrienne Rich, the American poet and Molodowsky's translator, noted that the poem voiced the difficulty of escaping old models of womanhood and the need to find new concepts of self:

> The faces of women long dead, of our family,
> come back in the night, come in dreams to me saying,
> We have kept our blood pure through long generations,
> we brought it to you like a sacred wine
> from the kosher cellars of our hearts.

And one of them whispers:
I remained deserted, when my two rosy apples
still hung on the tree
And I gritted away the long nights of waking between
    my white teeth.

I will go meet the grandmothers, saying:
Your sighs were the whips that lashed me
and drove my young life to the threshold
to escape from your kosher beds.
But wherever the street grows dark you pursue me—
    wherever a shadow falls.

Your whimperings race like the autumn wind past me,
and your words are the silken cord
still binding my thoughts.
My life is a page ripped out of a holy book
and part of the first line is missing.[14]

East European radicalism made a powerful impact upon those young Yiddish women writers who participated in these movements that gave their lives direction. In extreme instances, women who were trained in the underground Bund engaged in illegal revolutionary activities and were forced to emigrate to the United States in order to escape police arrest. Among them were Esther Luria, Shifre Weiss, Eda Glasser, and Rachel Holtman.

Esther Luria is particularly fascinating, since she reflects a type of Jewish woman revolutionary transplanted from Eastern Europe to the United States. Little is known about her life or her disappearance and possible death. Born in Warsaw in 1877, she was one of very few Jewish women not only to complete a gymnasium education but also to graduate from the University of Bern, Switzerland, with a doctorate in humanistic studies in 1903. In Bern she joined the socialist movement but returned to Russia to help fellow Jews as a member of the Bund. Involved in revolutionary activities in Warsaw, she was arrested several times and, in 1906, was sent to Siberia, from where she escaped in 1912 and fled to New York City.[15]

Luria discovered that the socialist movement in America was very different from Europe's. Socialists in America, who were permitted to establish legal parties, and to meet and publish freely, were part of the general reform movement of the Progressive Era and often encouraged alliances with and support of middle-class reformers. This was especially true for women's issues. Unlike Eastern Europe, where no one could vote and socialists isolated their party from liberals and feminists, American socialists supported liberal and some feminist causes. At the height of the American suffrage movement, between 1914 and 1920, Jewish socialists, especially in New York, made a special point of supporting women's suffrage, and the socialist Yiddish press frequently published articles on working women and the vote.[16]

Esther Luria tried to earn a living by writing for the Yiddish socialist press in New York: the *Jewish Daily Forward*, *Tsukunft*, and *Glaykhhayt*, the Yiddish edition of the International Ladies' Garment Workers' Union (ILGWU) paper *Justice*. Her articles about Jewish salon women in Germany, the poet Emma Lazarus, and the sociologist Martha Wolfenstein were meant to impress her working-class readership with the fact that women, even Jewish women, had made important contributions to society outside the home.[17] After 1920 and the passage of the Nineteenth Amendment, Luria's articles appeared with less frequency. She then tried to support herself by lecturing on general socialist topics, but there was no interest in her views that did not pertain to women's issues. Unmarried and without family, she lived in terrible poverty and died alone in the Bronx, New York. Even the *Leksikon* records her death as "192?."

THE EARLIEST WRITERS: BEFORE THE 1920S

At the turn of the century and well into the second and even third decades of the twentieth century, Yiddish women writers were considered by literary critics to be rare phenomena or, as Kadya Molodowsky noted sarcastically, "gentle, often exotic flowers of the literary garden."[18] Editors of Yiddish newspapers and journals, especially the anarchist and socialist press, were eager to publish the work of women poets and short story writers, as both a symbol of modernity and a way of increasing circulation. Editors and literary critics who were concerned with the quality of the emerging American Yiddish literature and felt that women might make a special contribution to this genre also encouraged female writers, among them, the literary editor and socialist Abraham Reisen, the anarchist editor of the *Fraye arbeter shtime*, Sh. Yanovsky, and the poet and literary critic A. Glanz.

The place of women in Yiddish literature, however, was rarely discussed. An article by A. Glanz which appeared in *Fraye arbeter shtime* on October 30, 1915, entitled *"Kultur un di froy"* ("Culture and the Woman"), was an exception. Glanz lamented the fact that culture had become stagnant because it was a lopsided product of male creativity; Yiddish culture had therefore become impotent. "Women are not in our culture, neither her individuality nor her personality." Women had a "new power, a new element" that, if introduced into literature, would also liberate the male and revitalize male originality. Men suffered from egoism and from blind selfish individualism; they thought only of themselves. Women were the opposite of men: "By nature women are not egoistical. By nature women are bound organically to other lives. Out of her body new life comes. Another kind of knowing exists for her. She has a second dimension and understands nature. She is a mother in the deepest sense of the word. Men are ephemeral, women are concrete." Therefore, "If these female characteristics are introduced into our literature, a true revolution would result."[19]

The revolution Glanz envisioned was, however, slow to arrive. In fact, most of the literary careers of young women writers, although received with some initial enthusiasm, really never matured. This was especially true for the writers of the period before the 1920s but was true to some extent later as well. The lives of two poets, Anna Rappaport and

Fradl Shtok, and one short story writer, Yente Serdatzky, are typical of women writers of this early period.

Anna Rappaport has been called "the first woman social poet" by literary historian Nahum Minkoff. Born in 1876, Rappaport emigrated to the United States from Kovna as a girl. Her father had been a famous rabbi in Kovna and her brother was studying for a medical degree at Columbia University. Anna went to work in a sweatshop and, after experiencing a personal sense of outrage because of conditions there, she became a socialist. In 1893, a year of depression and unemployment when male poets like Morris Rosenfeld and David Edelstadt were already well known for their social protest poetry expressing their responses to immigrant American life, Rappaport made her literary debut in the Yiddish socialist newspaper *Di arbeter tsaytung*. Her first poem, "*A bild fun hungers noyt in 1893*" ("A Picture of the Hardship of Hunger in 1893"), was of this social protest genre, describing the unemployment problems of Jewish women in New York City. Other poems followed, portraying the conditions of women in the factories and preaching a new world order through socialism. All her poems describe the painful plight of immigrant Jewish women, especially their attempts to control their own lives in the world of terrifying social realities. One of her most interesting poems, "*Eyn lebnsbild*" ("Picture of Life") relates how mother love becomes corrupted with opportunism in an industrial society and leads to the destruction of a daughter. The mother convinces her daughter to marry a man the girl does not admire. "You will be free of the machine and you will grow to love him," advises the mother. But the marriage ends in failure. The daughter explains her difficulties in the last stanza. The Yiddish style is intentionally simple, childlike and almost captures the mood of a folksong: "It is not enough I have no rest / from child and house / He counts out the pennies / and counts out trouble too."[20] Rappaport ceased to write in Yiddish after 1919. For a time she wrote a comic column for the socialist English-language New York *Call*, but after that she disappeared from the literary horizon.

Fradl Shtok did not write in the then popular genre of didactic social realism. Although her poetry appeared in the anarchist *Fraye arbeter shtime,* she wrote sonnets and lyric poems that explored the institution of marriage and the relationships between men and women. Erotic, exotic, turbulent, and audacious, her poetry challenged the passivity of women in love relationships. Courtship was central to her poems but women playfully dominated the interactions: "A young man like you, and shy / Come here. I'll coddle you like a child. / Why are you shy? Such a young man afraid of sin? / Come on, you can hide your face in my hair."[21]

Beautiful, young, and witty, Shtok became a popular figure in the literary cafes of the Lower East Side frequented by the Jewish intelligentsia. Both women and men admired her poetry and her romantic appearance.[22] In 1916 she began to publish short stories in the *Jewish Daily Forward* and in the new daily *Der tog.* In fact, the great demand for short stories in the growing Yiddish press provided opportunities for several other Yiddish women writers, such as Rachel Luria, Sarah Smith, and Miriam Karpilove, whose stories about women in the shtetl and in contemporary modern America began to appear regularly after 1915–16.[23] But Shtok was most admired, and a collection of her short stories, *Ertsey-lungen,* was published in 1919.[24] Many of the stories were subtle psychological studies of ordinary people caught in the anguish of a culture in rapid transition. Unfortunately, the reviews were unsympathetic, her severest critic being Glanz in *Der tog* on December 7, 1919. Glanz expressed the deepest disappointment in his unfulfilled expectations of women writers, and even intimated that Shtok was really a minor poet. An apocryphal story circulated in the literary cafes that upon reading the Glanz review, Shtok went to the editorial offices of *Der tog* and slapped her critic. But it is a fact that after her poor reception, Shtok stopped writing in Yiddish. Her first and only novel in English, *For Musicians Only,* appeared in 1917. Its plot involved the obsessional love of a young married Jewish woman for an Italian vaudeville orchestra leader. It was poorly written and not well received by American literary critics. Sometime in the late 1920s Shtok was institutionalized for mental illness.[25]

The fate of Yente Serdatzky, also a writer of short stories whose earliest work was published before the 1920s, was considerably different in that she remained a Yiddish writer despite adverse criticism and long periods of unproductiveness. In 1969, Sh. Tennenbaum, an essayist and short story writer, wrote a laudatory essay about Serdatzky called "Queen of Union Square." He portrayed her as cantankerous, articulate, intelligent, and still politically radical as she reigned in the proletarian public park of New York's Union Square in the 1960s.[26]

Born in the shtetl of Alexat, near Kavnas, Poland (Russia) in 1879, Serdatzky was the daughter of a furniture dealer and talmudic scholar who provided his daughter with an education that included a knowledge of Yiddish, German, Russian, and Hebrew. Their home was a central meeting place for young Yiddish poets, and Abraham Reisen was a frequent visitor. Serdatzky married, gave birth to two children, and was the proprietress of a small grocery store in Alexat until the revolution of 1905 stirred her literary imagination and prompted her to move to Warsaw. Her first short story, "Mirl," was published in Warsaw in 1905 in the journal *Veg,* which was then edited by the famous writer Y. L. Peretz. In 1907 she emigrated to New York, where she became a well-known writer, especially for the *Fraye arbeter shtime.* Her stories portrayed the fate of revolutionary Jewish women in the American environment. Isolated, left without ideals, often having sacrificed family life for the revolution, these women experienced mental depression, poverty, and lonely deaths. The stories written in the 1908–20 period reflect the author's unwillingness to adjust to American life. Her central theme remained one of relentless estrangement. Critics abounded; she was excoriated for the thinness of her plots, the sameness of her characters, and, as in the case of Fradl Shtok, male critics expressed their disappointment in the

long-awaited Yiddish women writers. In the 1920s she
stopped writing and returned to shopkeeping, only to reappear as an author in the 1940s.[27]

THE 1920S AND 1930S

Although mass East European immigration to America
ceased in the mid-1920s with the official termination of an
open U.S. immigration policy, Jewish immigrants did not all
become "Americanized" at that time. Nor was Jewish social
mobility into the middle class a uniform phenomenon, as
secular working class Jews defended their right to a Jewish
existence in America within a radical Yiddish culture. The
twenties also witnessed the emergence of large numbers of
women writers whose work appeared with greater regular-
ity in the Yiddish press and in anthologies and whose individual writings were no longer regarded as extraordinary
events. These women writers fell into two major categories:
Yiddishist writers, many experimenting with avant-garde
techniques, who were not formal members of a particular
political party (for example, Anna Margolin and Celia Dropkin, who wrote "pure" literature although they were published in anarchist and socialist papers as well as in such
journals of modernism as *Insikh*); and a group of mainly
communist writers whose literary work was motivated by
the propaganda needs of the party and by the new ideals of
writing a Yiddish proletarian literature.

At this time a Yiddish writer considered herself to be a
"radical" intellectual; that is, a person who combined the
quest for social justice with a search for personal authenticity, whether she actually belonged to a specific political
group or not. She wrote for an audience of other intellectuals, primarily from the Jewish working class, although there
were loyal Yiddishists whose economic circumstances
would certainly have excluded them from this category. Occasionally, women writers, like some male writers, prided

themselves on being "worker-poets," remaining in the factory and participating in trade union activities, but this was rare. Only a few actually did manual labor for a living. Writing was one way of escaping the factory without abandoning the ideals of working-class solidarity.[28]

However, the increase in women writers during the 1920s is not an accurate indication of the extent of their integration into radical politics and society. Despite their intense dedication, most women encountered difficulties in being accepted as equals by the Jewish male intelligentsia. Yiddish-speaking radicals treated women with ambivalence. While women's work appeared in socialist, communist, and anarchist papers, not one woman was permanently employed on a radical paper as part of its editorial staff. And when articles were accepted, they were almost never about general political or economic matters, but about "women's issues." If men found it difficult to earn a living by writing, women found it impossible.

Generally, women writers married and had children. The common pattern was to write before marriage and after widowhood. Intellectual isolation was something very real for them. There was little camaraderie among women writers, in sharp contrast to the long-term friendships and the intimate groups created by male writers. Women were only marginally tolerated in these circles. One had to be a wife, a sister, or a lover to gain admission into the inner sanctum of literary society where one could then share common intellectual and political interests. Many women writers did of course marry men who were active in Jewish Left political and literary circles, but the husbands were usually more famous than their wives, and in some instances wives depended upon their husbands' positions for their own publication. For example, Rachel Holtman married and later divorced Moishe Holtman, an editor of the communist daily *Frayhayt*. During their marriage she edited the Sunday women's page but apparently lost the position when their marriage was dissolved.[29]

Immigrant Jewish women intellectuals did not respond to

their exclusion from the centers of power or the implicit sexism of their male comrades by demanding access to power or by questioning the relationship between the sexes; nor did they organize a radical feminist movement. There were many reasons for this, rooted in the structure of immigrant American society. The women's isolation from other women and their reliance upon men, as mentioned earlier, was one factor, as was the reality that traditionally, Jewish men had been *the* intellectuals, and despite the late nineteenth century ideals of equality, echoes of earlier views could still be heard in radical circles. Cultural asymmetry was prevalent, and this meant that male, as opposed to female, activities were always recognized as having greater importance, authority, and value, even when women and men were engaged in the same activities. There were other factors as well. In the 1920s Jewish cultural life was undergoing transformation toward Americanization, and the Yiddishists were beleaguered. Many Yiddish women writers supplemented their incomes by teaching in the Yiddish *folkshuln,* which the children of socialist and communist parents attended in the afternoon following the public school program. These women focused their energies on keeping the next generation from defecting culturally. Championing Yiddish studies and contending with children might have contributed to their noncontentiousness about their own position as women.

In general, radical Jews did not feel secure in their new-found homeland in the 1920s. Political radicalism itself was under attack from the American government during the Red Scare. The radical movement was split into warring factions, and there was the added fear of anti-Semitism. These problems, faced by women as well as men, exacted a certain measure of solidarity.

Nevertheless, most women believed themselves emancipated and on an approximately equal basis with men in America. In contrast to the positions of their grandmothers and mothers, they were breadwinners, voters, "legal" revolutionaries, and cultural workers. No one seemed to notice that in the 1920s separate women's auxiliaries institutionalized the separate functions of the sexes in both socialist and communist organizations. It became accepted that men did the political work and women did the social and cultural work, although individual men and women transcended the barrier.

Individually, women writers explored their dissatisfaction with this state of affairs. New themes and experimental forms were introduced into Yiddish literature by both male and female writers in the twenties. Some women writers, encouraged to express themselves openly, described their intimate feelings as women and their criticism of traditional Jewish values. Anna Margolin and Celia Dropkin typified the intensely personal and iconoclastic tone of the twenties when they wrote about life's disappointments, ambivalent feelings, their sexual interest, and their hostility to conventional behavior and clichéd emotions.

Margolin's life was unconventional. She had lovers, was twice married, and left an infant son in the permanent care of its father.[30] Her sharp wit and intellectual acumen antagonized many of her male contemporaries and made it difficult for her to earn a living as a writer; they rejected her aggressive, self-confident behavior. It is particularly interesting that in her only book of collected poems, *Lider* (1929), Margolin chose as her first selection a poem entitled "*Ikh bin geven amol a yingele*" ("I Once Was a Little Boy") and as her second selection "*Muter erd*" ("Mother Earth").[31] Like other women of her generation who could not accept disdain even when they were unconventional, she eventually grew to pity herself. She wrote her own epitaph, a lament for a wasted life:

> She with the cold marble breast
> and with the slender illuminating hands,
> She dissipated her life
> on rubbish, on nothing.
>
> Perhaps she wanted it so, perhaps lusted after
> unhappiness, desired seven knives of pain,

And poured life's holy wine
on rubbish, on nothing.

Now she lies broken
the ravaged spirit has abandoned the cage.
Passersby, have pity and be silent.
Say nothing.[32]

Celia Dropkin's life was more conventional. She married,
reared five children, and kept house while, as her daughter
said, "she worked on pieces of noodle paper, on scratch
paper, on total chaos, on figuring out time."[33] Dropkin accepted the traditional role of women, but in her poetry she
expressed the ambivalence of anticipating freedom and fearing its consequences. Her poem *"Ikh bin a tsirkus dame"* ("I
Am a Circus Lady") illustrates this dichotomy:

I am a circus lady
I dance betwixt
Sharp knives that are fixed,
points up, in the arena.
If I fall I die,
But with my lithe body I
Just touch the sharp edge of your knives.
People hold their breath as my danger they see
and someone is praying to God for me.
The points of your knives seem
To me like a wheel of fire to gleam,
And no one knows how I want to fall.[34]

Dropkin also expressed hostility toward men—a theme
rarely expressed in Yiddish literature:

I haven't yet seen you asleep
I'd like to see
how you sleep,
when you've lost your power
over yourself, over me.
I'd like to see you helpless, strung out, dumb.

I'd like to see you
with your eyes shut,
breathless.
I'd like to see you
dead.[35]

Both Margolin and Dropkin wondered in their poetry whether they were not under the influence of some "pagan" power. Anxiously, Margolin wrote in 1920: "With fright, I hear in my mind the heavy steps of forgotten gods." Dropkin was more enthusiastic in *"Dos lid fun a getsendiner"* ("Poem of a Pagan"): "Silently, I came to the temple / today before dawn / Ah, how beautiful was my pagan god / Bedecked with flowers."[36]

In the 1920s the women who wrote for the communist press rarely dealt with such sensuous themes as did those who published in the anarchist and socialist papers. The communists tended to be puritanical and very much concerned with developing a "correct" working-class literature. But they were often more direct than other radicals in their distaste for female oppression. They openly advocated solidarity among women and pride in womanhood. In their poetry Esther Shumiatcher, Sara Barkan, and Shifre Weiss urged women to combat powerlessness by seeking self-respect and by acting in unison. In the December 1927 issue of *Hamer,* Shumiatcher called upon women to "Free yourselves from the dark lattices that imprisoned generations." In the late twenties, she and her famous playwright husband Peretz Hirshbein took an extended trip to China, India, Africa, and the Middle East. In a series of poems, *"Baym rand fun khina"* ("At the Border of China"), she lamented the plight of women: "Wife and mother / at the border of China / Baskets, filled with your sadness and weariness, hang from your shoulders. . ."[37] Sara Barkan, who had begun working in a factory at the age of nine and whose life was seriously affected by daily toil for herself and her daughter, wrote *"Mir, arbeter froyen"* ("We, Working Women"), commemorating International Woman's Day in 1925:

We, working women
We are raped in Polish prisons
We are decapitated in China;
And we forge hammers out of our fists,
In every part of the world, in each country
we have cut the rotten cords of yesterday's dark
    oppression.
Small, delicate, our hands have become hard and
    muscular.[38]

Although the social status of women in Jewish radical circles did not change in the 1930s, a new, more aggressive tone, criticizing male behavior, emerged in some women's writings. Golde Shibke, in an article entitled *"Di arbeter froy un der arbeter ring"* ("The Working Woman and Workman's Circle"), blamed her male comrades for limiting the role of women in that socialist "fraternal" organization to a mere women's auxiliary. Since women worked equally hard alongside men in the factories, it was unfair to discriminate against them in a socialist organization.[39]

Kadya Molodowsky, who emigrated to New York City from Warsaw in 1935, provided a role model for other radical women writers in the late thirties. Considered a serious journalist, poet, and intellectual among the Jewish intelligentsia in Poland, she was unhappy to discover that the New York radical literati considered women authors as "exotic flowers of the literary garden for whom direct and powerful thinking was alien." She protested the male categorizing of women as a breed apart. "Writing is more an expression of the spirit than of sexual gender," she insisted in her article *"A por verter vegn froyen dikhterin"* ("A Few Words about Women Poets"), which appeared in the New York communist literary magazine *Signal* in 1936. While admitting that there were some differences in male and female literary style, word conception, and personality presentation, she maintained that women writers were the equals of men in their insight, outspokenness, in their political and social awareness, and in their search for a profound understanding of reality. Molodowsky herself wrote some poems about critical political issues of the 1930s. One about the Spanish Civil War, *"Tsu di volontirn in shpayne"* ("To the Volunteers in Spain"), was published in *Hamer* in 1938:

> At night
> when the moon burns above you with death
> She awakens me
> And calls me to the window
> And the sky spreads itself
> with stars
> and a price tag . . .
> And the debt is so great
> And your blood falls on my mind
> heavy and red.[40]

It is difficult to assess in what way themes about women or poetry about politics affected the female readers of the radical Yiddish press and literature. Rachel Holtman's autobiography offers a rare glimpse into women's responses. In the mid-1930s Holtman traveled to Los Angeles, a city with a population of over 45,000 Jews, most of whom had arrived in the First World War period, and a wide range of radically oriented organizations and publications.

Holtman found that there were ten women's study circles affiliated with the International Workers Order that held meetings at least weekly and where members studied Yiddish literature. The women read both the Yiddish classics as well as works from contemporary Yiddish writers and discussed current political issues. Holtman described these women, most of whom were dressmakers and militant trade unionists: "The women in these study groups are quite another sort of woman—a *mentsh* [human being], who consciously educated herself. It is a pleasure to discuss things with her. She is sensitive, talented, understanding, straightforward. She takes a fine fresh look at the world."[41] Shifre Weiss, a member of one such Los Angeles study circle, shared her work with her group. Her writings included po-

ems about Rosa Luxemburg, Edna St. Vincent Millay, and
one "To My Black Sisters." She also wrote a poem entitled
"*Lern krayzn*" ("Study Circles"):

> We met as a minyan
> Eighteen or more;
> Building edifices of our culture
> Erasing the traces of tears and of pain
> Our dreams shall come true
> By creating and recreating.
> Happiness, Justice and Peace
> Shall come to this world."[42]

Immigrant Yiddish women writers such as Weiss created
an extensive literature that expressed their experimental
and highly complex perceptions. As Kadya Molodowsky
said, they were not exotic flowers of any literary garden.
Rather, they were a first generation of immigrant Jews, an
emerging female intelligentsia whose self-analysis and critical awareness are well worth exploring further. It is also
clear that they experienced, even if they did not always
directly confront, the profound contradiction faced by most
other radical women in the early twentieth century of living
within a pattern of seeming acceptance combined with implicit exclusion.

The literature of these radical Jewish women virtually
vanished as its audience disappeared. By the end of the
Second World War, Yiddish was hardly read by American
Jews, most of whom had become linguistically assimilated.
Anarchism, socialism, and communism, the radical movements that once attracted significant numbers of Jewish
American workers and intellectuals, were also in deep decline. Yet this literature is an essential component of the
American Jewish heritage, not only for its intrinsic value,
but also because it and the lives of those who created it
provide us with a much broader picture and deeper understanding of the cultural transformation of East European
Jewry in America.

NOTES

I acknowledge the kind assistance of Hillel Kempinski of the Jewish Labor Bund Archives and Dina Abramowicz of the YIVO Institute for Jewish Research. The original version of this essay including an appendix of over fifty women who wrote in Yiddish was published in *American Jewish History* 70 (Fall 1980), 68–90, and reprinted in *Decades of Discontent: The Women's Movement, 1920–1940* (Westport, Conn., 1983), ed. Lois Scharf and Joan M. Jensen, 131–52. This abridged and somewhat altered version appears here with the gracious permission of the American Jewish Historical Society.

1. Significant biographical information can be found in *Leksikon fun der nayer yiddisher literatur* (New York, 1956–68). See earlier versions and notes below for additional biographical sources.

2. For greater discussion of Jewish radicals' varying views on Jewish cultural expression, see Arthur Liebman, *Jews and the Left* (New York, 1979); Melech Epstein, *Jewish Labor in the U.S.A.*, 2 vols. (New York, 1959); and Nora Levin, *While Messiah Tarried: Jewish Socialist Movements 1871–1917* (New York, 1977).

3. Celia S. Heller, *On the Edge of Destruction: Jews of Poland Between the Two World Wars* (New York, 1977), 211–47.

4. Biographical information on Kadya Molodowsky (1896–1975) can be found in her serialized autobiography "*Mayn elter zeydes yerushe*" ("My Great-Grandfather's Inheritance"), *Sviva* (March 1965–April 1974), and in the Kadya Molodowsky Papers at the YIVO Institute for Jewish Research in New York City. For Devorah Fogel (1903–43) see Melech Ravitch, *Mayn leksikon* (Montreal, 1945), 188–90; Ephraim Roytman, "*Di amolike Devorah Fogel,*" *Israel shtime* (May 7, 1975); and I. B. Singer, "A Polish Franz Kafka," *New York Times Book Review* (July 9, 1978).

5. See Rachel Holtman, *Mayn lebnsveg* (New York, 1948); Malke Lee, *Durkh kindershe oygn* (Buenos Aires, 1958); and Molodowsky, "*Mayn elter zeydes yerushe.*"

6. Interview with Hinde Zaretsky. For *tkhines*, see chapter 4.

7. Charlotte Baum, "What Made Yetta Work? The Economic Role of Eastern European Jewish Women in the Family," *Response* 18 (Summer 1973), 32–38.

8. Heller, *Edge of Destruction.*

9. Ezra Korman, *Yidishe dichterins* (Detroit, MI, 1928), 57–58. Unless otherwise noted, the translations are by the author.

10. Lee, *Durkh kindershe oygn,* 25.

11. Lily Bes, "*Fun eygene vegn,*" *Frayhayt* (January 20, 1929).

12. For women in the Bund see Anna Rosenthal, "*Di froyen geshtaltn in Bund,*" *Unzer tsayt* 3–4 (November-December 1947), 30–31; and see citations in the original version of this essay.

13. Interview with Dina Blond, one of the leading women in the Bund, December 1978.

14. Kadya Molodowsky, "*Froyen lider,*" translated by Adrienne Rich, in *A Treasury of Yiddish Poetry,* ed. Irving Howe and Eliezer Greenberg (New York, 1969), 284.

15. *Leksikon fun der nayer yidisher literatur,* 5:30.

16. See Norma Fain Pratt, *Morris Hillquit: A Political History of an American Jewish Socialist* (Westport, Conn., 1979).

17. These articles appeared in the following issues of *Tsukunft*: 19:2 (February 1914), 189–95; 20:9 (September 1915), 835–38; 21:9 (September 1916), 792–97; and 22:4 (April 1917), 233–34.

18. Kadya Molodowsky, "*A por verter vegn froyen dikhterin,*" *Signal* (July 1936), 36.

19. A. Glanz, "*Kultur un di froy,*" *Fraye arbeter shtime* (October 30, 1915).

20. Nahum Minkoff, *Pionim fun yidishe poezie in America* (New York, 1956) 3:57–80. "Eyn lebnsbild" is quoted on p.68. Reprinted with the permission of Hasye Cooperman Minkoff.

21. Fradl Shtok, "Sonnet," *Di naye heym* (New York, 1914), 5.

22. Interview with Rashelle Veprinski.

23. Miriam Karpilove, "*Dos leben fun a meydl,*" *Yidishe arbeter velt* (June 30, 1916); Rachel Luria, "*Di groyse kraft,*" *Der tog* (June 13, 1919); Sarah Smith, "*Der man vil hershn,*" *Der tog* (July 23, 1916).

24. Fradl Shtok, *Ertseylungen* (New York, 1919).

25. A. Glanz, "*Temperment,*" *Der tog* (December 7, 1919); and see citations in earlier versions of this essay.

26. Sh. Tennenbaum, *Geshtaltn baym shraybtish* (New York, 1969), 47–51.

27. Zalman Reisen, *Leksikon fun der yiddisher literatur, prese un filologye* (Vilna, 1927–29), 1:684–85; S. Z. Zylbercweig, *Leksikon fun yidishn teater* (Warsaw, 1934), 1:1524–25.

28. Two poets who regarded themselves as workers were Sara Barkan and Rashelle Veprinski. Ber Green, "*Yidishe dikhterin,*" *Yidishe kultur* (December 1973), 33; *Leksikon fun der nayer yidishe literatur,* 3:491; and interview.

29. Holtman, *Mayn lebnsveg,* 79–100.

30. Reuben Iceland, *Fun unzer friling* (Miami Beach, Fla., 1954), 129–72.

31. Anna Margolin, *Lider* (New York, 1929), 5–6; Adrienne Cooper Gordon, "Myths of the Woman as Artist: A Study of Anna Margolin," paper presented at the YIVO Institute of Jewish Research Annual Conference, November 11–14, 1979.

32. Iceland, *Fun unzer friling,* 172 (author's translation).

33. Interview with Esther Unger, Celia Dropkin's daughter, August 1978, in New York City.

34. Celia Dropkin, "*Ikh bin a tsirkus dame,*" transl. Joseph Leftwich in *The Golden Peacock: A Worldwide Treasury of Yiddish Poetry* (New York, 1961), 672.

35. Dropkin, "Poem," translated by Adrienne Rich in Howe and Greenberg, *Treasury,* 168.

36. Anna Margolin, "*Fargesene geter,*" *Di naye velt* (July 23, 1920); Celia Dropkin, "*Dos lid fun a getsendiner,*" *Di naye velt* (May 16, 1919).

37. Esther Shumiatcher, "*Tsu shvester,*" *Hamer* (December 1927), 17,

and *"Baym rand fun khina,"* *Hamer* (July 1927), 5; interview with Esther Shumiatcher.

38. Sara Barkan, *"Mir, arbeter froyen,"* *Signal* (January 1925), 2; interview with Ber Green.

39. Golde Shibke, *"Di arbeter froy un der arbeter ring,"* *Lodzer Almanak* (1934).

40. Kadya Molodowsky, *"Tsu di volontirn in shpayne,"* *Hamer* (February 1938), 2.

41. Holtman, *Mayn lebnsveg*, 152–53.

42. Shifre Weiss, *Tsum morgndikn morgn* (Los Angeles, 1953), 59.

7 ◆ KATHRYN HELLERSTEIN

Canon and Gender: Women Poets in
Two Modern Yiddish Anthologies *

The formation of literary canons, through which a culture gives special authority to those texts it considers to be classic, timeless, and reflective of its values, is as much a part of literature as the composing of texts. The questions of canon in modern Yiddish poetry are especially interesting. The making of the canon in most literatures is a gradual process taking place over centuries. In Yiddish culture, this process was telescoped into the few decades in the twentieth century during which the literature reached its maturity.[1] This essay approaches this question in terms of gender, by considering how two early twentieth-century anthologies of Yiddish poetry represent women poets. These anthologies are M. Bassin's *Finf hundert yor yidishe poezye (Five Hundred Years of Yiddish Poetry)* published in New York in 1917, and

---

Ezra Korman's *Yidishe dikhterins: antologye* (*Yiddish Women Poets: Anthology*), published in Chicago in 1928.[2] By comparing the selection of poems by women in these works, I will investigate the editors' criteria of inclusion or exclusion as indicative of their conceptions of what poetry by women is and where it fits into the Yiddish canon.

Bassin's anthology is a monumental collection of poets in Yiddish from 1410 to 1916. The first volume encompasses Yiddish poetry through 1885, and tries to compensate for what the special editor of the Old Yiddish section there, Ber Borokhov, saw as Yiddish poetry's lack of a classical tradition. The second volume represents the modern period, beginning with Morris Rosenfeld and ending with M. Bassin himself. Bassin's general introductory remarks indicate that he intends his anthology to be inclusive and representative of all the kinds of Yiddish poetry. Yet the aims of this anthology to coalesce an available canon for Yiddish poetry has less than a neutral agenda. Going against the strongest ideas of poetry current then, which valued the individualism of the poet, Bassin's anthology embodies an idea of literary tradition that is political and nationalistic. Despite the individuating touches of the apparatus—including portraits, and biographical notes on the writers—the anthology emphasizes the way that each poet fits into a collective "harmony," and that each poem serves the greater ends of peoplehood and national culture. This nationalist agenda for poetry sounds something like the rhetoric of early anthologies of American poetry where, as Alan C. Golding has argued, "selection precedes as well as follows the formation of the accessible canon, affecting the form that 'accessiblity' takes."[3] Collecting poems as documents of a literary period broadens the canon and preserves a wide range of literature, while evaluating and selecting some poems over others narrows the canon. Even the most inclusive anthology selects out poems, thus narrowing the range of accessible texts.[4] Golding's notion of inclusion and exclusion provides the theoretical basis for asking a practical question about an anthology like Bassin's: What did Bassin leave out? In the first place, Bassin plays down, although without excluding entirely, poets who do not quite fit into his loosely defined agenda of nationalist harmony. But the most obvious and revealing underrepresentation is that of women Yiddish poets.

Bassin's second volume, encompassing the modern period and focusing, it seems, on America, contains 95 poets. Of these, 87 are men and 8 are women. Of the men, 32 poets are represented by 4 or more poems, and 55 are represented by 3 or fewer poems. Of the 8 women poets in Volume 2, only Fradl Shtok is represented by more than 3 poems. Two poets, Zelda Knizshnik and Yehudis, have 3 poems each; one, Sara Reyzen, has 2; and 4 (that is, half of the women writers), Roza Goldshteyn, Anna Rappaport, Roza Yakubovitsh, and Paula R. [Prilutski], are each represented by a single poem. While it must be taken into account that, as of 1917, many books of poetry by women had not yet appeared and other women poets had not yet published anything,[5] nonetheless, this list reveals clearly that Bassin represented women poets meagerly, both in the number of writers and in their works. That Bassin limited the number of women poets and the kinds of poems that represent them suggests this editor's perhaps unconscious sense of the place of women poets and of the kind of poetry he thought they could or should write. Bassin's implied feelings about uniformly "feminine" poems are in fact spelled out by contemporary critics like A. Glanz, writing in 1915 on women and culture, and Sh. Niger and Melekh Ravitsh, writing on women's poetry, in 1927 and 1928, who characterize a women's style as private, vague, conventional, intuitive, romantic, and appropriately emotional.[6]

We can speak of Bassin's exclusions and underrepresentations as significant because other historical alternatives were possible. Just eleven years later, Korman published his anthology. This volume was a direct imitation of (and improvement upon) Bassin's in its style and scope. It also attempted to provide a corrective for the canon in terms of women poets. The simple fact that Korman gathered a significant collection of women poets was in itself a canonical statement. Yet his attempt went deeper. In contrast to Bassin's 8 women poets,[7] Korman published 70, including some poets who had first come to light in the intervening decade. Moreover, in Korman's representation of the same poets chosen by Bassin, he clearly attempted to give a more varied and interesting view of these women's works.

In mere numbers, for example, Korman represents Zelda Knizshnik with 11 poems, as opposed to Bassin's 3; Yehudis with 7 poems, to Bassin's 3; Roza Goldshteyn with 5 poems (Bassin, 1); Anna Rappaport with 3 (to Bassin's 1); Roza Yakubovitsh with 10 poems (to Bassin's 1); Paula R. [Prilutski] with 3 (to Bassin's 1); Sara Reyzen with 14 poems (to Bassin's 2). The only poet represented comparably in both volumes is Fradl Shtok, with 12 poems in Korman and 11 poems in Bassin.

It is instructive to contrast the treatments of Zelda Knizshnik, who was born in 1869 in Vyazin, Vilna Province, and Yehudis, the pseudonym for Rokhl Bernshteyn, born in 1869 in Minsk, poets who are essentially unknown today. Bassin, though lamenting that "Yiddish poetry possesses very few women poets, and it is truly a shame that only a small part of Knizshnik's poems in Yiddish were published,"[8] chose only three lyrics, all of which depend upon rather conventional romantic tropes for sentiments of desire, wanderlust, and passion.[9] Korman's selection of eleven poems, which includes those in Bassin, presents a fuller sense of Knizshnik's poetic range, her more distinctive voice. The themes in her poems play as often upon the imagery of traditional religious life as upon romantic poetic conventions. Thus, in addition to the sentimental *"Baym fenster"* ("At the Window"), *"Vinter"* ("Winter"), and *"Morgen"* ("Morning"), we find poems called *"Kapores"* ("Atonement"), *"Un ven dayn neshome"* ("And When Your Soul"), *"O, heylike boyre"* ("Oh Holy Creator"). In *"Mayn letste likht"* ("My Last Candle"), for example, Knizshnik takes on the dramatic persona of a male yeshiva student who is left in the dark by his last candle, for both his poverty and his loss of faith have kept him from lighting another:

My last candle has burned out
And it's pitch-black at my reading table!
I do not know a single other prayer
To keep on praying as usual.

The night gleams at me in the dark,
Gray and cold;
Terrifying corpse-shadows
Fill up my old shul.

Fearful of death, I look all around
For a glimmer, a spark somewhere!
I stare and, creeping, crawl
Ever nearer to the door.[10]

With the familiar image of the candle, the poet puns ironically on the possibility of the student's enlightenment. The
device of the dramatic persona and the densely Hebraic
diction of this speaker, who edges ever nearer to the door
that will release him from the darkened house of study and
prayer, give the poem the edge of a wit more engaging than
the vague wanderlust in "*Volkns.*" Moreover, with the male
persona and "masculine" Hebraic diction, the poem disguises its female author. In "*Kapores*" ("Atonement"), Knizshnik again shifts the perspective from the personal by ex-
hibiting an unexpected pity for the ritual object, chickens
that will be made into the symbolic scapegoat in the ceremony of atonement before Yom Kippur. Knizshnik's last
poem in the Korman selection, "*Mayn man iz in amerike*"
("My Husband Is in America"), presents another dramatic
persona: a wife and mother who has stayed at home, alone,
as her entire family left *der alter heym,* the Old Country.
Again, Knizshnik plays upon this character's predicament as
the ironic embodiment of the ultimate homelessness of a
solitary woman, dependent upon her relationship to the
family to define her existence.

    Bassin includes three of Yehudis's poems, all of which are
spoken in a personal voice.[11] From these three poems alone,
one reads Yehudis as a poet essentially in the same vein as

Zelda Knizshnik—a poet relying upon the conventional tropes of the seasons and the diurnal cycle to express romantic themes. Even in these poems, though, Yehudis exhibits a more daring nonconformity, for her persona speaks of embracing her child in sleep, while tempted and then thrown into despair by the illicit passion in a "youthful dream" of her lover.[12] Her poem of romantic ennui, *"Brayte himlen, erd a groyse"* ("Ample Heavens, Earth Enormous"), speaks first in a generalized voice of despair, but breaks, mid-stanza, into rebellious individuality.[13] Even as Bassin allows Yehudis's bold voice to be audible, his limited selection of poems emphasizes a misleading similarity between Yehudis and Knizshnik, as in the conventional figure of a locked door that imprisons desire. Zelda Knizshnik writes: "Under lock and key remains / A restrained desire."[14] Yehudis writes: "In a corner of my heart / My youth is deeply hidden: Locked away from the years / With a rigid lock, an old one."[15] In Bassin, then, these two poets sound very much alike.

In contrast, Korman represents Yehudis with seven poems that show a far greater range of imagery and voice. At the center of one such poem is a trope of the womanly craft of weaving, suggesting an analogy between the making of a life and the crafting of a poem.[16] More importantly, Korman includes Yehudis's daring attack on a kind of poetry she considers old-fashioned, an attack addressed to her contemporaries, in *"Tsum dikhter"* ("To the [Male] Poet"). The collective voice in this poem of artistic protest has the bravado of political poems of the revolution:

> Enough! Don't repeat the old poems,—
> They aren't yours! . . . But, once, they,
> Like children, sang praise to God, love . . . stars in the
>   sky . . .
> Roses in the valley.
>
> That was then!. . . . They will not live again!
> Your poem now sounds false: your flower is colorless;

Your sun—not new; and God?—no one believes in him
    anymore.
Oh, shut up! You are not pious, your God is long since
    dead! . . .

You dream of your past happiness . . .
But your dream no longer provokes, it's sparse-gray, it's
    cold;
And you! . . . you're spiritless . . . you are weak!
    From your terrible illusions;
Of whom?—You forget; the world is old!

We are all long since grown up, sober.
Let the great sadness be,—we proudly inspect it, we are
    not going back.
Through flowers! Through the sun . . . through skies.—
And our gaze looks farther still.[17]

While Yehudis's poem does not succeed in creating a revolutionary poetics, it does invoke the problem of dead metaphors by citing and then appearing to discard them. And in
the penultimate line, the poem startlingly shifts the hack-
neyed poetic figures of flowers, sun, and skies, attacked in
the opening stanzas, into literal images. But the last line
makes these images fall back into figurative utilitarianism,
subject to the progressive gaze of the collective speaker.
Despite her effort, this poet cannot transcend the hack-
neyed forms of political poetry. Still, Yehudis's poem reveals a public voice, distinguishable from the private voice
that dominates Bassin's selection with the effect of making
Yehudis fit the stereotype of a "poetess," author of a "feminine lyric." The Yehudis that Korman presents works
against this stereotype. Korman also challenges the "selective canon of genre,"[18] limited to the ubiquitous lyric, by
including a part of Yehudis's long poem, *"Poeme far der
yugend (fragment)"* ("Long Poem for Youth [Fragment]"), a
descriptive piece about shtetl life, dedicated to the occasion
of the seventy-fifth birthday of the canonic Yiddish prose
writer Mendele Moykhr Sforim. By contrasting the Bassin

and Korman selections of these two now obscure poets, we see how the choice of poems can color a poet's appearance and place in a canon.

Finally, let us turn to the intriguing poet Roza Yakubo-vitsh. The ten poems with which Korman represents Yakubovitsh emphasize her strong personal voice speaking from a religious context. Thus, in Korman, Yakubovitsh's work stands out in sharp contrast to such sometimes bombastic protest poems as those by Roza Goldshteyn and Anna Rappaport, to whom Korman gives less emphasis.[19] In Bassin, these three poets appear in equal measure, with one poem each, and Yakubovitsh is essentially buried among them.[20] Yakubovitsh's single poem in Bassin, "*Tsu mayn tatn*" ("To My Father"),[21] while interesting in that the speaker sees God personified in her father's piety, does not convey the full range of this poet's achievement.

Yakubovitsh's work has a genuine originality and expressiveness that even Yehudis's spirited assertions lack. For example, she places the persona of the poem, "*On a statsye*" ("Without a Station"), in the midst of a struggle between desire and socially determined morality:

> Like a lightning bolt the train flies by
> The city of my love;
> A vision of him chases me,
> Oh, mercy, mercy God!
>
> I want to drink from his mild gaze
> And sip from his lips two,
> And take into eternal days
> My dream of what is true.
>
> But behind me someone stops me:
> Whither you want, my child,
> Another road there will not be
> Back to home and hearth.
>
> If you in fact get off the train
> Where there is no station,—

According to the Holiest Judge,
The train will not be waiting.

And thus you will trudge like an ox
Over sticks and stones—
And spend the night when it grows dark
In the wilderness alone.[22]

With skillful simplicity, Yakubovitsh embodies the idea of
the relentless moral code in the train on its determined
track and the inhibiting effect of this code in the thwarted
desires of a young woman, here addressed paternalistically
as *kind* (child). The poem ends on an inconclusive note,
with the threat of the unseen conductor's warning, and we
never learn whether or not the woman will follow her passionate vision to confront the solitude that he says awaits
her.

Yakubovitsh's dramatization of this conflict between individual desire and religious or social strictures on behavior
moves throughout her poems subtly and complexly. She
gives distinctive voice to stereotypes of traditional Jewish
women such as the *kale* (bride) and the *akore* (barren
woman). She also takes on the dramatic personae of biblical
women, including not only the matriarch Rachel, but also the
concubine Hagar. In these dramatic monologues, Yakubovitsh's innovation is that she offers a reading of the biblical
text at the same time as she develops each character in
modern terms.

Rachel
From palms and olives, shadows descend over wells.
The daughters of Bethlehem come there to water the
        sheep
And fragrant, blossoming, turn toward home with songs,
Flowing into the twilight glow of day.
But Leah, my sister, stays seated, alone and pale.
No messenger comes to her in the darkening field,
Her stars in soft, heavenly air give no light.
O, she loves Jacob, and he chose beauty,

Me, Rachel, the youngest!
O, tearful sister, do you remember?
How, for my sake, he rolled the stone from the well,
How he sold himself as a slave for my sake,
And he tends the camels of Laban with joy
For my sake—
Today I bestow him upon you!
I bestow upon you the one destined for me, my only
     desire,
O, Leah, my sister,
You don't know how great my offering, forever when I
     part from him
You don't know how great my offering
When I leave my happiness—

Hagar

This is how the mistress drove me into the desert.
I still feel the holy quiet
When the duke of the tribe of Abraham
Awoke me to a sunny vigil
Between bright haystacks and sheaves,
When he swore to me: You, Hagar, are
Chosen to bear a mighty tribe!
In the shadow of his camels
The light of his forehead still beams,
When he gave me a worldful of blessings—
This is how the mistress drove me into the desert.
Night falls, and the vulture descends to the carcasses,
The stars above ask: Where do you carry your sorrow,
     Hagar?
I know not where and to whom
My thirst will drag me,
But I am not alone in the night here,
I carry the fruit of his life under my heart,
And I drink the memories of love—[23]

These poems, from a longer series called *Biblishe motivn*
(*Biblical Motifs*), find their strength partly in the fact that
Yakubovitsh joins in them an awareness of three powerful
literary conventions: traditional Hebrew and Yiddish biblical interpretation, the Western European love lyric, and the

dramatic monologue. Korman's selection shows Yakubovitsh also to be capable of simple, direct expression, in *Goyrl*
(*Destiny*), a sequence of poems in a mother's voice, addressed to her child who has died.

In sum, Korman's generous inclusion of poems by Yakubovitsh reveals her to be a compelling, accomplished writer,
who developed beyond the earlier poets, Knizshnik and Yehudis. Yakubovitsh's treatment of religious themes distin-
guishes her from the antireligious, polemical strain in these
and other earlier poets, as well as from the aestheticism and
eroticism of her modernist contemporaries. In this respect,
too, Yakubovitsh foreshadows Itsik Manger's well-known
biblical monologues.

I do not want to misrepresent Bassin as finding no women
poets important. There is the case of Fradl Shtok, the modernist who is as well represented in Bassin as many male
poets (by eleven poems). In Korman, too, Shtok is among
the most widely represented poets (with twelve poems). In
the context of both anthologies, Fradl Shtok stands out as an
innovator in verse forms, enriching the meters and stanzas
of Yiddish poetry.[24] The musicality of her poems, almost
impossible to convey in translation, is evident in the six-line
strophes of a love song, "*Serenade*" ("Serenade").[25] Yet the
euphony of the lyric contrasts with the turn of her imagination, as eroticism takes on a threatening tone. In "*A vinter
ekho*" ("A Winter Echo"), the connotations of sweetness in
the diminutive nouns naming the lover give way to a metaphor likening marriage and burial:

> A little sleigh in the white snow,
> A trotting horse so small,
> A young, sweet couple in the sleigh,
> Voices chiming like a bell.
>
> He takes the whip in his darling hand
> And cracks it in the air,
> He takes a look at his dear girl,
> Her cheeks are flaming there.

> Burning kisses now are born
> Within his heart for his chosen—
> And landing on red little lips
> Immediately are frozen.
>
> Then a frisky little horse
> Overturns the sleigh—
> A snowy, stony canopy
> Buries their wedding-day.[26]

In another poem, *"Farnakhtn"* ("Dusks"), Shtok transforms the quietude of dusk into a threatening scene as she invents a startling metaphor for inspiration:

1

> In the quiet evening breeze
> The branches gently sway,
> A listless bird is flying through
> The orchard, silently.
>
> On the leaves, the larvae inch
> Toward fruits, to putrefy—
> And loneliness consumes me so,
> I'm lonely enough to die.

2

> Fly about in the sunset, you bee,
> Your body of golden rings
> Is shimmering into my eyes,
> Is luring me to sing.
>
> You fly in rings around me, too,
> Intolerably tiresome,
> Bringing no honey, for I know
> You want to leave me venom.[27]

By transforming the Romantic poets' singing nightingale into a stinging bee, Shtok shows herself to be a modernist, subversively employing literary convention and remaining alert to the risks of writing poetry. Shtok's sonnet cycle, which Malka Heifetz Tussman claimed was the first to be composed in Yiddish,[28] is an innovation both for Yiddish poetry and for the subgenre itself. Shtok imports to Yiddish the formal as well as the thematic tradition of European love poetry since Petrarch. At the same time, she distorts the very conventions of that love poetry, for the female persona controverts courtly convention in sonnets that most unconventionally declare love in the form of resentment and eros in the form of rage.

Both Bassin in 1917 and Korman in 1928 recognized Shtok as one of the innovative modernist poets in America. Yet she appears in Bassin as the only substantial woman poet of the moment, whereas in Korman, Shtok stands as one of a good number of strong, modern voices. Although Korman places Shtok's poems chronologically between the generous selection of Yakubovitsh and an extremely small group of poems by Rivke Rozental, her poems resonate with those of her contemporaries Tsila Dropkin and Anna Margolin, among other modernists on American soil.

Having said all this, we must nonetheless ask: What did Korman leave out? First, he omitted at least one significant modern poet, Malka Heifetz Tussman, who by her own account chose not to appear in this context, because, among other reasons, she said she did not want to be classified as a woman poet.[29] Second, although Korman expressed a poetic agenda in his introduction that favored the modern and the secular over the religious strain in Yiddish poetry, in fact his very inclusions contradict it. While arguing rather strenuously to deny any relationship between post-Enlightenment poetry by women and Yiddish devotional poetry, Korman's very juxtaposition of these two bodies of material supercedes his protestations of the distance between them, and suggests that there is a deep and important connection between them.

In conclusion, the question of canon is not merely academic. By looking back at earlier attempts at canonization in Yiddish poetry, we may better understand our contemporary efforts to make Yiddish canons, in particular, the recent bilingual anthologies published by Penguin and the University of California Press.[30] For Yiddish in the last decades of the twentieth century, canonization has a different meaning than it did in 1928. Now the anthologists are gathering poetry that translates well and appeals to an audience largely comprising non-Yiddish readers. This is an unfortunate but necessary broadening of readership that seems to call for some kind of "universal standards of excellence," in the phrase of Alan C. Golding. But establishing such universalities, which Golding attributes to a late stage of canonization, is a process that is itself illusory, for, as recent critics of canon note, "universality" is often determined according to culture, gender, and class;[31] "standards" are figurative,[32] and "excellence is historical, *not* transhistorical."[33] Since anthologies published today will determine what will remain and what will be remembered,[34] it seems advantageous that these anthologies reflect the diversity of literary values in our era. Eerily, none of the women from Bassin's anthology are included in the anthologies of the 1980's, not even Yakubovitsh (whom I regard highly) or Shtok (whom both Bassin and Korman recognized as a significant modern voice). Yet their absence from recent collections should hardly be taken as a final statement of their value as poets. Rather, it should make us think again about how we read, what we read, and why.

NOTES

This article is an abridged and somewhat altered version of my article "Canon and Gender: Women Poets in Two Modern Yiddish Anthologies," *Shofar: An Interdisciplinary Journal of Jewish Studies* 9:4 (Summer 1991), 9–23, reprinted here with the gracious permission of the Purdue Research Foundation. I am grateful to the Annenberg Research Institute and the Ratner, Miller, Shafran Foundation for generous fellowships supporting my work on Yiddish literature in general and this article in particular. All translations here are my own.

    1. See Avraham Novershtern, "Yiddish Poetry in a New Context," *Prooftexts* 8:3 (September 1988), 355–63.
    2. *Antologye: finf hundert yor yidishe poezye,* ed. M. Bassin, 2 vols.

(New York, 1917). *Yidishe dikhterins: antologye,* ed. Ezra Korman (Chicago, 1928).

3. Alan C. Golding, "A History of American Poetry Anthologies," in *Canons,* ed. Robert von Hallberg (Chicago, 1984), 279–307, 279.

4. An anthologizer of poetry often has an unstated agenda, which his or her selection of works and authors reveals. To a reader from a later period, the presence or absence of works and writers from an anthology is telling not only of the literary values of the times, but also of the broader political and cultural issues. The Yiddish writers of the late nineteenth and early twentieth centuries, for example, sought to justify their existence as representing a distinct national literature, complicated as this was by the socialist thought that pervaded the poetry, an ideology that eschewed nationalism. Although Yiddish literature did not have an actual nation, the language itself served as a kind of figurative territory for the Yiddish writers. Moreover, in Yiddish poetry, the early and late stages of canon formation were essentially simultaneous and compressed more or less into a single, brief period. In three decades, Yiddish modernists took on the double task of defining the texts that were to be considered "received" as well as of reacting against them. Both the conservators and revisionists of poetic tradition, these Yiddish writers made the initial and final stages of canonization simultaneous.

5. An example is Kadya Molodowsky, whose first poem appeared in 1921.

6. On these critics, see chapter 4 by Shmuel Niger and chapter 6 by Norma Fain Pratt.

7. An additional female poet, Gele, born in 1702, appears in Bassin's first volume.

8. Bassin, *Antologye,* 2:47.

9. Zelda Knizshnik, *"Unter shlos"* ("Under Lock and Key"), *"Volkns"* ("Clouds"), and *"A shpetige royz"* ("A Late-blooming Rose"), in Bassin, *Antologye,* 2:47.

10. Zelda Knizshnik, *"Mayn letste likht,"* in Korman, *Dikhterins,* 55–56.

11. Yehudis, *"In a vinkl fun mayn hartsn"* ("In a Corner of My Heart"), *"Di nakht iz tif, di nakht iz shvarts"* ("The Night is Deep, the Night is Dark"), and *"Breyte himlen, erd a groyse"* ("Ample Heavens, Earth Enormous"), in Bassin, *Antologye,* 2:49–50.

12. Yehudis, *"Di nakht iz tif, di nakht iz shvarts,"* in Bassin, *Antologye,* 2:49–50; in Korman, *Dikhterins,* 64–65.

13. Yehudis, *"Breyte himlen, erd a groyse"* ("Ample Heavens, Earth Enormous"), in Bassin, *Antologye,* 2:49–50; in Korman, *Dikhterins,* 63–64:

No! Enough! That'll do!
I want laughter, demon laughter,
Want to mock all forever after,
Laughing, laughing loud!

Let it thunder, let it lightning,
Laughter shall spew forth a frightening
Fire-flame and smoke-cloud!

And the skies shall roar and bellow,
They shall speak—for their mute wallow
Suffer I no more!

Speak! I want to hear which specter
And which devil, and which power
Holds you hitherto! . . .

14. Zelda Knizshnik, "*Unter shlos,*" in Bassin, *Antologye,* 2:47; in Korman, *Dikhterins,* 55.

15. Yehudis, "*In a vinkl fun mayn hartsn,*" in Bassin, *Antologye,* 2:49; in Korman, *Dikhterins,* 62.

16. Yehudis, "*Ikh endik mayn veben*" ("I Finish My Weaving"), in Korman, *Dikhterins,* 65.

17. Yehudis, "*Tsum dikhter*" ("To the [male] Poet"), in Korman, *Dikhterins,* 66.

18. Golding, "American Poetry Anthologies," 298–303.

19. Korman, *Dikhterins,* 84–92; 344. Roza Yakubovitsh remained within a traditional Jewish context, having been raised in a rabbinical household in the Polish province of Plotsker; she was educated in Russian and then Polish Jewish government schools, as well as by her father, a rabbi. She published in Peretz's collection *Yudish* (Warsaw, 1910), and her own volume, *Mayne gezangen* (Warsaw, 1924). Her second book, *Lider tsu Got (Poems to God),* was destroyed in World War II.

20. Of course, we have to take into account the fact that Yakubovitsh's book, *Mayne gezangen,* was not published until 1924, and thus Korman had more to choose from.

21. Roza Yakubovitsh, "*Tsu mayn tatn,*" in Bassin, *Antologye,* 2:125–26; in Korman, *Dikhterins,* 88–89.

22. Roza Yakubovitsh, "*On a statsye,*" in Korman, *Dikhterins,* 86.

23. Roza Yakubovitsh, "*Rokhl*" and "*Hagar*" (from *Biblishe motivn*), in Korman, *Dikhterins,* 89–91.

24. Melekh Ravitsh referred regretfully to the sudden silence of Fradl Shtok, the poet from Galicia, whom he accused of being more woman than poet in his review of the anonymous women poets in 1927. In the biographical notes, Korman simply reports that she was born in 1890 in Skala, Galicia, came to America in 1907, had a literary debut in 1910, and published a collection of short stories, *Gezamelte dertseylungen,* in New York, in 1919. On her subsequent life, see Norma Fain Pratt's essay in this volume, 122–123.

25. Fradl Shtok, "*Serenade,*" in Korman, *Dikhterins,* 93–95.

26. Fradl Shtok, "*A vinter ekho,*" in Korman, *Dikhterins,* 94–95.

27. Fradl Shtok, "*Farnakhtn,*" in Korman, *Dikhterins,* 96–97.

28. Conversation with Malka Heifetz Tussman, Berkeley, Calif., September 1978. Fradl Shtok published her sonnets in groups, for example, the eight sonnets in the anthology *Di naye heym* (New York, 1914). Zishe Landau's *Antologye* of the Yunge poets (New York, 1919) presents only one Shtok sonnet. A decade later, Itsik Manger includes a series of his

sonnets on biblical themes in his first book, *Shtern afn dakh* (Bucharest, 1929), 62–67.

29. Telephone conversations with Malka Heifetz Tussman, 1983. On Tussman herself, see Marcia Falk, "With Teeth in the Earth: The Life and Art of Malka Heifetz Tussman, A Remembrance and Reading," *Shofar* 9:4 (Summer 1991), 24–46.

30. *The Penguin Book of Modern Yiddish Verse,* ed. Irving Howe, Ruth Wisse, and Khone Shmeruk (New York, 1987); *American Yiddish Poetry: A Bilingual Anthology,* ed. Benjamin and Barbara Harshav (Berkeley, Calif., 1986).

31. Lillian S. Robinson, "Treason Our Text: Feminist Challenges to the Literary Canon," *Tulsa Studies in Women's Literature* 2:1 (Spring 1983), 83–98, examines the "feminist alternatives" to the accepted canon, which either include women writers or offer "alternative readings of the tradition." Robinson argues that unless the very rationale of canonicity— "literary quality, timelessness, universality"—is called into question, only a kind of token change results. If literary quality itself and "our received sense of appropriate style," are not redefined, she says, then it is impossible to recognize the value of writing by women, many of whom wrote not with canonical models in mind, but with other models. It is necessary to look at the place women take in literature, for only writing by women can speak for the literary experience of women.

32. Harold Bloom, "Criticism, Canon-Formation, and Prophecy: The Sorrows of Facticity," *Raritan* (Winter 1984), 1–20.

33. Golding, "American Poetry Anthologies," 283.

34. See Novershtern, "Yiddish Poetry," 355.

8 ◆ LAURA WEXLER

Looking at Yezierska

"What do you remember of Poland?" he asked, in a low voice.
—*Bread Givers*[1]

Anzia Yezierska, at one time a widely known and highly regarded twentieth-century Jewish American immigrant woman writer, is no longer so well known. Although a vigorous revival of her works and literary reputation is currently underway, it has not yet captured the imagination of a general audience. What is lost by this eclipse is the opportunity to encounter a forceful and distinctive voice in American writing that destabilizes habitual preconceptions of the immigrant culture of the Lower East Side, Yezierska's customary subject matter. What may be gained in her rediscovery is perhaps more subtle: it is the chance to envision Yezierska anew, to discover through her work a fresh appreciation of the place of her subject in the literary life of the nation.

Anzia Yezierska was born around 1881 in the village of Plotsk in Russian Poland. She immigrated to the United States, by way of Castle Garden, at the age of nine or ten, along with her scholarly and Orthodox Jewish father, her pious mother, three brothers, and three sisters. As her family scrabbled for a new life in the tenements of the Lower East Side, Yezierska labored hard on behalf of all, making and selling paper bags, enduring domestic service, and working in a variety of factories and sweatshops. But she also began to nurture a dream of something more for herself. As she later wrote, certain compelling questions seized her: "Who am I? What am I? What do I want with my Life? Where is America? . . . What is this wilderness in which I am lost?"[2] As Yezierska matured, the sense of existing in a double world of oppression and opportunity in America only grew more intense, and was not assuaged by conventional answers. Eventually her queries fueled a writing career that spanned nearly fifty years, beginning with the novel *Hungry Hearts,* published in 1920, when Yezierska was around forty years old, and ending with her last short story, published in 1969. All in all, there were six novels and collections of short stories, a long autobiographical memoir, further short fiction, and many uncollected book reviews and incidental pieces of journalism.[3]

The three distinct phases of this career have been well documented. The first stretches from her initial exposure to the genteel culture of the Lower East Side settlement house matrons, to certification in home economics from Columbia University Teacher's College, to a stint as a public school teacher, to brief unsuccessful marriages to Jacob Gordon and to Arnold Levitas, the second including the birth of a daughter Louise, to a lonely and determined period of self-dedication to writing, to her eventual discovery by the educator John Dewey, and his encouragement and practical support of her literary ambition. The second phase begins with the dazzling success of her earliest book, *Hungry Hearts,* and encompasses a cycle of ever greater recognition and renown as the public celebrated her production of five more books in twelve years, lovingly dubbed her "The Sweatshop Cinderella," and sent her to Hollywood as a writer for Samuel Goldwyn, where she met and worked with Elinor Glyn, Gertrude Atherton, Rupert Hughes, Alice Duer Miller, and Will Rogers. And the third incorporates the end of the American romance, in the long, hard, disillusioned years of the Great Depression and after, when Yezierska recoiled from Hollywood and returned to New York only to find that the always delicate relationship between a personal muse and a public zeitgeist had failed her. Yezierska joined the Work Projects Administration (WPA) in 1935 where she worked until 1938 in the company of such writers as Richard Wright, John Cheever, Harry Kemp, Maxwell Bodenheim, Edward Dahlberg, Claude McKay, and Harold Rosenberg, as her professional career continued to languish. Her publishers were now interested in other stories and heroines, but Yezierska persisted. In the late 1960s, the literary scholar Jo-Ann Boydston rediscovered an old, impoverished, and obscure Yezierska, but a Yezierska still at work. Still keeping her notebooks, Yezierska died, in her late eighties or early nineties, in 1970.

This describes *what* she did. But what has not yet been accounted for is *how* she did it. Where did this immigrant woman get the strength, despite every improbability and discouragement, to fulfill her stubborn, lifelong obsession to write for a national audience of the lives she knew and imagined? To try to answer this question, we must look at Yezierska more closely.

In a lovely photograph published in a recent biography, a young Anzia Yezierska appears radiant (see p. 168). This photograph is unlike many of the others that have been published of Yezierska. For one thing, it is an image of private life. "Anzia, a month after the birth of her child," the caption reads. "The smiling pride in her achievement remains on her face, although the baby has just been lifted from her lap."[4] For another, as a private picture this photograph holds no stake in constructing a public identity for the aspiring writer. Compared to the often reprinted publicity photograph taken from articles about Yezierska's writing in

such places as *Good Housekeeping, Cosmopolitan,* and the
New York Tribune (p. 176), this photograph lacks armor. It
does not display the social "mask" that American writers
since Ralph Waldo Emerson have complained about when
looking at their own expressions in photographs. Compared
to the sketch of Yezierska by the painter Willy Pogany
(p. 161), there is no ax to grind, no fortitude to demonstrate
to the ages. Instead, Yezierska's expression is charmingly
unselfconscious and candid. She does not even make eye
contact with the photographer, or hence the viewer. She is
composed. She knows she is facing the camera. But she has
been caught in the midst of a gesture, her gaze still fixed on
her invisible infant. The picture is, therefore, in another
sense private. We observe a glance of unexpected intimacy,
not of the author to her public, but of the mother to her
child. It is a portrait of Yezierska that gives an access to her
beyond what the stereotypes of an "up-from-the-ghetto"
writer allow.

I have stared at this photograph over and over and compared it to the other, more public images of Yezierska that
are to me so much more opaque. And I find that it has
become an invaluable supplement to my understanding of
Yezierska. In this private moment I perceive what it was
about her spirit that refused to inhabit forms or admit defeat, that was larger than the life she was born into, and that
attracted and held the heart of the silver-haired John Dewey
in their brief romance. Like Roland Barthes, who "found" his
deceased mother in a snapshot taken when she was a child,
I have in a sense "found" Yezierska in this image, in the
process discovering how much there is yet to learn about
the meaning of this writer's life. It is similar to the discovery
that results from comparing Alice Austen's rich and en-
chanting photograph of Jewish immigrant women in "Hester
Street, Egg Stand," with Jacob Riis's depressed and depress-
ing treatment of the same subject in *How the Other Half
Lives.*[5] The women in Austen's image are not extraordinarily
marked by ethnic difference, as they are in Riis. Nonetheless, on their ordinary, shoulders the burdens of ethnic vi-

olence sit. How do they manage? It is a discovery that suggests how little we still know about the lives and the images of the Lower East Side.

The photograph of Yezierska and its caption formulate what Roland Barthes calls a "blind field," a relation in which it is possible to picture a "before" and an "after" to the image—in other words, to imagine a historical relation.[6] Louise Levitas Henriksen, who wrote the caption to the photograph, is the daughter of Anzia and the author of the biography. Her language, which assigns the smile to the proud achievement of her mother's motherhood, also asks: How can my mother smile even when I am no longer in her arms? A double reading then: first the sentimental one, about the happy mother and her baby; and then the less easy one which concedes a place to history. Within a few years after this photograph was taken, in her determination not to lead an ordinary domesticated life but to have a serious career, Anzia Yezierska ended her marriage and gave up the care of her baby to her estranged former husband. These facts, which the biography recounts, give the picture and the caption a fierce poignancy. Yezierska's ambition, and Yezierska herself—especially what she would do—were more momentous than the sentimental category of working class immigrant women's writer within which her readers have regularly sought to restrain her. If, as Roland Barthes asserts, "the reading of a photograph is always historical," the reading of Anzia Yezierska's private photograph opens up complexities that are too often foreclosed, dehistoricized, and set aside. How much do we really see about the choices made by the immigrant generation of Jewish American women at the turn of the century, and what those choices cost?

The chief problem in coming to terms with Yezierska's genius as a writer is that she struggled so with form, and often lost. There has been no friendly critic yet—no patron, no rescuer, no appreciator—from the time of Yezierska's career to the present who has not felt compelled to point this out. Grace Paley (a "child of immigrants" herself) stated the problem vividly in a review of a recent collection of

Yezierska's short stories: "Muriel Rukeyser once described form as the vessel that enables the writer to give her story to the reader. Yezierska's stories don't quite fill the vessel, or else they drip, even overflow. But we take them away with us anyway. Their passion and awkwardness tell us about a female person, whose work—Yiddish accent and all— entered the English language first, and then literature."[7] Yezierska certainly felt this imperfection in herself, and expressed it with an almost palpable distress:

> I envy the writers who can sit down at their desks in the clear calm security of their vision and begin their story at the beginning and work it up logically, step by step, until they get to the end. With me, the end and the middle and the beginning of my story whirl before me in a mad blur. . . . I cannot sit still inside myself till the vision becomes clear and whole . . . in my brain. I'm too much on fire to wait till I understand what I see and feel. My hands rush out to seize a word from the end, a phrase from the middle, or a sentence from the beginning. I jot down any fragment of a thought that I can get hold of. And then I gather these fragments, words, phrases, sentences, and I paste them together with my own blood.[8]

But accepting Yezierska's assertion that she envied the poise and prose of other writers leaves something crucial unattended about her attitude toward her writing. Yezierska admired and was friendly with many native-born American writers who were her contemporaries. Most of them were gentiles, like Mary Austin, Zona Gale, and John Dewey, who seemed to her at first to embody all the virtues of clarity and self-restraint she felt she lacked. But in every case, it was the very self-command and command of form that had originally drawn her to these writers that eventually repelled her. Zona Gale turned into a "saint wrapped in cellophane."[9] With Mary Austin she found she "couldn't connect."[10] And, of course, John Dewey became for Yezierska the prototype of Anglo-Saxon coldness. The evidence is strong, in other words, that despite all her protestation to the contrary, Yezierska *chose* her lonely desk, and her piles of manuscripts and "scraps," her "mixed up feelings," and her "confusion of words in a second language." Yezierska was no victim. She preferred this disarray to more "logical" ways of writing because, as she said, "[I write] with my . . . blood."

What can she have meant? Form and self-restraint apparently signaled to Yezierska a fatal lack of "blood," that vital fluid that "drips" or "overflows" in Paley's description of her stories. If, as Rukeyser would have it, "form is the vessel that enables the writer to give her story to the world," then to Yezierska that gift had an extremely complicated signification. In the cross-cultural commerce that lies at the center of her writing life, the formal "vessel" apparently always bore, as it were, a secret cargo. Yezierska knew well that craft was a requirement for a writer, but she recognized that it was also an ethnic marker. Like the immigrant English she learned at first to speak, and like the immigrant "vessel" in which she herself had journeyed to the New World, the craft of her storytelling was not polished, nor even presentable or in good repair. Nevertheless, it would have to suffice, since it was her only chance of translating the East European Jewish past into the American present.

Such a journey could in no way be simple or assured. Its outcome was far too precarious. Probably, there was no way to do it in proper form. In the early twentieth century the word "blood," spoken by gentiles in relation to American Jews, meant simply "race." In the gentile view, the Jewish immigrants were a separate race: above all they were not Anglo-Saxon. According to the pseudo-scientific racial theory of that time, since the races were arranged hierarchically in relation to civilization, with the Africans on the bottom and the Anglo-Saxons on the top, the otherness of the Jews meant that they could never attain to that most highly evolved "form."

What Yezierska was saying, then, about her writing was that she wrote both *with* her "blood" and *about* her "blood."

She knew that her chief problem as a writer was the barrier
of form, against which she hurled herself bitterly all her life.
But rather than in any simple sense an issue of craft or style,
this question of form was also the issue of the social regulation of "race," and what that regulation hid or disguised
about the treatment of the Jews in the United States and in
Europe.[11] I have come to believe that it is because she lost
this battle with "form"—because she fixed the fight, in
fact—and not in spite of her failure, that we read her now,
and are beginning to find, after all this time, what richness
and complexity her writing holds.

Yezierska has often been read nostalgically, as a local
color writer, and sentimentally, as a primitive voice from the
ghetto. This she encouraged. She has also been conde-
scended to, and she has been pardoned for her many artistic
faults. Like the character Hannah Breineh in her story "The
Fat of the Land," Yezierska has developed an enthusiastic
following despite her many crudities. But it is time to reex-
amine our too simple image of Yezierska's stories. As with the
photograph, we must see how we ourselves are positioned
in relation to the blind field—the historical *tuché*—of Yezierska's life and times.[12] It is time to be surprised by the scope
of her vision, and her will, and to mark its extraordinary and
unexpected intimacy. The tale that Yezierska told is a Jewish
tale, though it is not only the tale of the Jews. It is also the
story of every striver and every stranger to American soil
who is faced with the demand for amnesia and assimilation.
Yezierska wrote of a necessary struggle with formalities, and
the impossibility for the working class or the racial "other"
to follow the codes of propriety and still be able to speak the
truth. Yezierska's choice to represent the Jews of her milieu
truthfully, however, was also a matter of "blood;" that is,
quite literally, a matter of life and death.

The conjunction of these themes can be illustrated particularly clearly by a reexamination of Yezierska's great
novel *Bread Givers*. *Bread Givers* has customarily been read,
as ethnic writing generally is, as thinly disguised autobiography, and as an ethnically "representative" text; one, that
is, that stands for the Jews as a group. But such a perspec-

1927 portrait of Anzia Yezierska by noted painter Willy Pogany. Courtesy of Yivo Institute Archives.

tive, while certainly illuminating, leaves out Yezierska's specific critique of the practical exigencies of her own writing career and, in particular, its entanglement with the issue of form. This is not a personal or an autobiographical or an ethnic issue merely; it is a sign of struggle for control of the meaning of cultural representation.

Yezierska's American career originally flourished because what she had to say about the colorful aspects of East European Jewish immigrant life on the Lower East Side fit—or seemed to fit—the need of the dominant, native-born, idealistic Anglo-Saxon class to see its own benevolence mirrored in the aspirations and achievements of the newcomers. The industrial elite at the turn of the century needed evidence that its domination of American life and labor could guarantee a certain progress for the urban immigrant poor. Otherwise, a revolutionary backlash might be in store. Yezierska's writing, like much other ethnic writing of the time, helped supply this culturally dominant class with the necessary before and after images. It was genteel men of good will, the liberal ideologues of the new corporate culture who occupied positions of intellectual leadership in Boston and New York, who originally supported her career. John Dewey's interest in Yezierska at Columbia University is a good example, but there are many more among her editors and promoters. These men expected Yezierska to fit the image they cherished of the striving immigrant. As Thomas J. Ferraro has shown, she played to their desires herself, carefully grooming the facts to fit the "up from the ghetto" image, even when it had become inaccurate.[13] Yezierska often chafed under this regime. Yet, when she left such sponsorship for the crasser brokerage of Hollywood, she was soon aware of what she had lost. It was one thing to reflect and reinforce the subtle stereotypes of the elite and the well-educated; it was quite a different thing to embody the cruder fantasies of racial difference that were to be found in the popular culture.

Of course, as a Jewish immigrant woman who did heave herself out of the the Lower East Side working class in the early twentieth century and make her way, eventually, from Columbia University Teacher's College to Hollywood, and back again to New York, Yezierska came to know how painful it could be to be affiliated with the wrong sponsor. She had been wounded in her dealings with the settlement house ladies of New York City, as a recipient of their charity and condescension. She had been badly hurt in her relationship with her demanding and inflexible father. And she had made and abandoned disastrous marriages with two conventional Jewish men. Not surprisingly, this problem of affiliation figures again and again in her characters' problematic relationships with men. The dilemma is especially clear in *Bread Givers.* But what Yezierska is examining through the relation of her heroine to these male figures is not only the restricted range of choices of men in an immigrant Jewish woman's private life. These choices also stand for three alternative moral relations that the immigrant Jewish woman might adopt toward the "blind field" of Jewish history—the before and after of America.

In the first instance, Yezierska brooded over the following scenario: a working-class immigrant Jewish woman has successfully finished a difficult intellectual task. She has escaped from the ghetto, gone to school, earned a diploma, landed a job. Buoyed by hope or success and wishing to share her plans with her semi-estranged father, an Old World talmudic scholar, she goes to visit him only to meet with a brutal rebuff. The father rejects her in a single, instinctive motion of disgust, much as if she were a piece of unclean food. Yezierska often included scenes such as this in her writing. *Red Ribbon on a White Horse,* for instance, recounts the following episode:

> "Woe to America!" he wailed. "Only in America could it happen — an ignorant thing like you—a writer! What do you know of . . . history, philosophy? What do you know of the Bible, the foundation of all knowledge?
>
> He stood up, an ancient patriarch condemning unrighteousness. "If you only knew how deep is your ignorance—"[14]

In *Bread Givers*, the incident is at its most extreme. The father is totally out of control:

> "*Schlang!* Toad! Wild animal! Thing of evil! How came you ever to be my child? I disown you. I curse you. May your name and your memory be blotted out of this earth."
>
> He rushed from me, slamming the door, a defeated prophet, a Jeremiah to whom the people would not listen.
>
> I knew now that I was alone. (207–8)

Many of her readers have pointed out the sexism of the father and his Old World ghetto prejudices, which Yezierska and her character, Sara Smolinsky, both rejected. The second-wave feminist revival of Yezierska as a writer was sparked, in fact, by the recognition of Alice Kessler-Harris and other feminist historians that as a protofeminist, the Yezierska of *Bread Givers* had much in common with the contemporary movement against gender-based restrictions. Affiliating with the old ways is, apparently, not a possibility for the ambitious American daughter. The nightmare image of the Old World patriarch intolerantly rejecting his child and her achievements because she is a girl is very resonant in Yezierska's writing. Not surprisingly, many feminist readers have concluded that Yezierska was counseling feminist rebellion against the traditions of the past.

However, there is another, white Anglo-Saxon Protestant version of the impossible male affiliate in *Bread Givers* against which it is crucial to read the Old World patriatrch. He is the New World patriarch, the dean of the small Midwestern college where Sara Smolinsky is a student. Sara meets this dean when, exhausted after working all day in a laundry and unable, therefore, to navigate the obstacle course required by her gym class, she is sent to his office by the gym teacher because she "seized the hurdle and smashed it to pieces." Insultingly, Sara has been inspected by the authorities and found to be physically inadequate: "Your posture is bad. Your shoulders sag. You need additional corrective exercises outside the class." Her physical culture—her very bodily form—is defective, and corrective exercises have been prescribed. Refusing them, she is expecting to get "locked up or fired." But instead, with the dean she finds understanding:

> "What can I do for you?" he asked, in a voice that quieted me as he spoke.
>   I told him how mad I was, to have piled on me jumping hurdles when I was so tired anyway. He regarded me with that cooling steadiness of his. When I was

through, he walked to the window and I waited, miserable. Finally he turned to me again, and with a smile. "I'm quite certain that physical education is not essential in your case. I will excuse you from attending the course."

    After this things went better with me. (217)

If the fuming father is modeled after Yezierska's own parent, whose relationship with his daughter was snarled in the fury and alienation of immigrant life as well as the traditional disdain for women's intellectual abilities characteristic of Old World Judaism, the figure of the rational, comforting WASP is a fictional version of the philosopher and educator John Dewey, with whom Yezierska shared a brief, improbable, and unforgettable flirtation in the middle 1920s, when he was fifty-seven and she around thirty-four. As Mary Dearborn has documented in her account of this relationship in *Love in the Promised Land,* Dewey felt that Yezierska represented an alternative to "his own stifled world, generations of Vermont farmers and tradesmen." For a while at least, Dewey imagined that her emotionalism was an avatar of a better American future than he and his kind had been able to create. One of his poems to her read:

> Generations of stifled worlds reaching out through
>   you . . .
> Generations as yet unuttered, dumb, smothered
> Inchoate, unutterable by me and mine,
> In you I see them coming to be,
> Luminous, slow revolving, ordered in rhythm.
> You shall not utter them; you shall be them,
> And from out the pain
> A great song shall fill the world.

It was a heady mantle for his young disciple.[15]

    Like Dewey, the dean in *Bread Givers* cites American history as the reason for his attraction to the immigrant heroine. As Sara recalls,

His house was always open to me. Once, while we were chatting in his library, I asked him suddenly, "Why is it that when a nobody wants to get to be somebody she's got to make herself terribly hard, when people like you who are born high up can keep all their kind feelings and get along so naturally well with everybody?"

He looked at me with the steady gaze of his understanding eyes.

"All pioneers have to get hard to survive," he said. He pointed to a faded oil painting of his grandmother. "Look! My grandmother came to this wilderness in an ox cart and with a gun on her lap. She had to chop down trees to build a shelter for herself and her children. I'm more than a little ashamed to realize if I had to contend with the wilderness I'd perish with the unfit. But you, child—your place is with the pioneers. And you're going to survive."

After that I could not go back to my little room. For hours I walked. I needed the high stars and the deep stillness of the night to hold my exaltation. (232)

Sara is swept away by this vision of herself, as Yezierska had been with Dewey's admiration. But is "exaltation" all that this passage promotes? Must we believe Sara's assertion that "after this, things went better with me"? In real life, social progress was not so simple. Yezierska lost Dewey's love and attention, and she seems to have missed it for the rest of her life. But she also seems to have found something in Dewey's conduct toward her to have been unforgivable. This is true as well in Sara's encounter with the dean. The "exaltation" of being the dean's object of admiration must be paid for by being his racial "other."[16] In fact, the dean's complacent self-location as one who would not survive the violence of the frontier is spoken to someone who is, herself, fighting for survival on the boundary between two worlds. The frankness of Sara's question to him—"Why do people like you . . ." is met by the frankness of his response: "You, child—your place is . . . ," but neither character seems aware of the power relations that inhere in such designations. Did Yezierska herself find credible the mappings of the social Darwinism over which the dean presides?

There are times when it is easy to underestimate the irony of Yezierska's voice. Her prose is difficult to penetrate. Much in Yezierska seems superficial, although often deceptively so. Grace Paley, for instance, warns us that she may be "hard to see." I think that this encounter with the dean is not one of her simpler moments. It is true that always, on the surface, Yezierska's heroines aspire to the American dream. They are on the move, yearning to relocate, to go "higher." In *Bread Givers,* Sara Smolinsky's own particular anguish is that "even in college I had not escaped from the ghetto. Here loneliness hounded me even worse than in Hester Street. Was there no escape? Will I never lift myself to be a person among people?" (220). As Sara sees him, the dean represents a class of "people who are born high up"; and plainly, to her, proximity with such a person is socially intoxicating. In that way, Sara can feel herself to be an American "pioneer." She will "survive." When the dean admires Sara, she grows "too big" for her "little room." Yet, in much of her other writing, and in her great short story "The Fat of the Land" in particular, Yezierska inveighs against placing one's faith in precisely the narrowness and emptiness of such an idea of social progress.

I would argue that in this encounter, Sara Smolinsky is getting a dose of something that is far more toxic than the dean's reassuring manner and "understanding eyes" would imply. At the college, as she shrinks before the "spic and span youngsters who . . . didn't even know I was there" and grows in stature by coming to know the "older and wiser professors," this Jewish Alice in a Midwestern Wonderland of "real Americans" comes to embody a version of Americanization as a self-transformation that requires the obliteration of historical memory. What Sara learns at college is that to become "American" she must be able to replace her own experience with distanced erasures and sentimental

circumlocutions that have been internalized and can be re-
gurgitated on demand. The epiphany Sara achieves in psychology class, for instance, when she learns that she was
"always" studying psychology when bargaining for herring
at the pushcarts of the ghetto, is of the same order of knowledge. "From that day on," she mused, "the words of psychology were full of living wonder. In a few weeks I was

Family photograph of Anzia Yezierska. Reprinted from
Louise Levitas Henriksen, with assistance from Jo Ann
Boydston, Anzia Yezierska: A Writer's Life *(New Bruns-*
wick, N.J., 1988), with permission of Louise Levitas Hen-
riksen.

ahead of anyone else in the class. I saw the students around me as so many pink-faced children who never had had to live yet. I realized that the time when I sold herring in Hester Street, I was learning life more than if I had gone to school" (223). Sara needs initially to "learn" that her life experience is outside of the master discourse of psychology, and then, that by an enormous act of will and imagination, even she, the working-class immigrant, can make it fit. It turns out that her early years were not "black," "barren," "thwarted with want" after all! Instead, they were preparation for a major in psychology. How wonderful was America! How wonderful was the college! "My anger did not get the better of me now. I had learned self-control. I was now a person of reason."

This ominous process of erasure of her own experience and interpretation and substitution of the values of another becomes even clearer at graduation, when Sara wins a contest. She has written the best essay on "What the College Has Done for Me." Her prize is a thousand dollars, donated by "the biggest newspaper owner of the town, who was a rich alumnus of the college." In awarding this glittering prize money, the wealthy newspaper owner, presumably himself an industrial success story of exactly the type promoted by the college, makes a moralizing, exemplary gesture toward the exotic immigrant labor that Sara represents. In accepting the prize, Sara is suitably grateful, bedazzled, and obtuse. She no longer notices the condescension that she at first had bridled against, as with the "hurdles" in her gym class. She will use the money to rent an apartment of her own, and to buy a good blue all-American girl suit at the Sport Shop on Fifth Avenue. There is nothing in her ears but the roar of the student body's applause. She has achieved the acceptance of the college.

But has not the newspaper owner himself learned at the college the particular version of westward expansion in which the dean instructed Sara? It is difficult, then, to imagine how the kind of accomplishments that the college admires—for instance, the writing that he must be publishing in his newspaper, including, presumably, Sara's own prizewinning

essay,—could "do" anything much for Sara. At a time of
Jewish suffering in Eastern Europe, from which Sara's own
family has fled, the Dean tells the Jewish heroine that Native
Americans were shot in the "wilderness" by strong and loving white women who carried guns on their laps as they
traveled in oxcarts simply in order to "protect" their children. And the star-struck Jewish heroine believes him.

The best indicator of what the American college has done
for Sara is that she never connects the dean's story with a
notion of the laws of American greed, conflict, or aggression
beyond the just-so stories she learns to tell about Hester
Street in her psychology class. She has learned, like most
Americans, to imagine the past as a separate and distinct
episode, sterile, innocuous, and already over. Here too, perhaps, Yezierska strikes a blow at Emersonian traditions of
American education and at John Dewey, who, like the dean,
was a progressive who could back off from the most somber
realities of cultural confrontation. And it is at least part of the
reason that Sara's (and Yezierska's) angry Orthodox father
despised her education. "An ignorant thing like you—a
writer! What do you know of . . . history, philosophy? . . . If
you only knew," he spits at her, "how deep is your ignorance."

By way of contrast, the Jewish lover who repeatedly
appears as an artist/teacher in Yezierska's writing is soft-
spoken and nonviolent. Faced with the young woman's reservoirs of rage, he is flexible, understanding, sympathetic,
and therapeutic. He also holds out a specific kind of hope
about "ignorance." Where the Old World patriarch hurls
invectives, and the New World patriarch fails to empathize,
the Jewish American lover quietly extends an intuitive embrace. The recognition scene between Sara Smolinsky and
Hugo Seelig at the end of *Bread Givers* is a prototype for all
of Yezierska's visions of redemption:

> "How strangely things work out," I said, with a new
> feeling of familiarity. "You got this blackmailing letter.
> And yet here we are born friends."

"Why shouldn't we be? You and I, we are of one blood."

We fell into a silence. All the secret places of my heart opened at the moment. And then the whole story of my life poured itself out of me to him. (278)

Although Hugo Seelig is a Jewish immigrant, as a school principal he has also integrated himself socially into the new life without undue self-laceration. This figurative new American berth sustains him. It is also what makes him desirable to Sara. It is opposed to the lack of place in America for Sara's infuriated father. Quite reasonably, then, she thinks about Hugo's face, and compares it favorably with "Father": "The features—all fineness and strength. The keen, kind gray eyes. A Jewish face, and yet none of the greedy eagerness of Hester Street any more. It was the face of a dreamer, set free in the new air of America. Not like Father, with his eyes on the past" (273).

But does facing the Old World and keeping one's "eyes on the past" really lose out in *Bread Givers*? Hugo and Sara are of "one blood." But what this means to them is not some external and essentialized concept of "race." It is that they share a history, a memory, a social past, and the responsibility not to forget what has happened to their people:

We got to talking about ourselves, our families, the Old World from which we came. To our surprise we found that our beginnings were the same. We came from the same government in Poland, from villages only a few miles apart. Our families had uprooted themselves from the same land and adventured out to the New World.

For a moment we looked at each other, breathless with the wonderful discovery. "*Landsleute*—countrymen!" we cried, in one voice, our hands reaching out to each other.

"What do you remember of Poland?" he asked, in a low voice.

"Nothing—nothing at all. Back of me, it's like black night."

"I remember a little," he said. "The mud hut where we lived, the cows, the chickens, and all of us living in one room. I remember the dark, rainy morning we started on our journey, how the whole village, old and young, turned out to say good-bye. When we came to the seaport, I couldn't eat their bread, because it had no salt. We thought we should starve going to America. But as soon as we got on the ship, they gave us so much that first meal that we couldn't touch another bite for days."

After that, all differences dropped away. We talked one language. We had sprung from one soil. (277–78)

It is extremely difficult for an American to read that Hugo's family lived in a one-room "mud hut" and to envision anything other than squalor. The complex physical heritage of the built environment of the Old World, with its ancient housing stock and traditional farm and village life, is precisely the sort of material recollection of cultural difference that mainstream American life is adept at obliterating. In just the same way it has speciously de-aestheticized and rendered primitive Native American housing practices while simultaneously valorizing white American norms. Yet there is no evidence that in their own setting the one room "mud" houses of the Old World were necessarily dirty, or undesirable, or even all that primitive, especially in comparison to the tenements the immigrants found in the New.

Indeed, many of Roman Vishniac's great 1930s photographs of just such houses in villages all over Eastern Europe present ample evidence to the contrary. In certain pictures an achingly beautiful village topography unfolds in the patterns of this architecture. In others a sense of social decay is unavoidable, but it is produced, as Vishniac notes in his diaries at the time, not by mud but by the fact of "no more money" and impending social disaster. Thus, if squalor is rightly to be pictured in such a home, it must be understood to derive not from the earthwork walls per se;

the disarray was produced by the frightening social tempest of ethnic violence in which the Jewish inhabitants were caught up, feeling themselves starkly unprotected and foreseeing a future desperate enough to make it desirable to leave behind everything they knew.[17]

Yezierska's heroine came from that kind of village, that kind of family, that kind of history, and that kind of house, only a few miles from Hugo's. When Hugo recalls his past to her, even as he uses the assimilated and uncomfortably supercilious term "hut," he gives her a chance to reclaim her own, non-American experience and recode her own previously forbidden pre-American truths. With Hugo, for the first time, Sara begins to emerge from the "black night" that is her historical amnesia, and to "face" the future from the foundation of her authentic heritage.

Sara's mother, also, had once tried to tell her daughters how lovely the wedding traditions were in the village, and how much more special the linens of her dowry were than any that could be bought on Fifth Avenue:

> ". . . the most beautiful thing of my whole dowry was my hand-crocheted tablecloth. It was made up of little knitted rings of all colours: red, blue, yellow, green, and purple. All the colours of the rainbow were in that tablecloth. It was like dancing sunshine lighting up the room when it was spread on the table for the Sabbath. Ach! There ain't in America such beautiful things like we had home."
>
> "Nonsense, Mamma!" broke in Mashah. "If you only had the money to go on Fifth Avenue you'd see the grand things you could buy."
>
> "Yes, buy!" repeated Mother. "In America, rich people can only buy, and buy things made by machines. Even Rockefeller's daughter got only store-bought, ready-made things for her dowry. There was a feeling in my tablecloth—."
>
> "But why did you leave that rainbow tablecloth and come to America?" I asked.

"Because of the Tsar of Russia! Worms should eat him! He wanted for himself free soldiers to make pogroms." (32–33)

The daughters don't listen, or they only half believe; but there is no reason for us to imagine that what the mother is saying is not true. What does Sara know of the Polish village? What do we really know of the village, and what was destroyed when it was destroyed? Why buy only the Saks Fifth Avenue story?

This is not to say, however, that European Jewish village life should be romanticized; only that it should be apprehended as materially complex. Russian Poland was not a Hollywood movie set or a Broadway play. In fact, a particularly vivid warning against accepting such an expurgated version occurs in *Bread Givers* when Mrs. Smolinsky tells her daughters why the family finally had to leave. Their father was about to be drafted into the Russian army, "to drink vodka with the drunken *mouzhiks,* eat pig, and shoot the people." This meant that

> There was only one thing to do, go to the brass-buttoned butchers and buy him out of the army. The *pogromshchiks,* the minute they smelled money, they were like wild wolves on the smell of blood. The more we gave them, the more they wanted. We had to sell out everything, and give them all we had, to the last cent, to shut them up.
>
> Then, suddenly, my father died. He left us all his money. And your father tried to keep up his business, selling wheat and wine, while he was singing himself the Songs of Solomon. Maybe Solomon got himself rich first and then sang his Songs, but your father wanted to sing first and then attend to business. He was a smart salesman, only to sell things for less than they cost. . . . And when everything was gone from us, then our only hope was to come to America, where Father thought things cost nothing at all. (33–34).

Mrs. Smolinsky's story leaves certain things unsaid, the details of both the raw violence of the pogroms and her husband's careless business practices. Nevertheless, one gets a sense of what her powerlessness, enforced by gender, must have cost her in exasperation, rebellion, and despair until "everything was gone from us" of her inheritance. The reader, like the daughters, is alerted by her refusal to speak on these topics that there is much more to the story of the mother and father than we are being told, and a more contested version of the violence in the Jewish past than percolates through the patriarchal discourse. What was left behind in Europe was not only a general Jewish culture and way of life, but the specific records of women's efforts to preserve it that have gone largely uncommemorated. Later, Mrs. Smolinsky actually brings Sara a featherbed, a somewhat diminished mutation of the enchanted tablecloth, in the apparent hope that if her daughter cannot "set things right" in the Old World, she might at least "make" a better history for women here.

Paula Hyman has written that "myth making about the Jewish family" is a response to Jewish history that clouds the existence of other issues:

> The last century has witnessed tremendous upheavals in Jewish life as a result of mass emigration, assimilation, and the Holocaust. Concern for continued Jewish group survival has led scholars and communal leaders alike to look for those social factors which accounted for Jewish survival in the past, even in the face of centuries of persecution. Often the Jewish family has been held up as a source of past stability in Jewish life; and a restored Jewish family has been proposed as a bulwark against further erosion of Jewish solidarity and consciousness. . . .
>
> It seems to me that such advice flies in the face of both history and common sense. It perpetuates a myth, when what we need is not myths, but a "usable past." A usable past is one which will provide us with mean-

Anzia Yezierska, 1925. Reprinted with permission of
Cosmopolitan *magazine.*

ingful role models for the present, one with which we
can feel a link. But building that past on myths is destructive; myths translate poorly into patterns for living.[18]

This problem pertains to the reading of *Bread Givers* as
well. It is time that Jewish feminists looking for a "usable
past" insist on expanding the terms of feminist revolt to
encompass all the issues of the racial and class construction
of the American Jewish family and modern American Jewish
history, as they interrelate with gender issues. It is time to
replace the insouciant myths of immigration and Americanization with the denser image of the refugee, to examine the
conflicts between and within Jewish families rather than as-

suming that the Jewish mother was able to compensate, and to illuminate the "black night" of historical amnesia out of which bitter American realities have grown. Hugo Seelig is the hero of *Bread Givers* not because he is unlike the heroine's father but because, like the unforgiving old man, and against all the efforts of early twentieth-century American society to make him conform, he does not choose to forget. He remembers Poland, as Sara's mother remembered it, and what the Jews did there, as well as what was done to them. He remembers why the Jews fled, and the hopes with which they fled, and the abjection with which they were grateful for enough to eat. He encourages connection to the dreams—both the historical nightmares and the revolutionary dramas—with which the immigrants, including Sara, sustain themselves in his ghetto schools. He does not adhere, therefore, to the proper American "form," or "forum." Against the odds, Hugo Seelig stands for "What the College Has NOT Done for Me."

Yet even as Hugo offers a welcome alternative to the humiliating denial of self and historical memory demanded by mainstream American culture, he does not resolve the problem of Sara's position in the present. Indeed, his masculine privilege of explicit connection to the Jewish past illuminates Sara's and her mother's fundamental exclusion from their people's most honored and status-conferring activities simply by virtue of their gender. When Hugo asks Sara's father to instruct him in Hebrew, he is at once welcomed into the males-only fold of Jewish learning. Sara's engagement to Hugo, on the other hand, proves to her father that she has at last accepted the talmudic precept that "A woman without a man is less than nothing. A woman without a man cannot enter Heaven" (294). For all of Sara's hard-earned education and her professional and personal success, "the problem of Father" (296) remains unresolved. *Bread Givers* does not end in the happy commencement of a promising marriage between two equal persons. Rather, the book concludes on a note of bitterness, as Sara recognizes that even among her own people her struggles, her accomplishments, and her intellectual aspirations will never be acknowledged: "It wasn't just my father, but the generations who made my father whose weight was still upon me" (297). Patriarchal sexism is just another of the barriers that are set against her, in the New World as in the Old. And Sara's protest will again be a story of female valor that is destined to be forgotten.

Sometimes a writer can be better known in her revival than she was the first time around. This is true for Yezierska. The gender, race, ethnic, and class conflicts of the past are encoded not only in the stories she wrote, but also in the definitive stumbling block of her career, the question of her relation to "form." These conflicts are perpetuated in the act of stereotyping and forgetting. To explore what has been ignored, forgotten, or distorted in the work of women writers like Yezierska who spoke from the ethnic, sexual, and regional margins of early twentieth-century American culture is to grow better able to appreciate the mission of these early modern literary witnesses. For readers of Yezierska, this process of revision offers a special chance not only to hear voices that have long been silenced, but also to make new connections to an ethnic past whose relation to the violent predicaments of our own time is more relevant than we have liked to suppose. The social conventions under which Yezierska labored during her lifetime have lost some of their inhibiting power, but the "living life" of memory beyond the forms has seldom been appreciated. More often she, like the other writers of the immigrant generation, has been sentimentalized and then dismissed; or to put it more accurately, as a woman she has been sentimentalized in order to be dismissed.

NOTES

I would like to thank Judith R. Baskin, Thomas J. Ferraro, and Susan Niditch without whose support over the years this project would not have come to completion. Thanks also to Cathy Caruth, Nancy Cott, Francis Courvares, Michael Denning, Julie Goldsmith, Joan Hedrick, Louise Levitas Henriksen, Paula Hyman, Indira Karamcheti, Franny Nudelman, Erika Penzer, Barbara Sicherman, Lynn Reiser, and Donald Weber for their ready exchange of ideas about reading Yezierska and their helpful comments on drafts of this essay. I am grateful to Louise Levitas Henriksen, *Cosmopolitan Magazine,* and the YIVO Institute for Jewish Research, for their permissions to use the photographs and drawing of Anzia Yezierska.

1. Anzia Yezierska, *Bread Givers: A Struggle Between a Father of the Old World and a Daughter of the New* (New York, 1925; repr. with new introduction by Alice Kessler Harris, 1975), 278. From this point on, page citations to this book appear in parentheses following quotations.

2. Anzia Yezierska, quoted in Louise Levitas Henriksen, *Anzia Yezierska: A Writer's Life* (New Brunswick, N.J., 1988), 16.

3. Crucial to the current reappraisal of Yezierska's writing have been Karen Braziller of Persea Books, Louise Levitas Henriksen, and Alice Kessler Harris's pioneering work in variously editing, reprinting, and writing critical introductions for *Hungry Hearts* (New York, repr. 1985); *The Open Cage: An Anzia Yezierska Collection* (New York, 1979); and with W. H. Auden's original introduction, *Red Ribbon on a White Horse* (New York, 1987). Important critical works include Jules Chametzky, *Our Decentralized Literature: Cultural Mediations in Selected Jewish and Southern Writers* (Amherst, Mass., 1986); Mary V. Dearborn, *Love in the Promised Land: The Story of Anzia Yezierska and John Dewey* (New York, 1988); *idem,* "Anzia Yezierska and the Making of an Ethnic American Self," in *The Invention of Ethnicity,* ed. Werner Sollors (New York, 1989); Thomas J. Ferraro, *Ethnic Passages: Literary Immigrants in Twentieth-Century America* (Chicago, 1993); Allen Guttmann, *The Jewish Writer in America: Assimilation and the Crisis of Identity* (New York, 1971); Henriksen, *Anzia Yezierska*; Wayne Charles Miller, *A Gathering of Ghetto Writers: Irish, Italian, Jewish, Black, and Puerto Rican* (New York, 1972); and Carol Schoen, *Anzia Yezierska* (Boston, 1982). Also see Vivian Gornick's introduction in her edited *How I Found America: Collected Stories of Anzia Yezierska* (New York, 1991); and Grace Paley's review of it, "Books: Telling Stories," in *Ms. Magazine* 3:3 (November/December 1992), 56–60. J. Hoberman, *Bridge of Light: Yiddish Films Between Two Worlds* (New York, 1991), contains a still photograph from the Famous Players-Lasky film production of *Salome of the Tenements* (1926), and Dearborn, *Love in the Promised Land*, contains a still from the Sam Goldwyn Hollywood film of *Hungry Hearts*.

4. Henriksen, *Anzia Yezierska*, 55.

5. See Alice Austen, *Alice's World: The Life and Photography of an American Original, 1866–1952,* ed. Ann Novotny (Old Greenwich, Conn., n. d.); and Jacob Riis, *How the Other Half Lives* (New York, repr. 1971).

6. Roland Barthes, *Camera Lucida* (New York, 1981), writes, 55–57: "The cinema has a power which at first glance the Photograph does not have: the screen (as Bazin has remarked) is not a frame but a hideout; the man or woman who emerges from it continues living: a "blind field" constantly doubles our partial vision. Now, confronting millions of pho-

tographs . . . I sense no blind field: everything which happens within the frame dies absolutely once this frame is passed beyond. When we define the Photograph as a motionless image, this does not mean only that the figures it represents do not move; it means that they do not *emerge,* do not *leave*: they are anesthetized and fastened down, like butterflies. Yet once there is a *punctum,* a blind field is created (is divined)."

7. Paley, "Books: Telling Stories," 57.

8. Anzia Yezierska, "Mostly About Myself," reprinted in Gornick, *How I Found America,* 132.

9. Yezierska, "Saint in Cellophane," in the Anzia Yezierska Papers, Boston University Libraries, quoted in Henriksen, *Anzia Yezierska,* 233.

10. Anzia Yezierska to Ferris Greenslet, quoted in Henriksen, 137.

11. Dearborn, "Anzia Yezierska," 122, reports that "critics called her fiction overemotional and uncontrolled, criticizing her for the 'ethnic' traits they had once enjoyed. W. Adolphe Roberts, in a typical review of *Salome of the Tenements,* called her work an orgy of the emotions, 'sentimental, illogical, hysterical, naive,' adding somewhat cryptically, 'I have assumed this incoherence to be racial. Yet I would hesitate to call it Jewish.' . . . Yezierska battled this kind of response tirelessly, pointing out to her critics exactly what they were doing: condemning the person they themselves had helped to create." Such statements often came with praise. Roberts also said she was a genius (Louise Henriksen in conversation with the author, January, 1994).

12. Barthes, *Camera Lucida,* writes: "The Photograph always leads the corpus I need back to the body I see; it is the absolute Particular, the sovereign Contingency, matte and somehow stupid, the *This* (this photography, and not Photography), in short what Lacan calles the *Tuché,* the Occasion, the Encounter, the Real, in its indefatigable expression" (4).

13. Ferraro, *Ethnic Passages,* 56–57, demonstrates that in *Bread Givers,* contrary to the "cult of Lower East Side authenticity that enveloped her in the 1920s and continues to frame our portrait of her . . . the arena of conflict for all but the opening moments of the novel are the developing institutions of the Jewish middle classes, institutions allied with if not embedded within those of more established Americans. The point here is not to delineate the concordances and discordances between Yezierska's actual experience and its subsequent fictionalization—we may never have enough biographical information to do that—but to challenge the still-prevailing identification of *Bread Givers* as solely an 'other half' novel." This read is important because until this identification is undone, it will be impossible to break through the binarisms of ethnic "bad faith" versus "authenticity" that have consistently drawn critical attention away from the complexity of Yezierska's actual literary achievement.

14. Yezierska, *Red Ribbon on a White Horse,* 216.

15. This incident is treated in Dearborn, *Love in the Promised Land*; Henriksen, *Anzia Yezierska*; and to a somewhat lesser extent in Robert B. Westbrook, *John Dewey and American Democracy* (Ithaca, N.Y., 1991). Yezierska quoted this poem, "Generations," which Dewey had apparently shown to her in *All I Could Never Be* (New York, 1932). Jo-Ann Boydston

has collected, dated, and written a critical introduction to Dewey's poetry in her edition *The Poems of John Dewey* (Carbondale, Ill., 1977).

16. On this point, see Mary Dearborn, *Pocahontas's Daughters: Gender and Ethnicity in American Culture* (New York, 1986), and Kristin Herzog, *Women, Ethnics, and Exotics: Images of Power in Mid-Nineteenth Century Fiction* (Knoxville, Tenn., 1983).

17. For Roman Vishniac's photographs, see, especially, *To Give Them Light: The Legacy of Roman Vishniac,* ed. Marion Wiesel (New York, 1993).

18. Paula Hyman, "The Jewish Family: Looking for a Usable Past," in *On Being a Jewish Feminist: A Reader,* ed. Susannah Heschel (New York, 1983), 19–20.

9 ♦ JANET BURSTEIN

*Mother at the Center: Jewish American Women's
Stories of the 1920s*

A significant development in Jewish women's writing of the
1920s is a new focus on the mother, both as central narrative
figure, and as a means of considering the effect upon women
of traditional assumptions about mothering. In a period during which "the ideal of femininity was changing so dramatically . . . that contemporaries began to speak of an entirely
'new woman,'"[1] several writers adopted the mother's point
of view, moving her from the periphery to the center of their
stories and clarifying the drama peculiar to her situation. In
one autobiography, one fictive memoir, and one novel, Rebekah Kohut, "Leah Morton" (Elizabeth G. Stern), and Emanie
Sachs looked, from a new perspective, at the cultural imperatives that had constructed the Jewish American mother.

Up to this time, Jewish mothers had rarely taken center
stage in women's stories. Even to other women, mothers'
lives probably appeared less interesting than the lives of
their children. Mothers, whose educations and romantic ad-

ventures were apparently behind them, whose ambitions were always subordinated to the needs of their families, and whose activities were determined largely by their husbands' status and income, seemed to lack the agency and the drama that could focus and hold literary interest. But in the twenties, Jewish American mothers became the subjects of their own stories, representing the tension they experienced between fulfilling their own aspirations and honoring the cultural imperatives that directed them toward service and duty to others.

This literary "re-vision"[2] of maternal service and self-denial had already begun in American women's literature, with stories like Charlotte Perkins Gilman's "The Yellow Wallpaper" (1892) and Kate Chopin's *The Awakening* (1899). But neither madness nor suicide, the last resorts of maternal protagonists in these earlier works, resolves the problems of Jewish American mothers in stories of the twenties. These Jewish characters, who remain in roles that demand self-sacrifice and self-abnegation, also bear little resemblance to non-Jewish characters in stories of the Progressive Era, which reflect the liberation of the "new woman" from marriage and maternal responsibilities.[3] Neither rebellious nor self-destructive, Jewish mothers in stories by Kohut, "Morton," and Sachs remain faithful to traditional imperatives even as their experience reveals the ways in which those imperatives constrain them. Their determination to sustain this tension links them to the "tradition" created by nineteenth century American Jewish women writers, recently described by Diane Lichtenstein, who by the turn of the century were struggling to "balance the claims of traditional and progressive" models of womanhood as their protagonists became more "self-conscious" in their "dedication" to their "own complex" selves.[4]

Behind this faithfulness to traditional imperatives is what Yiddish poet Kadya Molodowsky had called loyalty to the "kosher beds" of the "grandmothers,"[5] the generations of faithful East European Jewish mothers whose service at home and in the marketplace sustained Jewish life in a pre-

carious, often hostile, world. Yet women's service to children and husbands, however highly praised and however
essential to the Jewish family's well-being, was undervalued
by cultural priorities both before and after immigration. In
traditional European Jewish culture, the ideal of motherhood was secondary in status to study and prayer, activities
performed principally by men.[6] In America, Jewish mothers
responded to middle-class imperatives by withdrawing from
the marketplace to the home,[7] where their care of their
families still seemed secondary to wage earning activities.
Not surprisingly, then, beside the determination to be faithful to the model of the "grandmothers," the effects on
women of devaluation by a patriarchal cultural tradition,
analyzed in this period by Karen Horney, become important
issues in stories that place mothers at the center.

Rebekah Bettelheim Kohut (1864–1951), for example, in
her autobiography, *My Portion* (1925),[8] neither acknowledges her devaluation nor recognizes its effects. Indeed, her
life and its story testify to the public value, the resource-
fulness, and the power of the faithful, traditional Jewish
mother. But the persona created by this autobiographer
tells more than she intends of the costs of the ideal of service that dominated her personal and public life.[9] A Jewish
woman who lived entirely within a traditional culture as
both the daughter and the wife of rabbis, Kohut enjoyed
unusual advantages and suffered unusual deprivations. She
was educated beyond the norm for Jewish women of her
time, and made extraordinary contributions to the lives
of American Jewish women. But Kohut knew even more
pointedly than many other women the obligation to nurture,
for she was responsible first for her siblings in an otherwise motherless family, and later for a large number of
stepchildren. Kohut explains that a high school teacher had
reinforced and extended her early sense of obligation, directing the momentarily rebellious schoolgirl to serve not
only the family, but also the Jewish people, who "needed"
her: "there was work to be done in their behalf which was
more important than the state of my soul" (66). Responding

to this sense of need, Kohut devoted her life to the service of her own family, her husband's family, and the Jewish community.

American and traditional Jewish values overlapped for Kohut in a clear message, common not only among Jews but also among non-Jewish bourgeois women in late nineteenth-century America. From both cultures a woman learned to look outward to the needs of others, rather than inward, to the demands of her own "soul."[10] As modern Jewish men turned their attention from study to business,[11] Jewish women, like their non-Jewish counterparts, were encouraged to withdraw from the marketplace, "to restrict [their] activities increasingly to the home and homemaking."[12] But America also offered to aspiring middle-class women an opportunity to expand their caregiving beyond their families, for "philanthropic concern, particularly on a personal level, was considered one of the few activities that might legitimately draw a middle-class woman . . . from her home. Charity was considered an extension of the home and family obligations that women bore, and it became another example of her religiosity and purity."[13] Thus, like many other Jewish women who reentered the public world in America through voluntary work for the community, Kohut found in the domestic and social nurturer a culturally acceptable model for her own development.

She would be faithful always to this ideal of loving service to others. Her ambition and her spiritual generosity flowered in the light of tradition's chief imperative for women. She married a scholarly rabbi nearly old enough to be her father; he was a widower with eight children, his eldest daughter only a few years younger than herself.[14] Imagining her life with him, Kohut was "imbued . . . with the thought of spending myself in service, and in leading a life of significance" (118). "I go to New York," she told her disapproving sister, "to be the wife of a great man and to become a mother to the motherless" (119). By her own account, she served them well. And she took great pleasure in her service to both this family and, later, the larger Jewish community, becoming the first president of the World Congress of Jewish Women and of the New York chapter of the National Council of Jewish Women.

But she was also aware and proud of her "sacrifices." In them, and in the emotional context that surrounds them in the text, the tension engendered by the traditional ideal becomes visible. In every case, Kohut's "sacrifices" meant giving up her own gratification for the sake of someone else's comfort. "Thrilled," for example, when she was invited to address the first Congress of Jewish Women in Chicago, she accepted and wrote a paper. On the night she was to leave for Chicago, however, she noticed that her husband looked "unusually pale. . . . Finally he said, almost with tears in his voice: 'How shall we manage without you for a whole week?'" She reports, "My heart gripped me at his absolute dependence, and his sadness." After she sent her sister off to the conference to read the paper, she went to her room and wept (181). "The disappointment was keen," she confesses. But her consolation was even keener: "In later years I felt it was one of the finest sacrifices I had ever made for Alexander Kohut" (182).

Oddly, the magnitude of her disappointment rather than the gravity of his need appears to have measured the worth of the sacrifice. As her tradition and her teacher had promised her, she fulfilled herself (acquired "a finer soul") when she set aside her own satisfaction to serve her husband. But her tendency to take pleasure in self-denial reveals a dimension of the ideal of womanly service that throws a shadow on the face of its virtues.[15] After her husband's death, for example, Kohut gave up directing a school she had labored for years to build for the sake of her adolescent stepchildren, who "felt neglected" (230). Remembering that sacrifice, moreover, she recalls an even earlier one: "Friends have often wondered," she writes, "whether I did not miss having a child of my own. . . . Were I to have a child of my own, beside these stepchildren, mother love would come between me and the others, I should inevitably show the preference, and the family atmosphere would be inharmonious. So I elected undivided stepmotherhood rather than a divided motherhood" (232–33). In keeping with the ideal of womanly self-denial, Kohut sacrificed both the work she longed for and the satisfaction of bearing children because she believed the needs of others were more important than her own. In the text she does not even struggle with these decisions, so thoroughly has she internalized her culture's priorities. She takes pride in what she gave up because her culture encourages her to feel proudest of what she does for others. Beside the professional and communal achievements that distinguished Kohut's career beyond the family, then, her autobiography also identifies the pattern of motive and response that mark the woman who derives pleasure and pride chiefly from serving others.

Psychological analysis of female devotion to the service of others begins in this period with Kohut's contemporary, psychologist Karen Horney. From her clinical practice, Horney observed that the rewards of service can be deeply mixed. She believed that her female patients learned to love serving others from "masculine civilization" which preferred men to women and devalued women's needs.[16] As adults, such women would hold their own needs in check, and, in a culture that expected women to set others' needs before their own, that habit would be fixed for life. But, according to Horney and others, such behavior lowers self-esteem while also creating unacknowledged anger at those who have devalued, and taught a woman to devalue, her own aspirations. Finally, Horney argued, as a woman's fear of abandonment "wins out over her anger, she will defensively turn her anger against herself and will admire the devaluing adults, endowing them with idealized virtues and behaving as they demand in order to hide her own feeling of worthlessness. In this way admiring obedience procures safety by destroying the subjective basis of judgment" (136), but it also leads to denial of the "true self" in which authentic longings and judgments are acknowledged. Women who deny their "true selves" in this way often become "female altruists" whose generosity masks weakness.

Believing they are not worthy of love, female altruists "feel loved only if they are needed; they have a self only as a reflection of and response to someone else's needs" (137). Thus, in cultures organized to nurture men, daughters would grow up unable to "permit themselves to feel that their actions are for themselves . . . they translate their own intentions into doing for others" (125). When they become traditional Jewish mothers, this displacement is rewarded. What they do for others becomes, as it did for Kohut, a source not only of reassurance but also of personal pride and communal respect.

Neither the pride nor the pleasure of self-sacrifice, however, may satisfy the "true self" of the devalued woman who has lost awareness of her own needs. Traditional culture sustains her "ideal" self by rewarding her self-denials. But once she begins to question tradition, she experiences intense conflict. Stories by two other writers of the twenties who are more distant than Kohut from traditional Jewish belief and practice show how that conflict reveals to the woman who suffers it the individual needs obscured beneath the ideals that tradition has imposed upon her.

The title of Elizabeth G. Stern's (1890–1954) pseudonymous and largely fictive *I Am a Woman—and a Jew* (1926), written under the name of Leah Morton,[17] for example, reveals in each half of its neatly balanced title two centers of a single conflict that are exposed but never resolved in the narrative. The inward divisions that split her protagonist's professional and personal life and fragment her narrative persona arise out of the traditional dichotomy that empowered men and devalued women.[18] As a child, Leah learns from her father to be studious and self-assertive (55). But her mother epitomizes the conventional female values of self-denial and the rendering of service to others, socially, domestically, and religiously: "She lit her candles on Friday night, and she felt she served God in their lighting. She cooked the holiday meals and prepared them for honoring Him. She saved, denied herself even things she needed, to send her children to study Hebrew, that they might speak the language of her God. She gave, from her slender purse, to the poor and fed His children" (311). Leah spends her life attempting to incorporate both male and female models into one adult persona.

Once Leah resolves to forgo the approval of her traditional culture in order to satisfy her own needs, these gendered imperatives not only conflict, but also confuse her as she tries to define her own goals. Although she wants to become a writer, Leah silences this desire because she does not feel entitled to satisfy it; she chooses instead to be a social worker, "to do work for the oppressed, the poor, the hunted . . . to learn how to dedicate [myself] to something as beautiful as charity" (34). Twelve years later, her mistake becomes obvious: "There is nothing, surely, more disastrous than to choose the wrong profession," she realizes (39). Her sense of direction confused as she takes her first steps away from tradition, Leah tries, but fails, to honor conflicting cultural imperatives. Imitating her father, she achieves a professional life despite his objections. But, like her mother, she devotes this life not to the work she longs for, but to the service of others.

The impaired sense of entitlement that allows Leah to struggle toward but not to realize her own goals unless they serve the needs of others, appears again and again in the course of her narrative. Although teaching "was my happiness," she allows her husband's objections to turn her away from it (107). Her self-denial earns her, like Rebekah Kohut, the pleasure of sacrificing her own gratification to serve another: "Not many things in all my life have been to me what that short moment was when I felt his lean hand on my hair, and heard him thank me for giving up what I enjoyed doing most—to please his male pride" (108).

Unlike Kohut, whose acceptance of tradition silenced the troublesome voice of her own desire, Leah acknowledges here the existence of two strong inner voices, two opposing versions of self, that cannot become congruent. She resolves their incongruity by asserting the priorities she had learned from her "kosher" mother. What makes her happy must be secondary; what serves her husband's pride is primary. Service and responsibility to others always come "first of all" for her. But her distance from the culture that reinforced these priorities and made them spiritually significant denies her the reward her mother enjoyed. Now she appears simply to prefer subordinating her own needs to satisfying them.

Yet moving further and further away from the role tradition had ordained for her, this Jewish American protagonist holds on with one hand as she lets go with the other. Leah gives up traditional observances and behavior; she marries a non-Jew, leaving behind family, faith, and culture; she relinquishes communal approval and the spiritual confirmation offered to self-sacrificing Jewish women by their tradition. Leah achieves considerable success in the world, but hampered by the traditional devaluation of Jewish daughters, now reinforced by middle-class American ideology, she cannot validate her own needs or pursue her own goals without conflict. She cannot become aware of, much less express, anger at her husband's restrictions and derogations. And although she becomes a powerful administrator of a large social service organization, she must always protect her professional image from her husband's belittling. She clings, moreover, to the validation of an "ideal self" provided by his affectionate, but reductive, image of her as his "little girl."

Caught throughout her life in this conflict between two incompatible selves, Leah also sustains the tension inherent in her determination to reject traditional Judaism while still remaining a Jew. Her father's death reminds her that she is connected to the Jewish people even though she has married a non-Jew and will not "practice [Judaism's] precepts and its faith" (288). Although she has raised her children virtually innocent of any knowledge of their Jewish heritage, she is hurt by her son's denial of his Jewish identity (358). She cannot identify with other Jewish women in New York (347), but she insists on being recognized as a Jewish woman. Resisting to the end the ritual practices that belong to Judaism, she accepts "its history, its psychology" as her own (361). She knows she is a Jew "before everything. Perhaps not in my work or in my daily life. But in that inner self that cannot change, I belong to my people." Thus negation, as always in this memoir, is the companion of affirmation. Neither fully subordinated as a traditional wife and mother, nor fully liberated as a professional woman, neither pious believer nor rebellious agnostic, Leah manifests as both woman and Jew the deep, inward divisions that attend the Jewish American mother's first steps away from the imperatives that shaped her.

Emanie Sachs's (d. 1981) *Red Damask* (1927)[19] explores an even more intense conflict created by cultural imperatives that deny her protagonist both work and love. This novel demonstrates the impossibility of individual self-realization for a woman bound by conventional imperatives, but it also represents its protagonist's devotion to the imperatives that bind her. Most important, this novel analyzes both the effects of traditional loyalties upon the Jewish family and the cultural forces that defined middle-class women as nurturers and consumers.

To clarify the forces that act upon its protagonist, *Red Damask* looks as closely at the prosperous world of a German Jewish family in the United States in the early decades of the twentieth century as at the quest of its beautiful daughter, Abby Hahl. The image called up by the title becomes a metaphor for the intricate patterns that not only decorate the walls, the curtains, and the furniture of this world, but also suggest the elaborately interwoven social and familial pressures that create its structure and enrich its texture. Explicitly patriarchal, this world is dominated by Abby's grandfather. He is "majestic, powerful, a human engine fused to fight for the juice it ran on" (373). He controls the destiny of all his offspring and, to some extent, their mates and children. Abby envies him "the thrilling certainty that he was significant to something he considered significant" (373). His devotion to the ideal of "family solidarity" becomes the dominant value of the family.

The sacrifices exacted by this ideal are justified, for Abby, partly by the disappearance from her world of religious ritual and belief. With "no habitual religious responses, smoldering from childhood," Abby is chilled by a rabbi's "abstract holiness" and a synagogue service "not fervent enough to light new fires" (91). But residual religious fervor, "inherited from rabbinical ancestors, made her want to be good for the sake of being good. Denied its mystic outlet, it put emotion into her conduct; it flowed into dreams and ideals. Fighting her energy, fighting her brain, sometimes it betrayed them; sometimes it was betrayed" (2). In this world, then, religious feeling flows into a desire to "do the right thing" (33), and "any need for ritualism was filled by . . . family life" (2).

As family life absorbs the spiritual energies of its devotees, however, it becomes a patriarchal "tyranny" (193). Reckoning the sacrifices exacted of her relatives, Abby realizes that "her family thought they were gods, trying to create children in their own images." As often in the novel, she retreats, guiltily, from this insight (60). She grasps several times the understandings that might liberate her from the pattern imposed by her family. But duty, gratitude, loyalty, and fear weaken her grip on these revelations. Although she is capable of conceiving "a world where no words guided your way, where every step was separate, on its own responsibility, in its own time, and of its own place . . . a difficult world in which you couldn't stop thinking" (351), she is unable to enter that world. She moves briefly toward the dazzling pleasure of work she loves (39–40), but gives it up when her family belittle it as selfish and unpromising. She falls in love with an East European Jew, but gives him up as well when his rebelliousness threatens her idealization of her family. Trained to "obey her teachers" (38), raised by a childlike mother who follows "every herd formula" (274) and doesn't "believe in praise" (42), encouraged to doubt that women's work can succeed in the world (31), and guided always toward her "duty to others" (32), Abby falters and withdraws from every insight that would liberate her from the repetitive pattern that decorates, insulates, and dominates her world.

As she succumbs to that pattern, the novel explores the disappointments and defeats that mark the path of her submission. Her marriage contaminated by her husband's conventional assumptions about women's sexual passiveness, she renounces desire (262–63), sleeping at last in "a narrow, nunlike bed, made from an old oak chest, on which carved mermaids, forever stranded, wept on chiseled cliffs" (318). Her philanthropic work in the community subverted by the indifference of those she serves, she retreats to the nursery. Her efforts to mother frustrated both by her own natural impulses (239, 244) and her inability to "assert her adulthood" (248), she relinquishes her daughter's care to a professional. Her attraction to a married, non-Jewish architect obstructed by her faithfulness to the "kosher beds" of the "grandmothers," she turns away from adulterous romance as she has turned away from marital love, philanthropy, study, and training for a career.

Each new disappointment illuminates the hollowness of the ideals for which she has sacrificed herself. But disappointments also illuminate her "real" self beneath the beautiful clothes, the social rituals, and the dutiful behavior of her "ideal" self. In fact, she is amorphous, unformed, uncertain, full of incompatible possibilities (68, 159), all of them unrealized. She turns the talent that might have made her a successful architect or designer toward the intricacies of dress and domestic acquisition appropriate to women of her class. She turns the energy that sought outlet in work toward romantic and maternal fantasies, blaming herself for the intensity of feeling that then threatens her husband and unnerves her child. She feels the narrowness of the channel into which the pattern set by class and culture has directed her. And eventually she blames "the family for teaching her that 'helping others' was your first high duty, something you could hold to, no matter what failed. . . . Having guideposts recede when you needed them made you doubly lost. If she hadn't counted on them, she might have found her own way" (271).

The novel suggests, however, that besides Abby's belief in her "duty" to others, she harbors a powerful need for activity and a moral code that transcends her own personal interest.[20] The narrator punctures Abby's credulous illusions about duty to her family, her tendency to mix "moods with morals," (60) and her "need of love" (100). But her love of her child, her persistent longing for "an aspiration to tie to, greater than oneself" (229), and "her amazing energy, her eternal habit of finding future faiths" (294) are validated by the narrator. These traits dignify her and set her apart from other women in the novel, who amuse themselves in trivial or devious ways to offset the empty repetitions of their lives. When Abby's heart, like theirs, "ached with spring," when her "mind ached with servants' squabbles," she cannot still the pain by taking a lover or buying a new hat. She needs spiritual, not sensual or material gratification. Her inability to satisfy this need within a culture that discourages both religious fervor and professional development in its mothers creates the impasse in which her life is deadlocked, like the line that always turns back on itself in the red damask that surrounds her.

These stories of the twenties that place the experience of Jewish American mothers at their centers emerge from a historical moment in which the conflict between disparate needs can be seen, but not resolved, in terms of either cultural, individual, or spiritual priorities. Their authors begin to "re-vision" the dominant ideals of service and duty to others that shaped the lives of generations of Jewish mothers, a task that later writers like Tillie Olsen and Grace Paley would continue and expand. Kohut, "Morton," and Sachs cannot follow their protagonists beyond the conflicts that divide them, but they formulate one important element of an agenda for the future, by revealing the incompatible, equally precious alternatives that make movement, for the moment, impossible.

NOTES

1. Mary P. Ryan, "The Projection of a New Womanhood: The Movie Moderns in the 1920's," in *Decades of Discontent: The Women's Movement, 1920–1940,* ed. Lois Scharf and Joan M. Jensen (Boston, 1987), 113.

2. Adrienne Rich, "When We Dead Awaken: Writing as Re-Vision," in her *On Lies, Secrets, and Silence: Selected Prose 1966–1978* (New York, 1979), called "re-vision" the "act of looking back, of seeing with fresh eyes, of entering an old text from a new critical direction." She believed for women this was "an act of survival."

3. Elizabeth Ammons, *Conflicting Stories: American Women Writers at the Turn into the Twentieth Century* (New York, 1991), 9.

4. Diane Lichtenstein, *Writing Their Nations: The Tradition of Nineteenth-Century American Jewish Women Writers* (Bloomington, Ind., 1992), 129.

5. Kadya Molodowsky, "Women Songs," in *A Treasury of Yiddish Poetry,* ed. Irving Howe and Eliezer Greenberg (New York, 1969), 284.

6. On Jewish women's traditional roles in Eastern Europe, see Immanuel Etkes, "Marriage and Torah Study Among the "Lomdim" in Lithuania in the Nineteenth Century," in *The Jewish Family: Metaphor and Memory,* ed. David Kraemer (New York, 1989), 153–78; Paula Hyman, "The Jewish Family: Looking for a Usable Past," in *On Being a Jewish Feminist: A Reader,* ed. Susannah Heschel (New York, 1983), 23.

7. See Paula Hyman, "Gender and the Immigrant Jewish Experience in the United States," in *Jewish Women in Historical Perspective*, ed. Judith R. Baskin (Detroit, 1991), 222–42; and Susan Glenn, *Daughters of the Shtetl: Life and Labor in the Immigrant Generation* (Ithaca, N.Y., 1990) 77–79.

8. Rebekah Bettelheim Kohut, *My Portion* (New York, 1925; repr. 1975). An excerpt from this work may be found in *Writing Our Lives: Autobiographies of American Jews, 1890–1990,* ed. Steven J. Rubin (Philadelphia, 1991), 32–39.

9. For issues connected with reading women's autobiographies, see *Life/Lines: Theorizing Women's Autobiography*, ed. Bella Brodzki and Celeste Schenck (Ithaca, N.Y., 1988), and Sidonie Smith, *A Poetics of Women's Autobiography: Marginality and the Fictions of Self-Representation* (Bloomington, Ind., 1987).

10. A Jewish woman traditionally cultivated her soul by acts of self-sacrificing service to others. Sydney Stahl Weinberg, *The World of Our Mothers: The Lives of Jewish Immigrant Women* (New York, 1988), 17–19, describes the ways in which the religious piety of shtetl women was "intertwined with their daily functions," to create a "domestic religion" tied to homely rituals surrounding the family's life support system at home. See also Hyman, "Immigrant Jewish Experience," and especially Ellen M. Umansky, "Spiritual Expressions: Jewish Women's Religious Lives in the Twentieth Century United States," in Baskin, *Historical Perspective,* 265–88, and her introduction to *Four Centuries of Jewish Women's Spirituality: A Sourcebook,* ed. Ellen M. Umansky and Dianne Ashton (Boston, 1992).

11. Hyman, "Immigrant Jewish Experience," 225, reports that "full-time, lifelong and highly paid employment replaced the mastery of Jewish texts as the gender ideal for Jewish men in the United States."

12. Hyman, "Immigrant Jewish Experience," 225–26; Weinberg, *Mothers*, 196, 227.

13. Charlotte Baum, Paula Hyman, Sonya Michel, *The Jewish Woman in America* (New York, 1976), 30; Linda Gordon Kuzmack, *Woman's Cause: The Jewish Woman's Movement in England and the United States* (Columbus, Ohio, 1990), 27.

14. Nancy F. Anderson, "No Angel in the House: The Psychological Effects of Maternal Death," *Psychohistory Review* 11:1 (Fall 1982), 20–46, highlights the oedipal dimension of such a decision.

15. Kohut's "covert resentment" is noted by Baum, et al., *Jewish Woman*, 35.

16. Marcia Westkott, *The Feminist Legacy of Karen Horney* (New Haven, 1986), 1, 6–7. Westkott has drawn together Horney's work on the devaluation of women with that of later psychologists. Hereafter cited parenthetically in the text.

17. Leah Morton, *I Am A Woman—and a Jew* (New York, 1926; repr. with introduction by Ellen M. Umansky, 1986). An excerpt from this work may be found in Rubin, *Writing Our Lives*, 40–51.

18. Dorothy M. Brown, *Setting A Course: American Women in the 1920s* (Boston, 1987), 2, also points to the ambience of Stern's time and place in the twenties, when signs of struggle between the "new woman" and the genteel "true woman" were everywhere, as an important influence on her writing.

19. Emanie Sachs, *Red Damask* (New York, 1927). Jews from German-speaking parts of Europe came to the United States several generations before the large Jewish immigration from Eastern Europe that began in 1881. Generally speaking, by the early decades of the twentieth century, German Jews were far more Americanized and middle class than their East European co-religionists.

20. Patricia Meyer Spacks, "Selves in Hiding," in *Women's Autobiography*, ed. Estelle Jelinek (Bloomington, Ind., 1980), 112–132, argues that women's autobiographies reveal their writers' need for public commitments to both extend and escape from personal feelings.

10 ✦ CAROLE S. KESSNER

Matrilineal Dissent: The Rhetoric of Zeal in
Emma Lazarus, Marie Syrkin, and
Cynthia Ozick

I never meant to write essays.
                                        —Cynthia Ozick[1]

Out of the long and growing list of women who have made
significant contributions to American Jewish life and letters,
one rare type stands apart. Possessed of a morally serious
mind, she is a highly intellectual creative writer who passionately identifies with the Jewish past, present, and future. Such a woman joins her gift for language and literature
to a prodigious wit, not alone to further her own art, but
simultaneously to address critically the Jewish present as it
is and as it might be. Emma Lazarus, the first such important
American Jewish woman writer, spoke in a bold voice whose
echo can be heard down the generations in the words of her
literary and spiritual descendants, Marie Syrkin and Cynthia
Ozick.

All three women have been conscious of themselves as
Jews, as artists, and as women; they have also been aware of
the conflicts and paradoxes among these roles. Unafraid to
meet the challenge of those who would disagree, each has

dared to address the polarities of aesthetics and ethics, of American politics and Jewish life, and to assert an idiosyncratic feminism rather than to engage in sexual politics. Moreover, the details of Lazarus's, Syrkin's, and Ozick's careers are remarkably parallel: all three had excellent American secular educations; all three at an early age aspired to a life in English literature; all three are self-proclaimed Jewish autodidacts who did not begin to emphasize Jewishness in their writing until they were almost thirty. At that point, all three began to respond, both in their creative art and in their expository prose, to what they saw as the Jewish crises of their own times; all three ultimately developed strenuous polemical prose styles that won them renown in their own time as essayists; all three have argued vigorously the cause of Zionism. And each, while refusing to negate the Diaspora, has warned of its dangers. This essay will focus on the literary lives of Emma Lazarus and Marie Syrkin; Cynthia Ozick is discussed in another chapter in this volume, but from time to time I shall also point out Ozick's literary heritage as it derives from Syrkin and Lazarus.[2]

If Lazarus is recalled at all today, it is too often with overtones of piety; she is cited by feminists for having been a woman who achieved a certain fame in a patriarchal time, and she is remembered by historians and literary critics for the last four-and-a-half lines of the famous sonnet embossed on the pedestal of the Statue of Liberty. Few, however, remember that the title of that poem is "The New Colossus," or understand what that title implies; nor can many recall the first nine-and-a-half lines. Yet in the total fourteen lines of the sonnet lies the key to the extraordinary history of Emma Lazarus's personal journey of self-discovery and self-expression:

> Not like the brazen giant of Greek fame,
> With conquering limbs astride from land to land;
> Here at our sea-washed, sunset gates shall stand
> A mighty woman with a torch, whose flame
> Is the imprisoned lightning, and her name

Mother of Exiles. From her beacon-hand
Glows world-wide welcome; her mild eyes command
The air bridged harbor that twin cities frame.
"Keep, ancient land, your storied pomp!" cries she
With silent lips. "Give me your tired, your poor,
Your huddled masses yearning to breathe free,
The wretched refuse of your teeming shore.
Send these, the homeless, tempest-tost to me,
I lift my lamp beside the golden door!"

How did this very young, very unworldly, very upper-class American woman come to write an impassioned plea for the poor, for the immigrant, the oppressed "wretched refuse"? The answer is suggested in the first octave of the sonnet, which begins, "*Not* like the brazen giant of Greek fame," (italics added). In these words and in what follows, Lazarus rejects Western culture's Hellenistic glorification of male conquering power, of empty ceremony and aestheticism, and in its place she asserts the power of womanhood, the comfort of motherhood, and the Hebraic prophetic values of compassion and consolation.

Emma Lazarus's early years did not suggest that she would become a prototype for the modern Jewish woman writer, nor that she would become a Jewish nationalist in her poetry, a proto-Zionist in her aspirations, nor a socialist sympathizer in her politics,[3] nor assertive in her self-confidence as a woman. She was born on July 22, 1849, to Moses Lazarus, a wealthy sugar industrialist of Sephardic background, and his wife, Esther Nathan Lazarus, who was of Ashkenazic background. Both sides of the family had been in America since the Revolution. The Lazarus family lived in a fashionable section of New York City and summered in the popular watering spot of Newport, Rhode Island. Emma was educated at home by private tutors, and studied the curriculum thought suitable for well-educated young American ladies of upper-class status. In the introduction to two volumes of selected poems published posthumously in 1889, two years after her death, Emma's sister Josephine tells us that in Emma's early years, Hebraism was only latent, and it was "classic and romantic art that first attracted her. . . . Her restless spirit found repose in the pagan idea—the absolute unity and identity of man with nature, as symbolized in the Greek myths."[4] As we have seen, this is the very subject matter that was to be roundly rejected in "The New Colossus."[5] Certainly something profoundly transforming happened to Lazarus between the first volume of poems published privately in 1867 by her father, and *Songs of a Semite: "The Dance Unto Death" and Other Poems,* published in 1882, which has as its dedication: "In profound veneration and respect to the memory of George Eliot, the illustrious writer who did most among the artists of our day towards elevating and ennobling the spirit of Jewish Nationality."

During the course of her career, Lazarus struck up tutelary relationships with male writers; the first and most influential was Ralph Waldo Emerson, but she also became acquainted with such figures as Thomas Wentworth Higginson, Ivan Turgenev, the naturalist John Burroughs, Edwards Clarence Stedman, and finally Henry James. All of these men encouraged her, yet most were honest enough to suggest that she needed to find her own voice. In 1871 she published *Admetus and Other Poems.* The major poems of this volume are both curious and suggestive—*Admetus, Orpheus, Lohengrin,* and *Tannhäuser*—comprising two Greek myths and two medieval German legends about women who sacrificed themselves for the sake of men, and three accounts of poetic singers. Emma, it appears, was struggling to find her own voice, but looking in the wrong place.

As time went on she began more and more to reveal an awareness of her own traditions. She studied the Hebrew language and Graetz's *History of the Jews,* translated the German Jewish poet Heinrich Heine and the medieval Jewish poets of Spain, and began writing a few poems on Jewish subjects. Still her commitment to Judaism was more historical than spiritual, as she wrote in 1877 to Rabbi Gustave Gottheil, who had asked her to contribute hymns to a new Reform hymnal he was preparing for publication: "I cheerfully offered to help you to the extent of my ability, and was glad to prove to you that my interest and sympathies were loyal to our race, although my religious convictions (if such they can be called) and the circumstances of my life have led me somewhat apart from our people."[6] In 1878, Lazarus began a correspondence with the naturalist and popular author John Burroughs on the subject of Matthew Arnold's Hellenism as opposed to Whitman's Hebraism, a topic of increasing interest to her. Burroughs wrote in response to Lazarus's claim that Arnold is cold and lacks spontaneity: "Yes, Whitman is Hebraic, so is Carlyle, so are all the more vital literary forces of our century, I think."[7] It is interesting to see a similar perception in Ozick's interest in the distinction between Hebraism and Hellenism in her famous remark that the nineteenth-century novel in its moral seriousness is a Judaized novel.[8]

At this very time in Emma Lazarus's life, when she was searching for an authentic way to express her increasing Jewish consciousness, two related events occurred to fire her poetic imagination and social conscience. These were the Russian pogroms of 1881, and the increasingly harsh and restrictive anti-Jewish Russian legislation, epitomized in the May Laws of 1882. The result was mass immigration of East European Jews to the United States. Until this moment, Lazarus's interest in Judaism was mainly philosophical, and there was no active cause to which she could attach herself. But at this crux in history she responded immediately and passionately, and she was drawn into active battle, fighting on three fronts as poet, as political essayist, and as social activist.

Yet the transformation of Emma's consciousness was not quite complete. There was to be a critical moment. In April of 1882 Emma Lazarus published an essay, "Was the Earl of Beaconsfield a Representative Jew?" in *Century* magazine. In this still cool, rationalist, universalist assessment of Benjamin Disraeli, she concludes that indeed he *is* a representative Jew, "but he is not a first-class man." His qualities," she asserts, "were not those of the world's heroes; he possessed talent rather than genius. . . . Moses, Jesus, St. Paul, the prophets, Spinoza bear glorious testimony to the existence of first-class men. But centuries of persecution and the enforced narrowness of their sphere of action . . . have developed among the Jews a national character other than that of the above named scions of the race."[9] Lazarus's lament is for want of a great moral spiritual leader. She herself is on the threshold of accepting her own challenge. By some quirk of fate, in the same volume of *Century* there was to appear an article by Madame Z. Ragozin, a Russian journalist; Ragozin's essay was a defense of the mobs who were perpetrating the pogroms and a vicious attack upon Jewish character.[10] Before printing this article, George Gilder, the well-known liberal editor of *Century Magazine,* showed it to Lazarus, who immediately wrote an outraged response for the May 1882 issue. Gone is the cool detachment of the Disraeli essay; in its place is moral passion, irony, caustic wit, superb scholarship, rhetorical strategy, and a clear expression of her own identification as a Jew connected to all other Jews.[11] To Madame Ragozin's charge that there are two kinds of Jews, that a "vast dualism essentially characterizes this extraordinary race," Lazarus answers: "The dualism of the Jews is the dualism of humanity; they are made up of the good and the bad. May not Christendom be divided into those Christians who denounce such outrages as we are considering, and those who commit or apologize for them? Immortal genius and moral purity, as exemplified by Moses and Spinoza, constitute a minority among Jews, as they do among the Gentiles."[12]

Jesus and Paul are now absent from Lazarus's list of heroes; gone is her naive lament for the Jewish failure to produce "moral purity and immortal genius." This essay, entitled "Russian Christianity Versus Modern Judaism," is the first of a stream of polemical pieces in defense of her subject and in challenge to her people that Emma Lazarus would write over the next few years of her brief life. She had finally hit her stride, and she revealed it in a vigorous, muscular, prose—a prose style that elsewhere has been identified as the "rhetoric of zeal."[13] This double-edged rhetoric, which alternates between an extravagance born of idealism and devastating rapier thrusts, is characteristic of the zealous writer from the biblical prophets through John Milton to the passionate polemicists of the 1960s. Only the idealist with a high sense of moral purpose can turn the carpet over to expose the rough underside of moral indignation; the cynic has only one texture.

This, of course, belies the words of so many of Lazarus' admirers, including her sisters, who insisted that she was the consummate shy, restrained Victorian woman. She was not. All she lacked was an appropriate object for the passion of her "late-born woman-soul,"[14] a legitimate focus for the intensity of her moral and aesthetic passion. She found it in the wedding of her identification with her people and her decision to speak and act for them. She embodied it in poetry that rejects the high diction of the past and is charged with the prophetic urgency of the call for return to the land of Israel, and in vigorous prose, especially in the series of fourteen essays ironically entitled "Epistle to the Hebrews," written from November 1882 to February 1883, in which she undertook to "bring before the Jewish public . . . facts and critical observations . . . to arouse a more logical and intelligent estimate of the duties of the hour."[15]

Lazarus's commitment toward social justice, however, was not expressed in words alone, for she involved herself in the practical task of helping the new immigrants to resettle, and she was responsible for the founding of the Hebrew Technical Institute for Vocational Training. Moreover, in a series of twelve letters written to the influential political economist E. R. A. Seligman just before her trip to England in 1883, Lazarus desperately tried to form a Committee for the Colonization of Palestine. Seligman was uncooperative, and the venture appears to have failed.[16]

Lazarus sailed to London in 1883, armed with letters of introduction from Henry James to well-placed people in England, Jews and non-Jews, who could help her in her work toward the establishment of a Jewish national homeland.[17] Thus, a decade before Herzl's launching of political Zionism,

Emma Lazarus would argue in a poetic voice of her own and in powerfully persuasive prose for the land of Israel as a safe haven for oppressed Jews everywhere. It should be noted, however, that at no point did Lazarus advocate resettlement for all Jews.[18]

Emma Lazarus died on November 19, 1887, at the age of thirty-eight. She never married, and died childless; but twelve years years later her true child of the spirit, Marie Syrkin, was born. Syrkin was to become well known as a polemicist for the Jewish people and the State of Israel, whose keen arguments would appear in a wide range of publications for a period of almost seventy years. It is not as well known, however, that she recorded both the public and private aspects of her life and career in poetry written over the course of her long lifetime. For Syrkin (who lived over fifty years longer than Lazarus' brief thirty-eight years), the personal and the Jewish people became ineluctably intertwined. The close of her most intensely personal poem, "Memorial for a Child," an excruciating reflection upon the death of her son in his second year, is an example *par excellence* of the way in which she brought together her personal life and her life through her people:

> I have never gone back to Ithaca,
> Afraid of the small headstone,
> the weed-choked plot.
> Now there is a plaque with your name
> In a kindergarten in Jerusalem.
> In Jerusalem
> In a house for children
> With eyes dark as yours,
> Prattling in Hebrew
> And laughing,
> I took heart to face your name:
> Benyah.[19]

Marie Syrkin was born in Switzerland in March 1899, two years after the First Zionist Congress and six years before the 1905 Russian Revolution. She was the daughter of Nachman Syrkin, the erudite, moralistic theoretician of Socialist Zionism, and Bassya Osnos Syrkin, a headstrong revolutionary activist. Marie's personality undoubtedly was shaped by these two professional idealists. Psychobiography must take into account Marie's love-hatred for her father, who was an erudite ethical idealist, yet possessed a blazing temperament that vented itself publicly in scathing argument, and privately, as she herself described it, in a zealous "dedicated poverty." One must also consider the model of feminist activism and egalitarianism provided by her mother.

By the time Marie Syrkin was ten she had lived in five countries, finally moving to the United States in 1908, because, as she quipped, "Papa was always getting exiled—so we traveled a lot."[20] The Syrkins treated their unusually beautiful and exceptionally intelligent child, who at the age of ten was fluent in five languages—Russian, French, German, Yiddish, and English—as a prodigy. One might note here that Hebrew was not among the languages she learned, despite her busy father's sporadic attempts to instruct her in Spinoza in Latin, Marx in German, and the Bible in Hebrew when she was a child. As an adult she deeply lamented the fact that Hebrew had never become one of her languages.

If in these years the daughter admired her parents' dedicated poverty, she did not seem the slightest bit interested in the politics that inspired their chosen financial condition. She was fast developing a passion for romantic poetry equal to her parents' passion for radical politics. There was nothing at this stage to suggest that Marie Syrkin would become the doyenne of Labor Zionism. If anything, her adolescent diary suggests that she might become a woman of belles lettres; and indeed, this is probably what would have happened had she not made a conscious career choice to use her literary gifts in the service of Zionism and the Jewish people.[21]

When she was barely eighteen, Marie Syrkin eloped with Maurice Samuel, who was then twenty-two and had enlisted in the army and was about to leave for France. The two had met at a New Jersey summer resort and were instantly drawn to one another, not least by their mutual love for poetry. Nachman Syrkin, however, instantly had the marriage annulled, claiming that his daughter was underage. He successfully exercised his will, but it resulted in a resentment that Marie never quite conquered. In fact, Marie Syrkin and Maurice Samuel's subsequent common interest in Zionism and their activities in its behalf led to a resumption of their relationship in later years.

In 1918, as Nachman Syrkin went off to Versailles to represent the socialist-Zionists at the Peace Conference at the end of the First World War, his daughter Marie went off to Cornell University in Ithaca, New York, to pursue her literary studies, ultimately completing a master's thesis on the subject of Francis Thompson, the Victorian English poet to whose work she had first been introduced by Maurice Samuel. Here at Cornell, in 1919, Marie met and married a young instructor of biochemistry named Aaron Bodansky. They had two sons; the first child, however, tragically died at the age of two, only two months before the death of Nachman Syrkin, and three months before the birth of her second child. During these extremely painful years, Marie, who thought of herself primarily as a poet, devoted herself to writing verse. In order to make some extra money, however, she began to translate poetry from Yiddish, and by the time she was twenty-four she had published translations of Yehoash in *Menorah Journal* that were praised by Yehoash himself. This was one way of reconciling her love of poetry and her emerging sense of Jewish purpose. It was also during these years at Cornell that Marie's commitment to Jewish life and to Zionism began to develop. Now, in addition to poetry, she began to write prose essays as well. In fact, what appears to be the first example of her polemical Zionist writing is her 1925 article for *The New Palestine* in which she praises the new student movement Avuka over the more established International Zionist Association. In a prose style foreshadowing the sharp ironic wit alongside the roseate idealism that was to characterize her writing, she described the I. Z. A. as "a kind of painless dentistry which

temporarily filled spiritual cavities of a special nature."
Avuka, however, grew out of the postwar Mandate condition
and was "quickened by the beat of the *halutzim's* [pioneers']
pickaxes in Palestine."[22]

By the time Marie Syrkin was twenty-eight she had so long
a list of publications that she was asked to become an associate editor of the Anglo-Jewish publication *Reflex,* edited
by S. M. Melamed. By this time, too, Syrkin's feminist insistence on pursuing her own career inevitably led to a separation from Aaron Bodansky because of incompatibility.
However difficult the decision, she left Cornell and returned
to New York with her infant son, David. There she took up a
position as an English teacher at Textile High School in Man-
hattan. Despite the obvious problems of these years, her
separation and ultimately her divorce from Aaron Bodansky, along with unrelenting economic strain, Marie Syrkin
persevered in her single-handed efforts to maintain herself
and her child. She added to her meager teacher's salary by
doing translations from Yiddish and writing prose articles.
And she went on writing her own poetry despite her tedious
and detested teaching job.

Without doubt the mid-twenties marked the nadir of
Marie Syrkin's life, both personally and professionally. But
then, in 1927, she met the objectivist poet Charles Reznikoff,
whose poetry she had first come across at Cornell. They
married in 1930. Meanwhile her professional life began to
take a new turn as she became more involved in Zionist
activities. The 1930s (also her own thirties) were the real
beginning of a sustained and remarkable public career in
which she honed her poetic and polemical skills on an ada-
mant commitment to Jewish life. The more urgent the world
situation became, the more Marie grew intent upon doing
on-the-spot reporting. In 1933, during a sabbatical year, she
took the first of her many trips to Palestine. Later she was to
confess that on this trip, the romance of the Jewish pioneer
movement seemed more powerful than the news she heard
over the ship's radio about Hitler's edicts.[23]

When Marie Syrkin returned from her sojourn among the

Jewish settlers, her career took the signal turn that would propel her into an activist role as commentator, speech-maker, speechwriter for others, witness to great events, and firsthand reporter from the zone of conflict. While maintaining her job at Textile High School, she assumed a position on the editorial board of the newly established journal of the Labor Zionists, *The Jewish Frontier*. In this capacity she worked closely with the editor, Hayim Greenberg, with whom she had a deep professional and personal relationship. Like Emma Lazarus, Marie Syrkin had a penchant for the company of intelligent men. Indeed, Ben Halpern, her friend and colleague first at the *The Jewish Frontier* and later at Brandeis University, remarked that "Marie, of course, was accustomed from childhood to the delight that learned men, beginning with her father, took in the richness of their erudition."[24]

Later Syrkin herself became editor-in-chief of *The Jewish Frontier*, but in the early years under Greenberg's editorship she distinguished herself by writing firsthand reports from Palestine on the Arab disturbances, attacks on Jabotinsky and the Revisionists, and pieces on the pro-Nazi mufti (the leader of Palestinian Arabs), along with a stream of articles in praise of the *halutzim* and Youth Aliyah. Among her most prized achievements was her exposé of the Moscow show trials. At the suggestion of Hayim Greenberg she read through the six hundred pages of the Russian stenographic typescript of the trials. This resulted in a remarkable, full analysis that appeared in January 1937. She concluded that the defendants' confessions were false and that the trials were Stalin's method of liquidating dissent. Today the conclusion does not seem so remarkable, but the writer's insistence that "no service is done to socialism or to Soviet Russia by refusing to face what one conceives to be the truth" was not accepted so easily by the Left at that time.[25]

During the forties, Marie Syrkin continued to write articles in favor of the partition of Mandate Palestine, and a stream of essays and poetry as well, pressing for the opening of the gates of Palestine, and demanding liberalization of immigration quotas; she also wrote speeches for Chaim Weizmann and articles and speeches for Golda Meir, all the while holding down her own teaching job. As unpleasant as that job may have been, it gave her material not only for poetry, but also for her widely acclaimed book *Your School, Your Children*,[26] a vanguard analysis of the American public school system. She wrote in addition a number of essays on democracy and the schools in *Common Ground,* the official organ of the Common Council for American Unity. But perhaps the most celebrated episode in her journalistic career occurred in 1942, when the State Department received a cable from the Geneva representative of the World Jewish Congress to be forwarded to Rabbi Stephen Wise, president of the American Jewish Congress. The message contained the truth about Hitler's plan to annihilate European Jewry. At a small private meeting of Jewish journalists that Syrkin and Greenberg were invited to attend in August 1942, they learned of the horrifying report from Geneva that mass extermination was already underway. The next issue (November) of *The Jewish Frontier* appeared with black borders and contained an editorial by Syrkin that was the very first American report of the systematic annihilation that was already in process.

When the war was over, Marie took the first available ship to the Middle East in 1945 to gather material for her pioneering book on the Jewish Resistance, *Blessed Is the Match*.[27] It was the first of the eyewitness accounts, and it included a personal interview with the mother of Hannah Senesh, and Marie's own well-known translation of Senesh's poem *"Ashrei Hagafrur"* ("Blessed Is the Match"). During 1946 Marie Syrkin had her own personal adventure with underground activity when she was recruited to give the first English-language broadcast over the secret radio of Kol Yisrael (the Voice of Israel). In 1947 she went to work in the displaced persons camps in the American Zone in Germany to find suitable candidates for Hillel Scholarships to American universities. She characterized this task as "heartbreaking," because she could choose no more than fifty from the entire American Zone. This endeavor was followed by a return trip to Israel in 1948, just after the siege of Jerusalem. Syrkin's fears for the fate of the new nation had been expressed in a poem simply entitled "Israel: 1948," written in the wake of the Arab attack:

> Suppose, this time, Goliath should not fall;
> Suppose, this time, the sling should not avail;
> On the Judean plain where once for all
> Mankind the pebble struck; suppose the tale
> Should have a different end: the shepherd yield,
> The triumph pass to iron arm and thigh,
> The wonder vanish from the blooming field,
> The mailed hulk stand, and the sweet singer lie.
>
> Suppose, but then what grace will go unsung,
> What temple wall unbuilt, what gardens bare;
> What plowshare broken and what harp unstrung!
> Defeat will compass every heart aware
> How black the ramparts of a world wherein
> The psalm is stilled, and David does not win.[28]

One of Syrkin's primary tasks on this post-siege trip was to travel through the Galilee and other areas to draw up an official paper to be the basis of the Israel government's report to the United Nations about the continuing Arab exodus and about the accusation that the new government of Israel had destroyed mosques and other holy places. The conclusion she drew at this time, that the Arabs had responded to the direction of their leaders and that there had been no Jewish master plan to expel them, she held to for the rest of her life despite the later theories of revisionist historians.

At the age of fifty-one Marie Syrkin began a new career. Abram L. Sachar, now president of Brandeis University, invited her to join the faculty of the newly established school where, as professor of English Literature, she became the first female professor of an academic subject. While at Brandeis, Syrkin wrote a memoir of her father, Nachman Syrkin,

and a biography of her dear friend Golda Meir, whose fu-
neral she was to attend as an official delegate of the United
States at the request of President Carter. After Golda's death
she wrote the following tribute:

> For Golda
> Because you became a great woman
> With strong features
> Big nose
> And heavy legs,
> None will believe how beautiful you were,
> Grey eyed and slim ankled.
>
> The men who loved you are dead,
> So I speak for the record.
> Indeed you were lovely among maidens
> Once
> In Milwaukee and Merhavia,
> And sometimes in Jerusalem.[29]

Syrkin also took on in print such formidable adversaries
as Arnold Toynbee, Hannah Arendt, and I. F. Stone. She
wrote in praise of Nellie Sachs and in criticism of Philip
Roth. She introduced one of the first academic courses in
American Jewish fiction and one in the literature of the Holocaust. And all the while she continued to write her own
verse.

When she retired from Brandeis in 1966 as professor
emerita to return to New York to resume her life with
Charles Reznikoff, she assumed a desk at the Jewish Agency,
became editor of the Herzl Press, and was elected member
of the executive committee of the World Zionist Organization. After the death of her husband, she moved to Santa
Monica to be near her family. There she continued to write,
to lecture, to comment publicly on the current scene, to be
an active member of the editorial board of *Midstream,* and to
confound her critics on the Left by signing the first Peace
Now statement.

Syrkin's poetry is the least known of her writings; yet

some of her poems and translations have been included in major anthologies. In her eightieth year she published *Gleanings: A Diary in Verse,*[30] a volume of poetry that brings together all of the public aspects of her career, her commitment to Israel, her social commentary, and her devotion to literature, while it adds profoundly moving expressions of intimate emotions, private struggles, and personal sorrows. It is, moreover, testimony to the fact that the clash between a thinking woman's private life and public career is not a phenomenon of the current women's movement.

Syrkin died on Febrary 1, 1989, one month short of her ninetieth birthday. To the last she spoke out in that same "rhetoric of zeal" that was her hallmark. Indeed, in January of 1989, two weeks before she died, taking final stock of her lifelong work as a Labor Zionist and aware of the current tendency of some historiographers to debunk the accomplishments of Zionism, she said, "Something tremendous has been achieved." Yes, she recognized the present difficulties and failures of Labor Zionism, but she insisted in a still strong and contentious voice that "those who proclaim now that the 'myth' of Israel is dead are mistaken. It was no fable." She maintained that "Israel is an exemplar of what *can* be done. Even if it lasts only forty or fifty years, what that state achieved can never be erased because it shows the potential of idealism. It achieved something in the political structure of the world. The phrase 'next year in Jerusalem' became clothed in flesh as the vision became reality to a greater extent than one could have imagined." Not one, however, to gloss over even the most lamentable of facts, Marie admitted regret over the present state of affairs in which the Likud government of Yitzhak Shamir seemed entrenched; but she went on to explain that the adaptation of the dream to reality is "merely the price of survival." She sadly stated her regret over "the failure of Labor to increase its hold over the population—because of the errors of Labor and the megalomania of Likud—but still Israel has lived, it suffered, it flourished. It is not lost and there is no telling how history will unfold." By studying the record, she advised, "you will see that it was done with blood, sweat, and tears; the so-called 'myth' was created by people who did not participate."[31] She died before she could see her long-range optimism vindicated by the defeat of Likud and the Russian emigration and peace developments of the 1990's.

The essence of the rhetoric of zeal is found in the polarities that informed the lives of Emma Lazarus and Marie Syrkin: lofty ideals side by side with common-sense programs; vision come to terms with reality; passion and compassion; self-deprecation and self-assurance; and feminism without the politics of sex. And each of these American women, Lazarus, Syrkin, and Ozick, whose great gifts might have brought broad acclaim in a larger arena, discovered her true self through a life of passionate commitment in defense of the Jews and total dedication to her people's welfare.

NOTES

1. Cynthia Ozick, *Art and Ardor* (New York, 1983), ix.

2. Cynthia Ozick has virtually acknowledged this lineage in a personal letter to the author, August 31, 1990. where she writes that Marie [Syrkin] is one of her heroines: "a great model to aspire to, though never to reach"; and see Sarah Blacher Cohen's essay on Ozick in this volume.

3. In 1881 Lazarus wrote a sonnet "Progress and Poverty," inspired by Henry George's book by that name; she spent a day with the socialist-craftsman humanitarian William Morris at his workshop in 1883, and in her essay, "The Jewish Problem," *The Century* (February 1883), she wrote, "The modern theory of socialism and humanitarianism erroneously traced to the New Testament has its root in the Mosaic Code."

4. *The Poems of Emma Lazarus,* ed. Josephine Lazarus, 2 vols. (Boston, 1889), 1:3. "The New Colossus" is found in *Poems* 1:202–3.

5. The rejection of "paganism" also became a major theme for Lazarus's literary "granddaughter," Cynthia Ozick, whose fascination with the theme of Hebraism versus Hellenism was first announced in print in "America: Toward Yavneh," *Judaism* (Summer 1970), 264–82, and later embodied in the title of her short story "The Pagan Rabbi."

6. *The Letters of Emma Lazarus, 1868–1885,* ed. Morris U. Schappes (New York, 1949), 333.

7. *Letters to Emma Lazarus in the Columbia University Library,* ed. Ralph L. Rusk (New York, 1939), 30.

8. Ozick, "America: Toward Yavneh," 272.

9. Reprinted in *Emma Lazarus: Selections from Her Poetry and Prose,* ed. Morris U. Schappes (New York, 1944), 60.

10. Madame Z. Ragozin, "Russian Jews and Gentiles," *Century Magazine* 23 (1882), 919.

11. Analogous essays by Marie Syrkin and Cynthia Ozick include Marie Syrkin's rigorously argumentative "Who Are The Palestinians?" *Midstream* (January 1970), and Ozick's uncompromisingly tough "All the World Wants the Jews Dead," *Esquire* (1974).

12. Schappes, *Selections,* 69.

13. Thomas Kranidas, "Milton and the Rhetoric of Zeal," *Texas Studies in Language and Literature* 6 (1965), 423–32.

14. The first seven lines of Lazarus's poem "Echoes," *Poems,* 1:201, adumbrate the ideas in "The New Colossus":

> Late-born and woman-souled I dare not hope,
> The freshness of the elder lays, the might
> Of manly, modern passion shall alight
> Upon my Muse's lips, nor may I cope
> (Who veiled and screened by womanhood must grope)
> With the world's strong armed warriors and recite
> The dangers, wounds, and triumphs of the fight.

15. Prospectus for the fourteen essays under the general title "An Epistle to the Hebrews," *American Hebrew* (November 3, 1882).

16. Twelve unpublished letters from Emma Lazarus to E. R. A. Seligman held in the Columbia University Library.

17. Carole S. Kessner, "The Emma Lazarus—Henry James Connection: Eight Letters," *American Literary History* 3:1 (Spring 1991), 46–62.

18. As she wrote in "Epistle to the Hebrews," Schappes, *Selections,* 82: "For the most ardent supporter of the scheme does not urge the advisability of an emigration *en masse* of the whole Jewish people to any particular spot. There is not the slightest necessity for an American Jew, the free citizen of a republic, to rest his hopes upon the foundation of any other nationality soever, or to decide whether he individually would or would not be in favor of residing in Palestine."

19. Marie Syrkin, "Memorial for a Child," *Gleanings: A Diary in Verse* (Santa Barbara, Calif., 1979), 94–95.

20. Interview with Marie Syrkin, January 1989.

21. As Martin Peretz wrote of Syrkin's literary abilities and choices, *Jewish Frontier: Special Tribute Issue to Marie Syrkin* (January/February 1983), 9, "To be sure, had Marie Syrkin been less affected by the traumas and less committed to the aspirations of Jewry, her talents as a writer would have put her at the pinnacle of the literary elite, admired by the *goyim* no less than by the Jews, and in that case, more than admired by the Jews. I doubt, however, that she regrets the marginality which con-

viction and circumstance seem to have destined for her. In life and letters, after all, she has lived the modernist revolution."

22. Marie Syrkin, "The New Youth Movement," *The New Palestine* (August 14, 1925), 140.

23. Marie Syrkin, *The State of the Jews* (Washington, D.C., 1980), 3.

24. Ben Halpern, "Marie," *Jewish Frontier* (January/February 1983), 9.

25. *Jewish Frontier* (May 1937; repr. January/February 1983), 27.

26. Marie Syrkin, *Your School, Your Children* (New York, 1944).

27. Marie Syrkin, *Blessed Is the Match* (Philadelphia, 1947).

28. Syrkin, *Gleanings,* 70.

29. Marie Syrkin, "For Golda," *Jewish Frontier: Fiftieth Anniversary Issue* (November/December 1984), 13.

30. Syrkin, *Gleanings,* 1979.

31. Interview with Marie Syrkin, January 1989.

11 ◆ NAOMI B. SOKOLOFF

Expressing and Repressing the Female Voice in
S. Y. Agnon's In the Prime of Her Life

While the last fifteen years have witnessed an upsurge of interest in feminist critical thought and literary interpretation, few attempts have been made to explore the implications of gender as a thematic concern in modern Hebrew texts.[1] Yet Hebrew warrants special feminist examination because of its exceptional history as a holy tongue that for many centuries was studied almost exclusively by men. It was only the major cultural upheavals and transformations of the Jewish Enlightenment and Zionism—sources, as well, of the Hebrew linguistic and literary renaissance of the last two centuries—that led to significant changes in women's social and intellectual roles. The inevitable tensions between a male-dominated tradition and modern cultural change have left their mark on literary representations of women in Hebrew writing by men, even as they have fostered a singular set of obstacles and stimuli for the creation of a female literary tradition in modern Hebrew literature. In light of these considerations, *In the Prime of Her Life* (*Bidmi yameha,* 1923) invites a feminist rereading, since this novella by Shmuel Yosef Agnon, Nobel Prize winner and preeminent Hebrew novelist of the first half of the twentieth century, is centrally concerned with the sounding and silencing of female voice.

Much of the feminist critical agenda has aimed at documenting ways in which female figures have been represented by men, as well as ways in which women have spoken back, representing themselves through their own vocal self-assertion.[2] Agnon's novella, which features a female narrator, a young woman who marries her mother's former suitor and recounts her life story in the form of a written memoir, raises questions of interest for both modes of reading. Consequently, even as *In the Prime of Her Life* represents women through the filter of male perceptions, the text poses as a woman's account of her own experience and so calls attention directly to women's expression and language.

In this fiction such issues develop explicitly through insistent treatment of tensions between suppressed and emergent voices. Though critical appraisals have been curiously silent on this matter, Agnon in effect structures the entire novella around a series of verbal exchanges and keen thematic attention to talk. Virtually every paragraph centers on obtrusive reference to or citation of conversations, interior monologues, and varieties of written messages. In this way the text endorses the primacy of linguistic acts as plot actions that regulate matters of will, power, and social relations. It is noteworthy, too, that the representations of language, like the social conflicts they imply or convey, are marked by sexual difference. Just as men and women behave differently, so they express themselves differently, and their uses of words illuminate contrasting privileges and predicaments. The novella in this way highlights the protagonist's attempt to make herself heard by stating her convictions and expressing her own desires. This is not to say that the text necessarily applauds her efforts. At times it clearly decries them. Agnon himself was by no means a feminist nor an advocate of women's liberation, and he sometimes casts his character in a distinctly unflattering light. The narrative nevertheless maintains an intense scrutiny of women's voices, and for this reason feminist theory may provide a productive critical framework for examining *In the Prime of Her Life,* illuminating aspects of the text that have been overlooked, underestimated, or marginalized by critics.

From the start, *In the Prime of Her Life* concentrates on the silence of a female character, Tirza's ailing mother, Leah. In the process the text associates subdued voice with death and confinement. Describing the period of Leah's declining health, the opening paragraph relates: "Our house stood hushed [*dumam*] in its sorrow and its doors did not open to a stranger"(167).[3] The next paragraph reiterates and augments this introductory announcement: "The winter my mother died our home fell silent [*damam*] seven times over." Both passages play on the Hebrew root *d-m-m,* recalling the sounds of the title and the first sentence of the novella: "In the prime of her life [*bidmi yameha*] my mother died." *Demi,* "silence," functions in this last phrase to signify "in the prime" of her days. Submerged within it, too, heightening its ironic nuances, is reference to blood (*dam*). These lines thereby connect silence with the snuffing out of vitality in a young woman who died too soon. Subsequently the narrative illustrates the cruelty of Leah's fate by relating another image of suppressed language: letters Mother received from her true love, Akaviah Mazal, have been kept under lock and key for years. She opens them, it is recounted, only to destroy them, burning them in a room whose windows are locked tight. In this stifling setting of enclosure and repression, smoke rises in an allusion to the sacrifice of Leah's true desires.

After her death, Father's arrangements for the inscription on Leah's tombstone reconfirm the entire pattern of her life as silenced and suppressed desire. To understand this episode we should remember the feminist claim that patriarchal culture has often defined woman according to its needs rather than hers; it has also frequently represented females as passive beings unable to produce their own meanings. In this way, as Susan Gubar argues, men have attempted to create woman through masculine discourse, and women, serving as secondary objects in someone else's scheme of things, have been perceived as blank pages on which to write and be written.[4] In Agnon's story, these descriptions are apt; men have been writing the script for Leah all her life. Not allowed to sound her wishes, she has been denied intentionality. Most importantly, her father marries her to the wrong man, one who is better off financially and considered more socially desirable than the suitor she herself prefers. As a result she dies at an early age, her heart physically and metaphorically weakened because deprived of love. Through the incident of the tombstone Agnon creates a startling, culminating illustration of this phenomenon. The woman, her spirit extinguished, has been transformed into an object, her identity reduced to a name carved in stone. It is pointed out, moreover, that her husband thinks more about her epitaph than about her. Though he is genuinely and deeply aggrieved at the loss of his wife, in choosing the lettering for the grave he "all but forgot" (172) the woman. The writing, his defining of her, eases his pain. To Mintz's credit he does reject a highly formulaic epitaph, one which Mr. Gottlieb has prepared, in favor of one more meaningful. The first inscription is very clever; it is based on an acrostic of Leah's name that also incorporates the year of her death into every line of the poem, but there is nothing personal in it. Recognizing this shortcoming, the husband opts for something more authentic. He goes to Mazal, the former beau and author of those now burnt love letters, to commission a second inscription. Though it is finally too late, and though he acts only through an intermediary who is a man, Mintz makes at least some concession toward acknowledging his wife's suppressed desires and inner life: her ardent feelings for Mazal.[5]

Tirza, the daughter, who is at once the narrator and the primary focus of the narrative, establishes her own significance in opposition to these actions on the part of the men.

Her initial introduction of herself, for example, in the first paragraphs of the story, serves as a celebration of her mother's voice: "Lying on her bed my mother's words were few. But when she spoke it was as though limpid wings spread forth and led me to the Hall of Blessing. How I loved her voice. Often I opened her door to have her ask, who is there?" (167). While the rest of the paragraph insists on suffocation and enclosure, rendering the mother's thoughts inaudible, Tirza here emphasizes aperture (the outspread wings and the open door) along with sound, self-assertion, listening, and response. These emphases evolve into question about Tirza's identity ("Who is there?") and so constitute an affirmation of her own presence.

Tensions between the suppression and emergence of female voice develop further as the plot unfolds into a story of the daughter's search for independence. Tirza sets her heart on marrying Akaviah Mazal, falls ill in a kind of duplication or reenactment of her mother's final illness, and, surviving this, convinces her father that she and Mazal should be wed. The assertion of her desires, as a recuperation of her mother's lost life, progresses through any number of verbal encounters that disclose identifiably distinctive masculine and feminine aspects. When, for example, Mrs. Gottlieb invites Tirza to spend the summer at her home, the narrator recounts: "My father readily agreed, saying 'Go now.' But I answered, 'How will I go alone?' and he said, 'I will come and visit.' Kaila stood dusting by the mirror and she winked at me as she overheard my father's words. I saw her move her lips and grimace in the mirror, and I laughed to myself. Noticing how my face lit up with cheer my father said, 'I knew you would heed my words,' and he left the room" (175).

This passage could be a textbook illustration of sociolinguistic observations on female verbal behavior. Women, because of the more vulnerable status they occupy in many societies, often tend to avoid language that threatens or endangers the stability of relationships. Consequently, they rely heavily on a range of politeness strategies meant to deflect attack and help maintain interpersonal equilibrium.

These include attentiveness, approval, flattery or indirectness, the use of honorifics, appeals to a higher law, generalizations, and excuses of exigence.[6] In the passage cited, Tirza, too, is deferential because of her subordinate position. Accordingly, she restricts her comments to a question. Despite her unhappiness about the plans for the summer, she leaves the father's decision open and does not impose her own mind or views on him. The housekeeper likewise avoids straightforward declaratives. Trying to convince Tirza to agree with her father and respect his desires, Kaila expresses herself only by indirections and distortions. Tirza, aware of the preposterous incongruity of her servant's actions, laughs with amusement at the linguistic inequity prevailing in this exchange. Only fourteen, she does not yet take her own powerlessness quite seriously. She remarks innocently in the next paragraph: "Kaila, God be with you, speak up, don't remain silent, please stop torturing me with all your hints and riddles." For this she is reprimanded and reminded of the gravity of the situation: this trip is for the father's well-being, not hers, and would she but look at him closely she would realize that he is lonely and needs the opportunity to visit the Gottliebs in the country. In short, Kaila first acts on the conviction that she mustn't express herself directly, and then, when pressed, conveys this same message more overtly to Tirza. The girl's personal desires must remain unspoken. As a result of all the indirectness, Mintz for his part misreads Tirza entirely. "I knew you would heed my words (*lishmoa' bekoli*)," he says, thus reinscribing her back into his code of understanding. Using an expression typical of biblical discussions on obedience to God, he reinforces his patriarchal authority and reconfirms his failure to appreciate the inner thoughts of the women in his life.[7]

Other incidents as well contrast the discourse of men and women, demonstrating an imbalance of power between them. For instance, the matchmaker who comes to visit talks at great length, making tiresome chitchat and keeping Tirza a captive but courteous audience (193). Tirza's father, for his part, unselfconsciously exercises strategies to dominate conversations. Not only does he direct talk to his own preferred topics (generally, his personal misfortune due to Leah's death); he also extends his own words to encompass everyone: "We are the miserable widowers," he laments, and Tirza comments, "How strange were his words. It was as though all womankind had died and every man was a widower" (186).

In addition to these scenes in which Agnon neatly contrasts masculine communicative prerogatives with the women characters' cautions and insecurities about speaking, on other occasions male characters explicitly impute negative qualities to or give misogynistic interpretations of female speech. In an embedded tale recounting Mazal's past, Leah's father is quoted as chiding his wife for engaging in "woman's talk"—that is, talk he deems to be idle and impious (19). A comparably condemnatory comment surfaces when the doctor comes to visit the Mintz family after Mother's death. Remarking that the daughter has grown and that she has on a new dress, he asks if she knows how to sew. Tirza responds with a maxim, "Let another man praise thee, and not thine own mouth" (174). Restricting herself to a nonassertive stance, this character offers a formulaic reassurance of the male interlocutor's initiative in conversation. All the same he responds by saying, "A bold girl and looking for compliments." What the man takes as an act of boldness is more properly an evasion of confrontation and a highly reticent hint at a topic the daughter is actually eager for others to acknowledge: her budding sexuality, her own growing up which has been overlooked because everyone is preoccupied with mourning. This incident, like the scolding Leah's father gives his wife, underscores attention in the text to the characters' stereotypic notions of women's speech and to a conviction that female expression should remain sharply circumscribed.

In a pivotal scene concerned with these issues, Tirza at first submits to the discourse of men characters. Quelling her own impulses, she molds her expression to conform to their expectations. However, the episode quickly becomes a turning point, a moment of rupture in which she attempts to emancipate herself from male-dominated patterns of verbal interaction. This happens when Mintshi Gottleib, her hostess, discloses that Akaviah and Leah were once in love. Tirza, struck by melancholy and confusion, is then approached by Mintshi's husband, and the following exchange ensues: "'Look, our friend is boring a hole through the heavens,' Mr. Gottlieb said laughing as he saw me staring up at the sky. And I laughed along with him with a pained heart" (77). Afterwards, although she has humored him, Tirza remains deeply troubled by Mrs. Gottlieb's revelations about the past and she cannot let the matter rest: "Night after night I lay on my bed, asking myself, 'What would now be if my mother had married Mazal? And what would have become of me?' I knew such speculations to be fruitless, yet I did not abandon them. When the shudders which accompanied my musings finally ceased, I said: Mazal has been wronged. He seemed to me to be like a man bereft of his wife yet she is not his wife" (177). Shortly after that her ruminations resume:

> How I loathed myself. I burned with shame and did not know why. Now I pitied my father and now I secretly grew angry at him. And I turned my wrath upon Mazal also. . . . Sometimes I told myself: Why did Mintshi Gottlieb upset me by telling me of bygone memories? A father and mother, are they not man and woman and of one flesh? Why then should I brood over secrets which occurred before my time? Yet I thirsted to know more. I could not calm down, nor could I sit still for a moment's quiet. And so I told myself, if Mintshi knows what happened surely she will tell me the truth. How though will I open my mouth to ask? For if I but let the thoughts come to mind my face turns crimson let alone when I speak out my thoughts aloud. I then gave up all hope. More I could not know. (178)

Tirza's lengthy internal monologue offers an explicit meditation on her fears of speaking up. In its very length the

passage itself is an act of verbal self-assertion—a muffled
voicing of her anxieties, to be sure, but at least a way of
formulating and sounding her preoccupations in her own
mind. Here once more the character's remarks consist of
questions rather than declaratives or imperatives, but, in
contrast to her earlier silences and deferential reserve,
these questions are angry and searching. Language, moreover, serves specifically as a way of constituting a self. Probing her origins, Tirza asks overtly, who am I? and ponders
what she might have been had her mother married somebody else.

This character's progress toward self-expression is subsequently impeded but then also spurred on by her engagement, engineered by the matchmaker Gotteskind, with a
young man in whom she takes no interest. Recoiling at the
prospects of an arranged match, Tirza dreams that her father has married her off to an Indian chief and that her body
is "impressed with tattoos of kissing lips" (193). If, as feminist criticism has argued, the female predicament entails
the imposition of a male cultural script onto woman, a writing of her that determines her sexual life and social status,
in this passage we find a graphic image of a woman whose
destiny is being inscribed directly onto her body. The verbal
and sexual power so prominently featured in *In the Prime of
Her Life* as part of the male domain converge in this scene.
They are presented through a single dramatic symbol of
female disempowerment: the mouth, locus of both kisses
and speech, appears here as tattoo, sealing the young woman's dreaded fate of being married off by force to someone
entirely foreign and alien to her. This episode makes Tirza
all the more determined to have Akaviah Mazal, whom she
perceives as the true object of her desire.

As she pursues Akaviah and so expresses her own will,
Tirza again resorts to speech characterized by indirection
and generalization. She does so, though, with a new flare.
According to accepted protocol, she cannot easily speak
with her beloved. Mazal is not only older than she; he also
becomes her teacher when, turning sixteen, Tirza begins

attending a teachers seminary. With increasing daring she devises pretexts for making conversation with Akaviah. To reach him she pretends that a dog has bitten her hand, and so, under the guise of soliciting compassion and protective care, she dupes him into allowing her to reveal her erotic intent. (As many readers have noted, the dog in Agnon's texts is frequently an indicator of uncontrolled sexuality and also of madness, that is, of impulses threatening to the accepted limits of society.[8])

Tirza's most extreme declaration of desire occurs when societal constraints are further removed. During her illness, at the height of feverish delirium, she etches the name "Akaviah Mazal" many times into her mirror. She also writes Akaviah a letter, noting, "You shall dwell in my thoughts all day" (209). In both instances the young woman is trying to write him, to inscribe him, into her inner self or subsume his signature into the image of herself which she receives from the mirror. In this way Tirza attempts to reverse that early pattern, epitomized by the episode with the tombstone, in which the men inscribed Leah's name in their discourse. It is significant that she does this at a time when she is sick and suffering delusions. Literary equations of woman's rebellion with madness have been noted recurrently in feminist criticism. At times, too, feminist interpretations have considered this identification of aggression or self-assertion with insanity as an attempt to discredit female protest.[9] Tirza's temporary derangement conforms in part to such a pattern; her daring is a function of illness and irrationality. Agnon's text, however, is subtle in its judgment of her. The scene serves less as an attempt to trivialize Tirza's situation than as a sensitive acknowledgment of how profound are the disorders that plague the entire family and culminate in the events of the daughter's life. Yet, by contrast with those gravely disturbing matters, her efforts at self-expression do come to seem of diminished seriousness. What remains certain is that, opening a Pandora's box of emotional troubles, this character courts disaster. Something has gone fundamentally wrong in this home, and Tirza's sickness is highly overdetermined. Not only the occasion for speaking out, the fever is an expression of psychic dis-ease. Tirza invited a chill by wearing inappropriate attire (a summer dress in winter), and her illness then is instrumental in manipulating her father's (and perhaps Mazal's) sympathy. That this partially unwitting ploy is effective results from the susceptibility of the older generation to emotional blackmail as well as from their complicity, their willingness to arrange a new marriage to settle old scores. Each for his own reasons agrees to the match. Therefore, because of the complicated interpersonal context in which Tirza's development takes place, *In the Prime of Her Life* is only in part the story of a young woman's rebellion against social mores; beneath the surface there is another agenda, one in large measure pessimistic about the ability of a young woman to free herself of patriarchal imperatives.

Tirza's name has been understood as both "will" (*ratson,* from the Hebrew root *r-ts-h*) and "pretext" (*teruts,* from the root *t-r-ts*). A range of meanings delimited by these concepts underlies the events of her life and complicates the rather straightforward examples of incipient self-assertion brought forward in the first half of this essay. At issue, most crucially, is the protagonist's dangerous psychic involvement in the events of the past and in the unresolved tensions of her parents' youth. Her reliving of Mother's life turns out to be less a renewal than a repetition of mistakes, and in this light determination becomes a pretext for passivity and determinism. Agnon explores these matters by combining attention to mother/daughter relations—a central topic in current feminist criticism—with one of his own major thematic preoccupations: struggles between individual will and forces beyond the control of the individual, be those explained as destiny, divine intervention, or the workings of the unconscious.[10]

Many critics have claimed that Tirza's recreating of her mother's life enacts a variation on the familiar Agnon theme of the love triangle.[11] The young woman marries a father figure and continues to yearn for her father's company, even as Mazal marries the daughter instead of the mother he loved. Leah similarly married Mintz instead of her beloved, and Mintshi, enamored of Mazal, married Gottlieb and buried herself in ceaseless activity. Each case creates a threesome that interferes with the attainment of intimacy or displaces love from one object of passion to a dissatisfying substitute. What has not been sufficiently recognized and stated, though, is the degree to which Tirza's problems are those of an adolescent, specifically a female who must deal with the death of her mother, and the connection between these issues and that of emergent voice.

Adolescence is a time of gradually letting go, of loosening bonds with parents in preparation for making choices of all sorts, but most importantly erotic. As Katherine Dalsimer notes, this withdrawal from parents accounts for the unique place this stage of life occupies in psychoanalytic writing.[12] Deemed at once to be a time of possibility and aperture, it is also an age of pain. Because tensions present since earliest childhood are reactivated in adolescence, this is a moment of awakening that permits new resolution to old conflicts. At the same time, pulling away from parents is felt subjectively by youngsters as a profound loss or emptiness not unlike mourning. The actual death of a parent, occurring at this juncture, inevitably heightens that inner loss experienced in the normal course of growing up. It can also influence the reworking of psychic conflicts essential for the young person to attain new maturity. If all deaths are greeted by the living with some degree of denial, the impulse to disbelieve the finality of the loss proves that much more intractable for children or teenagers.[13] Unchallenged, unmodified by day-to-day experience, such wishful fantasy may prove even more difficult to abandon and may result in further magnified esteem for the lost figure.

Tirza's life is decisively affected by just such a turn of events. Matters are complicated further, because she is female. The field of psychoanalysis has increasingly recognized the enduring nature of a daughter's relation to her mother.[14] In adolescence there is heightened need for mother as the individual who provided crucial primary intimacy, and much as was true in the earliest days of childhood, the daughter often looks to her mother as a mirror through whose approval and disapproval she can recognize, define, validate, delimit, and forge herself. Tirza Mintz moves toward maturity with difficulty, for in her case the pull to identify with the mother is at once unhealthily strong and also exacerbated by Leah's death. Tirza's father, for his part, cannot compensate for the mother's absence. He is singularly unable to provide his daughter the mirroring she needs because he is deeply self-absorbed, preoccupied always with his mourning and his business dealings. Not only does he misread his daughter, as in the passage examined earlier; in addition he overlooks her awareness of her own emerging womanliness. When, for instance, concerned with her appearance, she puts on festive new clothes, his reaction of surprise leads her to feel deeply guilty; though the mourning period has passed, she comes to perceive her attentions to herself as a failure of devotion to Leah. As she moves one step toward embracing life, he encourages her to prolong mourning for her mother. Tirza notes explicitly: "In my grief I said, my father has forgotten me, he has forgotten my existence" (170). This passage alludes neatly to the two kinds of grief the reader can identify in Tirza's adolescent experience: she suffers a natural loss of intimacy, a withdrawal between parents and children, but this is a blow intensified many times over by the physical death of the mother. Both are made worse by the father's self-centered reactions.

It is in this context that Tirza tries to realize the fantasy of reenacting and revising her mother's life; she wishes to redress the (perceived) wrong done Mazal, even as she would like to reverse her mother's romantic disappointment, and so she tries to make the crooked straight (that is, *letaretz*— "to straighten"—a word that again recovers the sound of the protagonist's name). She attempts, too, to preserve a memory, to deny Leah's absence, and to find validation of herself as a woman. The implication raised by this set of circumstances is that, though Tirza believes she is pining away for love of Mazal, in effect and at a deeper level she attempts to hold onto childhood and maternal intimacy. That highly important psychic business of adolescence, the need to develop autonomy, is retarded and distorted by confusion of her own identity with that of her mother. The tragedy of this excessive attachment is then compounded by the incestuous quality inherent in the solution Tirza seeks out: her marriage to Mazal. Altogether, Tirza's adolescence, far from an emancipation, has become a subjugation to the parents' past and to her continuing need to imitate her mother. In a chilling scene Tirza, now pregnant, foresees for herself an early death parallel to Leah's. Part of this fantasy, moreover, is that she prays for a daughter—to take care of Mazal. This eventuality would result yet again in a displacement onto another of the maternal role; her wish hints that Tirza wants less to be a mother than to implore someone else to do some mothering.

The full extent of the protagonist's tragedy becomes apparent, like many other developments in the narrative, through the treatment of dialogue, talk, and matters of voice. For example, one of the first signs that Tirza has made a serious mistake in pursuing Mazal occurs early on in their courtship. She feels attracted to him precisely because she expects she can confide in him. Overcome with ennui at the seminary she notes, "I saw there wasn't a person to whom I could pour out my heart; and I then said, I will speak to Mazal." Her projected scenario does not materialize. Welcoming her into his house, Akaviah latches onto her as a listener and, telling her his life story, doesn't allow her to get a word in edgewise. Tirza, instead of speaking up, is drawn into his discourse. It is the long ago that remains dominant here, and not Tirza's newly emergent young life. It is significant that Mazal's monologue is presented as a long interpolated sequence in the novella; the very status of his speech as embedded narrative indicates that it is essentially extrinsic to Tirza's story, yet absorbs her attention and displaces the novella's focus from her present onto the past.

Subsequently, in another scene that relies on pointed reference to voice, Tirza's description of her illness testifies to the increasing intensity of her problems. She has come more and more to resemble her mother. The text observes, "My heart beat feebly and my voice was like my mother's voice at the time of her illness" (211). A similar remark appears, too, when her marriage fails to bring her the happiness she had expected. Pregnancy precipitates a crisis of depression that confirms and clarifies the nature of Tirza's discontent. She has not progressed to a mature autonomy, and when her father brings presents for the new baby, the mother-to-be speaks as if she were herself the child: "'Thank you, grandfather,' I said in a child's piping voice."

This scene also makes strikingly clear that forces operating in Tirza's life invalidate, alter, or bring additional layers of meaning to her vocal self-assertions. Noting, "The child within me grows from day to day" (215), the text here recalls the first description of Tirza listening to her mother's voice, which stated "I was still a child." Though the young woman is not aware of it, the reference to the child within may include Tirza as much as her offspring. Here, as throughout the narrative, what is said aloud is quite different from what the characters mean. If at first woman's speech is indirect, a kind of deferential duplicity determined by relations of power and powerlessness, later on words also function in another way to both conceal and reveal. They contain hidden significations, and Tirza at times unknowingly discloses deep motivations she herself would not recognize.[15] For such reasons voice cannot in any simple sense be synonymous with will. While Tirza's early attempts to make herself heard were intended to help her wield some power, it becomes clear in the course of the text that her unconscious desires, deeply powerful ones, exceed and elude the goals she has defined and willed for herself.[16] Nor does the birth of her child signal joy; her final melancholy is one more manifestation of the crooked that cannot be made straight.

At the end of *In the Prime of Her Life* the question of voice reasserts itself, complicated by such matters. Tirza seeks out a new kind of expression by composing a memoir. This fact has several implications. On a simple dramatic level, the effort to chronicle is plausibly motivated by Tirza's adolescence. Given the enlarged self-preoccupations typical of teenagers, keeping a diary is a natural activity for this time of life.[17] In Tirza's case such writing is a more formal attempt at the task begun earlier in the story: to constitute a self through language, to puzzle over her life and ask, who am I? (For Tirza this self-definition is crucial if she is not to subsume her identity totally within that of someone else.) That she is a female brings additional meaning to this act. She is, after all, a figure who has sought and is still seeking to assert her own voice in a society which discourages outspokenness by women. She turns, significantly, to the form of writing often favored by women: the diary or memoir not intended for publication but meant to provide an outlet for emotion and a forum for self-expression. Her purposes of self-definition and self-expression are stymied, though, because she finds herself unhappily trapped in a situation much larger than her own imagined script of events. Since other powerful forces are at play, and since even her public speaking up has led her to an all-encompassing, seemingly preordained pattern of relations, writing serves as a last resort, a way for her to seek solace and not as a way for her to arrive at an unambiguous enunciation of identity. As her persistent unhappiness and continuing restlessness lead her to one last act of speaking out, she brings the uncertainties of her stance to the fore in her closing comments: "Sometimes I would ask myself to what purpose have I written my memories, what new things have I seen and what do I wish to leave behind? Then I would say, it is to find rest in my writing, so did I write all that is written in this book" (216). Caught between the new and the old, she is left still searching for a context for her own voice, establishing it— only ambiguously—in a private realm of writing.

Yet Agnon's purposes extend beyond Tirza's private female predicaments to his concern with larger collective is-

sues. Throughout the history of Hebrew writing, female figures have often served to symbolize an entire reality or the
Jewish people as a whole—from the desolate widow of Lamentations, to the personification of Zion as beloved in medieval poetry, to A. B. Yehoshua's contemporary psychohis-
tories of Zionism. While Agnon deals in depth with Tirza's
personal tale specifically as a woman's experience, he also
uses her to alert readers to a series of questions, both historical and linguistic, connected with national rebirth. Tirza
lives in an East European shtetl at the turn of the century.
From an enlightened family, she receives a Hebrew education that is unusual for a girl of this time. As Agnon, at
various junctures in the novella, brings out the theme of
Enlightenment and transformations of tradition, there
emerges a parallel between his protagonist's individual efforts to revive the past and the communal effort to create a
Jewish cultural renaissance and to forge a rebirth of the
Hebrew language. Tirza's psychological dilemmas—especially her struggle for a context in which to make her own
voice heard—parallel the struggle of the Hebrew language
to achieve a new audience and new vitality. In addition,
attention to Tirza's Hebrew schooling makes for a specific
dramatic situation, in this sociohistorical milieu, that turns
questions about women's social roles into an integral part of
the collective issues treated here. It is a novelty for a woman
to have the opportunities Tirza has—to study and to insist
on her own wishes in rebellion against her father's plans for
her marriage. Her audacity becomes possible in a climate
that has begun to encourage human beings to shape their
own future. Within that context, where the question of individual freedom looms so large, Agnon examines the possibility of freedom for a woman whose expected lot in life is
very different from that of the men around her.[18]

Two major thematic concerns thus coincide and enrich
one another in *In the Prime of Her Life*: the return of what has
been repressed, and the repression of female voice. The
past of the mother resurfaces even as the daughter's early
inclinations reemerge in adolescence with destructive force.

Agnon's use of a woman's struggle for emancipatory language, together with the portrayal of the female adolescent as partially emergent voice, effectively symbolizes and conveys the drives at once present and absent in these lives. Tirza takes remarkable initiatives, but they become enmeshed in cultural and historical circumstances that irrefutably oppose her willfulness.

In *In the Prime of Her Life* it is the past both personal and mythic that fatalistically overshadows the future, leaving Tirzah Mintz Mazal incapable of determining her own fate. Yet, while he does not champion her cause, Agnon does pay serious attention to female predicaments and grants them credence as a legitimate topic for literary art, bringing remarkable insight and what can only be described as a brilliant synthesis of themes, narrative strategies, and stylistic sensitivities to his representation of a woman's voice. While designed to serve his own artistic aims, the treatment of women's speech and silence in this narrative renders *In the Prime of Her Life* exceptionally responsive to feminist readings.

NOTES

This essay is an abridged and somewhat altered version of my "Narrative Ventriloquism and Muted Feminine Voice: Agnon's *In the Prime of Her Life*," *Prooftexts* 9 (1989), 115–37. I am grateful to the Johns Hopkins University Press for permission to print this new version of the essay here. Research for this study was supported by a National Endowment for the Humanities Travel to Collections Grant and by the University of Washington Graduate School Fund for Overseas Travel. Thanks go also to Janet Hadda, Yael Feldman, Esther Fuchs, and Judith Baskin for their reactions to drafts of this paper.

1. Several books examining feminist perspectives have been published recently in English, including Nehama Aschkenasy, *Eve's Journey: Feminine Images in Hebraic Literary Tradition* (Philadelphia, 1986); Esther Fuchs, *Israeli Mythogynies: Women in Contemporary Hebrew Fiction* (New York, 1987); and *Gender and Text in Modern Hebrew and Yiddish Literature*, ed. Naomi B. Sokoloff, Anne Lapidus Lerner, and Anita Norich (New York,

234 *Naomi B. Sokoloff*

1992). This last volume contains my annotated bibliography of feminist criticism and gender studies in the field of modern Hebrew literature.

2. Women's silences and the suppression of female voice, both as literary theme and as political dynamic in matters of canon formation, have been primary concerns of contemporary feminist theory. For an overview of such issues see, for example, Tillie Olsen, *Silences* (New York, 1978), Adrienne Rich, *On Lies, Secrets and Silence: Selected Prose 1966–1978* (New York, 1979), Elaine Showalter, "Toward a Feminist Poetics," and *idem*, "Feminist Criticism in the Wilderness," in *The New Feminist Criticism,* ed. Elaine Showalter (New York, 1985), 125–43 and 243–76.

3. Hebrew citations are drawn from *'Al kapot haman'ul* in *Kol sipurav shel Shmuel Yosef Agnon* (Jerusalem, 1975). Quotations in English come from the translation by Gabriel Levin in *Eight Great Hebrew Short Novels,* ed. Alan Lelchuk and Gershon Shaked (New York, 1983), 165–216.

4. Susan Gubar, "'The Blank Page' and the Issues of Female Creativity," in Showalter, *New Feminist Criticism,* 292–313.

5. Yizhak Akaviahu, "Craft of Engraving and the Craft of Creating" [Hebrew], *Yediot ahronot* (September 4, 1976), offers a problematic reading of Mintz's reaction to the tombstone as an illustration of the artistic personality while overlooking the specificity of this episode as a comment on relations between the sexes.

6. See, for example, Robin Lakoff, *Language and Woman's Place* (New York, 1975); Dale Spender, *Man Made Language* (London, 1980); and Sally McConnell-Ginet, Ruth Borker, and Nelly Furman, *Women and Language in Literature and Society* (New York, 1980).

7. Yosef Ewen, "The Dialogue in the Stories of S. Y. Agnon" [Hebrew], *Hasifrut* (1971), 281–94, discusses at length how dialogue throughout Agnon's work functions to indicate failed communication.

8. See especially Baruch Kurzweil, *Masot 'al sipurei agnon (Essays on Agnon's Stories)* (Jerusalem, 1975), 104–15, and, in response, Avraham Kariv, "And the Straight Shall Be Made Crooked" [Hebrew], *Moznayim* (January 1978): 83–95.

9. Sandra Gilbert and Susan Gubar, *The Madwoman in the Attic: The Woman Writer and the Nineteenth-Century Literary Imagination* (New Haven, Conn., 1979), offer lengthy exploration of connections between madness and rebellion in literary images of women. According to this account, the woman who refuses to be selfless, takes initiatives, or has a story to tell is perceived to be monstrous or insane.

10. On mother/daughter relations see *The Lost Tradition: Mothers and Daughters in Literature,* ed. Cathy N. Davidson and E. M. Broner (New York, 1980). On the role of individual will in Agnon's writing see Dan Miron, "Domesticating a Foreign Genre," *Prooftexts* 7 (1987), 1–28.

11. For discussion see Eli Shweid, "In Way of Return" [Hebrew], *Gazit* 3 (1960): 17–20; Yair Mazor, *Hadinamika shel motivim (The Dynamics of Motives in Some Works by S. Y. Agnon)* (Tel Aviv, 1970); and David Aberbach, *At the Handles of the Lock: Themes in the Fiction of S. Y. Agnon* (London, 1984).

12. Katherine Dalsimer, *Female Adolescence: Psychoanalytic Reflections on Literature* (New Haven, Conn., 1986).

13. Dalsimer, *Female Adolescence,* 124.

14. See Nancy Chodorow, *The Reproduction of Mothering: Psychoanalysis and the Sociology of Gender* (Berkeley, Calif., 1978), and Dorothy Dinnerstein, *The Mermaid and the Minotaur: Sexual Arrangements and Human Malaise* (New York, 1976).

15. On Tirza's confusion about her own motives and about those of Mintshi and Mintz, see Gideon Shunami, "Gap in Consciousness as a Key to the Story" [Hebrew], *'Al hamishmar* (September 22, 1972); and Arnold Band, "The Unreliable Narrator in *My Michael* and *In the Prime of Her Life*" [Hebrew], *Hasifrut* 3 (1971): 30–47.

16. For overviews of the feminist angle on these issues see, for instance, Toril Moi, *Sexual/Textual Politics* (London and New York, 1985); Alice Jardine, *Gynesis: Configurations of Woman and Modernity* (Ithaca, N.Y., and London, 1985); and Kaja Silverman, *The Subject of Semiotics* (New York and London, 1983).

17. Dalsimer, *Female Adolescence,* 20.

18. The extent to which the particularity of women's experience has been recognized as a valid literary topic is a central and knotty problem for much feminist criticism.

12 ✦ ANNE LAPIDUS LERNER

The Naked Land: Nature in the Poetry of Esther Raab

Writing about Emily Dickinson in 1956, the American literary critic John Crowe Ransom claimed: "But it is common belief among readers (among men readers at least) that the woman poet as a type . . . makes flight into nature rather too easily and upon errands which do not have metaphysical importance enough to justify so radical a strategy."[1] Ransom's allusion to the facile stereotyping of women poets as nature poets offers one approach to the poetry of Esther Raab (1894–1981) who is known as the poet who first and perhaps best incorporated the landscape of the land of Israel into modern Hebrew poetry. Unlike Dickinson or Elizabeth Barrett Browning, Raab was not compelled to challenge a stereotype that women's natural proclivity draws them to nature. Her emergence as a modern Hebrew poet in the absence of any tradition of women poets allowed her to mold her poetic idiom as she pleased, and she conveys an experience of nature that can be both direct and threatening.

Because Raab's parents were among the small group who established the agricultural settlement of Petah Tikvah, nature was not merely a setting for her experiences, but essential to them. She felt that the primal landscape, barren and wild, threatening but beautiful, had been engraved on her consciousness as surely as sand crabs are imprinted with their initial surroundings. Indeed, nearly eighty years later she describes walking in the sand outside her house as a small child, feeling alone in the vast space of that landscape, the fright of feeling as though she "were the first and only creature within the infinite."[2] This stark landscape was virtually the only one she knew until she spent time in Egypt and France in the early 1920s.

Unlike the overwhelming majority of her contemporaries, particularly those who arrived in the Second Aliyah, Raab was born into loving the land of Israel.[3] This quality of her poetry was recognized by Shimon Ginzburg, who, in 1936, pointed out that "she grasps the appearance of the landscape of the land of Israel differently from most [of our Hebrew] poets who come from foreign countries, with a natural and authentic perception, with no trimmings, with no false sentimentality."[4] In fact, Raab took great pride in her role, asserting, with full justification: " 'I discovered the landscape of the land of Israel. From my mother's womb I inhaled it, as I emerged into the air of the world.' "[5] She plays a vital role in introducing a realistic, rather than a sentimental, picture of the land into modern Hebrew poetry through the specificity of her imagery, incorporating into her poems a wide range of plants and trees, flowers and thorns, as well as other natural referents such as the sea and the sky. Dan Miron asserts that "her affinity to the landscape was strongly emotional, but that to the emotion was joined in her case a strong sensual closeness, which mandated taking hold of physical details, an almost tactile recounting of rough or smooth textures, of bubbles of hot air and of odors which take shape and become concrete objects."[6] The breadth of her knowledge of the natural world is unsurpassed in Israeli poetry and gives her a distinctive poetic voice.[7]

Frequent references in her poetry to the eucalyptus, including the one that was the focal element in front of her home in Petah Tikvah, are illustrative of her use of natural themes.[8] Eucalyptus trees, which had been transported from their native Australia to Palestine in the mid-nineteenth century in the hope that they would help dry the malaria-infested swamps, were for Raab a focus of sight, smell, and sound. The allusions to eucalyptus trees in *A Garden Destroyed,* Raab's collection of autobiographical stories and sketches, and in *Qimshonim (Thorns)*, her first volume of poetry,[9] are but one indication of the preeminent position that these trees held in her life. They are fundamental in defining the speaker's relationship to father and lover, to the past, and ultimately to self.

References to the natural world are common in Raab's early poetry, appearing in all the anticipated contexts, as well as in some that take the reader by surprise, like her drawings accompanying the text. Thus, for example, the abundance of nature images in poems thematically tied to the landscape is in no way remarkable; their transformation into harbingers of pulsating sexuality in others is more original. The scene that Raab sets, particularly in her early poems, is often her childhood in Petah Tikvah or a broader canvas drawn from the same period.[10] Some of her poems seem to have as their major theme the celebration of that very landscape. An example is "My Heart Is with Your Dews, Homeland" (1923).[11] This poem rejoices in a wide variety of growing things and the way they meld. But while this paean to nature has universal implications, its details are quite specific. The opening line of this untitled poem addresses the land of Israel directly with the word "homeland." The only other appearance of the word in *Qimshonim* is in "Homeland Poems" as an additional title of the book.[12] That in itself is, paradoxically, an indication of her feeling for the land. While other Hebrew writers often felt pulled between two homelands, their birthplace and the land of Israel, Raab had no such conflict. Luz cites this poem as an example when he writes that Raab's poetry, unlike the poetry of those who immigrated to Israel, was not a love poem to the land, but a poem from within the land, with all its harshness:[13]

לִבִּי עִם טְלָלַיִךְ, מוֹלֶדֶת
בַּלַּיְלָה עַל שְׂדוֹת חֲרֻלִים,
וּלְרֵיחוֹת בְּרוֹשִׁים וְקִמּוֹשׁ לַח
כָּנָף חֲבוּיָה אֲנִי אֶפְרֹשׂ.
עֲרִיסוֹת־חוֹל רַכּוֹת דְּרָכַיִךְ
בֵּין גְּדֵרוֹת הַשִּׁטָּה שְׁטוּחוֹת,
כְּעַל פְּנֵי מֶשִׁי צַח
לְעוֹלָם בָּם אָנוּעַ
אֲחוּזַת קֶסֶם לֹא־נִפְתָּר,
וּרְקִיעִים שְׁקוּפִים רוֹחֲשִׁים
עַל מַחְשַׁכֵּי יָם עֵצִים שֶׁקָּפָא.

My heart is with your dews, homeland,
At night, above fields of nettles
And to the scent of cypresses and wet thistle
A hidden wing shall I spread out.
Soft sand-cradles are your roads
Spread out between fences of acacias,
As though across pure silk
Forever shall I move on them
Gripped by an unresolved spell,
And transparent skies whisper
Over the darkness of a frozen sea of trees.[14]

What gives this poem its distinct voice are the details of this place in this season. The critic Shifrah reminds readers that Raab's references can be understood only in the context of the particular Near Eastern climate from which they were written, in which summer is more a time of death than of ripening.[15] Even before the apostrophe to "homeland," the narrating voice indicates that her heart is with the dew, which is the sole source of water during the summer months. As she continues, involving all the senses except taste, she moves from the field of nettles, distinct to the touch, to the scent of the cypresses and the moist thistle.[16]

The roads, or paths, feel like sand-cradles, and the fencelike rows of acacias are seen. We are presented with a moment in time set, not under the hot sun of midday as in many of Raab's poems, but at night.

The first-person narrator in the poem is minimally present. The opening word, "my heart," the two verbs, "I shall spread out" and "I shall move," and the adjective "gripped" are the only indications of a human presence. The relationship between the human and the natural spheres is somewhat ambiguous. The outstretched wing intimates a protecting role for the human speaker and is sometimes used as an idiom of espousal. One might therefore conclude that there is a secret, intimate and binding tie between the land and the speaker, with the speaker assuming the dominant role. Even ignoring the possible allusiveness of the text, the human seems to have a privileged role in this first sentence of the poem, hovering above the land. In the second sentence she seems to come quite literally down to earth, moving eternally on the sandy paths among the rows of acacias.

While initially the bond to the land is expressed in compelling terms that are tied to a particular time and place, the conclusion of the poem reflects not the specific moment, but all eternity. The narrator presents herself as "gripped by an unresolved spell," facing the whisper of the "transparent skies" of dawn that stretch over the trees, still dark in the early morning light. Her desire is to preserve for all eternity this moment, the "frozen sea of trees." What is frozen here, in the heat of summer, is not the temperature, but movement.[17] The trees silhouetted in the morning light are undifferentiated and eternal, like the Reed (Red) Sea at its parting, embodying a threat to some while protecting others. The still of the moment gives the narrator the opportunity to articulate, subtly but surely, her bond to the homeland that is ultimately the source of her freedom, even as the walled waters of the Reed Sea frame the Israelites' path to freedom.[18]

In her poetry, Raab combines the feeling of the infinite, a feeling that is almost transcendent, reaching beyond itself, with carefully chosen and specific details of the landscape, which may seem, like thorns, to have been chosen for its harshness.[19] The leap to the infinite has been variously interpreted by critics. Zach, for example, sees it as a Romantic yearning for God.[20] Luz takes issue with him, claiming that it is often ill advised to move from the realia of the landscape, which is known, into the tenebrous shoals of amorphous abstraction.[21] In "My Heart Is with Your Dews, Homeland," Raab avoids these shoals by grounding her images specifically.

For Raab, nature is eternal, while the world built by human hands is ephemeral. She does not take pride, for example, in the rebuilding of the land of Israel, but laments its alien imposition on the pristine landscape. Her poem "Tel Aviv" (1928) is a dirge that opens with the initial word of the biblical book of Lamentations, and closes with the speaker's sob. To her mind, Tel Aviv spreads with the "mincing gait" for which Isaiah castigated the vain daughters of Zion (Isaiah 3:16); the city's feet are rebellious, in the term with which Samuel cursed Saul (I Samuel 16:23); and its furrows are as stale as the bread the Israelites complained about in the desert (Numbers 21:5). This torrent of biblical language, rare for Raab, indicates that the problem is so important that it warrants her assuming a quasi-prophetic tone.[22] The city she describes is starkly barren, unable to squeeze out even the single tear found on the cheek of mourning Zion in Lamentations (1:2). In fact the comparison between these two barren cities is instructive. The Zion of Lamentations has no future, for its inhabitants have been exiled. For Raab, Tel Aviv, which to many of her contemporaries seemed to represent the future of Israel, bespeaks calamity.[23] This city, which embodied growth and building, is for her a soulless, unnatural woman.

Raab recognizes that things change even in nature left untouched by human hands, but they change slowly. Thus, in "To My Unhappy, Storm-Tossed Sisters" (1924), her touching tribute to her friends who committed suicide by drowning, Lorette Pascal and Shoshanah Bogen, she describes the inexorable way the stream of water crumbles the stone. This metaphor of change, growth, and aging does not,

however, imply that anything is wrong with the process. In
fact, the subtle comparison with Isaiah 54:11, from which
the opening is drawn, intimates a positive resolution of the
tragic story. The building of Tel Aviv, on the other hand,
represents an unnatural incursion into the scheme of natural change.

When we think of literary themes informed by images
from the natural world, none comes to mind more readily
than love. The comparison of a woman to a frail, if convo-
luted, fragrant, and passionate flower is a literary common-
place for male writers.[24] Our expectations of female poets
are less fixed, since the tradition of poetry by women is
relatively underdeveloped. In her poem "Before Your Shining, Full Eyes" (1922), Raab draws a sexually charged analogy between her lover and a eucalyptus tree:

לְעֵינֶיךָ הָאוֹרוֹת, הַמְּלֵאוֹת
מַה טּוֹב חֲיוֹת;
לְאוֹרָן כָּל אֵבֶר מָתוּחַ
כְּאֶקָלִפְּטוֹס אַחַר סַעַר אָתָּה:
עָיֵף, אֵיתָן וְנָע עוֹד בָּרוּחַ —
רֹאשִׁי יַגִּיעַ עַד חָזֶךָ,
וְעֵינֶיךָ מִמַּעַל
חֲמִימוּת עָלַי תִּרְעַפְנָה.

Before your shining, full eyes
How good it is to live;
Before their light every limb is taut
Like a eucalyptus after a storm are you:
Tired, strong and still moving in the wind
My head will reach to your chest,
And your eyes above
Will distill warmth over me. (30)

The opening two lines seem hermetic and devoid of natural
referents, offering few clues to the identity of the addressee.[25] The poem continues, introducing the stormy
scene. The absence of punctuation after "taut" leads the

reader to assume first that the speaker's limb, not the listener's, is taut. The continuation indicates that the word
eiver (limb) refers to the penis, as is often the case in rabbinic
and modern Hebrew. The metaphor is transparently sexual:
the phallic tree, still moving, though tired, after the storm of
lovemaking; the female, shorter, certainly, than the tree,
reaching barely to his chest; the lover's eyes, distilling
warmth, even as "the skies distilled dew" (Proverbs 3:20).
The eyes frame the poem, implying that they and not the
phallus are the main source of initial attraction and of abiding
love. The parallel drawn by Raab between the lover and the
eucalyptus is particularly telling because it involves her fa-
vorite tree. In that sense, to the reader familiar with Raab's
outlook, the eyes of the lover balance the eyes of the poet,
for whom the eucalyptus is always at the center of the
scene.[26]

In Raab's early poetry, love is ordinarily experienced
within natural contexts. Thus, for example, there is a comparison between the lover and a wild animal implicit in "My
Palms Are Raised Toward You" (1926) :

כַּפַּי נְשׂוּאוֹת אֵלֶיךָ,
אֶל מְעַט הָאוֹרָה
אֲשֶׁר עוֹד לִי בְּעֵינֶיךָ,
וְאַתָּה — שִׁנֶּיךָ לוֹטֵשׁ
אֶל רֹךְ־בְּשָׂרִי הַצָּהֹב;
וְלוּ בָשָׂר זֶה עַל פְּנֵי שָׂדֶה יָשְׁלַךְ
וְעַיִט חָג מִמַּעַל לוֹ —
עוֹד כַּפַּי נְשׂוּאוֹת אֵלֶיךָ,
אֶל מְעַט הָאוֹרָה
אֲשֶׁר עוֹד לִי בְּעֵינֶיךָ.

My palms are raised toward you,
To the little light
Which I still have in your eyes,
And you—sharpen your teeth
For the softness of my yellow flesh;[27]

And were this flesh to be thrown upon the field
And would a vulture circle above it—
Still my palms are raised toward you,
To the little light
Which I still have in your eyes. (34–35)

The tone of this poem moves from what could be a religious opening, echoing the peaceful priestly benediction, to a violent metaphor that compares the person being addressed, clearly the lover, to a wild beast.[28] The narrator is the weaker in the relationship and further maintains her weakness by insisting that she will remain loyal to her vicious lover no matter how sadistic his behavior may turn. Raab spins out the conceit, picturing the speaker's dead body as having been thrown upon the field, encircled by a vulture. Nonetheless, she would maintain her devotion to the lover, as she frames the poem with her statement of loyalty. Given the sadistic nature of the relationship described, the reader may well find that the priestly benediction with its emphasis on peace has been ironically transmuted into the verse from the biblical book of Lamentations where, in a context of mass destruction, the speaker suggests: "Arise, cry out in the night / . . . / Pour out your heart like water / In the presence of the Lord! / Lift up your hands to Him / For the life of your infants" (2:19). As in Lamentations, here, too, the lifted hands serve as a gesture of supplication. They are the hands of surrender, not those of response or retaliation.

Raab's use of the metaphor of violent death at the teeth of a wild beast is intriguing in many ways. First, the speaker, whom we assume to be female, is the unprotesting victim of the attack, and we as readers are left to speculate about possible motivation. Second, the articulation of the death scene proceeds beyond the attack itself to the consequent threat of further violence to be visited upon the speaker's dead body by the vulture. Finally, no specific natural images refer to the speaker, whose body, alive and dead, is called "flesh." The lover, however, is metonymically compared to a wild beast, possessing eyes and teeth. A separate threat clearly comes from the vulture. Thus, the natural world plays a role that threatens the narrator, who seems somewhat outside it.

The natural world, however, does not simply provide fixed or static metaphors that consistently code Raab's poetry. Indeed, the beastlike lover in "My Palms Are Raised Toward You" becomes a rejected child in the following poem, "Not a Hearth and a Stove-Fire" (1926; *Qimshonim*, 35–37).[29] Here it is the narrator who possesses "the green eyes of a wild beast." She would replace the fires of domesticity with "blue bolts of lightning which will shoot sparks." This time, it is not the flesh of the female lover that is thrown upon the field, but rather the male lover who will rest on his beloved's knees "like a child thrown [out]." It is the male whose sad head will be surrounded by a multitude of white doves, a symbol of the peace that will follow upon his childlike submission. The male is not dehumanized, nor does he suffer a violent death, but he does end up being dragged, at least in sadistic sexual fantasy, behind her all night "in unbreakable chains." The apparent reversal of roles in this poem has occasioned some critical debate over the new female role. Miron claims that Raab is here presenting an image of feminine rebellion and anarchy, while Luz argues that this is simply the new image of women that has grown up in the thorny landscape of the land of Israel.[30] It is a rejection of the notion that the woman should always play the submissive role in a relationship.

The poem that most strikingly portrays the potential for erotic violence against a natural background is Raab's very first poem, "I Am Under the Thornbush" (1922), which describes a murder/suicide in the sun-blanched landscape of midday:

אֲנִי תַּחַת הָאָטָד
קַלָּה, זֵידוֹנָה,
קוֹצָיו צוֹחֲקֶת
לִקְרָאתְךָ זָקְפְתִּי;

אוֹר מַכֶּה עַל הַמֶּרְחָב,
כָּל קִפּוּל בְּשִׂמְלָתִי
לִי יִלְחָשׁ:
לִקְרַאת מָוֶת
לְבָנָה וּמְחוֹלֶלֶת
אַתְּ יוֹצְאָה.
אַתָּה מוֹפִיעַ —
וַאֲנִי קַלָּה צוֹהֶלֶת
מְנִיפָה חֶרֶב נוֹצֶצֶת
וּבְעֶצֶם צָהֳרַיִם
בִּשְׂדוֹת לְבָנִים מְאוֹר
אֶת דִּינֵנוּ גָּזַרְתִּי
בְּאַחַת!

I am under the thornbush
Nimble, menacing,
Laughing [at] its thorns
To greet you I straightened up;
Light beats on the vastness,
Every fold in my dress
Whispers to me:
To greet death
White and dancing
You go forth.
You appear—
And I nimble rejoicing
Brandish a sparkling sword
And at the height of noon
In very white fields
Decreed our verdict [31]
As one! (37–39)

This poem appears to make a strong personal statement: it opens with the word "I," the only poem in *Qimshonim* to do so, and closes with the feminine form of "one." Thus the speaker frames the poem. But the focus is equally the stark background against which the drama is played out. The speaker first locates herself crouching under a thornbush and describes herself as "nimble, menacing." The thorns themselves help mold the speaker's actions as she laughs at them, while straightening up to greet her unidentified male addressee. Yet this female figure coming forward to meet her beloved echoes not the sensuous language of the Song of Songs, but the crackly, harsh *k* sound that pervades the beginning of the poem.[32] As the speaker comes forward, each fold in her dress whispers to her a message oracular in its ambiguity, for she could be approaching either her own death or someone else's.

There are clearly echoes of different texts and myths at play here. On the one hand, there is, as Shifrah indicates, the Near Eastern myth of the death of Tammuz, where the male deity dies, or is held captive, by the female seductress during a period of summer barrenness.[33] But there are other allusions as well. The white of the scene, giving its aura of purity, recalls a wedding. In fact, the speaker twice refers to herself as *qallah,* meaning light in weight or significance, but at the same time exploiting the homonymic pun with *kallah,* "bride."[34] The shining sword she brandishes is clearly the transformation of the thorns. The couple's fate has already been determined by this Amazon, sword-wielding bride, for their union will be in death, not in life.[35] Here, again, there is an allusion, this time to a different love, the love of a person for God. What echoes in the last word of the poem is the story of the death of Rabbi Akiva, whose soul went forth as he was saying the word "one," concluding the recital of the *Shema* prayer. Rabbi Akiva's story tells of a spiritual union with God at death; Raab's macabre tale recounts a physical union in death.[36]

Why, one might ask, the unusual location? The thornbush constitutes an allusion to Jotham's parable (Judges 9:8–20), in which the apparently useless thornbush, chosen to rule over the other trees, warns that it has the potential to destroy even the greatest among them. While Luz reasonably suggests that the natural elements of her surroundings determine the fate of this female lover, he sees this as part of a new vision of love appropriate to a new country. Miron, on the other hand, sees her as a "decadent femme fatale,"

moved from the usual urban setting to a rural landscape in
her search for victims.[37]

The way the new land has occasioned a re-visioning of
love is paralleled by the way the land itself has been transformed into a pulsating, erotic crucible. In fact, Raab chose
to open *Qimshonim* not with her first poem, but with "Upon
Your Nakedness a White Day Celebrates" (1923):

עַל מַעֲרֻמַּיִךְ חוֹגֵג יוֹם לָבָן,
אַתְּ הַדַּלָּה וְהָעֲשִׁירָה כֹּה,
גֵּד הָרִים קָפָא,
שָׁקוּף כַּחֲזוֹן תַּעְתּוּעִים,
אֶל הָאֹפֶק דָּבֵק.
צָהֳרָיִם. מֶרְחֲבֵי שְׂדוֹתַיִךְ מִשְׁתַּלְהֲבִים
וּלְשַׁדֵּךְ כָּלִיל מִתְלַהְלֵהַּ וְעוֹלֶה
מוּל הַשָּׁמַיִם הַלְּבָנִים,
כְּמֻסָּךְ לֹא יִפְסַק
נִמְשָׁךְ וְרוֹעֵד.
בְּתוֹךְ הַמִּישׁוֹר
גִּבְעָה תֵּרוֹם כְּשַׁד עָגֹל
וּלְרֹאשָׁהּ קֶבֶר לָבָן חוֹפֵף;
וּבַעֲזוּבַת שָׂדוֹת קְצוּרִים
אָטָד בָּדָד רוֹבֵץ.
וְהָיָה כִּי תִיעַף הָעַיִן
מִזַּרְמֵי תַעְתּוּעֵי-אוֹר
וְטָבְלָה בִּירֵק הָאָטָד הַמַּכְחִיל,
כְּבְתוֹךְ בְּרֵכַת מַיִם צוֹנְנִים.
אַתְּ הַדַּלָּה כֹּה עַל חֲרִיצַיִךְ הַמַּאְדִּימִים
תּוֹךְ זְהַב הַמֶּרְחַקִּים
עִם קַרְקְעֵי נְחָלַיִךְ הַחֲרֵבִים, הַלְּבָנִים —
מַה יָפִית!

Upon your nakedness a white day celebrates,
You who are [so] poor and so rich,
A wall of mountains has frozen,
Transparent like a deceptive vision,
Attached to the horizon.
Noon. The vastnesses of your fields ignite
And your marrow totally revels and rises
Facing the white sky,

Like an endless screen
Stretched and trembling.
In the plain
A hill rises like a round breast
And its head a white grave covers;
And in the rubble of harvested fields
A lonely thornbush lies.
And it is when the eye tires
Of the streams of deceptive light
And is immersed in the green of the bluish thornbush,
As if in a pool of cool water.
You who are so poor with your reddening furrows
In the gold of the distance
With the ground of the wadis dry, white—
How beautiful you are! (9–10)

This poem presents the homeland as a woman's body in the white heat of a summer noon on the barren landscape. The erotic image of the day celebrating the nakedness of the land is a strange one. The day almost seems to be dancing, glimmering over the land. The very whiteness of the summer day would be unexpected for many readers who, not born into this landscape, might, like the great Hebrew poet, Hayyim Nahman Bialik, more readily connect white days with winter.[38] The day itself, in its whiteness, is a seamless part of the nakedness of the land, addressed in the second person, singular, feminine. The soupçon of sexuality inherent in the nakedness is amplified as the poem proceeds. The very marrow of the land rises against the white skies.[39]

Yet the land that rises is not the landscape of male metaphor. Rather the landscape is presented in the form of a woman's body, complete with a single breast in the form of a stone, sun-bleached hill, genitals (nakedness), veins in the guise of red furrows, and a head covered by a grave.[40] This re-visioned description of the land as a brazenly naked woman who is virtually "in heat," her breasts hard, is somewhat unexpected, particularly with the grave looming at its highest point. In this poem, overflowing with natural images, there is scarcely a line that does not surprise the reader with an unanticipated turn. The desertlike terrain, for example, offers us water, both when Raab subtly calls to mind Moses' Song at the Sea (Exodus 15) in her phrase "the wall of mountains has frozen," and when she overtly compares the bluish verdure of the thornbush to "a pool of cool water."[41] The land, twice referred to as "poor," despite the "gold of the distances," does not seem attractive in any sense. It is hot, dry, lonely, and mostly white. Yet, echoing both the Song of Songs and Bialik's "From the Winter Poems," Raab concludes her poem with the simple two-word line, indented for emphasis: *"Mah yafit!,"* ("How fair you are!") (Song of Songs 7:7).[42] The narrator's love for the land clearly defies rational consideration. One might venture that this reevaluation of standards for the beauty of landscapes might be matched by a reassessment of the standards for women's bodies, as well. They, too, are not to be denigrated on the basis of some arbitrary ideal.

Romantic love and sexuality are not the only relationships illuminated by metaphors and contexts drawn from nature. One of Raab's most moving poems was written for the fiftieth anniversary of her father's having gone onto the land of Petah Tikvah. "To the Father" (1929) describes the father in terms of the landscape that his hands have shaped and his eyes have seen. Curiously, in this most personal poem, there is no first person: the father could be an Ur-father sprung from the earth with no ties to the poet. The poem opens, "Blessed are the hands / which sowed / on winter mornings," and closes, "Blessed are the hands!" These hands have sown the fields, bent the vines, and planted eucalyptus trees, actions presented in order of smallest plant to largest, of most fleeting, in the annual winter sowing of the fields, to most permanent, in the planting of the eucalyptus trees. They also reined the horse and controlled the rifle used to defend the fragile home from the enemy. The father's actions are all cast in the past, although many of them, as demonstrated by Judah Raab's biography, continued long beyond the writing of the poem. In this poem, Esther Raab highlights the pioneer experience, describing, for example, not the house she knew as a child, but the fragile and temporary structure that was her father's first home in Petah Tikvah. She captures him at the moment when, with his green eye cast in the future, he is supervising the fledglings, transparent symbols of his young children yet to be born. The actions of the present are "plowing the furrow despite the desert / breaking through first in virgin land." But what is striking about the poem is not the moment in which Raab fixes her father, between the pioneering days of 1879 and the time when she was born, fifteen years later; it is the richness and the specificity of the images she uses to convey her father's power.

Much of this detail, as Miron points out, is taken from the world of nature.[43] The fields, sown in winter, to the rustling sounds of starlings circling, are of "red loam," a term Raab uses but one other time in her poetry.[44] The father's actions are symbolic of the faith of that pioneering generation, going out into the "winter" of the land's desolation and, despite the ever-present threats of predators, planting crops. Bending the vine so that it will strike new roots is also an action fraught with meaning, connecting the modern pioneers to the agricultural practices of their ancient Jewish forebears, as is the concomitant humility. Eucalyptus trees were planted "like flags of pleasant scent," a simile of possession, their scent redolent with the language of the biblical sacrificial system. Each element here is essential to the picture Raab is presenting.

The poem moves from the specifics of initial planting to the home, which rests "upon the sands and screwbean." The sands, of course, are shifting, but they are anchored by the carpet of screwbean. Even more pointedly, the vetch that covers these dunams, land at least subject to human measure, and the oxen lying in the swamps are images that appear only once in Raab's poetry. The singularity of the scene is underscored by the first breaking forth through the virgin land, a metaphor powerful in its sexual resonance. Thus, by using rich natural imagery to present the father's role, Raab makes her picture unique and specific. She also

presents the father as changing the face of the land, while
emphasizing the continuity of Jewish involvement with it.

Yet another perspective is supplied by the poem "A Thistle Burst Through the Red Loam." This parable about the
positive consequences for the world of productive human
relationships begins with the flowering of the thistle and the
integration of its spreading milky white flowers in a night
marked by the white of the moon and clouds. When the
screwbean surrounds the thistles and prevents them from
overtaking the sand, the two plants become intertwined like
lovers, filling the area with their abundance and complemen-
tary scents. Clearly, the thistle with its sharp odor is the
male bursting through the feminine red loam,[45] while the
civilizing force of the screwbean with its soft odor represents the feminine. Clinging to one another like lovers, they
are both essential for harmony and completion.

Raab's personal relationship with the land and the way it
fits into the historic Jewish experience is an important
aspect of the poem "Holy Grandmothers in Jerusalem"
(1930). Like the overwhelming majority of Raab's poems,
this one is untitled, deriving its identity from the first line,
addressed to the grandmothers, both characterizing them
and setting them and their sanctity in a separate and holy
place. The pious prayer that their merit will protect the
speaker indicates that while the poem might seem to focus
on the grandmothers, its center is actually the narrator's
search for self-definition.[46] The ambiguity of this search for
self is expressed in the narrator's veiling and revealing herself through possessives, verbs, and prepositions, but never
appearing as the freestanding word "I."

The world of piety so succinctly evoked at the outset of
the poem is first juxtaposed with the world of nature and
sensuality, eliciting concrete experiences from the narrator's infancy and childhood. While the sensual memory of
mother's milk reinforces the contrast with the distant grandmothers in Jerusalem, the next three lines move the sensuality clearly to the arena of childhood, recalling the early
memory of walking as a soft-soled barefoot child in the burn-

ing sand. Finally the "unkempt eucalyptuses" embody danger in their resident wasps and bees but, through their constant rustling, provide the narrator with a comforting lullaby.

In the two biblically based fantasies that follow, the narrator projects two different images of self. First, the narrator imagines herself as the beloved of King David; she immerses herself seven times in the sea, a reference to the ritual immersion of a bride before the wedding, and then rises through the mountains of Jerusalem to meet her lover. The awesome and regal Jerusalem intimated here is different from the pious world of the grandmothers, but the anticipated culmination of this fantasy, the meeting of the lovers, never takes place. Instead, there is a *Kaffeeklatsch*, a simple get-together, with the biblical leader Deborah (Judges 4–5) under her palm tree, where the two women discuss war and defense, topics very much on the mind of those living in Palestine in 1930. But it is not clear whether it is national warfare or interpersonal warfare that is intended in the words of this poet, whose romantic fantasies may, as we have seen, turn violent.

The poem is framed with the grandmothers, who are summoned in the same language used in the opening lines. Here, however, the description expands to include a reference to the candle wax and mothball scents of their clothing. The reader is pulled away from the secular world of nature and its scents, back to the odors of the relatively closed world of traditional Jewish piety. This image, which represents the completion of the circle, bespeaks preservation, warmth, and light. Yet while "Holy Grandmothers in Jerusalem" indicates that the sacred world of the grandmothers is important, they remain peripheral.[47] Both the childhood memories and the biblical fantasies locate the narrator firmly in the natural world, while the grandmothers evoke not "heroism and ancient glory but old age, the smell of naphthalene, the odor of the wax of Shabbat candles."[48]

In the poems of *Qimshonim,* Raab transmutes her place of birth into a living environment that plays an active role in her poetry. She makes no Ransomian "flight into nature." Hers is not the "feminine" landscape of pretty flowers and manicured shapes, but rather the teeming, sun-baked wilderness before it was brought under human dominion. This landscape serves as a reflection of human relationships and is, in turn, depicted in anthropomorphic terms. Above all, it is a landscape of different moods and seasons, sometimes bucolic, but more often full of "rebellion and anarchy."[49] Raab's unique perceptions allow her to transmit it to her readers in an idiom all her own.

NOTES

1. John Crowe Ransom, "Emily Dickinson: A Poet Restored," in *Emily Dickinson: A Collection of Critical Essays,* ed. Richard B. Sewall (Englewood Cliffs, N.J., 1963), 92.

2. Esther Raab, "On the Landscape and the Living and on the Periods of Landscape in the Land of Israel" [Hebrew], *D'var ha-Shavu'a* (October 20, 1989).

3. Reuven Shoham, *A Monograph on the Poetry of Esther Raab* [Hebrew], unpublished master's dissertation, Hebrew University (Jerusalem, 1973), 15.

4. Shimon Ginzburg, *Regarding Literature* [Hebrew] (New York, 1945), 279.

5. Moshe Dor, "'I Discovered the Landscape of the Land of Israel,'" *Ma'ariv* (October 3, 1971), 14.

6. Dan Miron, *Founding Mothers, Stepsisters: The Emergence of the First Hebrew Poetesses and Other Essays* [Hebrew] (Tel Aviv, 1991), 23.

7. Natan Zach, "The Landscape of a Landscape Poet" [Hebrew], *Amot* 11:4 (1964), 86–91, opens his essay on Raab with a long catalog of the plants she names and he does not recognize. Reuven Shoham, "Esther Raab and Her Poetry," in Esther Raab, *A Collection of Poems* [Hebrew] (Tel Aviv, 1982), 28, contributes a list of words drawn from nature which Raab was the first to use in Hebrew poetry. In the introduction to his unpublished volume of English translations, Harold Schimmel, "Poems of Esther Raab," (Tel Aviv, n.d.), 7–8, discusses in some depth the plants she incorporates in her work and their significance.

8. In "The Wasps' Nest," written in the early 1930s, Raab describes an event that took place in 1905 (published in *Ma'ariv* November 17, 1989). According to Hayyim Be'er, "I Am Lonely. Without Poems I Would Have Died Long Ago" [Hebrew], *D'var haShavua* (April 1, 1988), 14, Raab chose

her home in Hilwan, Egypt, after her marriage because it had a giant eucalyptus over it.

9. Esther Raab, *A Garden Destroyed* [Hebrew] (Tel Aviv, 1983); *idem, Qimshonim* [*Thorns*) (Tel Aviv, 1930).

10. There are poems that wander as far afield as Cairo, Hilwan, and Paris, but these are clear exceptions; indeed, they are often negative in tone. The poems that range farther around the land of Israel are more numerous and, when not focused on urban areas, more positive.

11. Raab's texts are cited from the original edition of *Qimshonim* (1930). Because none of them was dated in that edition, the dates are drawn from the complete edition of her poetry edited by her nephew and literary executor, Ehud Ben-Ezer, *All the Poems* [Hebrew] (Tel Aviv, 1988). I am also indebted to him for the wealth of material he has shared with me.

12. In the 1930 edition it appears on the page between her dedication of the book to her late husband, "In memory of my friend Yitzhak Green," and the first sketch. It was eliminated from the Masada edition of her poems, but restored to the 1988 edition, where it appears above the first poem.

13. Zvi Luz, *Existence and Man in Israeli Literature* [Hebrew] (Tel Aviv, 1970), 44–45.

14. Raab, *Qimshonim*, 11. The translations are mine, but they are informed by those by Schimmel, "Poems." They follow the texts and pagination of the 1930 edition.

15. Shifrah, "Summer Is Last Poppies: A Reading in the Poems of Esther Raab Five Years after Her Death" [Hebrew], *Iton* 77:80–81 (September/October, 1986), 23, 60.

16. Although it is difficult to translate the words Raab uses for some classes of plants, I have chosen to use a different English word in each instance to transmit some of the variety of the original.

17. A salient example of this usage is from Exodus 15:8, the Song at the Sea: "At the blast of your nostrils the waters piled up / The floods stood straight like a wall / The deeps froze in the heart of the sea."

18. Miron, *Founding Mothers*, 24, skillfully proposes two possible readings of the last few lines of the poem. One would have the last two lines, which are set off by the comma, stand as an independent syntactical unit, making them one of the many descriptive elements in the poem. The other would connect these lines with "gripped," leaving the central figure enmeshed in a landscape that is immobile after her brief, ethereal flight. My reading follows Miron's second suggestion in terms of the syntax but suggests that the import of the lines, because of the allusion to Exodus, is different.

19. The narrating persona takes pride in the thorny parts of nature, in the cacti and the thistles. See "Aha! For My Soul Has Taken Pride Within Me This Evening" (44–45).

20. Zach, "Landscape," 87.

21. Luz, *Existence and Man*, 50.

22. The language also proves that she had the resources to use biblical language more often, had she chosen to do so. See also Miron, *Found-*

ing Mothers, 193–4, who discusses this poem as an example of the antiurban theme in the poetry of this period.

23. In her 1974 essay "On the Landscape," Raab seems to have tem-
pered her antiurban approach, admitting that beautiful landscapes can
include those created by humans as well as those in the wild.

24. For comparison, consult the discussion of how late twentieth-
century American women poets use nature imagery in Alicia Suskin
Ostriker, *Stealing the Language* (Boston, 1986), 107–14.

25. There may be an echo here of the love poem "Commonplaces" by
Hayyim Nahman Bialik, *Collected Writings of H. N. Bialik* [Hebrew] (Tel
Aviv: 1938), 5, the most important Hebrew poet of the late nineteenth and
early twentieth centuries. His works had, and continue to have, an inor-
dinate influence upon Hebrew writers. In this poem the male, addressing
the female, says: "Your two eyes are beautiful, shining." For some discussion of the role of Bialik in Esther Raab's poetry, see Anne Lapidus
Lerner, "'A Woman's Song': The Poetry of Esther Raab," in *Gender and
Text: Feminist Perspectives on Modern Hebrew and Yiddish Literature,* ed.
Naomi Sokoloff, Anne Lapidus Lerner, and Anita Norich (New York, 1992),
27–28. Miron, *Founding Mothers,* 11–17, discusses the deleterious impact
of Bialik's influence on the development of Hebrew poetry by women in
the early twentieth century.

26. On the centrality of the eucalyptus one might read, in addition to
Raab's memoirs and interviews, "A Poem to the Eucalyptus" (1968) in her
All the Poems, 183–85.

27. Raab felt that her skin had been yellowed by the frequent attacks
of malaria from which she suffered as a child. See *A Garden Destroyed,*
95–97.

28. The priestly benediction recited as part of the synagogue service
is called *nesi'at kappayyim*, "the raising of the palms."

29. The order of the poems in *Qimshonim* is particularly important
because the texts are presented in run-on fashion; rather than each poem
starting on a new page, the text continues with eleven or twelve lines on
a page. The end of each poem is indicated by a small square. The format
of the book warrants further study; see Miron, *Founding Mothers*, 158–60.

30. Miron, *Founding Mothers,* 22, 96–97; Luz, *Existence and Man,* 47.

31. The idiom Raab uses literally means "to cut a judgment," returning
to the sword image.

32. The first eight lines contain twenty words, eight of which include
either a letter *kof* or a letter *kaf*; only one *kof* appears in the last ten lines.

33. Shifrah, "Summer," 23.

34. Adding another dimension to the double use of *qallah* is the double
use of *liqrat,* "to greet," an echo of the mystical Sabbath hymn "*Lekhah
Dodi,*" in which the beloved is invited to "come forth to greet the bride"
(*liqrat kallah*), who is actually the Sabbath Queen. Miron considers other
textual echoes, *Founding Mothers,* 22.

35. Shoham, "Esther Raab," 37.

36. "Hear O Israel, the Lord our God, the Lord is one" (Deuteronomy
6:4). The story is found in the Babylonian Talmud, Berakhot 61b.

37. Luz, *Existence and Man,* 47; Miron, "The Poetry of Esther Raab" [Hebrew], *Ha'Arets* (February 14, 1964) 10; idem, *Founding Mothers,*

38. It is possible that this poem reflects Raab's attempt to distance herself from Bialik, whose "Of Winter Poems" (1904) represents a harsh, hard, white winter landscape.

39. Edna Sharoni, "Edenic Energy: Esther Raab's Unmediated Vision of Nature," *Modern Hebrew Literature* 8:3/4 (Spring/Summer 1983), 64, sees this poem as "a glowing epithalamium to the land; full of light and color, it shimmers in all the rich hues of the rainbow but bridal white is triumphant"; while Shoham, "Esther Raab," 21, sees it as a meeting of the male and female landscapes. I do not find this barren scene so promising.

40. The phenomenon we see here is described by Ostriker, *Stealing the Language,* 108, who asserts that when women write in praise of the body, "their most significant tool is revisionist metaphor." This naturally bleak breast contrasts with the cement stone that rests on the chest of Tel Aviv in Raab's "Tel Aviv." Miron, *Founding Mothers,* 22, would extend the body metaphor to include the thornbush with its bluish thorns representing hair that does not quite cover its nakedness.

41. Raab's line is a confluence of two images in the verse: "At the blast of Your nostrils the waters piled up, / The floods stood straight like a wall; / The deeps froze in the heart of the sea" (Exodus 15:8).

42. Bialik, "See How Fair Is the Cold Light" ("From the Winter Poems" V), *Collected Works,* 44.

43. Miron, *Founding Mothers,* 110, further states that "the poem conveyed the image of the father only to the extent that it conveyed, marvelously, the image of the landscape."

44. "A Thistle Burst Through the Red Loam" (20–22); Raab did not substitute her own system of stock natural metaphors for an older collection, but varied her images considerably. Similarly, the word for screwbean appears only in these two poems. It is no accident that this poem follows "To the Father"; it may well represent her vision of the strong relationship between the daughter and father as it uses much of the same language.

45. In Hebrew each noun may be either masculine or feminine. The form of the word Raab uses for "thistle," *qimosh,* is masculine; the word *hamrah,* "red loam," is feminine.

46. See Bialik, "My Mother of Blessed Memory"; cf. *Mishnah Avot* 2:2.

47. I would disagree with Miron, *Founding Mothers*, 147, who argues that in this poem Raab attempts "to tie herself to the feminine-Hebrew tradition" through her evocation of the grandmothers and the biblical Deborah. It is significant that Raab does not allude to the major poetic work attributed to Deborah, the Song of Deborah (Judges 5), in the poem.

48. *Ibid.,* 111.

49. *Ibid.,* 22.

13 ✦ SARA R. HOROWITZ

*Memory and Testimony of Women Survivors
of Nazi Genocide*

In her 1943 lament for the murdered Jews of the Warsaw Ghetto, Rachel Auerbach asks, then answers herself: "Who can render the stages of the dying people? Only the shudder of pity for one's self and for others." Written from the "Aryan side" of the Polish city just after Nazi militia burned down the ghetto and shipped its inhabitants to death camps or killed them on the spot, "Yizkor, 1943" lists and elaborates the different people who fell victim to Nazi atrocity.[1]

I begin this essay by quoting and then analyzing Auerbach's essay so that my voice does not take precedence over the voices of the women whose memory and testimony constitute the focus of this inquiry. Working from the parts to the whole, from texts (and fragments of texts) to a broader conversation among texts and readers, I look at some of the ways women both experience and think through the complexities of memory, testimony, and survival. This project draws upon memoiristic reflections of women victims and former victims of Nazi atrocity: highly individualized accounts in diverse genres, including oral history, published and unpublished memoirs, interviews, and Holocaust-based fiction. These very different forms of testimony make different demands on readers or listeners. At the same time, each reflects the survivor's best attempt to recollect, recount, and understand what memory insists happened during those unimaginable years of atrocity.

Auerbach's eulogy represents part of a massive effort to document the ongoing events in the Warsaw Ghetto. Organized by social historian Emmanuel Ringelblum and operating under the code name *Oneg Shabbes* (literally "enjoyment of the Sabbath"), the project brought together a heterogeneous group of ghetto inhabitants committed to leaving a tangible trace of their life and death under Nazi rule. Working in secret, the group accumulated over one hundred volumes of diaries, reports, essays, and photographs. Like many of the *Oneg Shabbes* writers, both Ringelblum and Auerbach declined offers for safe passage out of Poland. After the ghetto's liquidation, they lived as fugitives in a presumably *Judenrein* Warsaw, continuing their work while in hiding. Eventually Ringelblum was captured, and sent to a death camp with his wife and child. Auerbach survived the war.

By the time Auerbach wrote "Yizkor, 1943," most of the *Oneg Shabbes* group—indeed, almost all the Jews concentrated in the Warsaw Ghetto—had been killed. Lyrical and moving, her eulogy seems as much a prayer as an eyewitness account, as her title reflects. *Yizkor*, the Hebrew third person imperative form of the verb *lizkor*, "to remember," is both the name and the first word of the Jewish memorial prayer, which begins *Yizkor Elohim*: "May God remember." Traditionally part of festival liturgy, the prayer takes the form of a Hebrew formula into which one inserts the names of dead loved ones. The prayer asks that God remember each by name, that God instate each one in *gan eden* (paradise) for eternity. In effect, the Yizkor prayer harnesses the eternal memory of the Jewish God to fortify the less reliable human memory. Through a ritualized act of human recollection, God recalls and, in recalling, eternally restores. To counter the truncation of death and the fallibility of human memory, the prayer imagines an everlastingly remembering God.

Auerbach's evocation of the Yizkor prayer on behalf of the murdered Jews of Warsaw is both wistfully nostalgic and bitingly ironic. She simultaneously places the Nazi genocide inside and outside the continuum of Jewish catastrophe. By drawing on the traditional memorial recitation she implicates the trope of Jewish survival, suggesting that Jews and Judaism will survive the present crisis, will absorb its events into Jewish collective memory (allied but not identical with Jewish history). At the same time, her essay suggests that this catastrophe may well mark the end of the Jewish people, and hence the end of the Jewish God and of Jewish memory. In contrast to the prayer, which begins by calling on God the rememberer, Auerbach's essay focuses on the human. She alone is the rememberer who enumerates the dead, and she cannot be certain of her own survival. Like all the other Jews under Nazi domain, Auerbach lives under a death sentence.[2] Her memory will not suffice, because she counts herself among those she eulogizes ("the shudder of pity for one's self").

Auerbach's essay raises a set of issues characteristic of Holocaust writing. Her eulogy utilizes the prayer form, but her intention is testimonial. Simultaneously chronicling and mourning the deterioration and destruction of Warsaw Jewry, the essay complicates our understanding of what constitutes testimony. Auerbach conflates roles usually kept separate: the victim who experiences, the eyewitness who sees and attests, the historian who certifies and verifies, and the imaginative writer who reconstructs or represents historical events. When Auerbach writes of the destruction of Warsaw Jewry, she does so as a particular type of eyewitness—one who both shares and does not share the experiences she describes. Having lived and worked in the Warsaw ghetto, having endured its indignities, hardships, and atrocities, she writes as former victim, from "inside" the events described. Having escaped the "liquidation," she also writes as eyewitness, close to but not a part of the events narrated. As eulogist to the ghetto dead, she speaks from the stance of the third-person witness who saw but did not share the events narrated, whose presumably "objective" testimony may be trusted. At the same time, the authority of her writing also obtains from the rigors of the professional historian, governed by a methodological training in "objective truth." No longer chronicling contemporaneous circumstances (as she did in the ghetto), she actively reconstructs the events (and people) of the past from the "outside." Moveover, in her eulogy, she imagines the deaths she did not see, imagines them because were she to have actually seen them—had she been present in the ghetto during the final roundups and shootings—she would not have survived to narrate them. Her act of imagining makes her testimony more comprehensive, but shifts the grounds on which its authority rests. Ultimately she imagines her way back into the fate she narrowly escaped, places herself "inside" rather than "outside" the testimony. The shifting voice of eyewitness, historian, imaginative narrator, and victim raises questions of perspective, memory, and experience, questions that surface not only in Holocaust testimony, but in the theoretical discourse that has emerged in Holocaust studies.

Further, the manner in which Auerbach chooses to structure her essay tells us something of the way she views the events narrated, and her relationship to them. Poised between the destroyed community and a posterity by no means guaranteed, Auerbach conveys both a sense of continuity and a sense of rupture with the Jewish past. As the structure and language of Auerbach's piece indicate, testimony shapes and takes shape within rhetorical form and genre. Not only the content but the shape of testimony connotes; the relationship between the said and the unsaid, the modulation of voices, and the cultural contexts constitute and complicate testimony.

As "Yizkor, 1943" indicates, women did indeed testify, interpret, and think deeply about their experiences under

Nazi atrocity. Their writing grapples both with immeasurable personal loss and with disturbing philosophical and theological questions raised by the Holocaust. And, as one reads Auerbach's writing, one wonders, following the few contemporary thinkers on Holocaust and women,[3] whether there is anything characteristically "female" about what Auerbach endured, or about her responses to it, the way she remembers, the way she narrates.

In his cartoon book *Maus*,[4] Art Spiegelman utilizes humanoid animals to tell the story of his parents, both concentration camp survivors. Vladek and Anja's personal history is conveyed through a combination of Vladek's words, as told to Art in a series of taped conversations spanning several years, and Art's graphics. Vladek's stories, which begin in prewar Czestochowa, Poland, and end up in postwar Rego Park, New York, depict Anja as a sensitive, loving, and emotionally fragile woman who survives the war thanks to her husband's enterprising shrewdness and pragmatism. By the time Art begins collecting material for his book, Anja has been dead for several years. Her suicide is one of the few segments of Spiegelman's book utilizing human rather than animal characters. The suicide sequence, originally published separately and interpolated into the text of *Maus*,[5] depicts a younger Art as doubly victimized: first by his mother's smothering love, then by her guilt-inflicting suicide. "You *murdered* me, Mommy, and you left me here to take the rap!!!" is his closing speech.

Intermittently, Art searches for his mother's diaries, to know "what she went through while . . . apart" from Vladek. Vladek repeatedly reassures Art that his narrative suffices to tell both of their stories: "I can tell you . . . She went through the same what me: TERRIBLE!" Only at the end of the volume does Vladek reveal that after Anja's death, in an attempt to "make order" with his memories, he burned her notebooks, and no longer recalls what she had written.

Anja's missing diaries exemplify the marginality of women's experience in constructing a master narrative of the Nazi genocide. Vladek burns her notebooks not out of malice but in response to his own pain, and then subsumes her memories under his own. In the absence of her own words (written, Vladek explains, in the hope that someday her son "will be interested by this"), Anja's story is recoverable only through the reconstruction of Vladek and Art's memories. In Art's recollection, Anja's love smothers and her suicide wounds. In Vladek's recollection, she appears weak and dependent; he repeatedly saves her sanity and life both before and during the war. In many male Holocaust narratives, women figure peripherally, as helpless victims (although the men were no less helpless), as absent loved ones (although the men, too, were absent), as needing rescue (although the men, too, needed rescue). A few of these narratives are openly hostile to women.[6]

Vladek's narration skirts moments of failure and loss. In *Maus II*, his testimony ends with memory of the reunion with his beloved Anja, soon after liberation. "We were both very happy, and lived happy, happy ever after," he tells his son, then asks Art to stop the tape recorder. Deliberately cut off at that moment is everything that happens next: Anja's suicide, Vladek's own incessant nightmares, recurrent thoughts of their murdered son, Richieu. How would Anja narrate her story of atrocity and survival? How would her diaries depict her life in the camps, her marriage with Vladek, her memories, her losses, her motherhood?

The rarity of women's voices is striking in the contemporary discourse about the Holocaust. Not that women survivors have failed to produce diaries, memoirs, journals, novels, vignettes. Women wrote in ghettoes and in hiding, as Auerbach's essays attest; some even managed to do so in Nazi slave labor camps.[7] Women continue to publish their reflections in many languages. Many women leave records of their experiences, in the form of letters, unpublished manuscripts prepared for their families, and oral or videotaped testimony, such as those gathered under the aegis of the Fortunoff Video Archive for Holocaust Testimonies at Yale University. Nevertheless, works by women survivors are cited less frequently in scholarly studies,[8] women's experience are rarely central to the presentation of a "typical" Holocaust story, and significant works by women fall out of print, becoming unavailable for classroom use. How we think about and how we teach the Holocaust has been based predominantly on the testimony—written and oral—of male survivors. As one survivor remarked to me during an interview about her Holocaust-based fiction, "No one has yet written the history of women in the Shoah."[9]

Does this matter? After all, one might argue, the Nazi program of genocide was not predicated upon gender but on a particular idea of "race." If biology was destiny, it was the "biological" fact of "Jewish blood" that consigned one to the "destiny" of genocide. Generally speaking, the testimony of male and female survivors corroborate one another and verify the same sets of historical facts.

Yet women's testimony reveals distinctly different patterns of experience and reflection. In recalling and grappling with memories of personal and collective loss, trauma, and displacement, and in reconstructing a sense of meaning and ethics, women may remember differently, or they may remember different things. Missing from male versions of survival are experiences unique to women, such as menarche, menstruation, and pregnancy in the concentration camps; the strategies some women devised to endure and survive; the ways in which other women met their death; the subsequent effect on women survivors in family, friendship, and civic relations; and the way women reconstruct shattered paradigms of meaning in the face of cultural and personal displacement.

The few studies on women and the Holocaust, primarily by historians, take one of two approaches. One approach asserts the equality of men and women, as victims, as resistance fighters, as sufferers and as survivors of Nazi atrocity.[10] In this view, the events of the Holocaust undermine "sexism." The second approach seeks to distinguish women's lives and deaths from those of men, and to bring into view uniquely female experiences.[11] These works tend to focus on pregnancy, menstruation, prostitution, and rape.

Both of these approaches yield valuable insights, and the concomitant research adds to the important store of knowledge about women during the Holocaust. But when posed antithetically, each approach skews the discussion, thereby misrepresenting the actual experiences of women victims and the recollections of women survivors. The first produces a unified (unisex) version of the Holocaust that unintentionally ends up occluding experiences particular to women. In this version, women are seen as identical to men, with the concentration camp universe functioning as a great equalizer. The second inadvertently reproduces the marginalization of women, by presenting their experiences almost exclusively in terms of sexuality. In this version, women are seen as particularly vulnerable—biologically vulnerable—to Nazi brutality, and at the same time as predominantly "bonding" and "nurturing" even in the face of extreme atrocity. All women become "mothers" regardless of actual circumstance.[12] Treating women as a more or less unified group with similar behavioral characteristics ignores important differences in cultural background, social class, age, economic standing, level of education, religious observance, and political orientation—differences that, like gender, contributed to the way victims responded to their circumstances. In addition, both versions tend to present an idealized portrait of women's behavior—strong (like men) or nurturing (like women)—that erases the actual experiences of women and, to an extent, domesticates the events of the Holocaust. The breakdown of values and resistance, whether spiritual, physical, or psychological, is one index of Nazi brutality.

Between these poles, I pursue a different tactic, suggested not by an a priori theoretical stance, but by the reflections of women survivors.[13] For example, Itka Zygmuntowicz, a survivor of Auschwitz, writes:

All on earth that I loved and held sacred I lost in the Holocaust, including nearly six precious years of my life. All on earth that I had left after liberation from Malchow, Germany, was my skeletal body minus all my hair, minus my monthly cycle, a tattered concentration camp shift dress without undergarments, a pair of beaten up unmatched wooden clogs, plus my "badge of honor," a large blue number 25673 that the Nazis tattooed on my left forearm of the day of my initiation to Auschwitz inferno. I was homeless, stateless, penniless, jobless, orphaned, and bereaved. . . . I had no marketable skills. . . . Jewish homes, Jewish families, and Jewish communities were destroyed. I was a displaced person, a stranger; alive, but with no home to live in. I had no one to love me, to miss me, to comfort me or to guide me.[14]

As Zygmuntowicz's recollection of her moment of liberation indicates, Jewish women survivors experienced and later reflect back upon the war both as Jews and as women. Zygmuntowicz's references to the cessation of menses and her lack of undergarments point to particular ways in which the Holocaust affected her as a woman, a subject she elaborates elsewhere. At the same time, her bereavement and displacement, the tattoo and wooden shoes, all place her as object of the genocidal practices aimed equally at Jewish men and Jewish women. The bringing together of both sets of details—one particular to women, one relevant to all Jewish concentration camp inmates—implies that survivors' reflections are inevitably gendered, and at the same time, that gender does not comprise the totality of one's experience.

Following her lead, I would like first to place the texts of women within the more broadly based conversation of Holocaust discourse. How do (and how did) different women reflect upon, recollect, and interpret their experiences of Nazi atrocity? How do they understand the allied acts of memory and testimony? Second, I would like to shift the representation of women as anomalous (and man as normative) and consider instead the gendering of Holocaust narratives generally. How is gender figured, for example, in texts by and about men? How are "man" and "woman" constructed in reflections of the Holocaust?

My point of departure and place of return are the words of women survivors. By the variety of details lived, remembered, and reconstructed, they give voice to the daily experience that constituted the events of the Holocaust. Holocaust testimony is fragmentary in nature, always incomplete. I would like to make the fragments speak to one another and to us as readers, but not to smooth over their gaps, tensions, and contradictions.

Because pregnancy and motherhood figure importantly in scholarly discussions of female "bonding," "nurturance," "biological vulnerability," and "biological resistance," I have chosen to focus here on those related themes, and to distinguish between their portrayal in testimony and in scholarship. As I will demonstrate, in the reflections of women survivors themselves, pregnancy and motherhood serve not only as touchstones of specifically female experiences, but also as a fulcrum for broader consideration of issues such as survival, morality, and remembrance.

As hard physical labor, scarce food and medical supplies, and the ever-present possibility of roundups, transports, and selections become the everyday experience of genocide, pregnancy becomes a life-threatening event, for the mother, the baby, and the community. Women's testimonies reveal the precariousness of childbirth during the Holocaust. One survivor recollects being too weakened from typhus to clear the mucus from the air passage of her newborn as he lay beside her; by the time others arrive, the baby has died.[15] When hiding from Nazi roundups, whether inside or outside the ghetto walls, the unpredictability of a baby's cries posed a threat to everyone else. Successful births in the ghetto required luck, courage, and ingenuity. Bella B. recounts assisting at the delivery of her sister's baby during a roundup. Hiding in a secret room, she muffled her sister's screams with her hand to escape detection; her hand still bears the scars of her sister's bites. Because no water was available, Bella's mother, "a very smart, an unusually smart woman," washed the baby in oil and butter.[16]

In the camps, matters were worse still. Women who were

visibly pregnant or who were accompanied by small children were selected for immediate killing. Sara Nomberg-Przytyk[17] recollects learning Mengele's rationale for procedures at Auschwitz:

> Mengele explained . . . why he killed Jewish women together with their children. "When a Jewish child is born, or when a woman comes to the camp with a child already . . . I don't know what to do with the child. I can't set the child free because there are no longer any Jews who live in freedom. I can't let the child stay in the camp because there are no facilities in the camp that would enable the child to develop normally. It would not be humanitarian to send a child to the ovens without permitting the mother to be there to witness the child's death. That is why I send the mother and the child to the gas ovens together." (69)

In Nomberg-Przytyk's memoir, Mengele's cynical "mockery of the tenderest of all feelings, a mother's love for her children" (69) serves as both illustration and ultimate symbol of Nazism's debasement of all human values. In spite of such orders, survivor accounts tell us that many pregnant women strove to conceal their condition rather than opt for a secret abortion. When discovered, such pregnancies were punishable by death.

While many survivors chronicle or depict pregnancy (sometimes their own) in the ghettoes and camps, pregnancy comes to mean different things in different accounts. It may serve as evidence of the special vulnerability of women, or of the predominance of the life force. The way a pregnant mother grapples with her condition, the response of other women, and the Nazi reaction make pregnancy testify to the strength or the fragility of the intimate bonds that tie human life together. Individual testimonies may affirm or shatter the ideal of motherhood. By pointing to the triumph or the eclipse of the life force, the kindness or cruelty of people, the selfishness or altruism on which survival hung, such testimony may affirm or deny important cultural, religious, and philosophical values.

The related tropes of pregnancy and motherhood have led later scholars to focus on one of two distinct forms of narrative: those of atrocity and those of heroism. In narratives of atrocity, pregnancy and motherhood render women especially vulnerable to Nazi brutality. In narratives of heroism, the same representations provide an arena for resistance against genocide.

Central to narratives of heroism is the portrayal of women conspiring against the genocidal will of the Nazis to save a newborn or a child. The accounts often focus on a secret pregnancy, with a baby born healthy and being either hidden with its mother or smuggled out of the camp or ghetto to safety. Resistance finds concrete expression in preserving the well-being of the pregnant woman, ensuring that the pregnancy and later the baby remain undetected by those who intend harm, feeding the child, and guaranteeing its safety. These narratives valorize not only the protective agency of women, but also motherhood itself. The mother's determination to carry to term at the risk of her own life proves powerful enough to prevail over the forces of death. Pregnancy (biology) becomes a form of "inner resistance" that triumphs over external forces of evil. Because the mother's success requires the help of others, individual pregnancy becomes a form of community building. In a sense, all the women become the baby's mother, its lifegiver.

By contrast, in narratives of atrocity, the mother is not strong enough to keep her baby alive. The fetus may be aborted, the infant stillborn or killed soon after birth. In some instances, Jewish women kill the baby to preserve their own or the mother's life; in other cases, the Nazis kill the child, often together with the mother. The narrative of atrocity reverses the conventional symbol of pregnancy as hope and regeneration. Instead, birth becomes synonymous with death, continuity with truncation. Even the intended kindness of women becomes a cruelty; not only can they not protect the baby, but their efforts to help it and the mother may cause both additional suffering.

When writing about women in the Holocaust, scholars tend to emphasize one or the other of these two types of narratives, and the conclusions each entails. Such selectivity, while elucidating an aspect of life and death under Nazi rule, leads to partial interpretations of women's behavior. Narratives of atrocity convey the overwhelming magnitude of the genocidal forces, which rendered meaningful resistance impossible or negligible. Reading through or listening to a sequence of such testimonies imparts a sense of the immeasurable losses women suffered, their sense of powerlessness, and their lack of meaningful choices. Narratives of heroism, on the other hand, focus our attention on those few moments when women were able to overcome, sometimes only provisionally, the genocidal forces that engulfed them. By drawing our attention to "happy endings"—the few babies saved, the few pregnant women protected—such stories create a feeling of optimism in the face of a destruction that we know, historically, was almost completely achieved.

In the actual testimonies of women survivors, the strands of these two narratives come through intermeshed. In Buchenwald, for example, Anna K. did not realize she was pregnant until the fifth month, when she felt the baby move.[18] While at the other labor camp, Starzysko Kamienna, she had asked for a transfer to the "awful" section where her husband was interned. Later, in the summer of 1944, they were placed on the same train to Buchenwald, where they were again separated. Because Anna K. had not menstruated since she was interned, and because the starvation rations left her emaciated, her pregnancy came as a shock. "You're crazy, where do you have it? You're so flat!" she was told by a friend who remained near her throughout the pregnancy.

As rumor spread of a pregnant woman, an SS officer lined up the six thousand women in the camp and announced: "Whoever is pregnant is going to be hanged to show you all that it's not right. Here's a camp, and you should work." Anna K.'s identity was revealed a few weeks before the liberation of Buchenwald by Allied forces. She remembers going to sleep each night not knowing whether she would be killed the next morning. Only the late date saved her from certain death. The day Buchenwald was evacuated, Anna K. went into labor. With the assistance of a Russian nurse, she gave birth to a healthy girl. Eventually, Anna K. was sent to Switzerland with her baby, uncertain of her husband's survival. In a letter that eventually reached him she wrote, "Try to be strong. You have for what to live." Her husband made his way to Switzerland, and the family began life anew in the United States.

In Anna K.'s remembrance (and in her husband's[19]), pregnancy and the birth of her daughter held out a beacon to her husband in his own struggle. One is tempted to read in Anna K.'s testimony solely a typical narrative of heroics exemplifying "biological resistance." Not only does the family unit remain intact, but, we learn, the daughter grows up to earn a master's degree and have children herself. At the same time, however, Anna K.'s story contains more somber undertones. We hear about other women in the camp, pregnant "ahead of me," whose destiny remains undisclosed. Anna K.'s own survival hung in the balance, effected only by the Allied victory. Her fate remained unknown to her family until the receipt of her letter. Holding her husband responsible for the pregnancy that jeopardized Anna K.'s life, her older brother threatened to kill him: "If something happened to Anna I will kill you with my hands that you could do it to her." Thus, pregnancy simultaneously stands for the continuity and the termination of life. While both Anna K. and her husband speak with obvious delight about their family—in particular about their grandsons—Anna K.'s plunge into memory brings her a feeling of pain rather than triumph. At the close of her testimony, she says, "When I started talking about how they killed my son I was hysterical, and how I was pregnant with mine daughter, it was also—it was a horrid story."

As reconstructed in memoirs and as refracted through the lens of fictional representation, narratives of heroism and of atrocity qualify, oppose, and undercut one another. Sara Nomberg-Przytyk's memoir, *Esther's First Born,* further complicates our notion of what pregnancy meant to women in concentration camps. The narrative plays the hopes of the pregnant Esther, a naive nineteen-year-old, against the fears of the older, more experienced narrator. Esther responds to her pregnancy with all the hope and joy of an expectant mother in the free world; Nomberg-Przytyk considers the perils of pregnancy in Auschwitz. Feeling life quicken within her, Esther embraces the impending motherhood, without a thought to her own safety or her child's survival, as evidenced by the "happiness that emanated from her whole body" (68). Viewed from the outside, however, Esther's is clearly an Auschwitz pregnancy: like Anna K.'s, virtually undetectable by anyone but herself. The narrator notices only that, while generally emaciated, Esther was "peculiarly thick" (68).

For Esther, the pregnancy promises a future, an antidote to the losses she has suffered. "I want to give birth to this baby. It's my first baby. It moves. It kicks me. It will probably be a son. My husband is not here anymore. That's his son" (68). As Esther joyfully anticipates the birth of her child, Nomberg-Przytyk struggles to save other women from the deadly repercussions of pregnancy in Auschwitz. Esther wishes to "go to the hospital to give birth to a baby like thousands of other women in the world" (70), but Nomberg-Przytyk learns that the infirmary doctor has women deliver in their own blocks rather than in the infirmary barracks, because she can keep it secret more easily, thus preserving the mother's life. "Our procedure now is to kill the baby after birth in such a way that the woman doesn't know about it" (69). Initially, the killing is done by lethal injection; later, in the absence of medical supplies, the doctor drowns the newborn, telling the mother, "The baby was born dead" (70).[20] In the grotesque situation of the death camp, cruelty becomes kindness, and murder, lifegiving. The doctor tells

Nomberg-Przytyk, "I want so much for the babies to be born dead, but out of spite they are born healthy" (69).

As Nomberg-Przytyk struggles with her deadly knowledge, Esther remains serenely certain that she and her child will survive. She dismisses Nomberg-Przytyk's suggestion to deliver in her own block, and refuses to relinquish her child. "I am sure that when Mengele sees it he will let me raise it in the camp. It is going to be a beauty because my husband was very handsome" (70). Briefly, the narrative allows us to hope that Esther's gamble will be rewarded. The infirmary supervisor does not report this birth. A selection takes place in the hospital block on the first day of Passover, and Esther anticipates Mengele's compassion. Momentarily, the young woman in Auschwitz is placed against the pantheon of heroic Jewish women: the biblical Esther, who saves her people from the genocidal decree of King Ahasuerus; the midwives, mother, and sister who rescue the infant Moses from Pharaoh's genocidal order, initiating the liberation celebrated at Passover. The invocation of the festival promotes the possibility that Esther's son may, indeed, survive. The first night of Passover holds special meaning for first-born Jewish males. On that night, the book of Exodus tells us, the Angel of Death enacted the tenth plague by killing the eldest son of each Egyptian household; however, the angel *passed over* Jewish households, sparing the Jewish first-born (hence the name of the holiday). But Jewish memory and a mother's wishes are spectral vestiges of a vanished world. As the narrator knew all along, Mengele selects Esther and her first-born for death.

Nomberg-Przytyk's narrative unsettles our notion of right and wrong. Both Mengele and the infirmary doctor commit murder, but for different reasons. Mengele implements the "final solution," while the doctor attempts, within narrowly constrained parameters, to save at least one life of two. In this horrible context, Esther's determination to carry to term and save her child is both heroism and a foolish, and deadly, romanticism.

Ilona Karmel explores these complexities further in her

novel *An Estate of Memory.*[21] Its central focus evolves from
the crisis of one woman's pregnancy in a slave labor camp.
In an enactment of group purpose rather than individual
survival, and at great personal risk, three keep secret the
pregnancy of a fourth, provide for her from their own inadequate ration, deliver her baby in secret, and arrange to
smuggle it from the camp to safety. The survival of Aurelia
Katz's baby girl symbolizes to them the triumph of the life
force over the machinery of death. "So the child, carried like
a parcel out of the camp, kept growing, until it was big
enough to take upon itself the burden of their longing for a
proof, for the sign that out 'in the Freedom' they still mattered" (277). By mothering Aurelia Katz and rescuing her
baby, they each may claim the child as their own, a form of
continuity should one or all of them not survive.

At the same time, their moral victory is undercut by a
counternarrative, the story of another baby born in the
camp and left to starve upon doctor's orders: "The child
should be laid in cotton wool. . . . The child should not be
fed anything, not even water" (255).[22] Moved by compassion, women feed that infant sugar water, at great risk to
themselves. The clandestine feedings, however, only prolong the baby's agony—a kindness that becomes a cruelty.
This brutal story, part of the oral history transmitted among
the camp women, serves as a touchstone to Nazi cruelty. It
also undermines the sense of heroic possibilities asserted
by the rescue of Aurelia Katz's baby.

In all of these reconstructions, the chasm between "normal" life—the life the victims remember, the life survivors
reenter—and atrocity is exemplified by the differences in
what pregnancy connotes in the camps and in memory.
Rather than an occasion for celebration, pregnancy threatens the mother's life. Karmel's novel contrasts one woman's
prewar "longing for a child" (166) with another's sense of
her unborn baby as "a tormentor who sucked her strength,
snatched every crumb away" (242). Like other Jews, the
fetus exists under a death sentence.

In Karmel's novel, the conspiracy to protect Aurelia
Katz's pregnancy provides the author with a fulcrum upon

which to explore the moral dilemmas inherent to the struggle to survive. While the women in the novel form "makeshift families," that bond remains tentative and fragile, subject to heuristic needs. Initially, Karmel presents such bonding as an enactment of ethical choice. Fighting to retain moral agency under dehumanizing conditions, the women forge a code of behavior: to act on behalf of the group's survival, to struggle for "us" rather than solely for "me," constitutes altruism, while to look out for one's own interests constitutes selfishness. In this framework, women fight aggressively to preserve the group they have formed.

While the makeshift families Karmel depicts in her novel, drawn from her own labor camp observations, support the view of women as forming "nurturing" bonds even in extremis, the actions they perform on behalf of the group do not differ from the behavior depicted by men, often described as individualistic and enterprising rather than cooperative. In actuality, the women in Karmel's novel and in other women's testimony navigate their precarious existence in much the same way as the men in Primo Levi's memoirs and David Rousset's sociological study: by "organizing," trading, peddling, begging, smuggling, and sometimes stealing.[23] And men and women alike often seem torn between meeting their own desperate needs and those of their families, real or constructed.

In Karmel's novel, even the women's simple code unravels in the hardships of camp life. As the novel progresses, one of the women begins to question the group ethic. "What is it? Anything done for someone else is a sacrifice, a noble deed; but try to do the same thing for yourself and the sacrifice becomes a disgrace. Why? I too am someone; I've no contract for survival, I too am afraid" (342). The novel asks, then, that we differentiate not between selfishness and altruism, but between selfishness and what Lawrence Langer calls "self-ishness." In his meditation on the videotaped testimonies of Holocaust survivors, Langer draws an important distinction between these terms. "Motivated by greed, indifference, malice" when one could choose otherwise, "the selfish act ignores the needs of others through

choice when the agent is in a position to help without injur-
ing one's self in any appreciable way" (124). Langer contrasts this with the "self-ish" behavior of the Holocaust survivor who remains "vividly aware of the needs of others but
because of the nature of the situation is unable to choose
freely the generous impulse that a compassionate nature
yearns to express" (124).[24]

Because the war against the Jews was launched in the
home and the community rather than in a distant battlefield,
it was first encountered and fought in the domestic realm.
Unlike traditional war narratives, survivor reflections often
focus on intimate settings made unfamiliar by atrocity: the
home, the synagogue, the marketplace. Perhaps because the
struggle against genocide often took place in women's
spaces and transformed women's work into resistance—
keeping a family fed, healthy, clean, clothed, and shel-
tered—Holocaust narratives frequently reverse the traditional dependence of women upon men in war stories.[25]

Karmel's work inverts the conventional war narrative
wherein heroic men protect endangered women. Most frequently portrayed as weak and passive, the men in her writing become increasingly reliant upon women for survival as
conditions worsen. In moments of crisis, and Karmel's narratives depict an enchainment of such moments, men re-
gress to a childlike dependence that threatens everyone's
survival. The protagonist of *Stephania,* for example, remembers her father paralyzed with fear in face of an impending
roundup. He cannot manage the simplest of tasks, such as
trading ration coupons for flour, and his daughter must in-
tervene. His helplessness diminishes him in her eyes; her
parting cry to him, as she pulls her mother out of danger, is
"Idiot!"[26] Pathetically seeking the reassurances of a vanished domesticity the morning of a roundup, he asks his
wife, "Myrele, what should I put on?" (270), just as in *An
Estate of Memory,* Aurelia Katz's husband asks, on the eve of
his death, "Aurelia, should I shave tomorrow?" (160).

By contrast, mothers figure importantly in memoirs by
women survivors. Especially women who had been adoles-

cents during the war remember their mother's competence, daring, and ingenuity as instrumental in their own survival. In her videotaped testimony, Anne J.[27] recollects her mother's offer to sew a special dress for the mayor's daughter, prior to the deportation of Jews to ghettoes and mass graves. In so doing, the mother purposefully sets up an important connection to people in power that later saves her family from the Yom Kippur "action" (mass murder). As the Jews assemble in the market square, Anne J.'s mother calls out to the mayor's wife that she has not yet completed the dress. The mayor pulls the family out of the crowd, retaining them among the "useful" Jews of his town. Later, Anne J.'s mother strategizes ways to save her husband, whose physical condition would not withstand the harsh manual labor demanded of Jewish men. Similarly, Ilona Karmel credits her mother with keeping Ilona and her sister alive and together during the war. "My mother always knew what to do." When Ilona was hospitalized with typhus, her mother stole her out of the hospital because Jewish patients were frequently murdered. Later, to escape a labor camp "selection" (a Nazi euphemism for choosing murder victims), the mother hid her daughters under a mattress, an incident Karmel uses in *An Estate of Memory*.[28]

As women survivors remember them, mothers protected not only their families but other endangered members of the community. Zygmuntowicz recollects that her mother endured beatings at the hands of the Gestapo rather than give away the identity of a Jewish man who had defied a Nazi order to turn in valuable possessions. The memory is a complicated one for Zygmuntowicz, who was also beaten, in earshot of her mother, who remained silent. "Why did my mother care more about a stranger than about me? . . . At that time I was really too young to understand it. And later . . . I started to understand . . . if my mother could risk her life and mine for a stranger, if she could love a stranger and be that *mentschlich,* how much more did she love me? I think that she left me the greatest legacy that I could ever have."[29]

Reflecting on the aftermath of Nazi atrocity, women frequently evoke the murdered mother whose absence concretizes their vast sense of loss. This becomes particularly noticeable when survivors marry and have children of their own. Zygmuntowicz recollects that when she first went into labor, she bicycled to the hospital to deliver her baby. Because in adolescence—in Auschwitz—she had not seen a normal pregnancy run its course, she explains, and because she had no mother to initiate her into the intricacies of womanhood, she had no idea what to do. Similarly, Bella B. frames the intensity with which she misses her mother in terms of child rearing. She is certain her mother would have known how to better cope with her sons' sibling rivalry. When Edith P. describes the cattle-train journey to a concentration camp, she remembers her mother complaining of the suffocating heat. At the time, Edith P. recalls, she was puzzled; she did not find the heat oppressive. However, she explains, since becoming a mother herself, she understands that her mother was oppressed not by the temperature, but by the knowledge of what awaited her children. As Edith P. narrates this remembrance on video tape, she flushes and breaks out into a sweat. Uttering her mother's words, "I'm so hot, I'm so hot," she momentarily becomes her mother.[30]

In retrospect, memories of the absent mother serve also to fortify the women as they grapple with deep anguish. One recurrent feature of women's testimony involves a final conversation with the mother who perished. Itka Z., for example, invokes her mother's parting words, uttered just before joining her two youngest children bound for the gas chamber at Auschwitz: "Itkaleh, you are a big girl. I cannot leave the small children. Remember, Itkaleh, no matter what happens to you, don't become bitter and hateful, don't let them destroy you."[31] Similarly, Dorothy F. recalls that after her mother was shot, she received a note from her that read: "My dear child, you are young and strong, and hopefully you will survive. But if you do survive, remember to tell the world how those barbarians treated us."[32] As these examples illustrate, the mother's parting words, as remembered

by their surviving daughters, fulfill several important functions. On a psychological level, they give the daughter permission to survive and to rebuild her life. In addition, the
mother's words contain a moral imperative, both collective
and personal. On a personal level, the message urges the
daughter neither to imitate the Nazis nor to absorb the image they project of her, but to retain a sense of self predicated on the mother's values. On a collective level, the
words make of the daughter a witness, enjoining her to remember the victims, to tell the story of those who perished
and cannot speak for themselves. For many survivors, this
entails a commitment to speak out against contemporary
cruelty and injustice.

Invoking the mother's memory is double edged, simultaneously attesting both to her presence (in memory) and her
absence (in actuality). Like all Holocaust victims, the
mother is present *only* in memory, and only at the moment
remembered. Moreover, the testimonies do not present a
vision of motherhood untouched by the horror of genocide.
Indeed, survivors invoke the shattering of mother-child
bonds as the ultimate emblem of Nazi evil. Bella B. remembers the importance of guarding one's meager bits of food in
the concentration camp. "We were not human beings. . . . A
mother took away the piece of bread from her daughter. . . .
The will to be alive is so strong you will do anything. You
will rob your kids from the bread, from the food." Other
testimonies mention women who disavow their small children, hoping to be spared the gas chamber. These anguished memories depict the infiltration of atrocity into the
most intimate recesses of one's life, disabling mothers from
being mothers. Ilona Karmel refers to the "spiritual suicide"
of women forced by harsh circumstances to go against their
compassionate nature. Such women, she notes, appeared
"monstrous from the outside and destroyed the self."[33] By
setting the welfare of the mother against the welfare of her
child, the Nazi system turned the mother into an instrument
of her own torture.

In response to the relentless system demanding that one

betray oneself and others, the intricately nuanced recollections of female Holocaust survivors reveal an unraveling of
self even in the midst of more affirming memories.[34] One
survivor reflects that by corrupting the motherhood and
wifehood so integral to the shtetl woman's sense of identity,
the Nazis deeply corroded a woman's sense of self.[35] This
corrosion sometimes distances survivors from their children, or makes them fearful of raising children, redoubling
their sense of isolation and loss. Some survivors express a
fear of passing along the aftereffects of atrocity, like an in-
fection or genetic defect. When Bella B. met her husband, "I
was afraid to have kids. . . . Let's not have children. I was
afraid that my kids will be not normal. I was afraid what I
went through I will give to the kids." These Holocaust memories indicate not that mothers or fathers, daughters or sons
have willfully betrayed one another, but that the Nazi machinery of atrocity deliberately and relentlessly aimed to
sever the links to family and community.

As these women's testimonies reveal, the Nazi genocide
radically ruptured the lives, families, and values of its victims. Even with a new family, isolation sometimes hits survivors of Nazi genocide, whose violently painful memories
surface of their own accord. Sometimes in the midst of celebration—a bat mitzvah, a wedding—tentacles of intense
memory may seize them, distancing them from events at
hand. Perhaps for this reason, when Rachel Auerbach
"list[s] the various kinds" of Jewish men, women, and children who perished, she categorizes them according to family relationships. Through an act of memory and imagination
she struggles to reclaim them, to restore lost connections,
asserting, "They are all mine, all related."

NOTES

1. Rachel Auerbach, "Yizkor, 1943," transl. Leonard Wolf, reprinted
in *The Literature of Destruction,* ed. David G. Roskies (Philadelphia, 1988),
459–64.

2. Emmanuel Ringelblum, *Notes from the Warsaw Ghetto,* transl. Jacob Sloan (New York, 1958), described the Jews as "*morituri*—sentenced to death" (320).

3. See, for example, Joan Ringelheim, "Women and the Holocaust: A Reconsideration of Research," *Signs* 10:4 (1985), 741–61, and an updated version in *Jewish Women in Historical Perspective,* ed. Judith R. Baskin (Detroit, 1991), 243–64; and Marlene E. Heinemann, *Gender and Destiny: Woman Writers and the Holocaust* (Westport, Conn., 1986).

4. Art Spiegelman, *Maus* (New York, 1988).

5. Art Speigelman, "Prisoner on the Hell Planet," *Short Order Comix* 1 (1973).

6. For example, in his monograph composed in the Warsaw Ghetto, "The Moral Decline of Jewish Women During the War," in *Kiddush Hashem: Jewish Religious and Cultural Life in Poland During the Holocaust,* ed. Jeffry S. Gurock and Robert S. Hirt, transl. David E. Fishman (New York, 1987), 240, Shimon Huberband explains that he does not wish to engage in "God forbid, a smear campaign of horrors against all Jewish women." Nonetheless, he asserts, "Rarely did one notice a Jewish woman open her purse to give a groschen to a starving Jew."

7. Two sisters, Ilona Karmel and Henia Karmel-Wolfe, wrote poetry on the backs of pilfered work reports while in a slave labor camp. Some of these poems were collected and published in the original Polish in *Spiew za Drutami (Song Behind the Wire)* (New York, 1947).

8. A recent collection of essays examines Holocaust studies in light of certain theoretical positions of postmodernism. *Probing the Limits of Representation: Nazism and the "Final Solution,"* ed. Saul Friedlander (Cambridge, Mass., 1992), thoughtfully examines the ways in which contemporary culture remembers or reconstructs the Nazi genocide. Friedlander speaks of "keeping the record of this past through some sort of 'master-narrative'" (3), inviting a group of scholars to collectively think through its shape and boundaries. Striking in an excellent volume representing new ways of thinking about the Nazi genocide is the marginalization of women both as remembered and as rememberers. Both Friedlander's provocative introduction and the excellent essays make clear that whatever its parameters, this *master*-narrative is gendered. Despite the voices of women as ghetto writers and memoirists, despite their thinking as imaginative writers, historians, and theorists, in Friedlander's volume women do not surface in reflections of the past, and only rarely as reflectors on the past. Of the twenty contributors to the volume, purposely solicited to expand the horizons of Holocaust discourse, only two are women. And they, too, write almost exclusively about male authors.

9. Interview with Irene Eber, February 4, 1992.

10. Cynthia Haft, *The Theme of Nazi Concentration Camps in French Literature* (The Hague, 1972), asserts that "the camp system grants complete equality to men and women" (121).

11. For example, Heinemann, *Gender and Destiny.*

12. Heinemann sets up "three categories of mothers," including "mothers and women above age forty-five" (22), a category that inexplicably subsumes all women under the heading of mother.

13. Cultural studies and postmodernist theory teach us, of course, that each of us reads texts with cultural and ideological assumptions that frame our interpretation. I do not naively claim here to exclude myself from this understanding of reading practices, but rather, I indicate that I have allowed the texts I have read to interrogate theory, to serve in some fashion as a test limit case for some theoretical positions within feminism.

14. Itka Frajman Zygmuntowicz, with Sara Horowitz, "Survival and Memory," in *Four Centuries of Jewish Women's Spirituality: A Sourcebook*, ed. Ellen M. Umansky and Dianne Ashton (Boston, 1992), 290.

15. Cited by Lawrence L. Langer, "Memory as Time," *Yale Journal of Criticism* 6:2 (Fall, 1993), 266–67.

16. T-306, Bella B., Fortunoff Video Archive for Holocaust Testimonies, Yale University Library (hereafter FVA).

17. Sara Nomberg-Przytyk, *Auschwitz: True Tales from a Grotesque Land*, transl. Roslyn Hirsch (Chapel Hill, N.C., 1985).

18. T-1115, Anna K., FVA, Yale University Library.

19. T-1114, Abraham K., FVA, Yale University Library.

20. Not all such killings were done to save the mother from death. Joan B. witnessed the camp commandant drown a newborn (T-82, FVA, Yale University Library).

21. Ilona Karmel, *An Estate of Memory* (Boston, 1969; repr. New York, 1986).

22. Like much else in the novel, the description of the baby left to starve to death is not Karmel's fictional invention. Bella B. recalls that the Nazis in her town would place babies on a table in the synagogue, and forbid anyone to feed them (T-306, FVA, Yale University Library).

23. For example, Primo Levi, *Survival in Auschwitz: The Nazi Assault on Humanity*, transl. Stuart Woolf (New York, 1959); David Rousset, *The Other Kingdom* (New York, 1947).

24. Lawrence L. Langer, *Holocaust Testimonies: The Ruins of Memory* (New Haven, Conn., 1991).

25. Karen Alkalay-Gut, "Women and the Gulf War," *Kerem* 2 (Winter 1994), 27–34, makes a related claim for the behavior of Israeli men and women during the Gulf War of 1991.

26. Ilona Karmel, *Stephania* (Boston, 1953).

27. T-1150, Anne J., FVA, Yale University Library.

28. Interview with Ilona Karmel, September 13, 1992.

29. Interview with Itka Zygmuntowicz, June 8, 1989. My thanks to Mary Kate McDonald for transcribing the text of the interview.

30. T-107, Edith P., FVA, Yale University Library.

31. T-1984, Itka Z., FVA, Yale University Library.

32. T-1312, Dorothy F., FVA, Yale University Library.

33. Interview with Ilona Karmel, September 13, 1992.

34. Langer, *Holocaust Testimonies*, elaborates on two chronologies that unfold in videotaped testimony.

35. Interview with Irene Eber, February 4, 1992.

14 ♦ SARAH BLACHER COHEN

Cynthia Ozick: Prophet for Parochialism

The waning of the immigrant experience and the depletion of the Yiddish culture which so enriched that experience have prompted some critics to write an epitaph for the dying body of Jewish-American writing in the postwar period. Thus, Ruth Wisse has written that Jewish-American literature "derives its strength from the peculiar tension of the Jew who is native to two cultures while fully at home in neither; hence the more fully the Jew becomes integrated into the larger culture, the less the tension and the fewer the creative energies generated by it."[1]

This charge may apply to the totally assimilated Jewish writers who, like Philip Roth's Portnoy, say the equivalent of "stick your suffering heritage up your suffering ass. I happen also to be a human being."[2] But it doesn't apply to a new group of American Jewish writers of the 1970s and 80s who have attempted to express their artistic vision in Jewish terms. Unconcerned about real or imagined charges of parochialism, they have freely explored the particularistic aspects of Judaism and have even speculated on the impoverishment of English as a literary language. They have worn their ethnic label conspicuously for they have proudly defined themselves as Jews. As Wisse observes, "their interest is not in the sociological or even the psychological legacy of a Jewish background, but in the national design and religious destiny of Judaism, in its workable myths."[3] Graduating from jumping in and out of the melting pot and creating a great splash for the spectators, they have concentrated on replenishing their minority puddles to sustain themselves rather than becoming inundated by the American mainstream.

The movement's prime diver into the reservoir of Jewish sources is Cynthia Ozick, who delivered a prophetic address at the American-Israel Dialogue of 1970, exhorting American Jewry to move "Toward Yavneh," that is, toward the creation of an authentic Jewish culture in the Diaspora. In this pronouncement, Cynthia Ozick admonished the Jews to stop whoring after the false gods of assimilationism and devote themselves to cultivating their own peculiar treasure: a new literature of cultural rebirth, "a liturgical literature [that] has the configuration of the ram's horn: you give your strength to the inch-hole and the splendor spreads wide."[4] The image of the shofar, or ram's horn, associated with biblical history and the most holy days of the Jewish New Year, was to rally the Jews to repent their sins to God and humanity so they could be redeemed. The shofar also sounded the call to the Jews to remember the tragedies of Jewish history, to avoid the forbidden lure of idolatry, and to return to their own origins. The shofar's piercing sound was meant to chastise all those universalist Jews who denied their own heritage by blowing into the wide or wrong end of the shofar: Bernard Malamud for his protest, "I am not a Jewish writer; I am a writer who is a Jew"[5]; Allen Ginsberg, with his loud persuasion that religions are "allee samee";[6] and even Saul Bellow, who wanted to be regarded as a great public writer and thus resented the Protestant majority for labeling him a Jewish writer or, as he said, for "giving a dog a bad name in order to hang him."[7]

Taking issue with this universalist stance, Cynthia Ozick contended that nothing produced by Jews in the Diaspora would last except what was produced in their own literary ghettos. For she had argued elsewhere, "all genius is parochial. Shakespeare wrote out of a tiny island, Yeats out of a still tinier one. Tolstoy had all the spaciousness of Russia, yet imagined the world mainly out of the French-speaking fraction of the Russian nobility."[8]

In "Toward Yavneh" Ozick further maintained that the only surviving Jewish literature would be that written in a Jewish tongue. Or as she said, "Literature does not spring from the urge to Esperanto but from a particular tribe, with its particular language."[9] This particular language she termed "Judeo-English," or "New Yiddish," the mode of expression for a new liturgical literature, not didactic or prescriptive but "Aggadic, utterly freed to invention . . . experiment, enlightenment, profundity, humanity."[10] Just as the Jews introduced Jewish ideas and Jewish intonations into the German language and created Yiddish, so, she claims, they can inject the Jewish sensibility, the Jewish vision, into English and create a distinctive language for their need in the American Diaspora. Ozick believes Jews have a choice. They can totally embrace Gentile culture and entirely lose their identity, or they can refashion the Diaspora language into their own unique linguistic gift. As she powerfully expresses the alternatives: "If we blow into the narrow end of the shofar, we will be heard far. But if we choose to be Mankind rather than Jewish and blow into the wider part, we will not be heard at all."[11]

These impassioned comments sound more like those of an inspiring prophet than a perspiring writer, able to realize such lofty visions. Yet Cynthia Ozick's fiction through the years has provided substantial evidence for her claims. Her most effective stories and novellas, notably "The Pagan Rabbi" and "Envy; or, Yiddish in America," are modern-day parables grounded in Judaic teachings in which Ozick functions as a prophet in Abraham Joshua Heschel's sense of the term: her narrative voice is neither that of a "singing saint" nor a "moralizing poet," but that of an "assaulter of the mind."[12] In contrast to many twentieth-century American novelists whom the Hemingway code of physical heroism made ashamed to think, she has "brain on the brain," a phrase she uses to describe Saul Bellow.[13] Like him, she is intoxicated with a wide range of ideas that have produced a heady brew of original thought.

The assaulting mind of the prophet is especially evident in the title story of Cynthia Ozick's first collection, *The Pagan Rabbi and Other Stories,*[14] where her protagonist, Isaac Kornfeld, a talmudic scholar of "piety and brains," is torn between worshiping the beguiling world of nature and obeying the prohibitions against pantheism contained in Leviticus and Deuteronomy: "Ye shall utterly destroy all the places of the gods, upon the high mountains, and upon the hills, and under every green tree. And the soul that turneth after familiar spirits to go a-whoring after them, I will cut him off from among his people" (16). The pagan, however, exerts a greater force upon him than does monotheism. And for a time he becomes an unfettered creature of the woodland, as opposed to the shackled occupant of the study and synagogue. In this respect, he is like those fictional heroes of Yiddish literature who yearned to free themselves from the bondage of rigorous talmudic study, from the narrowing confines of shtetl culture, to experience the physical raptures of the natural world.[15] But nature for Isaac is not just a hedonistic playground or a welcome respite from rabbinical burnout. It is a powerful heathen force that draws him away from traditional Judaism so that he becomes a Pagan Rabbi committed to the belief that "Great Pan lives" (17).

Isaac, however, suffers the consequences for his rabbinic dereliction of duty. According to the story's epigraph, which Ozick has chosen from *The Ethics of the Fathers,* "He who is walking along and studying, but then breaks off to remark, 'How lovely is that tree!' or 'How beautiful is that fallow field!'—Scripture regards such a one as having hurt his own being" (3). Similarly, Isaac Kornfeld "hurts his own being" by attempting to have his Torah-bound soul commune with a free-souled woodland nymph. Though he derives orgiastic pleasure from his florophilia and plant sodomy, he pays a terrible price for it: the loss of his immortal Jewish soul. Too late he realizes that "The sound of the Law is more beautiful than the crickets. The smell of the Law is more radiant than the moss. The taste of the Law exceeds clear water" (36). Abandoned by his soul who would have sung him David's songs in his grave, Isaac, in despair, hangs himself with his prayer shawl and in death is rejected by his fickle flower-child.

Ozick has us initially sympathize with the rabbi's desire to become a noble savage who is at one with the natural universe and sees creation with original eyes. But she ultimately rejects Isaac Kornfeld's nature-loving Hellenism for his observant widow's law-revering Hebraism. Just as the prophets reproached the Israelites for worshipping nature deities and foreign idols, Ozick, through this story, warns modern-day Jews of the injurious effects of choosing pagan aesthetics over Jewish ethics and spirituality. Like the prophets, who were more conservative than revolutionary, "calling men back to an older obedience rather than breaking new religious ground,"[16] Ozick chastises Isaac Kornfeld for wanting to be a creature of nature, leading a life of ease and spontaneity. She rebukes him for turning his back on painful Jewish history and living in the sensual present. She warns of the dire consequences of choosing the verdant tree of beauty over the unadorned tree of knowledge. Finally, like the prophets who "can speak words which clarify God's will,"[17] she makes necessary distinctions between the pagan and the holy in her story by instructing us to appreciate the marvels of nature, but not to worship them "instead of" God. She cautions us not to revere "the rapture-bringing horizon instead of God, the work of art instead of God."[18]

Thus Ozick would not have us read Isaac Babel's "The Awakening" to heed the old man's admonition to the young narrator, a studious urban Jew: "And you dare to write! A man who doesn't live in nature, as a stone does or an animal, will never in all his life write two worthwhile lines."[19] By standing *apart* from nature and differentiating between the natural and the sacred, Cynthia Ozick has written liturgically in "The Pagan Rabbi." As a contemporary prophet of powerful inspiration bidding us worship God who transcends nature, not a deity within nature, she has, in her deft fusion of art and revelation, transformed "the divine afflatus into divine sentences."[20]

Even more divine are the sentences in Ozick's "Envy; or, Yiddish in America," her most inventive and profound liturgical piece of fiction.[21] As in "The Pagan Rabbi," she is the hortatory prophet censuring American Jewry for its self-destructive embrace of an alien culture's aesthetics, but she is also the ironic prophet inveighing against the abandonment of an authentic Yiddish tradition and the inflation of an inauthentic talent in its place. Employing the prophet's style, which is both sardonic and "charged with agitation, anguish, and a spirit of nonacceptance,"[22] she berates American Jews for their peremptory dismissal of the best Yiddish authors. By translating into English only those inferior writers who specialize in the sensational and the modish, they, along with the Holocaust, have consigned to death the formerly vibrant Yiddish culture.

Filled with what Heschel terms the prophet's "sympathy with the divine pathos, the communion with the divine consciousness,"[23] Cynthia Ozick creates Edelshtein, a sixty-seven-year-old Yiddish poet, desperately striving for the past forty years to have his talents recognized in America. In one respect, he is still the fearful little man of the shtetl who has a Chaplinesque sense of himself as the accidental and insignificant creature barely surviving in the hostile world. In another respect, he has the hauteur of the high priest of Yiddish culture, deriding superficial Jewish-American writers and a facilely translated Yiddish author, Yankel Ostrover, who have made financial killings in the literary marketplace.

Edelshtein's feelings of extreme inferiority and extreme

superiority incur Ozick's ironic treatment. When he is the insecure shtetl figure, she compassionately views him as a saintly fool in his valiant efforts to keep Yiddish alive for American Jews: "Sometimes Edelshtein tried to read one or two of his poems. At the first Yiddish word the painted old ladies of the Reform Temples would begin to titter for shame, as at a stand-up television comedian. Orthodox and Conservative men fell instantly asleep. So he reconsidered and told jokes" (43).

Ozick acknowledges the ruefully comic incongruity of Edelshtein's mourning the death of Yiddish in synagogues that have become Cecil B. DeMille amusement parlors and fancy catering halls. Like Micah and Amos, ironically railing against the "idolatry of wealth, . . . and self-indulgence,"[24] she ridicules the gastronomic Judaism and edifice complexes of nouveau riche American Jewry: "The new Temples scared Edelshtein. He was afraid to use the word *shul* in these places—inside, vast mock-bronze Tablets . . . prayerbooks printed in English with made-up new prayers in them. . . . Everything was new. The refreshment tables were long and luminous [with] . . . snowheaps of egg salad . . . pools of sour cream . . . pyramids of bread . . . Hansel and Gretel houses of cream cheese and fruitcake"(44). Such lavish display, including the "soaring" architecture with "Scripture riveted on in letters fashioned from 14-karat gold molds" (44), cannot, however, distract Edelshtein from his mourner's grief. Comparing him to a "wanton stalk in the heart of an empty field" (70), as he declaims his Yiddish verse before a vanished audience, she makes us weep for him.

But Ozick transforms her sympathy into castigation of Edelshtein when he becomes the supercilious Yiddish purist. This is not to suggest that she totally disagrees with his assessment of American Jewish literature. With the exception of Saul Bellow, whom she respects as the "most purely and profoundly ideational"[25] of the Jewish-American novelists, she shares Edelshtein's belief that they are largely ignorant of their Jewish heritage, yet reviewers praise them for their ethnic wit and perception. Indeed, much of the

story's amusement stems from the fact that Edelshtein acts
as the stringent literary critic who employs the quaint accent and fractured syntax of Yiddishized English to pro-
nounce his unkind judgments. He deplores, for example, the
cheap way Jewish-American novelists add Yiddish local
color to their work: "Their Yiddish. One word here, one
word there. *Shikseh* on one page, *putz* on the other, and
that's the whole vocabulary. . . . They know ten words for,
excuse me, penis, and when it comes to a word for learning,
they're impotent" (79–80). Or he mocks his best friends' two
sons, "literary boys" who had "spit out the Yiddish that had
bred them" (45) to become experts of gentile literature, with
their Ph.D. theses on Sir Gawain and the Green Knight and
the novels of Carson McCullers.

However, Edelshtein is most envious and thus most mer-
ciless in his lampooning of Yankel Ostrover, the third-rate
Yiddish writer who enjoys national and international acclaim because his modernist English translators have "freed
him of the prison of Yiddish" (47). Edelshtein maliciously
calls the Polish-born Ostrover *der chazer,* the pig, "because
of his extraordinary white skin, like a tissue of pale ham"
(46), and because of his pornographically grotesque subject
matter—"men who embraced men, women who caressed
women, sodomists of every variety, boys copulating with
hens, butchers who drank blood for strength beneath the
knife" (47).

But what most hurts Edelshtein is that Ostrover is the
only Yiddish writer whose works have been saved, that is,
translated into English. He plaintively asks: "Why Ostrover?
Why not somebody else? What occult knack, what craft,
what crooked convergence of planets drove translators to
grovel before Ostrover? . . . Who had discovered that Ostrover was a "modern"? His Yiddish . . . still squeaked up to
God with a littleness, a familiarity, an elbow-poke, it was still
pieced together out of *shtetl* rags, out of a baby *aleph,* a
toddler *beys* —so why Ostrover? . . . Ostrover was to be the
only evidence that there once was a Yiddish tongue? . . . And
all the others lost? . . . Snuffed out . . . As if never?" (51).

Clearly, Ostrover, whose fiction about imaginary Polish villages reeks of the occult and the pornographic, is Ozick's caricature of Isaac Bashevis Singer.[26] But rumor also has it that Edelshtein is Ozick's thin disguise for the Yiddish poet Jacob Glatstein, whose views of Singer were even harsher than those of Edelshtein. In a 1965 essay, "The Fame of Isaac Bashevis Singer," Glatstein censures Singer for his "tales of horror and eroticism," infected with "all kinds of spiritual and physical depravity," and populated with heroes sullied by "villainy, brutality, and cynicism at every turn." Glatstein further claims that Singer's stories are "more attuned to the non-Jewish than to the Jewish reader," to whom Singer's themes "are a distasteful blend of superstition and shoddy mysticism."[27]

Sharing Glatstein's views of Singer, Ozick utilizes her prophet's irony as a "way of telling the truth" about the fraudulent Ostrover. "Extending a partial perspective into a more comprehensive one," she thus depicts Ostrover not as a serious author committed to his subject matter and craft, but as a joke machine mechanically rattling off one wisecrack after another.[28] She reveals him to be a titillator of the masses with his simplistic aphorisms, "dense and swollen as a phallus" and his "naked swollen sentences with their thin little threadbare pants always pulled down" (51). Moreover, she compounds her ironical treatment of him by having his shallow public honor him in the same room as the pantheon of great Jewish figures—Moses, Einstein, Maimonides, Heine— whose names are emblazoned on the majestic frieze lining the ceiling of the Ninety-second Street Y. Because she has the Yiddish Yankel Ostrover Americanize himself to become "Yankee Doodle" Ostrover, she makes him into a "worldwide industry" (62), who "can stand up forever and dribble shallow quips and everyone admires him for it" (63).

Departing from drollery to prophetic denunciation, Ozick, like Jeremiah inveighing against the false prophet whose "disingenuousness was the mark of a charlatan,"[29] has Edelshtein attack Ostrover for being an obscene literary faker and for perpetrating hoaxes of translation to gain fame. If reading an author's work in translation is, as the Hebrew poet Bialik notes, "kissing the bride through the veil,"[30] then so many deft hands have improved the appearance of Ostrover's bride that she scarely resembles his flawed original. Because Ostrover, a cripple in English, hires a stable of skillful translators to make the bride ravishing for the avant-garde and commerical reading public, Ozick reveals that the talent Ostrover has is not for the invention of innovative fiction but for pressuring his translators to transform his lackluster Yiddish into polished English. Because he woos one translator and drops the other, he keeps them in a "perpetual frenzy of envy for each other" (55), so that Ozick's story becomes a prophet's exposé of authorial rivalry as well as translator rivalry.

Ozick, like the prophets who took the populace to task for their false judgments, condemns the idiocy of the literary establishment for valuing lifeless prose cosmetically touched up by multiple translators rather than the vitality of a living language created by a talented single author zealously committed to Yiddish. But Edelshtein is not that impassioned devotee and practioneer of Yiddish. What Ozick finds most objectionable about him is his hypocrisy. Much as he mocks Ostrover, he also prefers to escape from the "prison of Yiddish" (47), or from being Jewish, if he could achieve fame. Thus, Ozick criticizes him for lamenting the waning of Yiddish when he actually laments the waning of an audience to appreciate his creativity.

Edelshtein's hypocrisy is attacked not by the author but by Hannah, a twenty-three-year-old American woman, fluent in Yiddish, whom Edelshtein implores to be his translator. The more desperate he becomes to obtain her services, the more anguished is the language he employs to depict the fate of Yiddish during the Holocaust. "A little while ago there were twelve million people—not including babies—who lived inside this tongue and now what is left? A language that never had a territory except Jewish mouths and half the Jewish mouths on earth already stopped up with German worms" (74). But Edelshtein immediately berates himself for exploiting the grisly details of the Holocaust to gain sympathy for his literary plight, for using international tragedy to call attention to his personal crisis.

No matter what Edelshtein's motives are or how impassioned his pleas, Hannah refuses to be his personal messiah and save his dying poems. Acting as a midwife to his creativity would prevent her from giving birth to the poetry gestating within herself. To guard against being exploited, she indignantly lashes out at him: "You jealous old men from the ghetto . . . You bore me to death. You hate magic, you hate imagination, you talk God and you hate God, you despise, you bore, you envy, you eat people up with your disgusting old age—cannibals, all you care about is your own youth, you're finished, give somebody else a turn!" (94, 97–98) .

On one level Hannah's diatribe appears to be a legitimate feminist complaint of an emerging woman artist who wishes to develop her own talent and not waste her energies translating the oeuvre of an old Yiddish male she doesn't respect. She accuses him of being too Jewish, of clinging to suffering, of revering history, and most damning of all, of producing works that were "little puddles," not the "mainstream" (95). The only Yiddish writer she admires is Ostrover, for being an author of many visions: "A Freudian, a Jungian, a sensibility . . . A contemporary" (95).

We are not to side with the young woman, however. Her devotion to the worldly Ostrover, who speaks for humanity, and her scorn of the ghetto poet, who speaks for Jews, shows the limitations of American-born Jewish youth who would readily sacrifice the parochial for the universal and in so doing lose their claim to any distinctiveness. Because Yiddish is an indigenous part of Edelshtein, who had the misfortune of living at a time when Yiddish "died a sudden and definite death" (42), Ozick sympathizes with his desire to communicate and be understood in an alien land. She can even forgive his envy for those who achieve a spurious kind of communication, and she endows him with a sense of pride to compensate for his maltreatment.

Thus, when Hannah banishes Edelshtein from her universalist house of fiction, claiming he doesn't interest her, he is compelled to view his ghetto identity not as a burden but as a blessing. In the Jewish equivalent of a Flannery O'Connor revelation, Edelshtein has an epiphany:

> He saw everything in miraculous reversal. . . . What he understood was this: that the ghetto was the real world, and the outside world only a ghetto. Because in actuality who was shut off? Who then was really buried, removed, inhabited by darkness? To whom, in what little space, did God offer Sinai? Who kept Terach and who followed Abraham? . . . Suppose it turns out that the destiny of the Jews is vast, open, eternal, and that Western Civilization is meant to dwindle, shrivel, shrink into the ghetto of the world—what of history then? Kings, Parliaments, like insects, presidents like vermin, their religion a row of little dolls, their art a cave smudge, their poetry a lust. (96)

This "miraculous reversal" that Edelshtein envisions represents Ozick's championing, like the prophets before her, of the superiority of the Judaic contribution to civilization. This passage contains her refutation of the belief that Jews are a culturally backward people, bereft of intellectual curiosity, totally consumed with obscurantist learning. Rather, she proudly asserts that the Jews' text-centeredness and monotheism have enriched a spiritually impoverished world.

"Envy," however, does not end with such an optimistic vision, but a pessimistic one. In a random telephone call Edelshtein encounters the anti-Semitic venom of a Christian proselytizer: "Christianity is Judaism universalized. . . . Our God is the God of Love, your God is the God of Wrath" (100). When Edelshtein refutes his position, he retaliates with standard Jew-baiting insults: "Even now, after . . . how many years in America, you talk with a kike accent. You kike, you Yid" (100). These remarks are offensive in their own right because they echo the sentiments of anti-Semites through the ages. But Edelshtein finds them even more painful because many Jews, themselves unaware of the grandeur of their own heritage, accept such pejorative views of Judaism and unassimilated Jews. Such self-hatred prompts a sizable number of Jewish artists to abandon Jewish sources of creativity in pursuit of worldly fame. It also causes the majority of American Jews to abandon Yiddish for fear of being considered "kikes." Thus the final words Edelshtein shouts at the bigot are: "Amalekite! Titus! Nazi! The whole world is infected by you anti-Semites! On account of you, children become corrupted. On account of you, I lost everything. My whole life! On account of you I have no translator!" (100).

The forlorn, vulnerable Edelshtein resembles the fate of Yiddish itself that Maurice Samuel described as an exile language "in a double sense, with the language of the people in exile and long in exile among the elite of that people."[31] Edelshtein is also bereft of supporters just as Yiddish literature is bereft of a physical territory, a supportive nation, a lengthy tradition, and a sustaining culture. Finally Edelshtein is rejected by the Hebraists and the American avant-gardists just as Yiddish literature has been shunned by the towering giants of the Hebraic past and the post-Enlightenment present.

As the title "Envy; or, Yiddish in America" suggests, Cynthia Ozick has written two stories.[32] The first, "Envy" is a ruefully amusing tale of a crotchety old man seeking translation for his sentimental poems while seething with jealousy of a slickly translated rival author. The more profound second story, "Yiddish in America," is about a thousand-year-old Jewish language and culture, almost destroyed in a decade by the Holocaust, and its precarious fate in America. Since Yiddish poetry for Ozick has a "liturgical impulse" and is a "continuation of Scripture," the story is about the struggle of the liturgical to find a place in the secular.[33] But the secular has been overrun by the pagan, and even its most learned and artistic inhabitants have had a "memory operation" (97) and suffer from cultural amnesia so that liturgical Yiddish is in danger of being forgotten and doomed to extinction. But Cynthia Ozick, the writer as prophet, has roused our concern for Yiddish, stimulated a reawakened interest in it, and, for a time, rescued it from oblivion.

Cynthia Ozick's aim as a prophet who strikes when her irony is hot[34] is to lift human beings up, not to push them down, to remind them of their commitments: "God has a controversy with you."[35] Thus Ozick wages a controversy with her fictional characters for abandoning Jewish sources of creativity and choosing the more universal; in real life she also takes issue with self-hating Jews who have no knowledge of the worth of their heritage. In a 1978 *New York Times* reply to Anne Roiphe for her article "Christmas Comes to a Jewish Home," Cynthia Ozick chastises her for being an unsuccessful assimilationist "because she has no gift of her own to offer the majority. . . . Bankrupt, she borrows from her neighbor's spiritual house all its furnishings; or else moves right in and calls this universalism. She cannot invite her neighbor into her own historic house because it isn't only that her cupboard is bare; all the rooms are empty. She has taken all her worldly notions from the majority culture, including the majority's mistakes, even when they are mistakes about herself."[36] Of her own Jewish identity, Ozick asserts: "It is not sufficient for me to be someone's symbol. I am not a Jew only under duress; my Jewish conviction derives not from what Anne Roiphe repeatedly calls the ghetto, but from the voice of Sinai."[37] Indeed this voice of Sinai, blending with Cynthia Ozick's ironic prophetic voice, will make her fiction heard a long time, for she has blown loud and clear into "the narrow end of the shofar."[38]

NOTES

1. Ruth Wisse, "American Jewish Writing, Act II," *Commentary* 61 (June 1976), 40.
2. Philip Roth, *Portnoy's Complaint* (New York, 1970), 84.
3. Wisse, "American Jewish Writing," 41.

4. Cynthia Ozick, "America: Toward Yavneh," *Judaism* 19 (Summer 1970), 280.

5. Bernard Malamud in a question-and-answer period. University at Albany, State University of New York, April 9, 1975.

6. Quoted in Wisse, "American Jewish Writing," 41.

7. Quoted in Cynthia Ozick, "Hanging the Ghetto Dog," *New York Times Book Review* (March 21, 1976), 47.

8. *Ibid.*

9. Ozick, "America," 275.

10. *Ibid.,* 280.

11. *Ibid.,* 282.

12. Abraham Joshua Heschel, *The Prophets* (New York, 1962), 10.

13. Cynthia Ozick, "What Drives Saul Bellow," in her *Metaphor & Memory* (New York, 1989), 13.

14. Cynthia Ozick, "The Pagan Rabbi," in her collection *The Pagan Rabbi and Other Stories* (New York, 1971). Further citations to this story are in parentheses in the text of the essay.

15. Ruth Wisse, "American Jewish Writing," 41–42, points out that in the works of Mendele, Sholem Aleichem, Peretz, Bialik, Feierberg, and Tchernikhowsky, the physical world of sun, storm, trees, and rivers provides a model of freedom counterposed to the self-denial of shtetl culture.

16. Daniel Jeremy Silver. *A History of Judaism: From Abraham to Maimonides* (New York, 1974), 80.

17. *Ibid.,* 79.

18. Cynthia Ozick, "The Riddle of the Ordinary," in her *Art & Ardor* (New York, 1983).

19. Isaac Babel, "Awakening," in *The Collected Stories of Isaac Babel,* ed. and transl. Walter Morison (New York, 1934), 311–12.

20. Silver, *History,* 79.

21. Cynthia Ozick, "Envy; or, Yiddish in America," in *The Pagan Rabbi and Other Stories.* Further citations to this story are in parentheses in the text of the essay.

22. Heschel, *Prophets,* 6.

23. *Ibid.,* 37.

24. Israel Knox, "The Traditional Roots of Jewish Humor," *Judaism* 12 (1964–65), 331.

25. Ozick, "America," 266.

26. In Yiddish circles Edelshtein has been identified with the poet Jacob Glatstein, who publicly deplored the rising fame of Isaac Bashevis Singer and criticized his work for being shallow. Cynthia Ozick, however, has denied these associations.

27. Jacob Glatstein, "The Fame of Isaac Bashevis Singer," *Congress Biweekly* (December 27, 1965), 17–18.

28. Knox, "Traditional Roots," 329.

29. Silver, *History,* 83.

30. Hayyim Nachman Bialik (1873–1934), quoted by Sarah Blacher Cohen, "The Jewish Folk Drama of Isaac Bashevis Singer," in her edited collection, *From Hester Street to Hollywood: The Jewish-American Stage and Screen* (Bloomington, Ind., 1983), 198.

31. Maurice Samuel, *In Praise of Yiddish* (New York, 1971), 8.

32. Joseph Lowin, *Cynthia Ozick* (Boston, 1988), 20.

33. Cynthia Ozick, "Prayer Leader," *Prooftexts* 3 (1983), 1.

34. For an extended analysis of irony in all of Cynthia Ozick's fiction, see Sarah Blacher Cohen, *Cynthia Ozick's Comic Art: From Levity to Liturgy: The Fiction of Cynthia Ozick* (Bloomington and Indianapolis, Ind., 1994).

35. Lowin, *Ozick,* 21.

36. Cynthia Ozick, "The Holidays: Reply to Anne Roiphe," *New York Times* (December 28, 1978), C6.

37. *Ibid.*

38. Cynthia Ozick, "America," 282.

15 ✦ NORA GLICKMAN

Jewish Women Writers in Latin America

Esther Seligson, a Mexican writer, recalls a story of a woman who escaped from the Warsaw ghetto. Her grandfather's advice before she left was: "Always remember you are a Jew!" Her grandmother also had some advice: "When you leave this place, forget you are a Jew!" These same contradictory messages can be derived from the distinctive literature produced by Latin American Jewish women writers, of which some representative examples are discussed in this essay.

A Jewish presence in Latin America has been recorded since the time of Columbus. In order to protect themselves from the Inquisition, early Jewish writers in Spanish and Portuguese hid their religious identity. In the nineteenth century, as each Latin American nation gained independence, the Inquisition was abolished, and more liberal policies were implemented, the situation of Jews improved. Large-scale Jewish immigration from Europe at the beginning of the twentieth century contributed to an increase in

Jewish self-confidence. While some of the new immigrant writers continued writing in Yiddish and contributed to Yiddish newspapers in Buenos Aires, New York, and Warsaw, most were soon writing in Spanish and Portuguese. Despite social and cultural differences among the countries in which the immigrants settled, Jewish writers in Latin America are remarkable in the similarity of their concerns.

The year 1910 can be singled out as the official beginning of Jewish writing in Latin America as it marks Alberto Gerchunoff's publication of *The Jewish Gauchos,* a romanticized account celebrating Argentina's hundred years of independence, and the arrival of large waves of East European immigrants. Gerchunoff's positive views of the experiences of the agricultural colonists, however, were not shared by all the chroniclers. The following generation of native-born Latin American Jews, anxious to establish themselves in their respective countries, were preoccupied with social, political, and economic realities. They were not afraid of pogroms, as their parents had been, but they did not expect to find the promised land either.

Latin American Jewish writers share a need to search for their identities.[1] Some are involved in this search through associations and images. Others are more explicitly preoccupied with Jewish issues. Starting from their own memories, they seek out those of their ancestors. Through this process, individual and historical, collective and personal memories merge into one. These authors share a history of exile that consists of memories of uprooting, persecutions, pogroms, and irrational hatreds. They also share the warnings and advice they received from their elders. Having shed the burden of religious rituals after they emigrated, they recover it decades later, as they begin to write. Writing, then, becomes a unique way of searching, understanding, and explaining; a way of finding identity. Judaism becomes a complex process that, far from disappearing into assimilation, becomes dynamic, stimulating, and enriching.

At the same time, the authors reviewed here are also affiliated with the general culture of their country. They regard their hybrid condition—Jewish at the same time as Argentine, Peruvian, Venezuelan, and so on—as both a challenge and an asset. They insist on being regarded above all as writers, rather than as nationals of their respective countries. Their personal experience often provides material for their fiction. Although they identify with the concerns of their particular country, their Jewishness comes across through their writing.

With the exception of Sor Juana Inés de la Cruz, a seventeenth-century mystical poet, few women's voices had much impact in Latin American letters until the appearance of the poets Delmira Augustini, Juana de Ibarbourou, and Gabriela Mistral at the beginning of the twentieth century. Since the 1950s, with the proliferation of literary journals, women like Victoria Ocampo, editor of *Sur* in Buenos Aires, have begun to gain international recognition. The "boom" of women writers, however, was eclipsed by that of men like Fuentes, Vargas Llosa, and García Márquez. Not until the 1970s and 80s did women such as Rosario Castellanos, Elena Poniatowska, Clarice Lispector, Isabel Allende, and Luisa Valenzuela begin to have an impact on world literature. Among these women writers are many Jews.

Second- and third-generation Latin American Jewish women authors tend to be professionals—lawyers, journalists, analysts, teachers, translators. They experiment with a variety of literary genres, including novels, plays, poems, testimonials, and drama. Some, who rebel against the paranoid mentality of the immigrant generations, write denunciatory literature in order to exorcise their past. Their intention is to demythologize the Jew, and to understand him or her better. They all touch upon generational differences, assimilation and integration, and the dissonant elements between Latin American culture and their own East European Jewish heritage.

A close description of taking root in the new land can be found in the work of Rebeca Mactas (b. 1924) a journalist, poet, and translator. Mactas's collection of short stories, *The Jews of "The Acacias,"* provides vignettes of life in the

Jewish agricultural establishments of Argentina settled by
East European immigrants.[2] Mactas's depictions differ from
the romanticizations of Alberto Gerchunoff and from the
versions of Samuel Eichelbaum and César Tiempo, whose
plays provided their gentile public an image of the assertiveness and combativeness of the new Jewish settlers.
Rather, Mactas focuses on the disintegration of the colonies,
which meant the end of Jewish life, religion, and tradition in
the countryside. *The Jews of "The Acacias"* presents a microcosm of Jewish life in the colony, as it portrays the idio-
syncrasies of the people, their belief in the coming of the
Messiah, their need for solace in liturgy and music, the intolerance of the elders toward intermarriage, and the deser-
tion of the young people to the cities.

Mactas observes in particular the roles of women, especially mothers who have sacrificed everything to follow
their spouses to the new country in pursuit of freedom,
leaving behind a culture and submerging themselves in the
barrenness of the Pampas for the sake of educating their
children. From the male perspective, the woman remains
the nameless "wife of . . ." She is a female whose "mission"
it is to blindly obey her husband, and who shares with other
women the qualities of "goodness, honesty, hard work,
courage, and generosity." Her feelings, however, are atro-
phied by boredom and poverty. Young, marriageable
women have no options for eligible men, as they have all left
the colonies.

Mactas's romantic sensibility comes through in her keen
observations of the relationship between woman, nature,
and language. Her younger women, who seem to make their
own choices, are actually the product of a patriarchal mentality. They feel trapped by adverse circumstances, without
options in the isolation of the Pampas. In "Simple Heart,"
Eva's widowed father dies after she has spent a lifetime
caring for him. Given the choice between the younger man
whom she loves, or a much older man who needs her, she
opts for the latter. Mactas equates need with virtue, because
it allows one to give. "One only lives when one gives; such
is the law of the world" (50). To give, she insists, is peace.

For this and other ethical considerations, the parallels drawn from the animal world provide women with their most important lessons. Watching the agony of a cow dying after numerous births, the protagonist identifies with the animal's pain: "One could say that her shout was the real shout of solitary flesh, kneaded for death and created to be torn apart." The farm girl, who learns from the cow the strength of giving birth, kneels next to her with the concern she would have for an unfortunate, loving sister: "Poor, poor little Chilena!" (54).

In spite of being rather obvious, Mactas's animal imagery does not lose its freshness and naiveté over time. When Miriam, of "Springs," condemned by poverty to a wretched existence on the land, attempts to protect a defenseless sheep from the horseman's whip, she is told by the local shepherds that "her" newly adopted sheep is on the way to the slaughterhouse. Their callous joke consists of "herding" her along with the sheep, saying, "What a lovely sheep, what a pretty calf! They'll pay a lot for her!" (130). There is a tragic sense of the injustice of the land, which is generous to some and withholding to others. The joyful celebration of a wedding, marked by the slaughtering of a sheep, leads Miriam to ponder that while "the fields burst with life, misery makes life unbearable" (155).

Mactas's style is permeated by lyrical imagery and with spirituality. Miriam's fantasies of love are both sensual and surreal: "Suddenly she felt she was growing wings. And she undertook a flight in space, like a nocturnal bird, with the impression that the spring night was hers, much like her dreams" (148). Sexual imagery is effectively conveyed through animal rather than human feelings. Miriam's somber, painful future is forecast by the image of a bull, "panting in the purple dusk the beast was a dense stain of blood, heavy and evil blood, blind and powerful" (156). Teachings of the Bible, Kabbalah, and other works of Jewish literature are also adapted to Mactas's own philosophy. In a story reminiscent of I. B. Singer's "Yentl," a girl in the Pampas who is versed in religious subjects, only permitted to boys, is less likely to obtain an easy match for marriage.

Mactas's legacy is both her nostalgia for the secular Yiddish culture of the Old World ("Birds") and her hopes for Jewish utopia in Latin America. She is also sensitive to the bitterness resulting from the harsh and barren life in the colonies. Her most accomplished stories, which deal with the dichotomy of city/country life and the generational conflicts, follow in the tradition of Argentine Gauchesque literature, which is best represented in the plays of Florencio Sánchez. In "The Home," an old immigrant despairs of his lost pioneering dreams. He rejects the lifelong care of his wife as a "nuisance" and a "shadow," and provokes his own fall into the hole he is digging for himself, rather than accept a more civilized death in the new farmhouse his bourgeois son has built for him.

The voices of the past that keep pounding in the minds of these women writers are perhaps best captured in a short story by the Uruguayan Teresa Porzekanski, in which memories shift back and forth, driven by the confusion of a ninety-year-old woman in a hospice.[3] As the evening progresses, Rochl Eisips repeats, with variations, a vague litany that gives rhythm to her words:

> Over and over the cossacks had murdered her parents and over and over her aunt from Vitebsk made cakes to sell in the market. Then the ship appeared over the horizon from the port, and a fifteen-year-old with her kerchief tight around her head came down and mingled amidst the crowd with kitchen utensils, only to get pregnant and give birth to five wise children. All that outline strung together again and again in the fable-cadenza of the afternoons. (228)

The Genealogies (1981), by the Mexican author Margo Glantz, an elaborate tableau of Jewish life, reconstructs the history of her own family as it migrated from the Ukraine to Mexico in the 1920s.[4] In *The Genealogies* Glantz utilizes a long conversation with her father, interrupted by multiple digressions, to write a story that will help to unravel her past. In recording the experiences of Jacob Glantz—a Russian immigrant, cafe owner, artist, and Yiddish poet—his daughter traces ways of life that are both her own and also culturally different. Glantz raises her quest to the sphere of epic, comparing herself to Telemachus and her father to Ulysses.

Jean Franco observes that in this novel, "family is represented as a space of survival, as a space where the dominant ideological values are questioned and negated."[5] Yet Glantz does not negate; rather she succeeds in salvaging her elusive past through her journey back to the shtetl, the recovery of scraps of sepia photo albums, and the records of voices and faces handed down by older generations. In this manner, Glantz's act of writing leads to self-discovery. When listing the important items she has inherited over the years, she discovers the heavy burden of her Jewish past:

> Whether we come from nobility or not, we all have our genealogies. I descend from Genesis, not out of pride, but out of need. My parents were born in the Jewish Ukraine, very different from the present one and far more different from the Mexico where I was born, where I was lucky to grow amidst the shouting of the merchants of La Merced, those merchants my mother looked at in astonishment, all dressed in white. . . . Perhaps what attracts me most to my past is the awareness of the garish, cheap colors of profuse baroque, the grotesque, the conscience that makes real Jews seem lesser people with a greater sense of humor, their ill-ventured, placid warmth, and even their occasional shamelessness. (15)

And yet, because she collects pagan monsters and popular saints that make her look "un-Jewish," the narrator feels compelled to explain her duality: "It is all mine and yet it isn't; and I seem Jewish and yet I don't, and for that reason I write these genealogies" (106).

Margo Glantz's Venezuelan counterpart is Alicia Freilich

Segal, a journalist, whose first novel is a Chagallesque portrayal of Jewish life in Latin America.[6] *Cláper* (1987)—a Yiddish term for a door-to-door peddler—alternates between
two narrative voices, using rhetorical questions, interviews,
monologues, letters, and even the "I and Thou" of Buberian
dialogue. Freilich adopts the voice of her father Max for
memories and witty anecdotes. She adopts the voice of the
daughter, a professional woman and first-generation Venezuelan, for more analytic, autobiographical fiction. Following a parallel construction, the father's actions are repeated
thirty years later by the daughter, to show how certain values and traditions are preserved through the generations
and how the Jewish heritage is maintained.

At the same time, the novel interprets events that affected
Jewish life in the Americas and touches upon other subjects
of concern to Jewish writers of Freilich's generation. These
include the heritage of Yiddish journalism, with its contacts
with Yiddish newspapers from Buenos Aires and New York;
the shadow of a Jewish white slave trade that lasted until
the 1930s; the acceptance by several countries of German
refugees, and their refusal to allow Jews to immigrate after
the war; the sense of guilt, shared with Holocaust survivors;
the tentative encounters with Sephardic Jews.

Cláper is a saga of the Diaspora that recreates the mystical atmosphere of the Hasidic world in Poland, characterized by the teachings of the Hebrew Bible, Yiddish proverbs,
and Jewish humor. As in the case of Margo Glantz, here too
the father is the dominant influence. While the mother at-
tends to family business, the father solves larger, communal
problems. Several parallel situations affect both generations
as they undertake their lives' adventures: the father abandons his parents' home in Lendaw, and the daughter leaves
her parents' house in Caracas, to attend university; both
father and daughter experience freedom upon contact with
the gentile world; and both open the doors to outsiders—
the father by inviting out-of-towners for the Sabbath in Poland, and later the daughter by hosting gatherings of intellectuals in Caracas. When in 1929 the father returns from

Cuba to Poland, he finds that the Hasidic world is already dead, and that despite the blatant anti-Semitism and the dire poverty, many still refuse to leave.

With his constant good humor, the father holds on to the Yiddish of the European immigrants, rescuing it from oblivion. His effective correspondence with the New York Yiddish newspaper *Di Prese* is providential in securing his safe deportation from an American prison to Cuba, when he cannot secure a resident visa in the United States. More than a language, his Yiddish is an instrument of survival and an expression of nostalgia. As the son of the real-marvelous world of I. B. Singer and Elie Wiesel, Freilich describes to his daughter the paradoxical encounters of trauma-ridden immigrants with a generous, hospitable Venezuela.

Cláper is also Freilich's avenue of expression for recording the changes that took place in Venezuela through the twentieth century in the fields of art, music, film, politics, and history. She voices her criticism of deficient education and corrupt university politics, of the corrupted state of journalism, the deficient teaching methods used in universities, and the excessive reliance of the middle class on psychoanalysis. As a writer and a journalist, she perceives language as freedom and uses it to understand her past and present. Freilich shares with Margo Glantz and with Gloria Gervitz the destiny of the immigrant's daughter who debates whether or not she belongs to the Jewish tradition.

Gloria Gervitz's prayerlike poetry is both confessional and colloquial.[7] In *Yizkor* (1987), this Mexican poet commemorates the strength of the bonds between mothers and daughters, and ponders the fears of old age and death. Rather than addressing a patriarchal God, here is a woman who speaks to an absent mother Goddess. Gervitz subverts the "sacred" attributes assigned to mothers and their children, bringing a female voice to the male preeminence of the Torah. In *Yizkor*, whose title refers to the traditional Jewish prayer service for mourners, the female poet prays in a language "that is not mine" (male, and Hebrew), referring to the traditional exclusion of women from the obligation to

recite the kaddish, the mourner's prayer. Anticipating that
there may be no man present to perform the ritual for her
when she dies, she says "Kaddish for you and for me." Gervitz's ambiguous feelings toward religion are evident when
she quotes from Christian prayers: "Mother of God, pray for
us." In her secular answer to the religious prayer, Gervitz
equates remembering with creating, as she pieces together
fragments of the past Jewish world to which she belongs.
After the traditional month of mourning, the Grandmother's
voice still struggles to have a dialogue with the living:
"Thirty days after your death you hear voices through this
heap of earth and small stones left by those who remember
you. . . . I remove the stones so the words can penetrate"
(65).

Gervitz gives voice to exiled Jewish women who arrived
from Russia to a world of which they knew nothing. *Yizkor* is
an homage to the spirit of those women who fought bravely,
yet silently, to build a home for themselves and for their
children. These were the altruistic women who had no time
for crying because mere survival consumed all their energies. And yet, what sustained them were their dreams and
determination. Gervitz weeps for them, so they are not forgotten.

Sabina Berman, mostly known for her plays *Heresy, Yankee,* and *Hopscotch,* wrote *The Bobbe* (1991) as a way to
understand the relationship between a young Mexican and
her immigrant grandmother.[8] This novel, which spans over
twenty years (from the fifties to the seventies), is told
through three feminine voices: those of the grandmother,
her daughter, and her granddaughter. In this way the reader
acquires a consciousness of the historical trajectory of Mexican Judaism in this century, from Orthodoxy to atheism.

The Bobbe is a testimonial, impressionistic novel cen-
tered in the conflict between religious experience and logic,
embodied in the confrontation between the mother and the
grandmother. The latter transfers her Jewish Viennese
world to Mexico, where she lives anachronistically like an
aristocrat, isolating herself in her religion, tradition, and

multiple languages (Yiddish, Polish, and German), while ignoring any contact with the Mexican world. The mother, for
her part, has become acculturated, and changed her religion
for the more universal ideology of psychoanalysis. The third
generation is looking for a new experience that combines
these two worlds. The new synthesis, based on the message
the girl gathers from her daily contact with her grandmother, consists of a series of revelations that go from the
discovery of words to the realization of death itself. Simple
acts are made sacred and transformed into celebrations.

The *bobbe*'s (grandmother's) secret is her gift of alchemy,
capable of transforming the prosaic into the sacred. She
also transmits to the child the mystical experience of Jewish
religion, through the perception of the *Ein Sof:* the Light of
the Eternal. Like the *bobbe,* Berman's poetic prose can
charge everyday moments with beauty and dignity. The curious mind of the grandchild is nursed in her mother's pragmatism and the grandmother's spirituality:

> As I kept feeding myself one grape after another, I went
> on explaining to my grandmother about the hypothet-
> ical God. I told her about the visit to a church I made
> with my mother. The parishioners were praying and
> the Father, next to a golden altar, mentioned the Lord.
> Then everyone said: Amen. My mother asked me if I
> saw the Lord the priest was talking about. And since
> I did not, because he was invisible, she asked me if I
> could hear that Lord answering him or the parishio-
> ners, by word or by sign, perhaps a creak on a bench,
> a change in the glance of the Virgin's statue, any pro-
> digious or commonplace event. For half an hour I paid
> close attention to the Virgin, the parishioners, the
> benches. No; that Lord doesn't answer, I said. And nev-
> ertheless, they still cry out to him, my mother pointed
> out. That, she said, is what having faith means. . . .
> And my grandmother, absorbed in her thoughts,
> made a jigsaw puzzle of the broken plate. Suddenly I felt
> sad. I kept silent. The water kept running from the tap

into the sink. Finally Grandmother said: "Close your eyes." I lowered my lids.

"What do you see?"

"Nothing."

"And in that nothing, do you see light?"

I paid attention. Under my lids, in that blackness, something like a yellow and white dust, a vibration, a light. "Yes," I said. "But I always see it like that."

"Always?"

I thought about it. That light was nothing out of the ordinary.

"Yes," I said, "always."

"Always," Grandmother repeated. "Well, that is God, and He has many names." (36–37)

Like Berman, Marjorie Agosín, a Chilean poet, human rights activist, and college teacher residing in the United States, is intrigued by the legacy passed on through women's generations, and observing cultural taboos and forbidden desires. Her writings, collected in *Happiness,* make use of interior monologues and stream of consciousness to convey a young woman's view of the world in delicate and poetic prose.[9] Agosín focuses on the injustices caused by political repression, on the unhealed scars left by past wars and persecutions. Her Jewish tales are striking for their depiction of women who are immersed in their own private worlds as a means of surviving the horrors that surround them.

The protagonist of "The Seamstress of St. Petersburg" is a kind of wandering Jewess who sews for the "tsarina," and is caught up in the turmoil of the Russian revolution: "When they began to kill Jews and trees, to burn Jewish children and chickens, Estefanía was not worried about her chafed skin, her crooked back, she simply felt an immense terror for the precious remnants of brocade she kept. . . . When one day they burned her room, Estefanía leisurely, calmly strolled out through the streets towards the outskirts of St. Petersburg" (36). Years later, Estefanía's greatest moment is her chance encounter in London with a benefactress who gives her a few rubles. In the seamstress's mind, the world froze in 1917 and never changed since that time.

Agosín's literature, like that of other Jewish women writers, shows an attraction for the Christian world and its rituals: the mass, communion, incense, and of course, the *goy*. In some cases the subject is treated with humor, in others with gravity. Agosín's "Church Candles" is a story about the conflict of a Jewish girl brought up in a Catholic society. Here, the influence of the superstitious housemaid is juxtaposed to the leniency exercised by assimilated parents. The narrator's attraction toward the shape of the cross (as opposed to the jagged edges of the star of David) goes hand in hand with her willingness to taste the communion wafer during Mass. She is "terrified," however, when she learns that what she had been eating was the body of Christ.

Recurrent images of the horrors of the Holocaust are often found in the works of Jewish women authors, even when they have not directly witnessed these events. Allusions abound about the transport trains, the camps, the gas chambers. The reconciliation of past with present, however, is a departure from the earlier identification of Jews with suffering and with death. Agosín's "Plains" is about the strange friendship forged between two girls in Chile; one, the daughter of Austrian-Jewish immigrants who survived the Holocaust, the other German-born. Their mutual questions about the past lead to painful disclosures: "I asked her what her parents did during that war, when my grandmother Helena resigned herself to leave behind her books, her sacred candelabra, and walk toward the horror chambers. . . . She told me, with her head lowered: 'My parents worked for the SS in Auschwitz. I saw women with your eyes, burning . . . I saw children charred, climbing into the death trains, while some Bach sonatas were being played'" (81). The guilt of one and the pain of the other result in forgiveness, in a mutual loss of fear, and in friendship. The narrator's initially shocked response gives way to a new comprehension of reality: "I sensed an icy, very fine blade riding up my back. . . . I offered her a white wine of the kind people drink in my country so they'll be filled with love and forget hunger. I offered her things that only silence could keep, and she, defenseless, arrogant, asked me to walk with her along the immense poplar groves" (81).

The novels of the Argentine writer Alicia Steimberg reflect generational conflicts between immigrant grandparents and their offspring, the preoccupations of urban middle-class women and of their immediate families, and the dualities of growing up in a Catholic world. These novels, equipped with large doses of black humor and sarcasm, refer to contemporary politics and to the contrast between the ideological socialism of the grandparents and the farce that democracy has become two generations later. Steimberg contends she should not be classified as a Jewish writer "because I have never written on this subject. I write about matters related to family and to childhood, inspired by my own history." Thus, Steimberg's protagonist in *Musicians and Watchmakers* (1971) insists that her Jewishness is the result of a series of transplants and uprootings (98).[10]

Musicians and Watchmakers is a novel of transgressions in which Steimberg caricatures the rules set by a Jewish bourgeois family that puts excessive emphasis on material success. But rather than depicting harmonious relations among family members, she focuses on the malice, the envy, the crass taste, and the constant quarreling that permeates this household:

> Mother was the only one of the four that studied.
> "We're starving so you can study, you bitch," her sisters often reminded her.
> "Living with a bunch of snakes like you, I'd shoot myself if I couldn't study," mother answered. (98)

The grandfather in this novel is the ideologue and spiritual teacher, while the grandmother—as in Mactas's stories—is the one who takes care of the family and is not rewarded even with the pleasure of seeing her children succeed:

"Grandpa José, unfortunately, was not a farmer. He was devoted to teaching children history and Jewish religion, while Grandma Ana became a Jewish *gaucha*. She did all the work, and kept having kids and fed them on milk and noodles until they were fifteen, when they grew up and left and some never returned" (100).

The protagonist's skeptical aunts warn her to guard her tradition by holding fast to it: "Jews make better husbands, while *goyim* only play billiards and call their spouses 'dirty Jew' when they have a fight." When it comes to disclosing her identity, they insist she should always wear a Star of David round her neck.

In response to their prejudice, Steimberg's heroine reveals another kind of wisdom, more cynical and street-smart:

> During an explanation on Jews and Christians her fifth-grade teacher asked all the Jewish girls to raise their hands. Some did so, meekly, like when they finished solving a problem. My hands remained on my desk. . . . I was learning not to be stupid, by pretending to be stupid. When the teacher finished going over the faces of those who had raised their hands, she told them to put them down, and continued with her explanation. She said the Jews were still paying the price for a crime committed two thousand years ago. The proof was the number of Jews who died in the war. (Poor Jews, she added.) Their punishment would end when the Jews converted to Christianity and received Jesus who was, she said, infinitely merciful. (70–71)

The neurotic narrator of *Madwoman 101* is the girl-adolescent-mother-woman-wife, all in one, who wants to transcend her drab reality by becoming a writer.[11] Steimberg caricatures her social group that seeks assimilation into *porteño* life and begins by adopting some of its customs, such as drinking *mate*.

As a child and as an adolescent the "Madwoman" feels

rejected because of her Jewish origin, and would like to conceal it. All she wants is to be like everyone else. As in the case of her two Argentine contemporaries, Mario Schizman in his novel *The True, False Chronicle,* and Germán Rozenmacher in his play *Simon, Knight of the Indies,* Steimberg's protagonist invents a past for herself in order to make the present more bearable. Now she has illustrious ancestors to compensate for her East European grandparents.

Steimberg's latest novel, *When I Say Magdalena* (1992), set in Buenos Aires and narrated through the obsessive thoughts of a "crazy" woman in a mental hospital, is a reappraisal of Steimberg's old identity issues, and an attempt to redefine her own identity:[12] "After a while I came to think that it wasn't so bad to have a past of pogroms in Russia, a poor tenement house in Buenos Aires, and an old Yiddish newspaper in which to wrap a jar of cherry jam. . . . It's curious how at my age my heart beats faster and I get goose bumps when I say I am Jewish and that I have to think carefully whether to say that I'm Jewish and Argentine or that I'm Argentine and Jewish, so that nobody cares about the order of the terms" (23- 24). The novel considers how Jews and non-Jews differ; and how Jews reveal themselves to others. It explores their private ethnic jokes; the stigma caused by having Jewish surnames in a Catholic society; the confusion caused by demeaning names such as "Ruso" or "Israelita," rather than "Jew"; the constant reminders of World War II; the obsession with grim details of the Holocaust; and the difficulties of living in the same lands as Nazi oppressors:

> To be Jewish is a mixture of many things: childhood memories, a special way of crying and moaning, a language one refuses to learn, a need to always remember that Einstein and Freud and Marx were Jews, a feeling that one is very ancient, more ancient than the Catholics. To be Jewish is a swastika, a Star of David, a Sholem Aleichem story, a page from *Di Prese* used for wrapping tomatoes, a caravan of somber beings march-

ing to the crematory, a need to say *I am Jewish,* even
when it isn't called for. (65)

Steimberg's characters refer to the changing role of Yiddish for each generation. To the immigrants Yiddish was
their everyday language, but it was also an obstacle to their
integration. Their children deliberately ignored it. The protagonist, belonging to the grandchildren's generation, confesses to a mixture of shame and pleasure when she hears
Yiddish spoken: "In spite of it, I understand it when I hear it,
and it pleases me . . . and yet I feel ashamed, as if I found
myself at a gala function at the Teatro Colón in my under-
pants" (28). Elsewhere she muses,

> Borges used to say that one of his grandmothers spoke
> one way, the other another way; but in time he learned
> that one of them spoke Spanish while the other spoke
> English. Well, the same happened to me, except that
> Spanish was one way of speaking, the other was Yid-
> dish. Since Yiddish sounded harsh and disagreeable to
> me, I systematically refused to learn it; it was a lan-
> guage that could uncover who I really was. . . . Yiddish
> hid, I can't express what shameful secrets; I didn't like
> the way it sounded, and if in spite of all my efforts, I still
> understood the meaning of a word, I tried not to reveal
> it under any circumstances. I would rather die than
> disclose in a smile, or in a positive gesture, that I un-
> derstood it. (61)

Some women writers express Jewish themes through religious fiction. The novels of Angelina Muñiz explore Jewish
mysticism, Kabbalah, biblical sources, and popular beliefs.
Some of the stories gathered in her *Enclosed Garden* (1985)
are inspired by the Song of Songs, and paraphrase Hasidic
teachings and prophetic pronouncements.[13] Muñiz's style is
hermetic and metaphorical. In "Searching for a Name," about
deciphering the secret name of God, her Sephardic Jewish
character undertakes a pilgrimage over unknown lands. In

"The Sarcasm of God," Muñiz makes reference to the founder of Hasidism, and invents an alchemist who foretells an incredible event that will change the order of things. After much adversity, he discovers that he arrived too late—and that is the sarcasm of God. "The Son of the Rabbi" forecasts the coming of the Messiah, and the Devil's manner of preventing it. Other stories, such as "Christian Knight," deal with the disguises a Marrano Jew has to employ to hide his religion.

The plays of Diana Raznovich deal with uprooting and alienation.[14] Pervading images of displacement and loss suggest a metaphysical need of all human beings to understand who they are and where they are heading. In spite of her deliberate avoidance of explicit Jewish themes or characters, Jewishness is the essence of her writing. Raznovich reveals her own Jewish perspective through lonely characters entrapped in a world that fails to understand them and blames them for being different. Raznovich describes this experience with knowledge from within, because having emigrated to Spain on two separate occasions and returned to her native Argentina in 1992, she is a Jewish wanderer herself. Her heroines are twentieth-century equivalents of the wandering Jew, always in search of a home, a country, an identity.

The source of the title of her dramatic monologue *Lost Belongings* is the warning often heard in airports: "Do not forget your personal belongings"; Raznovich, however, associates this with the belongings Jews had to abandon when entering a concentration camp.[15] The play deals with a condition that Jews know well, suffer from, and even enjoy: the absurdity of living in a world that makes no sense.

The last name of the protagonist, Casalia Belprop, an amalgam of "belle" and "property," is intended to parody the many changes Jewish names have undergone through misspellings and mispronunciations, to the point that an original name becomes utterly unrecognizable. Casalia is in constant panic as she searches for her matching ticket in an airport luggage claim. Her travails epitomize the many migrations Jews have had to experience through the ages. The profusion of suitcases surrounding her represent a mythical stage, a shifting country in which objects get lost along the way. When Casalia opens one of her suitcases to discover what may still be rescued, she finds her grandmother's and her lover's bones. Memories of the past are thus brought out through death. Although Latin American readers may immediately associate this scene with the disappearances of thousands of victims during the recent military repressions, to a Jew it also represents the remains of one's ancestors transplanted from one place to another.

Casalia finds herself in an anonymous place, with no one to welcome her, except for a voice like her own coming over the loudspeaker, with a warning: "Be careful, watch your number" (46). Casalia's obsessive fears may be related to the Jewish survival instinct, along with the hope that however terrible things seem to be, there is still another chance that death will not take over yet. Like Gregor Samsa in Kafka's *Metamorphosis,* Casalia knows the meaning of uncertainty and utter confusion. Surrounded by suitcases, she finally opts to turn into a chameleon. By enclosing herself in a suitcase and merging into the luggage, she ceases to be.

Autumn Garden can be regarded as a local Argentine play on the basis of its allusions to the social conditions in that country.[16] Two spinsters, in love with a television hero, make him live out his soap opera life with them as the heroines. But to the extent that the protagonists are concerned with a life they could have lived but did not, the play presents a Jewish way of looking at life. The nostalgia for the unattainable is related to the plight of Jewish immigrants and refugees who never recover from the past, and never cease to ask: What might have become of us had we had not been expelled, persecuted, tortured? The confrontation between myth and crude reality gives a comic and pathetic quality to the characters. Raznovich regards the choice between a life not lived and myth as another trait of the Jewish spirit. The alchemy fails when the women break away from their daily routine but still are unable to experience a trans-formation.

As in *Lost Belongings,* the paradox of waiting is another aspect of this play. For Jews the end of waiting would mean the loss of hope that something better will take place. The arrival of the Messiah remains a myth as long as it can be postponed. The paradox of this Jewish trait is the expecta-tion of a better world, while being aware that the world is growing worse. At the end of *Autumn Garden,* the actor is finally ready to make love to the women, but they show him the door and switch on the television to see their myth in action.

Through the ritual of soap opera, Raznovich creates a universal metaphor that applies to everyday actions and idealizations. When the alchemy of translating the theatrical into the real fails, and the women, who consider themselves the "Chosen People," do not turn into goddesses, they de-stroy their God instead. The effort of reconciling two com-pletely different worlds also relates to the idea that wherever the Jew goes, she is forced to adapt, to create a new fiction representing different scenes, or to die. The author's choice is obvious: she opts for invention, defiance and creativity.

Aída Bortnik, the Argentine journalist and dramatist whose screenplay of *The Official Story* was awarded an Oscar in 1984, depicts the spiritual destruction of the traditional fam-ily in response to the uncontrollable conditions taking place outside their home. In *Poor Butterfly,* Bortnik traces the pro-cess of deterioration that started in 1945, the year in which Juan Perón came to power.[17] The collapse of the middle-class family is portrayed in *Father Dear,*[18] in which the burial of the father is a powerful symbol of a family and of a country gone astray without the unifying force of its leader. During the eight-year "reign of terror" (1976–83) of the military dicta-torship in Argentina, Bortnik wrote *One by One,* an allegory about a disjointed family gathering and a reflection on the denials practiced by the members of a typical family.[19] Bort-nik alludes to the self-imposed silence and complicity of large numbers of Argentine families who chose to ignore the blatant abuses of human rights and preferred not to talk about the *desaparecidos,* when they should have spoken out. In this play, as people begin to disappear, limbs and voices emerge from under the tablecloth—which becomes a common grave, a specter of the untold horror. Bortnik's message of commitment is expressed through one of her characters: "One cannot live without witnesses and without memory" (5).

Bortnik's filmscript for *Poor Butterfly* sets the grounds for the political coup that began in 1945, and follows the rise of fascism through its developing stages. Clara Merino, the protagonist, is an assimilated Jew in search of her past after her father's suspicious murder. When she has to confront her daughters as they argue over their newly discovered Jewish identity, she calms them down, insisting that "There is no war here; nobody here gets killed." But even as she states these facts, she knows the evidence points to the large numbers of Nazis entering Argentina illegally in 1945, and she also knows she is a target. Nevertheless, Clara chooses to ignore the gravity of the situation broadcast in radio bulletins and continues with her own work, advertising soaps and beauty aids. When she finally does take action and divulges the list of the Nazi criminals, it is too late. Like the "poor butterfly" that flies too close to the light and burns its wings, Clara is killed in what appears to be an accidental street skirmish.

Bortnik sought exile in Spain during the Argentine repression of the late seventies and early eighties. Alicia Dujovne Ortiz lived in Paris during that period, and took French citizenship there. For Dujovne, the experiences of writing both Spanish and French and of living in exile have been enriching. Parody and humor permeate her novels. To distance herself from her subject matter, she plays at being a Catholic among Jews. Dujovne considers herself "a double being: a Christian and a Jew; a centaur and a siren." She writes about her roots out of a need for reassurance, and a fear of not belonging to either past, Jewish or Christian, Sephardic or Ashkenazic.

Like Glantz and Freilich, Dujovne feels compelled to write
about her own roots. In her novels *The Corner Mailbox* (1977)
and *The Hole of the Ground* (1982), she includes the biography
of her father, one of the founders of the Communist Party in
Argentina, who went back to study in his native Russia in
1923, went to Chile in 1932, founded the Soviets Party in the
University of Santiago, and became, for a time, a translator
for Stalin. Yet he ended his life by committing suicide because "the Pampas were too big for him." In her novel *Let's
Go to Vladivostok,*[20] about the pioneer years of search for a
promised land in South America, Dujovne pays tribute to
both her Christian Genovese and her Russian Jewish ancestors. The summary of Dujovne's ancestry is a composite of
losses and failures, of heroic adventures and disastrous defeats.

The condition of exile provides a particular style for Luisa
Futoranski, an Argentine poet, narrator, translator, radio
host, and essayist residing in Paris. Futoranski observes the
intricate relationship between exile, language, and travel: in
exile one develops the defense mechanism of camouflage.
But rather than suffer from it as a burden, as is the case of
Raznovich, Futoranski's writing is permeated by an inherent
humor: "I want to see the world without having to carry its
weight. I want to move at ease with all my handicaps: being
an older woman, a Jew, poor, Argentine and alone . . . I am
a frog in someone else's mudhole. I'll remain a foreigner
forever."[21] After a very prolonged search into her roots,
Futoranski regards the results of her adventures as a Babel-
like enigma: Andean, biblical, Mediterranean, oriental, Pari-
sian, Argentine, Israeli. The umbilical cord with her native
country has been cut, and only language and writing can
restore the connection. However paradoxical the transformation of language through exile, Futoranski asserts, "[I] am
fragments of Buenos Aires," and yet that city remains "my
greatest bond" (35).

The writings of all the authors discussed in this essay are
characterized by a searching, self-examining attitude, and a
deep identification with the past. Deeply dissatisfied with

women's traditional roles within Judaism, they have been able to move beyond them by the very act of writing. What these women have retained in common with their ancestors is their continuing close attachment to their families and their familial histories. The way these authors so persistently incorporate their families into their fiction attests, both positively and negatively, to their enduring attachment to the richness and pain of the Jewish experience.

Latin American Jewish women writers enrich the indigenous cultures of their own countries while contributing at the same time to the international hybrid, or *mestizaje,* of Jewish-European-Latin American literature. As they have become more comfortable with their own identities, their themes have become universal. Issues such as language, coming to terms with the Holocaust, and being marginalized for their differences cease to be purely Jewish and become human dilemmas. Nonetheless, in spite of liberated and progressive attitudes and active social and academic success, their commonality of concerns gives these writers a particular imprint. The duality of living within two groups simultaneously, as women in a dominantly male Jewish literary tradition, and as Jews in a dominantly Latin American Catholic culture, is an inherent trait they all share. They insist on belonging to two worlds, but ideally, what they strive for is an intangible, liminal space, for "between both worlds lies the wonderful space of the writer, a space overflowing with mysteries, waiting to be discovered."[22]

NOTES

All translated excerpts from the works discussed here are by the author.

1. Several authors of Ashkenazic origin have recently been incorporating Sephardic components of Jewishness into their writing. Sabina Berman, *Herejía (Heresy,* 1985), explores the tragedy of the *converso* Luis de Carbajal, who continued practicing Judaism in Mexico and was burned at the stake. In this play Berman deconstructs official versions of history

by exposing topics that many would rather keep hidden. Alicia Freilich, *Colombina Discovered* (1991) creates an anachronistic Christopher Columbus who is transformed into Biná Colon, a woman living simultaneously in 1492 and in 1992. This experimental novel can be interpreted as an allegory of America as a refuge for the pariahs of the world. The contemporary Sephardic Jew, less frequently portrayed by women writers, is depicted in the humorous tales of Esther Seligson, who points out some of the misunderstandings and prejudices of Ashkenazic Jews.

2. Rebeca Mactas, *Los judíos de 'Las Acacias'* (*The Jews of 'Las Acacias'*) (Buenos Aires, 1936).

3. Teresa Porzekanski, "Rojl Eisips," from *Ciudad impune*, in *Cuentos judíos Latinoamericanos* (Buenos Aires, 1989) 237–39.

4. Margo Glantz, *Las genealogías* (*The Genealogies*) (Mexico City, 1981).

5. Jean Franco, *Plotting Women* (New York, 1989).

6. Alicia Freilich Segal, *Cláper* (Caracas, 1987).

7. Gloria Gervitz, *Yiskor* (Mexico City, 1987).

8. Sabina Berman, *La bobe* (*The Bobbe*) (Mexico City, 1990).

9. Marjorie Agosín, *La felicidad* (*Happiness*) (Santiago, 1991).

10. Alicia Steimberg, *Músicos y relojeros* (*Musicians and Watchmakers*) (Buenos Aires, 1971).

11. Alicia Steimberg, *La loca 101* (*Madwoman 101*) (Buenos Aires, 1973).

12. Alicia Steimberg, *Cuando digo Magdalena* (*When I Say Magdalena*) (Buenos Aires, 1992).

13. Angelina Muñiz, *Huerto cerrado, huerto sellado* (Mexico City, 1985); *Enclosed Garden* (Pittsburgh, 1988).

14. Elisa Lerner, a Venezuelan dramatist, touches upon the same themes as Raznovich, but her Jewish content is explicit, especially in her intergenerational conflicts and in her treatment of the Holocaust.

15. Diana Raznovich, *Objetos perdidos*; *Lost Belongings*, trans. by Nora Glickman and Gloria Waldman, in *idem, Anthology of Argentine Jewish Theatre* (Bucknell University Press, 1993).

16. Diana Raznovich, *Jardín de otoño* (Buenos Aires, 1981); *Autumn Garden*, transl. Nora Glickman (unpublished).

17. Aída Bortnik, *Pobre mariposa* (*Poor Butterfly*), in *Escritores judíos Latinoamericanos* (Buenos Aires, 1990).

18. Aída Bortnik, *Papá querido* (*Papa Dear*), in *Teatro abierto* (Buenos Aires, 1981), 11–20.

19. Aída Bortnik, *De a uno* (*One by One*), *Hispamérica* 15:43 (1986), 57–72.

20. Alicia Dujovne Ortiz, *Vamos a Vladivostok* (*Let's Go to Vladivostok*); published in French as *L'arbre de la gitane* (Paris, 1990).

21. Luisa Futoranski, *Noaj* 3–4 (1989), 35.

22. Interview with Moacyr Scliar in Nora Glickman's *Tradition and Innovation: Jewish Issues in Latin American Writings* (Albany, N.Y., 1993), 56.

16 ♦ YAEL FELDMAN

Feminism Under Siege: The Vicarious Selves
of Israeli Women Writers

> I live on the top floors now, she summed it up to
> herself, where there is a constant commotion, work-
> rooms, children's rooms, the kitchen, the living
> room, all kinds of things. [Only] the cellar is locked,
> and I don't even know where the key is [any more].
> Perhaps one should not know.
> —Shulamith Hareven, *A City of Many Days*[1]

In this passage the age-old metaphor of the house as the
image of its tenant is given an added twist. The vertical
division of this dwelling, whose upper floors are full of
movement and light in contrast to the locked cellar below,
offers a clear analogue to Freud's topographic model of the
human psyche. The female voice using this metaphor, however, seems to question the very foundation of the Freudian
quest when she suggests that one may do better to leave the
underground room of the unconscious inaccessible.

This questioning of the usefulness of introspection grows
out of the experience of Sarah Amarillo, the protagonist of
the novel in which Shulamith Hareven reconstructs life in
Jerusalem under the British Mandate, before and during

World War II. Although the impulse for self-knowledge is
quite palpable here, it clearly stops short of breaking into
the locked psychological "cellar." Self-knowledge is thus
displaced to externally observable facts, and a potential
psychological exploration turns into a sociocultural inquiry.
Situated as it is a few pages before the end of the novel (184
in the Hebrew edition; 199 in the English), this arrested introspection functions as the author's culminating reflection
on the uneasy coexistence of modern psychology within a
society of collective persuasion in which female roles have
been traditionally limited.

As *A City of Many Days* indicates, contemporary Israeli
women novelists have seemed to shy away from telling their
life stories directly.[2] While the Hebrew literary canon has
featured a long list of women poets, until the last decade
Hebrew prose was mostly the domain of male writers. The
few women who excelled in fiction wrote short stories and
novellas, mainly in the lyrical impressionistic mode (for example, Dvora Baron). Indeed, as early as the turn of the
century, women were cast in a well-defined role by the ar-
biters of the renaissance of Hebrew, who declared that
"Only women are capable of reviving Hebrew—this old, forgotten, dry, and hard language—by permeating it with emotion, tenderness, suppleness, and subtlety." This generous,
as well as limiting, evaluation was offered in 1897 by Eliezer
Ben-Yehuda, the first propagator of spoken Hebrew; and it is
not easy to determine today whether the encouragement or
the limitation was more effective.[3]

It took more than half a century for the old barriers to
begin crumbling. And it is only in the last two decades that
a number of women have made the shift from short stories
to novels, many of which are set in the past. Until very
recently, however, none of these narratives came close to
fictional autobiography, even in the "arrested" form found
among Israeli male writers.[4] I would nevertheless argue, using the examples of Hareven and Shulamit Lapid,[5] that it is
in these apparently historical novels that one must look for

the representation, however indirect, of the "self" of the Israeli female author.

This generic choice is neither accidental nor arbitrary, for these quasi-historical novels camouflage a contemporary *feminist* consciousness, and express, in different degrees of displacement, their authors' struggles with questions of female subjectivity and gender boundaries.[6] In fact, one can point to a process of regression in the choice of historical settings, from Jerusalem of the 1920s and 30s in *A City of Many Days* (1972) through Palestine of 1882 in Shulamit Lapid's *Gei oni* (1982). However, this chronological regression is counterbalanced by a diametrically opposite progression in the "feminist" consciousness of the protagonists of these novels, who move from traditional gender roles in a patriarchal society to a utopian new womanhood, paradoxically projected back into the historicomythical past.

That they do this "under siege," in a society that is fundamentally unfriendly to their quest, is part of the explanation of their literary choices, but also part of the paradox. For it is precisely those pressures that have rendered Israeli male subjectivity different from its western counterparts, that have also prevented the direct expression of Israeli female subjectivity. For contemporary European and American women, issues of selfhood and gender definition are inextricably bound up with feminism; as such, they automatically become politicized. But in Israel such an agenda would necessarily collide with the larger political issues that are always at the center of attention. Israeli women writers are therefore trapped in a double bind: unwilling to relegate themselves to marginalized "women's journalism" and "female thematics," they are obliged to enter the mainstream "in disguise," registering their social critique vicariously via their presumably historical protagonists.

This phenomenon results, in part, from woman's problematic place in the Jewish tradition, which by and large excludes her from participating in man's public roles.[7] However, as in the writing of their male contemporaries, the sociopolitical pressures of Israel's reality and the major historical events of Israel's collective memory also work to inhibit psychological introspection and the quest for individual autonomy. It is precisely this embeddedness within a larger, collective order that is at odds with any feminist aspiration; and it is the slow and vicarious realization of this unavoidable conflict that is the subject of the following analysis.

For Sarah Amarillo, the protagonist of *A City of Many Days,* the pivotal historical moment is the breakdown of the Jewish-Arab equilibrium in Jerusalem of World War II. As the tension heightens, the narrative is permeated by a sense of an ending: "Something was ending, and something was about to begin" (136; 146 [see also 75; 77]). Jerusalem's oriental design, which the novel recapitulates in its lyrical impressionism, is doomed to oblivion, except in the literary reconstructions of its mourners. Jerusalem's polyphony of voices will be replaced by the "first-person plural" of the next generation, as the male protagonists wistfully observe:

> "All these men will be coming home from war now," said Professor Barzel. "They'll all have learned to fight. The country will change again. Everything will become more professional, the fighting too. The individual won't count any more—only the stupid plural. The plural is always stupid."
>
> "And what will be then, Elias?" asked Hulda worriedly.
>
> "We will be then," said Elias, so quietly that they couldn't be sure they had heard right. "For better or worse, we will be." (182; 197–98)

This is the notorious "we" of the Jewish defense forces ("We are everywhere the first we, we, the Palmach," as their song proudly announced). Hareven's characters grieve this loss of the first-person singular, while rationalizing it as the unavoidable result of the political situation. Her ambivalence is further demonstrated by her treatment of Sarah's interior monologue quoted above. On one hand, she allows Sarah a measure of self-awareness, the admission that she lives "on the top floors." But then she lets her state flatly, without any change of tone, that "the cellar is locked, and I don't even know where the key is any more" (184; 199). Moreover, the attentive reader may note not only what is marked as "locked" but also what is marked by its absence: the curious omission of a bedroom from the list of rooms on the top floor, which passes unremarked.

Apparently, to join the war effort, Sarah must, like Professor Barzel before her, "skip over her own self" (*ibid.;* see 122; 130). Barzel, the German-born physician who had trained her as a nurse in her youth, now insists that she help him prepare paramedics for the insecure, threatening future. It would seem that in this society under siege, male and female share the same lot. But this is not quite true, since it is Sarah and not Professor Barzel who registers the loss in psychological rather than social or intellectual terms. While he is reported to "have lost the key" to his hobbies and philosophical ideas (122; 130), Sarah is aware that what she misses is nothing less than the key to her own "underground room," to the cellar of her psychic apparatus (184; 199).[8] Yet this insight does not lead to any action. Neither the protagonist nor the authorial voice shows any signs of rebellion ("Perhaps one should not know"). On the contrary, despite the great losses, the novel closes on a poetic note of mystical transcendence:

A silent presence, the whole city spread at her feet, and [she] looked at the lambswool light out over the mountains, over the houses drowning in radiance, as if once this city, long, long ago, soon after Creation, had burst from some great rock and its truth flown molten and shiny over the hills. She could feel the moment to the quick. Now this is me, she told herself, now this is me, here on this hill, with this feeling of great peace [reconciliation] that will never last, or standing in the

street, people know [recognize] me: I have three sons
and so little time. Now this is me in this moment of
hers. Tomorrow I'll be gone and the street will be gone.
Or another street and another time. And always, forever, this fleecy pile of light, that rock tumbled halfway
down the hill to a lonely stop, a terraced alley, a drip-
ping cypress tree, a caper plant in a wall. A place to
walk slowly. A place to touch the sky: now it is close. To
breathe in mountain-and-light. Now.

It is hard to exaggerate the contrast between this recon-
ciled woman and the spunky girl that Sarah once was. Described by herself and others as a chip off the strong and
feisty (mostly male) Amarillo block, those who "are always
quarreling with life" (36, 113; 36, 119), this "big" emancipated woman now takes a turn toward submission, "lying
low in realities, the wick trimmed all the way down" (179;
194). The woman who prided herself on her sharp tongue
and unabashed "meanness" is now growing emotional over
her motherly duties. And the daughter who as a young girl
vented her rage against her absent father by screaming "No
father! No mother! No grandpa! No grandma! No nothing!"
(16; 14), is now processing poetically her discovery of his
helpless insanity: "I went down into a garden of nut trees [to
see the fruits of the valley]. Down down down. To the rock-
bottom beauty of madness" (187; 202; cf. Song of Songs
6:11). Again, the anguish is camouflaged by the indirection
of metaphor. And again, both protagonist and narrator stop
on the brink of the abyss: "Sarah looked at him for a long
while, the great question that had haunted her for so long,
now a spent little answer cast mindlessly before her." This
is all Hareven grants her protagonist by way of self-scrutiny.
Staged as it is two pages before the end of the novel, this
encounter loses its potential force as an all-embracing psychological explanation.

Even Sarah, whose "education" is at the core of the plot,
is rendered only by brief surface brush strokes. Moreover,
she does not occupy center stage by herself; as the lyrical

fusion of her last narrated monologue makes clear, she shares it with another female, the city of the title of the book. It is Jerusalem who is the strongest presence in this novel, because, ironically, it is "she" who embodies the powers of history ("This city abides no one's decision about who they are. She decides for them, she makes them, with the pressure of stones and infinite time. She teaches humility" [121; 129]). In the final analysis, it is history rather than psychology that circumscribes human action in this novel, subsuming both anguish and pleasure under its impersonal workings.

Yet the closing statement of the poetic coda makes clear that there is a place for the female subject: despite the constant effort of the authorial voice to decentralize its focus, to multiply its points of view, Sarah emerges as the central consciousness of the narration. The more the rich mosaic of the past disintegrates, the more her introspective voice usurps that of the ironic narrator, culminating in her final monologue.

It is perilous to see in Sarah any sort of direct self-representation. For Shulamith Hareven has not followed the lead she herself suggested. She never adopted the autobiographic modality in her writing, and except for one collection of stories partially addressing women's issues (*Loneliness,* 1980; available in English as *Twilight and Other Stories,* 1992), she has shunned female protagonists altogether. *A City of Many Days* stands alone in her oeuvre, written after two books of poetry and two collections of stories (1962–70), and followed by more collections of poems, essays, short stories, and two possibly allegorical novellas whose narrated time is the biblical past.[9] Moreover, Hareven is notorious for her refusal to participate in any forum dedicated to "women's literature"; she does not believe in women writers as a category; and she has often claimed that a writer is a writer regardless of gender. At the same time, she is politically active, voicing her ideological positions in her oral pronouncements and excellent essays.[10] But when critics tried to read her political convictions into her latest "biblical" novellas, she vehemently protested that art is art and should not be confused with one's worldly preoccupation.[11]

In other words, the woman behind the novel is an engaged person of clearly drawn convictions and priorities. Feminism, however, is not among them, as *A City of Many Days* complexly demonstrates. On the one hand, cross-gender equality as a realistic possibility is an unquestioned premise of this novel, for without it the characterization of Sarah would be totally spurious. In fact, in her independence of spirit, intolerance of weakness, and provocative sexual freedom, she is almost a parody of the typical male adolescent. On the other hand, by equipping her with a weak father who is easy prey for false female charms and a victim of mental illness, and a "strong" paternal aunt, the colorful, single but happy Victoria (no less), Hareven seems to exaggerate the feminist cliché of "transcending gender roles."

Sarah starts from a non-genderized dichotomy, unproblematically rejecting one model and adopting another. Yet it is marriage and maternity that pose the real test. How would this male-modeled, autonomous woman function as a wife and mother? Superbly, of course, but at a "cost." After giving birth to her first son, Sarah for the first time allows "weakness" to penetrate her hitherto armored psyche. The self-centered, unrelational ego restructures itself, but reacts with a sense of loss and fear: "Help me, Grandpa," she prays from her maternity bed, "because a frightening vulnerability has opened up in me today" (111, 118). But if we think that motherhood is the end of "androgyny," we are mistaken, at least as far as this novel is concerned. It is the father, not the mother, who verbalizes the effect of parenthood on the self: "The first child forces you to define yourself. When the second comes you are already defined. Not just as a parent. Whatever you are and aren't, you can be sure that's what your child will learn to demand from you" (112, 119).

At this point of the narrative, just past the midpoint of the story, the myth of male/female equality still holds. But not for long, as in the following pages we witness the deterioration of Arab-Jewish relations and the palpable echoes of World War II. Life is disrupted; individual destinies get farcically and hopelessly entangled in plots they do not comprehend. The dichotomy of weak/strong, so hopefully deconstructed in the human sphere, ominously sneaks back into people's political discourse. Against this background, Sarah slowly emerges to her difference only to realize that under these circumstances she cannot take this difference anywhere.

The motive power behind her emergence is, predictably, a chance rekindling of a youthful love. But just as predictably, this emotional reawakening is painfully cut off, undermined by the historical moment of underground activities and military voluntarism of men at war. All that she has left is "acceptance" of her unexamined inner life. So that when her self-conscious "I" is finally vocalized, it is only to be defined in terms of others: "They recognize me: I have three sons and so little time." The irony could not be any greater: Sarah Amarillo, the paradigm of the "new," Jerusalem-born Jewish woman (echoes of the social-Zionist ethos of the "new man/Jew" not unintentional here!), falls back on the most traditional and often maligned Jewish definition of womanhood. Like the biblical Sarah, she gains status through motherhood, and more significantly through the recognition of others. In the Hebrew phrase *makirim oti* ("they recognize me"), she is clearly the passive receptor of the action.

In this novel, the celebration of the self, feminist or not, is temporarily compromised by the historical circumstances dramatized in this novel. The sociopolitical conditions that have given rise to the ideology of "we," the "stupid first-person plural," have also dictated the suppression of the Freudian quest and the throwing away of the key to the psychic underground room. But all this is historically, not universally or essentially, determined.[12] And if the female subject of this narrative cannot be privileged with a fully autobiographical voice, she is allowed the empowerment of existential transcendence. It is the eternal female Other, Jerusalem, that offers a moment of ecstasy, of metonymic submersion: "Now this is me, she told herself, now this is me, here on this hill, with this feeling of great peace [reconciliation]. . . . Now this is me in this moment of hers. . . . A place to touch the sky: now it is close. To breathe in mountain-and-light. Now."

The uniqueness of Hareven's position on feminism (among Israeli writers) is paralleled by the splendid isolation of her heroine among Israeli female protagonists. In no other novel has the gap between lofty ideals (authorial and Zionist, intratextual and contextual) and the limitations of reality been so sensitively, if ambivalently, dramatized. In some sense, this novel was ahead of its time. In the early seventies, the horizon of expectations was not yet ripe for a literary discussion of feminism, even in its moderate, selective form. It is not surprising, then, that *A City of Many Days* was received as another nostalgic tale about Jerusalem, "lacking highly significant themes and conceptual contents."[13] That the issues of gender and female subjectivity, as well as their conflict with the historical constraints, are central to the novel passed totally unnoticed. It goes without saying that the potential critique of Zionist ideology implied by this material was not even surmised.

It would take a whole decade, and the stimulus of the Yom Kippur War (1973) and its aftermath, for the next attempts at female self-representation to materialize. Although Shulamit Aloni's treatise on women's deplorable status within the Israeli legal system, *Women as Human Beings,* appeared in 1973, the 1978 report of a Knesset commission on the status of women still concluded that "their contribution to society was marginal and supportive by nature . . . a reflection of their political status and the inclination of the Labor Movement elite to view them as voters but not as decision makers."[14] In the following decade and a half only a gradual and incomplete change has taken place.

Still, the distance traveled by Hebrew readers in the seventies can be readily measured by the openness with which

Shulamit Lapid's *Gei oni* (1982), a highly popular historical novel, tackled the very issues upon which Hareven had circumspectly touched a decade earlier. Here we do not find metaphoric indirection and nuanced play of voices. On the contrary, in a realistic, rather coarse style, in which dialogues and interior monologues are stylistically indistinguishable, the third-person narration weaves its way through a maze of "relationships" that would easily rival those of any Hollywood or television romantic melodrama. Nothing is implied here, not even the characters' most intimate reflections. Thoughts, emotions, ideology, and popular psychology are all evenly spread out as if illuminated by the bright Israeli sun.

Yet despite its limitations, *Gei oni* caught the imagination of Israeli readers in an unprecedented manner. In the first place, it played into the wave of nostalgia that swept the country in the eighties, when the first centenary of the earliest Jewish Aliyah (wave of immigration) to Palestine was celebrated. Indeed, Shulamit Lapid, until then a rather obscure short story writer,[15] wrote her first novel in anticipation of this anniversary. In that year the Galilean settlement Rosh Pinah, whose earlier name had been Gei Oni, celebrated one hundred years of its existence. Judging by the reception the book enjoyed, the timing was right; readers exhibited great hunger for the richly documented panorama of that distant past filtered through a fictional prism. And this was not the only reason for the novel's success. Readers were no doubt responding to the novelty of being introduced to a "serious" historical reconstruction through the eyes and mind of Fanya, a young Russian immigrant who joins Gei Oni in the opening scene and remains the central consciousness through which the narrative is vocalized throughout the novel.

Yet one must inquire why a strong independent female settler was considered such a novelty. Wasn't the pioneer movement, indeed the Zionist ethos in general, supposed to have promoted the equality of women? In fact, wasn't "the woman question" one of the basic issues debated—and

deemed solved—by the early communes and kibbutzim?[16]
The answer is, of course, yes to all of the above, but only as
long as we remember to add the qualifier "in theory." For
what recent research has shown is that in practice, neither
the early settlers nor the second wave of immigrants at the
turn of the century had transcended the patriarchal norms
of their home communities in Europe.[17] And as Shulamit
Lapid herself has recounted, she could find no historical
model for her heroine in the archival records of Gei Oni/
Rosh Pinah.[18] As the jacket of the book states, the names of
those "giant women" who were part and parcel of the early
settlement wave "are absent from history books because
the records of the saviors of the motherland list only men."
Even among the figures of the Second Aliyah, Lapid could
make use only of one exceptional personality, Manya Shohat
(1879–1959).[19] Fanya had to be invented; here is a woman
who "did not know she was a feminist," but whom the contemporary reader recognizes as such.

Gei oni succeeds in creating a narrative frame that authentically preserves the patriarchal way of life of the 1880s
while at the same time accommodating a fictitious protagonist whose own norms would satisfy contemporary "feminist" expectations by piecing together two novelistic
genres: the settler epic and the romantic melodrama. On
one level, *Gei oni* is a typical settlement drama, realistically
depicting the struggles against all odds of the small Galilean
group in the early 1880s. The chief antagonist of this plot is
nature itself, the mythic Mother Earth. In this story she is no
welcoming bride; as we join the narrative, she has been
holding back her gifts for two consecutive years. Severe
drought has chased away most of the pioneers, leaving behind just a few tenacious and idealistic families, including
that of Yehi'el, the male protagonist.

On another level, this is a typically euphoric "heroine's
text,"[20] a predictable love story whose models are not only
the canonic texts adored by Fanya (Tolstoy's *Anna Karenina*
and the novels of Jane Austen [161]), but also popular modern romances. Fanya is the self-conscious budding young

woman, who struggles to preserve her independent spirit while falling in love with her enigmatic "dark prince." The latter, for his part, is "handsome like the Prince of Wales" (34, 69, 85) and "wise like King Solomon" (117); he falls in love with Fanya's looks the moment he sees her but keeps the secret to himself. Since neither the reader nor Fanya gets to know the truth before half the story is over, a chain of romantic misunderstandings and jealousies constitute the better part of the plot.

One must ask if Lapid has wandered too far afield from "founding mothers," since the conventions of the romantic novel cannot contain a fighting, independent spirit like Manya Shohat. Lapid could not have sustained her model and satisfied her feminist quest had she kept the model intact, nor could she write a true historical novel while staying as close to Fanya's consciousness as she did. She resolved this problem, however, by splicing the two genres together; from this intersection a new model emerges, one that generously accommodates contemporary expectations.

To begin with, Fanya's romance deviates from the romantic model in one crucial detail: its denouement does not coincide with the closure of the novel. Nor does its culmination lead to a proposal or an engagement, since her love affair takes place within the boundaries of a marriage. And our two protagonists are atypical as well: Fanya is not only an orphan, she is a sixteen-year-old survivor of a Russian pogrom (the infamous pogroms of 1881–82, especially devastating in the Ukraine, that are credited with inspiring the first wave of immigration to Palestine), who finds refuge in the Promised Land, accompanied by an old uncle, a deranged brother, and a baby, the initially unwanted fruit of her rape in that pogrom. Yehi'el, who happens to see her upon her arrival in Jaffa, is a twenty-six-year-old widower and a father of two, one of the few courageous souls still left in the nearly desolate Gei Oni.

As the narrative opens, we are privileged to hear Fanya's reflections after a hasty betrothal in Jaffa. While Yehi'el's motives are not disclosed, it soon becomes clear that for

Fanya this is not just a marriage of convenience but also a marriage of appearances. On arriving in Gei Oni she insists on separate sleeping arrangements, a rather unexpected turn within the conventions of the romance but a perfectly plausible step for a psychologically conceived character who is still in pain from her traumatic past. The attentive reader, however, will notice a structural and symbolic analogy in this otherwise realistically motivated action. It is not only the human bride who denies her husband her favors; with the drought continuing, the fertilization of Mother Earth is also prevented.

There is a perfect symmetry, then, between the two plots: the psychological and the mythic, the romantic and the historical. In both, the male principle is initially defeated and no consummation is possible. This symmetry does not escape Yehi'el himself, who, unaware of Fanya's trauma, reacts to her refusal by saying: "When you change your mind, let me know. I ask for favors only from the land" (45). To get the story rolling again, both female protagonists must give in; it is against the background of the long-awaited rains (117, 121, 123) that the passionate (and confessional) reunion between Fanya and Yehi'el finally takes place (119–28) and the euphoric plot seems to have reached its happy ending.

But not quite. For in the second part of the narrative, the settlement plot comes back with a vengeance, leaning down heavily on the delicate balance of the new romantic attachment. Not unlike Hareven's Jerusalem, the Galilee, or Mother Earth (or perhaps the pioneering quest itself), exerts pressure on the human subjects of this story, limiting their freedom of choice and forcing them into its mold. But unlike Hareven, Lapid seems less willing to accept the verdict of the historical moment, of the Zionist "dream of redemption, burning like fire in the bones" (103–4, 144, 175). She does not have Fanya "skip over her own self," as Sarah did in *A City of Many Days,* but rather lets her develop her female subjectivity despite and against the pressures of the collective vision, with all its tragic consequences. By so doing, Lapid has unwittingly blended her two models into a third, a novel of experience and education that may be rather fanciful for the 1880s but is totally satisfying to readers one hundred years later.

Predictably, Fanya achieves her independence through a series of tasks that she undertakes in order to save her husband and home from the devastation wrought by Mother Nature. We find her breaking into the male-dominated worlds of commerce, political discussion, even armed self-defense. At the same time, she does not deny her difference from the male world surrounding her (104, 144, 175). Her personal code is defined, then, as the freedom to choose the best of the two worlds, to move freely from one to the other. More than her predecessor in Hareven's novel, this heroine fully embodies cross-gender equality as she shuttles between home and "world," Gei Oni and Jaffa, taking care of husband and children, and conducting business. Yehi'el turns out to be just as exceptional. Although he does not fully approve of Fanya's "androgynous" tendencies, he does not stand in her way, which is more than can be said of any of his peers (109, 172–73, 188, 236). The result is a virtual reversal of conventional gender roles (with Yehi'el staying close to home and Fanya going into the world), and more importantly, the transformation of Fanya from a child-bride into a mature wife-companion, fully aware of her choices, sexual as well as social.

It is only natural, then, that as the novel comes to a close and Yehi'el succumbs to exhaustion and malaria, the reader is ready to embrace Fanya's experience as a necessary training for her ultimate task in the perpetuation of the mythical male quest. But in an ironic twist Fanya, though ready to undertake the role, perceives it as something alien, not her own script: "Should she sell their home? Driving Yehi'el out of his dream? This home and this land were the purpose of his life. Once again fate has decreed that she realize others' dreams. Has she ever had her own dreams? But perhaps everyone is like this? Everyone realizes someone else's dream?" (256). Is this a "feminist" protest lamenting the lot of women in general, or a specific charge against the andro-centric Zionist dream? And who is the "everyone" of the final questions: women? all people? The lines seem to blur here, leaving the reader with a sense of an unfocused griev-ance. For what is read throughout the novel as a critique of a male-engendered ideology ("Her father's dream of rebirth has turned into sacred madness that now consumes her youthful years, her life" [102]) is now taking an existential turn, possibly hiding behind "the human condition."

We should not be surprised, then, that Lapid does not give her heroine the chance to try to make it on her own. In the last page, the plot of the romance prevails. Sasha, an old acquaintance, himself a survivor of the Russian pogroms in the Ukraine, reappears, asking permission "to help and be helped." With this new beginning, the novel reverts to its original two models: the historical and the romantic. Sub-jective experience is embedded again in Jewish collectivity ("This is what we Jews do. Start all over again. Again. And again. And again"), only to be taken over by an old/new romance closure: " 'I need you, Fanya! Will you allow me to help you?' Fanya looked at him wondering. Then she thought that if he hugged her, her head would barely reach his shoulder. And then her eyes filled with tears" (266).

It is evident that this quasi-historical, quasi-feminist ro-mance set a century ago may be read as a vicarious repre-sentation of a contemporary female quest. Lapid's lack of distance from Fanya (ironic or other), as well as the narra-tor's narrow point of view, undermines the work's claim to be a historical novel. Rather, the reader receives the impres-sion that the development of the historical heroine repre-sents the concerns and expectations of a contemporary con-sciousness that present-day Israeli reality cannot satisfy. In some sense, *Gei oni* is a feminist novel of education mas-querading as a more acceptable genre, the historical novel. Lapid obviously felt that Israeli society of the early 1980s would accept a "feminist" identity as a historical projection but would find it difficult to digest as a realistic proposition for the here and now.

This impression is further reinforced by the unmistakably contemporary feminist protest of one of Lapid's earliest stories, "The Order of the Garter,"[21] and by the totally female orientation of her oeuvre in the last few years. Although, like Hareven, she does not consider herself a feminist, she has been limiting herself, by her own confession, "to women's thematics," and perceives herself as "small, delicate, and becoming more and more aggressive" at the "ripe age of fifty-four."[22] Thus, her recent novel, *Local Paper,*[23] features Lisa, a lower middle-class woman journalist in a contemporary provincial town (Beer Sheva). In this popular quasi-detective story, Lapid does what she did not dare to do in *Gei oni*. She imagines a female character more common in contemporary America than in Israel: an unmarried woman who is proud of her work ethic, of her "professionalism," and whose priorities are "working" and "being in love." Yet despite this daring move, Lapid's penchant for romance is operative here as well, although from a more ironic perspective. For if matrimony has totally lost its appeal ("I have seen my sisters," Lisa explains), the romantic attachment has not. Like Fanya, Lisa gets her reward in the form of a "dark prince," updated for the 1980s: a tawny, handsome, rich, and worldly divorcé, whose timely "information" rescues Lisa from the imminent danger of losing her job.

Working within the conventions of the popular romance, Lapid has created female subjects whose identity seems to be much more seamless and unconflicted than those created by Hareven and other women writers. While Hareven, for example, consciously questions the place of individual autonomy, gender difference, and psychological determinism in a society under siege, Lapid uses the historical and ideological materials as a setting against which her protagonists reach toward their optimal development. By the same token, she does not subject her own premises about gender to a serious scrutiny. "Motherhood," for example, is never really problematized (Lisa rejects it out of hand, and Fanya just weaves it into her busy schedule, although it is never clear how). Nor does she indulge in a true psychological exploration of her characters. In a curious way, the wealth of information we accumulate about them, even about their past, does not allow any meaningful conceptualization. Lapid is content to follow their present entanglements to their happy endings without delving into the larger questions posed by the issues she has dramatized.

These deeper concerns are explored in the latest work of other writers, including Amalia Kahana-Carmon and Ruth Almog, who attempt to overcome the state of historical siege so convincingly demonstrated by Hareven and Lapid.[24] In doing so they uncover new sets of limitations and other kinds of psychological and existential states of siege for women, an inevitable ironic consequence, perhaps, of the artistic endeavor and the human experience it attempts to represent.[25]

NOTES

This essay is an abridged and somewhat altered version of my "Feminism Under Siege: The Vicarious Selves of Israeli Women Writers," *Prooftexts* 10 (1990), 493–514. I am grateful to the Johns Hopkins University Press for permission to print this new version of the essay here. The original version contains more detailed theoretical and linguistic analyses than the present format allows. Work on this essay was made possible by an National Endowment for the Humanities Fellowship during the summer of 1989.

1. Shulamith Hareven, *'Ir yamim rabim* (Tel Aviv, 1972), 184. Subsequent references appear in the body of the text. The second page numbers given refer to the English version, *A City of Many Days,* transl. Hillel Halkin (New York, 1977),

2. This is not to say that women do not use autobiographic materials—Naomi Fraenkel, Rachel Eitan, Amalia Kahana-Carmon, Dahlia Ravikovitch, Hedda Boshes, and Yehudit Hendel do—but rather that their narratives generally do not take the shape of autobiographical retrospection. On the obvious exception, Netiva Ben Yehuda's *Bein hasfirot (Between the Calendars,* 1981), see my article, "Gender In/Difference in Contemporary Hebrew Fictional Autobiographies," *Biography* 11:3 (Summer 1988), 189–209; reprinted in *Sex, Love and Signs: European Journal for Semiotic Studies* 1 (1989), 435–56.

3. It was also easier to write verse without the training in classical Hebrew traditionally reserved for males. It is no coincidence that the first modern Hebrew prose writer, Dvora Baron, had been raised "as a son," instructed in the sacred sources by her father who was a rabbi. (See Ruth Adler's essay in this volume). On the emergence of women's poetry see Dan Miron, "Founding Mothers, Stepsisters" [Hebrew], *Alpayim* 1 (June 1989), 29–58; and see a translated excerpt from this work, "Why Was There No Women's Poetry in Hebrew Before 1920?" in *Gender and Text in Modern Hebrew and Yiddish Literature*, ed. Naomi B. Sokoloff, Anne Lapidus Lerner, and Anita Norich (New York and Jerusalem, 1992), 65–91.

4. See my "Living on the Top Floor: The Arrested Autobiography in Contemporary Israeli Fiction," *Modern Hebrew Literature* 1 (Fall/Winter 1988), 72–77.

5. Shulamit Lapid, *Gei oni* (Tel Aviv, 1982). All further page references will appear in the body of the text, with quotations in my translation.

6. Another example of this phenomenon is Amalia Kahana-Carmon, "The Bridge of the Green Duck" [Hebrew], in her *Lemalah bemontifer (Up on Montifer)* (Tel Aviv, 1984), 59–184.

7. See, for example, *On Being a Jewish Feminist,* ed. Susannah Heschel (New York, 1983).

8. Although the precarious position of Freudian psychology is most palpable in the language and plot of this narrative, it is not easy to determine whether it derives from the historical materials themselves (the 1930s-40s), or from the personal ambivalence of the author, who expressed her contempt of classical Freudian psychology in her conversation with me (August 16, 1989). The problematic reception of psychoanalysis in Hebrew literature is the subject of my *Freudianism and Its Discontents* (work in progress), and is partially presented in my "Back to Vienna: Zionism on the Literary Couch," in *Vision Confronts Reality*, ed. Sidorsky et al. (Rutherford, N.J., 1989), 310–35.

9. *Sone' hanissim* (Jerusalem and Tel Aviv, 1983) was published in English as *The Miracle Hater*, transl. Hillel Halkin (Berkeley, Calif., 1988); *Navi (A Prophet)* (Jerusalem and Tel Aviv, 1988) was also translated by Halkin (Berkeley, Calif., 1990).

10. *Tismonet Dulcenea (The Dulcenea Syndrome)* (Jerusalem, 1981).

11. See, for example, her essay "The First Forty Years," *The Jerusalem Quarterly* 48 (Fall 1988), 3–28, especially 25–26; and an interview with Helit Bloom in *Bamahaneh* (March 1, 1989).

12. See on this point the succinct analysis by Naomi Chazan, "Gender Equality? Not in a War Zone!" *Israeli Democracy* (Summer 1989), 4–7.

13. Gershon Shaked, "Imbued with the Love of Jerusalem," in *Gal ahar gal (Wave after Wave in Hebrew Narrative Fiction)* (Jerusalem, 1985), 13.

14. See Dafna Sharfman, "The Status of Women in Israel—Facts and Myth," *Israeli Democracy* (Summer 1989), 12–14.

15. Lapid's earlier collections of short stories are *Mazal dagim (Pisces)* (Tel Aviv, 1969); *Shalvat shotim (Fools' Paradise)* (Tel Aviv, 1974); *Kadahat (Malaria)* (Tel Aviv, 1979).

16. See, for example, Elkana Margalit, *Hashomer hatsa'ir: me'adat ne'u-*

rim lemarksizm mahaphani (*Hashomer Hatsa'ir: From Youth Movement to Revolutionary Marxism*) (Tel Aviv, 1971).

17. See Dafna Izraeli, "The Labor Women Movement in Palestine from Its Inception to 1919" [Hebrew], *Cathedra* 32 (1984), 109–40; and Deborah Bernstein, "The Status and Organization of Urban Working Women in the 20s and 30s" [Hebrew], *Cathedra* 34 (1985), 115–44.

18. Private communication, 1984. Literature does not score much higher on this point, the few exceptions such as Rivka Alper's *Hamitnahalim bahar* and Moshe Shamir's *Hinumat kalah* notwithstanding.

19. Rachel Yanait Ben-Zvi's fascinating biography of Shohat, *Before Golda*, was recently published in English, transl. Sandra Shurin (New York, 1988); it was also the basis of a documentary film. See also Shulamit Reinharz, "Toward a Model of Female Political Action: The Case of Manya Shohat, Founder of the First Kibbutz," *Women's Studies International Forum* 7:4 (1984), 275–87. On the situation of women in this period, see the essays in *Pioneers and Homemakers: Jewish Women in Pre-State Israel,* ed. Deborah S. Bernstein (Albany, N.Y., 1992).

20. Nancy Miller, *The Heroine's Text* (New York, 1980).

21. In Lapid, *Mazal dagim,* 1969.

22. See interview with her in *Lilith* (Summer 1989), 20. The same issue also includes a translation of one of her new "aggressive" stories, "The Bed."

23. Shulamit Lapid, *Meqomon* (*Local Paper*) (Jerusalem, 1989).

24. Ruth Almog, *Shorshei avir* (*Dangling Roots*) (Jerusalem, 1987). For Kahana-Carmon see above, n. 6. See my "The 'Other Within' in Contemporary Israeli Fiction," *Middle East Review* 22:1 (Fall 1989), 47–53, for a discussion of some of these issues.

25. See my "Feminism and Its Discontents in Israeli Literature," in *Voices of Postmodernism in Israeli Fiction 1973–1993*, ed. Alan Mintz (Hanover, NH, 1994).

17 ◆ MIRI KUBOVY

From "Data Processing" to "Sex, Car and
Love Later": The Poetry of
Maya Bejerano

Maya Bejerano is one of the most important contemporary Israeli poets. She entered Israeli poetry in the 1970s; her seventh published volume, *Whale,* which includes the major poem "Sex, Car and Love Later," follows *Ostrich, The Heat and the Cold, Data Processing, Song of the Birds, Voice,* and *Selected Poems.* Bejerano is a "Tel Aviv poet," uniting the Israeli view with the broader cosmopolitan awareness of our time. The daughter of Sephardic Jews who immigrated to Israel from Bulgaria and settled in Jaffa and Bat Yam, she addresses philosophical and universal issues of political injustice, representation, language, and media in the framework of Israeli existence today.

Independent and highly committed both politically and artistically, Bejerano reflects in her life, as well as in her poetry, the current crises in women's existence. Female poets, such as Rachel and Leah Goldberg, have always held a central position in modern Hebrew poetry; they expressed in lyrical poetry their personal emotional worlds, including disappointment in love and loneliness, a trend that characterizes even Dahlia Ravikovitch, a major revolutionary poet, whose early poems came out in the late fifties. Yet, Ravikovitch's feminist protest poem "Mechanical Doll," a milestone in the history of Hebrew poetry, still shied away from the direct confrontations with social, political, and scientific subjects that are essential to Bejerano's poetry. Among Israeli women poets only Yonah Wallach preceded Bejerano in introducing questions of philosophical and social truth, metaphysics, language, and gender to Israeli women's poetry; to these themes Bejerano has added the components of media, simulacra, high tech, and scientific innovation.

This study surveys Bejerano's poetry as a whole, emphasizing the transition from the search for truth in the "real" physical world by means of lyrical epistemology, to the internal truth, the knowledge of existence by way of tormented insatiable love, and finally, the celebration of sex and temporal love in *Whale*. In all her poems Bejerano also examines the various discourses of language, using not only the language of the arts, but also scientific discoveries, to explore the universe and the human condition.

Data Processing and *Song of the Birds* are poetic philosophical tractates, focusing on consciousness and observing the world, human existence, and themselves.[1] The critic Ariel Hirschfeld[2] has categorized *Song of the Birds* as a "philosophical poem," and found in it a parallel to a "medieval encyclopedia" in its concern to define and give value to phenomena by selecting and analyzing them. The book as a whole deals with such eternal problems as the relationship between consciousness and the observed world, ultimately inquiring whether human consciousness can ever comprehend the world and discern reality and truth. Bejerano's poetry illuminates these ancient questions, together with the question of language itself, in an original way. In her work, modern existence, the relationship between individuals, love relationships, ethical values, scientific discoveries, and technology all combine to create the importance and excitement of this poetic cosmos.

Bejarano asks if phenomena can exist as external objects, outside and beyond consciousness, or does the world exist only within the human thought that conceives it? Should the natural sciences be understood as an a priori system or as a construction created by the human consciousness, which attempts to structure the natural phenomena it perceives? As the philosopher Kant pointed out, the human being who seeks to know the world of phenomena has first to structure it; the transcendental structures in which human beings live are their own creations.[3]

Data Processing and *Song of the Birds* are series of poems that deal, in various ways, with consciousness as a separate entity that reacts to the world and seeks a connection with it, observing the wonderful structures in existence, the processes developing, the metamorphoses of phenomena, becoming excited by the miracle of finding an echo of itself within them. This wonder becomes enhanced when consciousness finds an echo not only in known objects but also in the discovery of strange, unimagined combinations of which it was not previously aware.

Bejerano is interested in all aspects of natural phenomena, including science and technology, and she uses them creatively. She discovers their beauty, their "wondrousness," and develops from them a poetic system of "the new laws of natural phenomena." Although there have been other poets who used science as a subject of their poetic works, the meaningful innovation in this poetry is the discovery of the profound nature of a new epistemology, apparent in new states of mind that transform the concepts of reality, imagination, and art. The discovery of X-rays and optical fibers, for instance, which can literally penetrate the heart and the lungs, has completely altered the meaning of the biblical phrase "Sees the veins and the heart" (Jeremiah 20:12). Phrases like "landing on the moon," which used to belong to the realm of imagination, change their meaning, their logical position, and their emotional impact from the moment they acquire a literal meaning or external existence within reality. Scientific innovations break down epistemological laws and define in a new way the boundaries between the possible and the impossible, object and subject, reality, imagination, and art. Bejerano believes that despite the dehumanization it causes, technology also carries some advantages when it creates a new mode of thinking, bringing forward new kinds of beauty, aesthetics, language, and syntax, new genes, and the essentials of a new kind of poetry.

For Bejerano, consciousness tries to unite itself with reality by understanding reality's systems and laws. Phenomena that disprove common conceptions and the refute complacent expectations create the atmosphere of surprise in her poetry. Thus, optical fibers are exciting because they break accepted rules. She prefers the description of phenomena that are in themselves miraculous, powerful, and surprising, such as the making and structure of a synthetic sapphire or a botanical guide to unusual plants, to augmented metaphors that strengthen and broaden the subject described ("your eyes are like an ocean in flames"). The subjects she chooses for her poems represent the unexpected and the preciously rare, independent of the poet's emotions or imagination. She selects them from all aspects of reality: rare corals, optical fibers, the process of studying, the nature of photography; all are described in a direct, factual, and concrete way within the framework of their own terminology, as if classified in a scientific lexicon. The infinity of possibilities, the exhilaration of the imagination, and the sense of being faced by the miraculous: these derive from the intrinsic properties of the phenomenon itself, rather than from the elaborations and metaphors of the poet. The infinite journey "To the Star of the Soul" (5) is a revelation of the many qualities and diverse aspects that break down all barriers of definition and allow terminological elasticity. The "star of the soul" is indeed the goal of emotional, intellectual, and metaphysical craving; as the innermost part of the soul, it is the nearest and the most intimate of all, and as a star it is celestial, unreachable, and the most distant. The voyage is the transition, the ascent, the closing of the gap. The most physical aspect contains within itself the most metaphysical.

> To the Star of the Soul
> Let there be let there be let there be
> Half my way half my way
> To the star of the soul—
> Riding an invisible optical fiber
> I was a beam of light, the shortest voice frequency
> A beam of light, a voice frequency moving towards my
>   explosion
> And right after that—a tiny ball
> I was a young UFO
> invulnerable and transparent,
> seeing yet unseen
> And in front of me—a watery blue-gray screen
> The whole universe, and in it—a panel of buttons
>
> * A button for wondrous events—situations and
> * A button for wondrous people—relationships and
>   deeds
> * And a button for wondrous places—happenings and
> * A button for wondrous things—tools materials and
> * A button for wondrous plants, colors and
> * A button for wondrous animals—life and
> All of them set in the star of the soul like spice beds
>   without spices
> Distant, blind from Earth's vantage point
> Planet Earth—an alarm button
> On the panel of buttons in the blue screen
> In the star of the soul far away in silence.

The language used in this poem expresses its nature: "Let there be let there be let there be." Cosmic creation is being renewed rhythmically, a broadcast, the music of rhythmic energy. The same energy at the same time has an impact on several senses. When searching for structures similar to itself, consciousness looks for contact, sense, and compatibility. Understanding may be intellectual, but its motivation is emotional, prompted particularly by fear of death. Clas-

sification, one scientific methodology used to systematize
the phenomena of the world, at the same time expresses the
human need to control, derived from the feeling of loss and
disorientation. As Bejarano writes, "And the classifier is terrified of death; numbers are his mighty shield in the face of
death" (3). To classify is an attempt to exhaust, to survey, to
understand, to quantify, to distance oneself without objec-
tifying, without being carried away, and in this way to survive:

> Classification   For Clara S.
> To classify, to cleanse yourself
> To classify, to purify yourself
> To classify, to remain
> To number the flesh, to frame so as not to be swept
>   away
> A frame intangible and weightless
> Hovering in the mind of the classifier; who is he, who is
>   she, what is this?
> Death is approaching, hopping; crumb-shaped birdfood,
>   a wind is blowing
> They rise into the air, light death crumbs, islands of
>   ruins around him and he,
> Who is he, she, who is she
> Sitting in an armchair and classifying death;
> Seneca and Diogenes were smiling peacefully,
> Carolus Linnaeus, Mr. Dewey in his later work
> Archimedes sitting in the shade, Socrates shakes his
>   hands, the schlemiel;
> And the body of Moses our teacher;
> They all accept death crumbs like lovers,
> Innocent and weak, singing birds.
>
> And the classifier is terrified of death, he classifies it,
> Numbers are his mighty shield in the face of death,
>   his sword,
> Numbers are at his expense;
> He's choking slowly, perpetually sealed ledger
> You can't find an open window that's not numbered
> The number stuffs every mouth and orifice

That lets in air, only in dreams can it be stamped
How can we classify death? What's this,
What is it to classify murder? The heart rooted up
From a girl's body? The Loch Ness monster, the rape
By plural bodies of a singular, the strangler with a
    golden wire
The gold is one thing, the last breath another;
A number for each crumb, the rattle of the sick,
    the miserable;
The starved noise, how is it possible—the remotest
    death,
Love and the passion of reason?
How is it possible to classify the motion flowing into
    stars,
Even the revenger's steel hands, the terrorist's,
Who runs with a leader's decorated head sunken in
    frozen breasts;
To classify the terrible impulse, in precise relation to
    perverts less terrible;
How to input them, classify
The passing moment, before everything is wiped out
In the big boom, the collision of exploding gamma rays
A wondrous laser beam like a pewter wand, basking
And generating power cells for the world;
How to classify imagination, breathing not only outside
    the mouth
But in a square-edged frozen ark
Thicker and foggier inside, in the mass of the magma;
And he sits apart from all this magma
And has to come up with tranquil numbers.

This poetry revives the contacts and the proximity between the seemingly contradictory drives in human nature
and nature as a whole: fear and understanding, science and
imagination, the factual and the poetic, the mundane and
the miraculous. It is intelligence, based on the deep connections among the plethora of appearances, which unites the
multiplicity of points of view into one, unified entity.

When searching for the unifying and common elements in
reality, the individual is striving to "touch himself" (*Space-*

ship), and "be in touch with himself" as a path to the solace
which will enable him "to be happy being here" and to "return to life" (50). Humankind tries to save itself first by
isolation, to flee to the remotest realms like space, and then
to return to earth and be united, to feel in touch with the
various aspects of existence. In this way God, nature, existence, and consciousness are fused together. Consciousness returns to itself from the totality of the universe, from
its depth as well as from its external realms, from outer
space. The poetry of consciousness written by Bejerano is
reminiscent of the philosopher Spinoza's conception of God:
"The greater the number of things the mind understands by
the second and third kinds of knowledge, the less subject it
is to emotions that are bad, and the less it fears death,[4] and,
the more we understand particular things, the more we understand God."[5]

In "The Bamboo" the poet discovers an echo of herself:
"Like me, once in a hundred years the bamboo flowers . . ."
(28). Similarly, she discovers happiness in the understanding of the miraculous elements in her own life, which, in the
very concept of its uniqueness, enriches the observer. Here,
too, the poetic element is found in the phenomenon itself
rather than in the poet's imagery; the excitement results from
the "objective" observation, and not from attributing emotion to objects or creating exciting situations. Observation
becomes part of the phenomenon. Poetic imagination is neither symbolic nor surrealist; it does not derive from other
realms; it is concentrated in the objects themselves and their
evolution. This way of observing the miraculous in all aspects of existence is interwoven into all the poems of this
collection.

The miraculous expands and is intensified by its connections to each of the wonderful phenomena, and thus the
whole poetic cosmos is constructed. At the moment that
consciousness succeeds in relating to the world of phenomena by means of excitement and discovery of systems, the
facts themselves are transformed into poetry. In that instant
the center of events is transferred to the observer him-

self, who becomes emotionally awakened by the phenomenon: "once in a hundred years the bamboo flowers / *like me*," or "He is *in me and in you, yes, in me, the wondrous,* a wondrous animal" (28; italics mine). Humans are the "wondrous animal."

Within a world equipped with modern, developing technology, the concepts of the near and the distant dramatically change. It is possible to reach distant places by missiles, satellites, swift vehicles, and instantaneous communications. Cameras and television enable humankind to visit every corner of the earth and to penetrate into the depths of the globe and the human body. Everything that until recently was regarded as remote in all spatial dimensions, internal as well as external, and even in time, has become accessible. Scientific discoveries have brought to light things that were hidden, reducing distances to a minimum or completely annihilating them. We receive information in "real time," without time intervening between an event and its reaching our consciousness. The camera may bring things closer or make them more remote, upsetting the accepted "order" of space. It can also alter time: the process of a flower's growth, which may take several months in nature, can be presented by a movie camera during several seconds. This, and other technological means, has transformed the hidden realms of existence, once described only in an imaginary manner, into observable facts.[6] Television screens can show an apple larger than a building, and this will not seem, as did the painting of the apple by Magritte, surrealistic. Films have accustomed us to observing ancient cultures interwoven with modern traffic jams, without distinction between the historical and the contemporary.

Technological inventiveness thus completely upsets our previous conceptions concerning space and time and all the laws derived from them, creating new states of consciousness, states of mind, which demand a new epistemology. What does closeness mean, in the sense of both proximity and intimacy, in a world where the annihilation of distance does not create it? The various means of overcoming phys-

ical distances give us, emotionally, only the illusion of proximity and intimacy. The problem is transferred to the realm
beyond the physical; our craving for "realness," intimacy,
truly touching the object of our desire, is on a different level
from the closeness provided by technology. In our world of
simulacra, there is always an illusion: objects only seem to
be accessible to the touch, whereas in fact they retain their
remoteness. In this new structure, human craving is transformed. The meaningful task is no longer to overcome physical distance, to reach the moon or the bowels of the earth.
The human search is directed now toward the sense of
reality, the true contact, "the real thing," instead of sub-
stituted simulations and demonstrations that are the by-
products of technology. Scientific triumphs over physical
space created new emotional and philosophical distances,
deep in human consciousness, that express themselves in
the sense of fallacy and of "missing the right thing."

The desired proximity is achieved when consciousness
becomes aware, and discovers and systematizes a way to
relate to variegated phenomena, to recognize them and discover their intrinsic meaning. Even if technology itself is
rational and abstract, in its understanding consciousness
discovers and creates elements of connection, solace, and
intimacy. In the last poem in this collection, "Spaceship,"
which is to some extent a "Space Odyssey," we find an ode
to the beauty of space, of the spaceship itself, and of space
technology; the book ends with the sentence: "But—how to
go back home, we wish; . . . we are happy to be here/sane . . .
in the knowledge that we have touched ourselves and returned to life" (50).

Bejerano's poems explore states of mind and the disrup-
tion of the familiar laws of consciousness and their rele-
vance. Consciousness, which searches for intimacy, reacts
in wonder, surprise, fear, frustration, alienation, despair, humor, or joy. In all phenomena consciousness looks for contact, for an echo of itself, even when they are difficult to
understand, like "how to copy a scent," "genocide," the
innermost aspect of an object or its disappearance:

Data Processing 60
My face is beautiful when I am understood;
Something in my innermost core that turns
To the depths, sunk in darkness
Awakens to life and slowly slowly hovers

The angel of my privacy, fly angel of my spirit
Stretching his finger toward "my other"—a human
    countenance upon me
Because understanding is germination
Touched by inspiration and electric beauty . . .

My face is beautiful when I am understood
It expands to the dimensions of a broad gate
In hundreds of hues of color in the paper
In the clay's facets and its shavings.

The world described in these poems is one conceived through a screen or a monitor. The screen appears in almost every poem in this collection. It governs everything and represents everything, at the price of misrepresenting the world, shrinking and reducing everything to its own size. It becomes the window and the mirror of modern consciousness. All the senses are transformed, "translated" on the screen, into a visual language of imaging. Modern technology constantly creates situations evoking synesthesia, a response by one sense to the impressions of another.[7] Bejerano does not create synesthetical metaphors but describes situations with such structure and characteristics. Musical sounds, electromagnetic currents, and the "feel" of materials are transformed by technological means into visual images on the screen; even the senses of taste and smell, the movements of bodies ("Radar"), and the body's limbs are measured and undergo a process of quantifying so they can be viewed on the computer's monitor. The whole world of the senses is translated into the imaging language of the screen. In scientific work, for instance, the colors presented on the monitor are used as signifiers of different categories, as in medical tests, where blood in the veins can be marked by the color blue, evoking all the associations of "blue blood" and

all those resulting from the absence of the red. The screen
is thus one of the most important reasons for the confusion
of our conceptions relating to space, time, and dimensions.

The poem "Song of the Birds" (39) stresses the multiplicity of discourses and aspects of all worldly phenomena. In
contradiction to the past concepts that viewed science as
inimical to art and nature, in Bejerano's world view art and
science, like all other realms, are segments of nature. Her
poetry emphasizes the lyrical element in all phenomena,
revealing the poetic aspect that is added to the factual in the
laws of reality and science. She brings to light hidden aspects or destroys accepted notions when she uses optical
fibers as a one would use a horse or a broom for riding:
"She rides an invisible optical fiber" (5). She surprises the
reader, because usually we do not conceive the fiber as a
stick used by a rider, even though we know that energy
flows in it. Means of communication are transformed into
means of transportation. Bejerano transforms functions
usually thought unchanging by playing with them, expressing their many elastic possibilities:

> The Optical Fiber
> Let there be let there be let there be
> Half my way half my way
> To the star of the soul, riding
> A transparent optical fiber,
> I was a beam of light, a frequency—
> A binary number; and inside me a word
> And another word and another word
> Like beatings of light and darkness from an electric
>   heart
> Sending quivering signals, waves, rows of waves as a
>   storm
> From one end of the earth to another;
> And there, at the end of earth, the bewitched number
>   will return
> Into a regular number within a fraction of a second,
> And from the thin optical fiber a cooing
> Is heard as if from a pit of sleep: "I love you"

> Words and angels out of blooming fibers
> Beaming hundreds of flowers in the velocity almost of
>   light
> And all of this is only a laser light call inside a fiber
>   optic stomach
> Reliable and refined, thin and hollow as a string
> Transparent as glass and impenetrable as a riddle.

Every phenomenon is both functional and, at the same time, an idea, a logical entity. The singing of the birds becomes a physical-biological phenomenon with a neurological aspect, since the voice box producing the sounds contains many nerve ends ("Syrinx: The Name of the Box of Singing in the Bird's Chest" [39]). The factual-scientific description evokes the lyrical-metaphysical one: the nerves are also the material creating the singing, the producers of the music that evokes an emotional response. The nerves are also the strings of sadness. On the behaviorist level, the singing of the birds is a communicative language, a code of behavior. The physical aspect does not exclude the lyrical one; on the contrary, it enriches the emotional response of the audience, who moves from one aspect to another and ascends to the musical-poetic level of the singing. In this way, the sentiment and the idea present in all natural and scientific phenomena must be discovered by the poet and the reader. This poetry is focused on physical, biological, chemical, and factual changes rather than psychological processes. The psychological is reflected in the apparently scientific description.

Every phenomenon is automatically charged, becoming a metaphor. Whether UFOs, chemicals, spaceship, accident, cave, or crime, we respond to the subject matter of the poetry of Maya Bejerano with fear, shock, calm, happiness, or excitement, surprised at the discrepancy between her representation of the phenomenon itself and our expected response, like an empty camera that takes no pictures (6). Her art accepts the contradiction, celebrates it, and gives it life as a poem inquiring into the meaning of the breakup of old physical laws and their transformation into new realities. In the poem "The Story of Pedro Rolan and Maria Cortes (Empty Love)" (7), the prisoner Pedro assumes that Maria will marry him. This assumption is based on a wrong interpretation of her behavior. Their relationship is "lots of activity, unformed as yet." Consciousness discovers, when the poem unfolds, that in every act of interpretation there is an element of misunderstanding, a revelation that brings consciousness into harmony with "form," a new law. The ending of this poem surprisingly presents Maria marrying, "as a simple fact," another man whose name is also Pedro; the prisoner Pedro is astounded and shocked, as is the whole world around him. But consciousness understands that all the pieces of information and the hints in Maria's behavior were, from the very beginning, misleading: "They were just pantomime," meaningless gestures. The prisoner remains bound "in his imagination, his prison," while consciousness has already understood a new kind of order— the impossibility of knowing the truth.

The poem "Empty Camera" also addresses the destruction of expectations and the understanding of a new law through constant movement between the charming and fascinating on the one hand, and the frightening and threatening on the other. The photograph is supposed to give eternity to the "moment in gesture," but there are no such moments; a photograph cannot impart eternity "to the moment of the surfacing of the most profound elements of a personality" (6). In this poem, like the one on the unrequited but short-lived love of Pedro Rolan, "there was a mistake, just a mistake."

Bejerano's most recent book, *Whale,* is a lyrical tractate investigating the subject of "true" love. A new kind of knowledge is introduced: emotional knowledge, a readiness to devote oneself to disappearing love, to the "evasive, slippery lover." Both husband and lover figures are gone in this volume and so is the illusion of stability and security. All that remains is the realization that most loves are temporary although not conceived as such. Experiences as well as concepts and metaphors in *Whale* are taken from the cinematic world of vanishing images, the sciences, especially physics, the Song of Songs, and from the narrative of S. Y. Agnon.

Bejerano's innovation is in the fusion of science, technology, classical Jewish texts, famous works of art, prose, and poetry. These do not merely provide images; they constitute the lyrical world itself as it is present within the drama of nature and science, human existence and literature.

Whale is a courageous observation and acknowledgment of what actually happens even to the greatest of loves. The uniqueness of this cycle of poems is that, even after the sad realization that there is no eternal love, it is still a celebration of the perfection of ephemeral love. People refuse to acknowledge and come to terms with the reality that passionate love is usually short lived. Bejerano makes the most of what actually exists and is possible for lovers, denouncing false hypocritical clichés, rejecting the accepted lies and pretense: "Only truth, because we have rejected / all the falseness and pretense, / transferring them to others, for another time" ("Sex, Car and Love Later," *Whale,* 9).

Despite its temporality, love ignites our emotional life, hope, freedom, longing, and imagination and brings changes that outlive the relationship itself. *Whale* explores aspects of temporal love, its power, excitement, meaning, madness, and sickness. Being in love is both elating and unbearable. Bejerano's poetry attempts to overcome these tormenting feelings and transcend them by reliving and exhausting and celebrating the beauty, and intensity of short-lived love.[8]

As in *Song of the Birds,* in which the ultimate destination of the space odyssey is to come back and touch Earth to reunite with it from a different perspective, the purpose of the Peter Pan-Agnonian love journey in *Whale* is a poetic analysis of a woman who, having lost great love, makes sense of her life and her "emotional truth," of what is "right" and precise, and ultimately sees herself from a new, unexpected vantage point.

While Western culture usually sees a contradiction between science and love, and science and poetry, in Bejerano's world, love, poetry, and science have a great deal in common. Love is unpredictable and uncontrollable; similarly, science and technology develop in unpredictable ways. Bejerano is bewildered by all the manifestations of exotic beauty, the mystery, and the irrationality of science. The contents and the form of her poems impersonate and recapitulate rhythms, velocity, states of mind, abstract laws, and structures of science. Not only does she denounce the traditional contradiction between the two, but on the contrary, she adopts scientific structures and discourse as materials and structures for her poetry. The two great languages of Western culture, Marxism and psychoanalysis, have long insisted on the division between poetry and science, the mind and the soul. Moreover, both tend to demystify and reduce love and show that love is actually something else. In *Whale,* Bejerano disputes this and suggests a new conception of love.

The central poem in *Whale,* "Sex, Car and Love Later" (7–9), is an odyssey of love in the same way that her previous book, *Song of the Birds,* was an odyssey of human consciousness, oscillating between being and nothingness, reality and imagination or fiction. The mature and ripe woman who "was abandoned, and abandoned her husband" is in love with a young man who refuses to marry her:

> Sex, Car and Love Later
> I am telling my friends that
> I wouldn't be able to come
> You won't see my face
> I am in the innermost chambers
> Having casual sex.
> Eros, smiling in the fields, turns me on
> And the dance of cry and laughter caresses, hurls my
>   creatures
> blooming in full blossom,
> in bouquets of daisies, bunches of ormenises,
>   dandelions, and cyclamens,
> One Sicilian snapdragon, and a yellow henbane,
> half awake half asleep
> Because of one "bouquet of wrinkles" saturated with
>   silicon perfume
> Finally Ms. Missed Opportunity mastered Mr. Moment
> And he dropped her and she—him . . .

The young lover has many attributes. He is a prince who awakens her from her sleep, he is God, Lord of the World, he is a mythical creature, a whale, he is a sex god, Mr. Eros, he is adventurous, he is Time itself, the Master of the Moment—like the handsome naked young men in allegorical Renaissance paintings—and he is also a tough guy, a selfish calculating man who does not want any commitment, and who puts his interests first. The woman wants to hold on to the man, even at the price of her identity. She is willing to sacrifice everything, and blames her independence as the obstacle to her love (*Whale,* 40):

> A Man of Principle
> A man loves a woman and desires her
> But he does not want her,
> He cannot want her as a wife
> His love will not help him in this matter
> It will only obstruct
> His desire, lust, and yearning all together will not be
> strong enough against his will;
> And his will is the essence of his identity, the marrow of
> his fate
> That removes her from his ways.
> If she were only something softer that could be
> added to
> Something kneeling and bending, "but she is too" she
> screamed,
> It is just that the train on the dress of her past
> entangles and clouds
> In a blinding, distracting light and she does not cross
> The gate of his iron divine will
> That denies, recedes
> And is closed.

That love could also be an encounter, a dialogue between two literary texts, is congruent with the postmodern notion that the self is a text. Bejerano weaves her poem through a love dialogue with the Hebrew writer Agnon's most famous story of lost love, "Another Face" (or "Metamorphosis," as it is called in another translation), to express her belief that every love is a mode of transcendence and transformation. Like Agnon's story that begins at the end, at the moment of the divorce, and describes in retrospect the relationship between husband and wife, this poem starts at the point of separation between the lovers and relives the relationship after it is over. Although the relationship no longer exists, Bejerano unites past and future from the position of "the superiority of lovers," where the lover basks in the glory of the idealized godly beloved, and fears that life would not be worth living if the beloved were to leave, but the reader knows that the lover has left. The voice in the poem lives the past as if it were present and as if time had stopped.

In the poem "A Whale" Bejerano talks about the tormenting danger of losing the beloved. The reciprocity of the beloved becomes the reason to live. Without it the lover feels repulsive and worthless. This lover is reminiscent of the lover in "Sex, Car and Love Later," a mythical young man, taken from a legend or a fairy tale. Here he appears as a whale:

> My friend is a whale who is twenty years old
> And I am hospitalized between his eyes;
> I am a raft on the hills of flesh
> Struggling at the end of his nails
> On high and cold ranges of mountains
> And danger is far away
> And danger is far away
>
> In streets strangled by cement, gray,
> Colored in pipe shades
> I am walking, my bracelets are thrown away
> The straps of my skin are stripped,
> And my smooth cheeks, my thighs are addicted
> And danger is far away
> And danger is far away
>
> Every moment is wondering outside the time frame
> Every moment I am his—my moment

A precious moment, thrown and lost
A moment of skin getting ready to burn
Get ready my skin in the oil of light,
The oil of the whale is flesh,
That the sea of time had given
Had given me to nurture and anoint

Because danger is far away
Because danger is far away.

The young man does not want any commitment. However, he enables the woman to arrest the moment and experience the beauty of the adventure, the excitement of danger, and the risk, and living the present, which is very real.

"Sex, Car and Love Later" is, to a large extent, a love odyssey of the nineties. It is a classical cinematic car chase, in which the lovers are both the chasers and the target. In "Sex, Car and Love Later" (*Whale*, 7–8) the lovers go on a ride and they strike a deal. The young man says: "I came to pick you up, / In your car you'll drive and the gas is mine." The energy and rhythm of the fuel is like the energy-message moving in the optical fiber, like a sperm flowing toward orgasm, or a missile breaking the atmosphere: "The gas is running boiling in the pipes and we are speeding / in a different velocity, almost zero friction with any external foreign object / which means infinite movement, smooth, uninterrupted, and eternal." Not only love is likened to a car, but the heroine herself is a car: "And once more I became beautiful and glamorous / Like the headlights of a racing car / At night."

Bejerano is also keen on cars as salvific chariots of ascension. Whereas in "Sex, Car and Love Later" the heroine owns her car, in the earlier poem "Has He Got the Wheels" ("The Heat and the Cold"), the protagonist, in a moment of despair, goes out to the street praying for a miracle, a knight who will come in a car, abduct her, and sweep her far away from her mundane unbearable existence (*Selected Poems*, 146):

Has He Got the Wheels?
Has he got the wheels?
Chariot of fire with swift and hidden lightning horsemen
Come and take me . . .
This is not real gutsy
To be ravished madly, climbing like sapphires
On my fingers, spreading in me
A moaning jungle beast, a city beast
Poor thing; Wow!
What a fright she is;
The leaves freeze as she walks, an ancient legend;
Bushes are resting, long hedgerows of the cold wind.

She won't give her skies away;
Her changing skies: blue and cloudy.
To break through and smash her up—

her skies sure know
How to devastate her.

The whole of the imagery, movement, and rhythm of "Sex, Car and Love Later" is taken from film language. This union of message and medium is reminiscent of Bejerano's earlier cycle of poems about the "Optical Fiber," where the poem itself was a reconstruction, a recapitulation of the pace, the energy, and matter of waves transformed from auditory to visual, so that telephone calls consist of a human message flowing within the almost unseen fiber used in telecommunication.[9] Indeed, even the title "Sex, Car and Love Later" brings to mind the movie *Sex, Lies and Videotape*. The protagonist of the movie, who has lost faith in honesty and love, can reach his own truth and have sexual satisfaction only through watching video tapes of women who tell him about their sexual lives. But he cannot have sex in any other form, with any of these women themselves, and is dependent on the tapes as an agent. This poem, the journey, the crazed car race signifying lost love, is made of scenes like video clips of flashbacks, cuts, nature picture, fairy tales, photomontage, blowups, slow motion, strong technicolor—all played forwards and backwards, changing scale and speed, and thus changing the order of time and space. Love in this poem is the sensation of being lost, losing control, and losing the sense of space and time. It is both frightening and freeing; the lover experiences the world as in a science fiction movie.

Bejerano's awareness of the deep mutual relation between cinema and poetry was present even in her early work, where the theme of the car, the rich description of nature appealing to all senses, the field, the flora, and the lovers as heroes of a fairy tale all appear. In "Data Processing #15," a poem that also evolves around a dialogue with another work of art, Henri Rousseau's renowned "primitive" painting *The Dream,* the language of cinema is central (translation by Linda Zisquit):

> The influence of movies on poetry is tremendous.
> Crushed, I was pressed to the anemone's trunk
> as I went out to my lofty deeds,
> tortured by light, banishing the cars off me
> with my breath.
> Casually we fell into the valley and the silence
> covered my head green and sweet.
> A gorgeous scarecrow, a horseman and I without
>   provisions
> three hunters, survivors.
> The work flowed on around when a tiger emerged from
> the leaves. Therefore I was pressed into deep slumber,
>   properly dressed.
> And above us the sky took our pictures.
> With blowing hair, with a red gloomy face and in the
>   end, trembling.
> The fishermen arrived at three. Three fastidious men
>   stuck each on his way,
> we shook each other's hands
> sniffing in horror. And the bells were playing,
> and the mustard flower and the cyclamen got what was
>   coming to them.
> When I left the weak spot,
> everything shrank in relief, returned to its course.
> The ants started their silly boat-dance and weeds—

flared up.
I fell into them and the time of the tiger was over.
My heart went out to him at four o'clock, consumed
     with lust.
Like an amethyst, breathless, I was gathered
with the last rays into tomorrow
glowing on the hilltops
in an unfinished whisper,
that the influence of poetry on movies is tremendous.[10]

In Maya Bejerano's poetry, materials taken from many areas of existence enrich both the realm of phenomena and the realm of poetic experience. The poetic element is found within the phenomenon itself, into which the poet's observation is incorporated. Her originality is expressed in the human apprehension of the miracles, the beauty, and the structures hidden in the state of things or in the phenomena, and the ways in which scientific advances create new relationships between human consciousness and the natural world, bringing the previously unattainable within human grasp. Yet nostalgia and cravings remain, for even if physical differences can be overcome, the poetic desire to bridge the gap between the new realities and the absent essences remains. This gap is the eternal field in which imagination and poetry flourish.

NOTES

1. Maya Bejerano, *Data Processing* (Tel Aviv, 1983) [Hebrew]; *Song of the Birds* (Tel Aviv, 1985) [Hebrew]; *Selected Poems* 1972–1986 (Tel Aviv, 1987) [Hebrew]; *Whale* (Tel Aviv, 1990) [Hebrew]. All quotations, unless otherwise noted, are from *Song of the Birds*; page numbers are indicated in parentheses. With the exception of "Data Processing no. 15 (see n. 10), all of the translations are mine, with the assistance of John Felstiner, whom I thank very much for his interest and insightful help.
2. Ariel Hirschfeld, in his review of the book in *Yediot Ahronot*, November 1, 1985 [Hebrew].

3. See Samuel Bergman, *God and Man in Modern Thought* (Jerusalem, 1947) [Hebrew], 6: "Kant, indeed, reversed the order: it is not the objects that determine a man's mind, but it is the mind that determines the objects by its creative activity, that endows our world with its fundamental forms. This human creative activity is relevant only to the world of phenomena in which we live, and not to the objects themselves, in their objective existence."

4. Baruch Spinoza, *The Ethics,* part V, proposition 38, transl. S. Shirley, in Baruch Spinoza, *The Ethics and Selected Letters,* ed. S. Feldman (Indianapolis, 1982), 222.

5. Ibid., proposition 24, 216.

6. Walter Benjamin, quoted in Rudolf Arnheim, *Film als Kunst* (Berlin, 1932), 138, realized the infinite possibilities of the camera, and made the analogy to psychoanalysis in terms of its immense power to destroy conventional worlds and recover worlds that were unknown and unseen to us: "Then came the film and burst this prison-world asunder by the dynamite of the tenth of a second, so that now, in the midst of its far-flung ruins and debris, we calmly and adventurously go traveling. With the close-up, space expands; with slow motion, movement is extended. The enlargement of snapshots does not simply render more precise what in any case was visible, though unclear: it reveals entirely new structural formations of the subject. So, too, slow motion not only presents familiar qualities of movement but reveals in them entirely unknown ones which, far from looking like retarded rapid movements, give the effect of singularly gliding, floating supernatural motions." And, as he wrote elsewhere, "The Work of Art and the Age of Mechanical Reproduction," in *Illuminations,* ed. Hannah Arendt (New York, 1968), 236–37: "The camera introduces us to unconscious optics as does psychoanalysis to unconscious impulses."

7. Synesthesia is a well-known device used by poets in all cultures and generations, intermingling impressions of various senses to create a poetical-emotional unity (e.g.: "the people see the sounds" [Exodus 20: 18]).

8. In an interview in the Tel Aviv newspaper *Ha'Ir,* March 10, 1990 [Hebrew], Bejerano related:

> I was completely shattered during the whole experience of love: at the beginning, in the middle, and at the end, keeping an innermost core, the equilibrium—everything was in a great upheaval. I felt worthless, helpless, as if I hit bottom, and all the poems were written while going through this experience—love and friendship perceived and felt as passing. The whole time I was aware of my finality. . . . "Sex, Car and Love Later" was written after we broke up, and then, one stands all alone in the world. . . . The poem was written out of excruciating pain. I wanted to salvage that which was. . . . I wanted to preserve the magic, to touch that realness, which I knew would vanish, which is vanishing, the pain of the realization that a human being is ephemeral and of the constant

illusion of eternity. This is an ode to the moment, to the impermanent, not a lamentation or an elegy, in spite of the terrible state I was in, because Mr. Moment is indeed our master.

9. In the same interview (see n. 8), Bejerano pointed out: "The feeling in the book . . . is of meta-cinema, of filming, of a production, while the participants are completely real, but also meta-realistic . . . because at this point what interests me in literature, in my poems, in the stories I have been writing is to create a reality, superimposed on another reality. . . . I want the directing . . . the language notating the movement of the characters, you may say—the choreography itself—to be the sole expression of the most intense concentration of what I want to say about life, about people, and about the world. Not rhetorical poetry, not making an argument or taking a position, rather poetry of happening . . . and by that I mean the intensity of the present, of the moment. It may be a moment that lasts a long time, a month, even a year. But if we go back to films, then this whole book is like a filming experience of shooting that takes seven months, perhaps six months . . . as if someone were directing us, some supreme reason, and everything happens in the most accurate and right way."

10. This unpublished 1993 translation is printed here with the gracious permission of its translator, Linda Zisquit.

INDEX

Abramovich, S. Y. [Mendele Mocher/
 Moykr Sforim], *Fishke der krumer*,
 73, 91, 92, 103, 104, 142
Abravanel, Benvenida "the Princess,"
 51, 62
Abuse, women and, 52, 56, 103
Adelman, Howard, 22–23
Adler, Ruth, 25
Admetus and Other Poems (Lazarus),
 200
Adolescence, 227–28; in *In the Prime of
 Her Life*, 226–29, 232–33
Agada, 75–76, 79
"Against Women Who Pursue Reli-
 gious Studies" (Frances), 60–61
Agnon, Samuel Yosef, 97, 217–18, 356;
 "Another Face," 359–60; *In the
 Prime of Her Life*, 25–26, 217–18,
 220–22, 226–29, 232–33
Agosín, Marjorie: "Church Candles,"
 311; *Happiness*, 310; "Plains," 311–
 12; "The Seamstress of St. Peters-
 burg," 310
"Agunah" (Baron), 103
Aharonson, Yosef, 108
Akiva, Rabbi, 247
Alchemy, 309, 316, 317–18
Aleichem, Sholem, 91, 92
Alharizi, Judah, *The Book of Tahke-
 moni*, 41
Alienation and uprooting, 316, 322n14

Allende, Isabel, 301
Almog, Ruth, 340
"America: Toward Yavneh" (Ozick),
 284–85
American diaspora, literature in,
 284–85
Americanization, 126, 167–73. *See also*
 Assimilation; Historical amnesia
American Jewish Congress, 209
American Judaism, 30
American suffrage movement, 119
"Ample Heavens, Earth Enormous"
 (Yehudis), 141
Anarchists, 113
Androgyny, 330, 337
"And When Your Soul" (Knizshnik),
 139
An Estate of Memory (Karmel), 273–76,
 277, 282n22
Animal imagery, 243–45, 303
Anna Karenina (Tolstoy), 334
"Another Face" (Agnon), 359–60
Apoteker, Avrom, 77
Argentine Gauchesque literature, 304
Aron ben Shmuel: *Lovely Prayer*, 77;
 *Powerful Medicines for Body and
 Soul*, 77
Ascarelli, Debora, 62
Asceticism, 54
Assimilation, 30–31, 132, 313–15; ef-
 fects of, 283–84, 294–95, 296

Feminist theory, 218–19
Ferraro, Thomas J., 162
"Few Words about Women Poets, A" (Molodowsky), 130–31
Film language, 362, 363, 366n9
"First Day, The" (Baron), 98, 106
Fishke der krumer (Abramovich), 73
Five Hundred Years of Yiddish Poetry (Bassin), 136–38, 141, 148
Flaubert, Gustave, *Madame Bovary*, 108
Fogel, Devorah, 113–17
Folklore, 71
Folkshuln, 126
Folksongs, 71
For Musicians Only (Shtok), 122–23
Fortunuoff Video Archive for Holocaust Testimonies, 263
"Fradel" (Baron), 97, 102
Frances, Immanuel, "Against Women Who Pursue Religious Studies," 60–61
Franco, Jean, 305
Fraye arbeter shtime, 120, 122, 123
Frayhayt, 125
Freud, Sigmund, 323, 331
"From the Winter Poems" (Bialik), 250
"*Froyen lider*" (Molodowsky), 117
Fuentes, Carlos, 301
Futoranski, Luisa, 320

Gale, Zona, 158
Garden Destroyed, A (Raab), 238
Gedaliah ibn Yahya, 61
Gei oni (Lapid), 325, 332–34; narrative form in, 334–38
Gender, 64, 107–8; Holocaust narratives and, 262–64, 281n8; Holocaust studies and, 262–67; language and, 217–18, 220–22, 231–33, 344; writing and, 62–65, 130–31, 329
Gender boundaries, 164, 325–26
Gender conflicts, 26, 28–29, 177–78, 185–87, 188–91, 191–94, 216–17; language and, 217–18, 220–22. *See also* Women: traditional Jewish culture and

Gender differences, 31–32; in shtetl life, 105–7
Gender roles, 117, 232, 325–26, 337; in *A City of Many Days*, 330–32
Genealogies, The (Glantz), 304–5
Generational conflicts, 31, 304–7, 308–9, 312–13. *See also* Fathers; Mothers
"Geniza" (Baron), 106
Geniza ceremony, 96, 110n12
Genocide, 259–60, 264, 279–80; resistance to, 269, 271; women's experience of, 262–64, 281n8
Gerchunoff, Alberto, 302; *The Jewish Gauchos*, 300
Gervitz, Gloria, 307; *Yizkor*, 307–8
Gilbert, Sandra, 20
Gilder, George, 202
Giles of Rome, *De regimine principum*, 60
"Gilgulim" (Baron), 99, 105, 107–8, 109, 110n32
Gilman, Charlotte Perkins, "The Yellow Wallpaper," 183
Ginsberg, Allen, 284
Ginzburg, Shimon, 237
Gioia, Dona, 51
Glantz, Margo, 306, 307, 320; *The Genealogies*, 304–5
Glanz, A., 122, 138; "Culture and the Woman," 120
Glasser, Eda, 118
Glatstein, Jacob, "The Fame of Isaac Bashevis Singer," 291
Glaykhhayt, 119
Gleanings: A Diary in Verse (Syrkin), 212
Glickman, Nora, 31
Glückel of Hameln, 23–24, 73, 84–86, 88n12, 90n35
God-Fearing Song in Honor of Women and Girls, A, 74
Goldberg, Leah, 343–44
Goldberg, Rachel, 343–44
Golding, Alan C., 137, 149
Goldshteyn, Roza, 138, 139, 143
Gonzaga, Elizabeth, 51
"Goose" (Baron), 109
Gordon, Jacob, 154